"I have been a fan of Marv Weisbord's for years. His thoughts and understanding of how people and organizations accomplish work improves with each update of *Productive Workplaces.* He is a master of this subject and, most importantly, he helps us practice what he teaches."

—Richard G. Haworth, Chairman Emeritus, HAWORTH, INC.

"Weisbord has been a major voice in the theory and practice of organization development (OD) since the early 1970s. This book is a wonderful history and reinterpretation of many of the events, schools of thought, and controversies that have punctuated the field from its beginnings. It should be required reading for every organization behavior and development scholar. Among its many virtues, the book is beautifully written."

—Peter Vaill, Senior Scholar and Emeritus Professor of Management, Antioch University Ph.D. Program in Leadership and Change, author of *Learning as a Way of Being: Strategies for Survival in a World of Permanent White Water* and *Spirited Leading and Learning* (Minneapolis, MN, USA).

"During my thirty-three-year career, I have been involved in publishing well over one thousand books. *Productive Workplaces* is certainly among the top five most influential in terms of its impact on the organizations in which I worked as well as on my personal leadership, management concepts, and practices."

—Steven Piersanti, President and Publisher, Berrett-Koehler Publishers, Inc. (San Francisco, CA, USA, formerly president, Jossey-Bass Publishers)

"Reading the 1987 version of PW in the early nineties was a major stepping stone for me towards a more fulfilling, creative, and dynamic way of thinking and working."

—Richard Wilkinson, HR Director, International Training & Education Center for Health (I-TECH) a partnership of the University of Washington and University of California–San Francisco (Seattle, WA, USA)

"I discovered *Productive Workplaces* when I began teaching in the Pepperdine MBA program in 1990. I loved that Marvin had gone back and read the primary resource material written by the great management thinkers of the twentieth century: Taylor, McGregor, Lewin, Emery, and Trist. The book provides a cogent overview of management thought and how it has evolved over the last century."

—Miriam Y. Lacey, Ph.D., Academic Director and Professor, MSOD Program, Graziadio School of Business and Management, Pepperdine University (Malibu, CA, USA)

"PW illuminated a path that would become my life's work. Future Search gave me the practical understanding and tools to take the journey."

—Shem Cohen (USA), Change Events, Inc.

"Reading *Productive Workplaces* we encountered a vision of a workplace in which people matter, teams collaborate, and direct participation enables individuals to contribute their full range of talents. That vision is just as relevant today as in 1987—perhaps more so—as change becomes constant and speed becomes imperative."

—Frederick A. Miller and Judith H. Katz, The Kaleel Jamison Consulting Group, Inc., authors of *The Inclusion Breakthrough: Unleashing the Real Power of Diversity* (Albany, NY, USA)

"Organizations that value 'dignity, meaning, and community' are not born overnight. The wisdom I have gained from *Productive Workplaces Revisited* has provided me with techniques, processes, and the openness I need for consulting to organizations that aspire to build these values into their cultures."

—Richard Beckerman, President, Richard Beckerman Consulting (Seattle, WA, USA)

"I have a much-dog-eared copy of *Productive Workplaces,* which I read while managing an R&D lab at NYNEX (then the 'Baby Bell' in New York and New England). The book was a turning point for me. It inspired me to run against the grain of re-engineering with a participative work design project for a critical business process. That project was one of the most successful among a spate conducted during the re-engineering craze at NYNEX (and it required no new technology!)."

—Jim Euchner, Visiting Scientist, MIT Sloan School of Management (Cambridge, MA, USA)

"As a professor in graduate studies in leadership and business psychology, I see my role as passing on to a new generation the values and lessons learned from a twenty-five-year career in organizational effectiveness. Marvin Weisbord is a master whose wisdom I encourage my students to seek out. *Productive Workplaces* has been an anchor in my life and career. It is my mission to see that it becomes the anchor for a new generation of practitioners."

—Connie S. Fuller, Ph.D., Associate Chair and Assistant Professor, Business Psychology, The Chicago School of Professional Psychology (Chicago, IL, USA) co-author, *Bridging the Boomer-Xer Gap: Creating Authentic Teams for High Performance at Work.*

"I devoured the first edition of *Productive Workplaces.* Here was a book that confirmed everything I had experienced in my consulting career. I felt validated. Today when people ask me where they can learn about the history of the field, this is the one book I recommend."

—Dick Axelrod, The Axelrod Group (Chicago, IL, USA), author of *Terms of Engagement: New Ways of Leading and Changing Organizations.*

"PW has shaped the way I have approached my consulting practice for nearly twenty-five years."

—Loretta Raider, Principal, The Raider Consulting Group (Melrose Park, PA, USA)

"*Productive Workplaces* (PW) is more than a book about the field of organization development; it also shows the possibility for aligning yourself with basic values about [organization and management] and some hints about trying new ideas for yourself. This takes courage, of course, and courage has meaning only in situations where you are in doubt. With PW in your hands you are not alone."

—Henrik Simmelkjær, Consultant (Kolding, Denmark), former secretary of European Institute for Transnational Studies in Group and Organizational Development (eit).

"This is the OD book of the century."

—Bengt Lindstrom, Ander & Lindstrom, AB (Stockholm, Sweden)

"Marvin Weisbord's story of his own encounter with worker participation in his family business was a 'me-too' story of great power. To read the unfolding argument in favour of letting 'those with a stake in the problem help define and solve it' was riveting—it affirmed and informed my research and my practice as a consultant to industry then, and continues to do so now."

—Verna Blewett, Associate Professor, Occupational Health and Safety, University of South Australia (Adelaide, Australia)

"If somebody asks me to name just one good book on management, or organization development, or social psychology, I give them the same answer: *Productive Workplaces.* It addresses the heady topic of meaning and dignity in work with writing that is as engaging as a well-written novel."

—Gil Steil, Gil Steil Associates (Boston, MA, USA)

"So far as I know, PW provides the only systematic review of multiple cases over the longer term, fifteen to thirty years after the intervention."

—Tonnie Van der Zouwen, Ph.D., Van der Zouwen Consultancy, author of *Building an Evidence Based Practical Guide to Large Scale Interventions: Towards Sustainable Change with the Whole System* (Vlijmen, Netherlands)

"While I can't say that *Productive Workplaces* saved me from a burning building or plucked me from a raging river, I can say that this book slowly, systematically changed my thinking, my career, and my life."

—Birgit C. Olsen, Higher Education Consultant, doctoral student in organizational psychology, Walden University (Los Angeles, CA, USA)

"*Productive Workplaces* has been required reading since 1987 in Seattle University's Organization Systems Renewal (OSR) graduate program (formerly at Antioch Seattle). OSR's founding principle is to learn the theory, acquire the knowledge, and practice the skills required for putting theory into action. That is exactly what PW shows you how to do."

—Bob Woodruff, The Woodruff Group and Institute for Systemic Learning; former director and faculty, OSR (Seattle, WA, USA)

"For the past quarter of a century and for the foreseeable future, the clear and elegant expression of Marvin Weisbord in his books and his personal support have inspired untold numbers of practitioners dedicated to organizing and managing for dignity, meaning, and community. We are indebted to him and love him for his contribution to our work."

—Neil Watson, Independent SocioTechnical Systems Consultant (Sydney, Australia)

"Reading the preface of *Productive Workplaces*, I was touched by these words: 'There are no technical alternatives to personal responsibility and cooperation in the workplace.' To me, that sounded like coming home!"

—Hans Begeer, co-founder, Ubuntu4u (Brussels, Belgium)

"Learning from experience is somewhat of a cliché, but as the reader enters Marvin's thoughtful insights and reflections, the trip becomes an exciting journey."

—From the Foreword by Billie Alban

ABOUT THIS BOOK

Why is this topic important?

Productive Workplaces, 25th Anniversary Edition, traces the origins of and validates "getting the whole system in the room," a principle that has influenced large scale projects ever since the 1987 edition. The book was voted one of the five most influential books in the field by the Organization Development Network in 2004. It provides a model, guidelines, and successful methods for improving organizations under conditions of nonstop change. This may be the only book of its kind, for it includes follow-ups to ten projects done fifteen to thirty years earlier; the author not only reports what happened afterward, but also draws implications for managers and consultants today. With this glance backward, the book challenges the myth that you can "build in" practices that ensure continuity of new norms when leadership, staff, markets, technology, and ownership are constantly changing. "Each new generation," says Weisbord, "must learn all over again for itself." In this edition he supports his contention with forty new stories from practitioners who read earlier editions and applied the ideas to their own work.

What can you achieve with this book?

You can learn how to establish conditions for success before undertaking complex change projects. You will gain a deeper appreciation of key management practices and why some work better than others. The book will lead you to rethink, appreciate, and learn from your own experience and confirm that values matter more than techniques. It will help you become more secure and competent to face unprecedented dilemmas of nonstop change and cultural diversity.

How is this book organized?

The book contains five sections, revised to enhance the original by cutting some parts and adding contemporary material. Part One provides the bookends of Weisbord's story, starting with a summary of his conclusions after fifty years of practice, then backing up to tell the story of how he got started as a manager. Part Two tells key stories from management history, comparing the work of Frederick Taylor, "father of scientific management," to that of social scientists who came after. Part Three presents cases involving typical managerial dilemmas that illustrate an evolution in practice from expert problem solving toward involving everyone in whole-systems improvement. The cases were updated in the 2000s, with implications for today. Chapters added in 2003 on seminal workshops in primary medical care and steel production show the benefits of having whole systems study themselves. Part Four presents a practice theory for managing and consulting in the new millennium. It includes key guidelines for success and how-to methods by which the theory can be applied. It also shows how one company saved itself from oblivion using these guidelines. Part Five has new chapters on choosing among large-group methods and a summary chapter answering critical questions about the nature of change and the practice of effective workplace improvement.

What other *Productive Workplaces* resources are available?

An Instructor's Guide is available highlighting key points and questions raised by each chapter at www.pfeiffer.com/go/weisbord. At www.organizationaldynamics.upenn.edu you will find the Marvin Weisbord Archive, containing video interviews with many people mentioned in the book, plus cases studies and documentaries illustrating the themes. At MarvinWeisbord.com you will find downloadable versions of several cited articles.

Productive Workplaces

Productive Workplaces

DIGNITY, MEANING, AND COMMUNITY IN THE 21ST CENTURY

25th Anniversary Edition

Marvin R. Weisbord

The workplace classic, revised and expanded to include six new chapters and forty reader stories

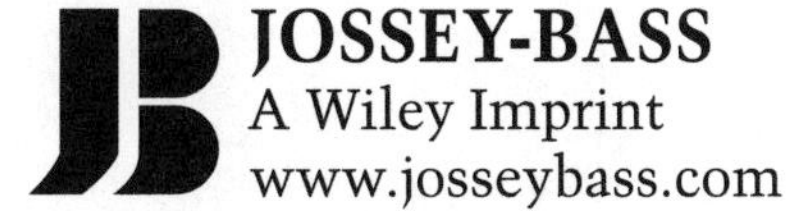

Published by Jossey-Bass
A Wiley Imprint
One Montgomery Street, Suite 1200, San Francisco, CA 94104-4594—www.josseybass.com

Jossey-Bass books and products are available through most bookstores. To contact Jossey-Bass directly call our Customer Care Department within the U.S. at 800-956-7739, outside the U.S. at 317-572-3986, or fax 317-572-4002.

Wiley also publishes its books in a variety of electronic formats and by print-on-demand. Some material included with standard print versions of this book may not be included in e-books or in print-on-demand. If the version of this book that you purchased references media such as CD or DVD that was not included in your purchase, you may download this material at http://booksupport.wiley.com. For more information about Wiley products, visit www.wiley.com.

Library of Congress Cataloging-in-Publication Data

Weisbord, Marvin Ross.
Productive workplaces : dignity, meaning, and community in the 21st century / Marvin R. Weisbord. – 3rd ed., 25th anniversary.
p. cm.
"The workplace classic, revised and expanded, including six new chapters and forty reader stories."
Includes bibliographical references and index.
ISBN 978-0-470-90017-8 (cloth); ISBN 978-1-118-09906-3 (ebk); ISBN 978-1-118-09907-0 (ebk); ISBN 978-1-118-09908-7 (ebk)
1. Industrial management. 2. Industrial management–Employee participation. 3. Quality of work life. I. Title.
HD31.W424 2012
658.3′14–dc23

2011029049

Printed in the United States of America
THIRD EDITION
HB Printing 10 9 8 7 6 5 4 3 2 1

Sitting in my local movie theater one Saturday at age eight, I was astonished a monochromatic film changed into brilliant Technicolor. *The Wizard of Oz* became my initiation into the illusory power of technology. Dorothy and her terrier Toto, blown by a Kansas tornado to a magic land, learn that only the Great and Terrible Oz can send them home. On the Yellow Brick Road to Oz, they meet a Tin Man, Scarecrow, and Cowardly Lion, each seeking a missing part: heart, brains, courage. The creatures join Dorothy and Toto, hoping the Wizard will make them whole.

The Great Oz awes them with his magic, appearing as a giant head, a lovely lady, and a ball of fire. He booms out that to have their wishes they must kill the Wicked Witch of the West. The quartet and Toto take on this risky quest. With axe, straw, and loud roar they defeat the wolves, crows, and bees sent to stop them. When all looks hopeless, Dorothy, protecting her friends, pours water on the Witch. To her astonishment, this simple solution melts the evil hag into oblivion.

They return for their rewards, and Toto, poking around, tips over a screen to reveal the Great and Terrible Oz as an old bald guy creating illusions with a homemade contraption. "Oh, you are a very bad man!" says Dorothy. "Oh no, my dear," says the Wizard, "I'm a very good man. I'm a very bad Wizard."

He then pretends to deliver heart, brains, and courage to Dorothy's companions, knowing that they already found these qualities while questing to kill the Witch.

"How can I help being a humbug, when all these people make me do things that everybody knows can't be done?" asks the Wizard. Later he suggests that Dorothy return to Kansas by clicking her heels three times, a capability she always had. Until that moment, she did not know that she had it.

I dedicate this book to Dorothy Barclay Weisbord, my lifelong companion on the Yellow Brick Road.

OTHER BOOKS BY MARVIN R. WEISBORD

Campaigning for President

Some Form of Peace

Improving Police Department Management (with Howard Lamb and Alan Drexler)

Organizational Diagnosis: A Workbook of Theory and Practice

Discovering Common Ground (with thirty-five international authors)

Future Search: An Action Guide (with Sandra Janoff)

Don't Just Do Something, Stand There! (with Sandra Janoff)

Other Resources

Visit the Marvin Weisbord Archive of interviews and case studies bringing to life people, cases, and stories from this book on the website of the Organizational Dynamics program at the University of Pennsylvania www.organizationaldynamics.upenn.edu/.

CONTENTS

UPDATES FROM THE FIELD

FOREWORD: THE EXISTENTIAL QUESTION

Years ago I was traveling on a tanker off the West Coast of South America crossing the equator into the southern hemisphere. It was a brilliant starry night. I had never seen the Southern Cross before, and there it was on the horizon. I was joined on the deck by a crew member. We stood there, the two of us, tiny, human specks under the dome of this incredible night. He turned to me and asked, "Señora, do you think we make any difference?" I have pondered that question most of my life.

I invited one of the people who contributed a story to the current edition of this book to tell me what she thought the word "meaning" signified in the subtitle of the first edition (*Organizing and Managing for Dignity, Meaning, and Community*). She responded, "The opportunity to make a positive difference in your workplace or organization."

Marvin Weisbord, with the publication of the first edition, made a major contribution to the field of organization development. This third edition of *Productive Workplaces* contains forty new stories and examples, interspersed among the chapters and contributed by people from all over the world: Scandinavia, Australia, South Africa, the U.S., UK, Europe, Canada, New Zealand, and Afghanistan. These managers, consultants, teachers, and students found that the concepts and ideas in Weisbord's book have resonated for them and influenced what they have done in their workplaces and communities.

The first chapter, "A Mythology of Organizational Change," sets the framework for the book. Marvin Weisbord, my colleague for four decades, points out that people's behavior is based on the myths and assumptions they hold as true. The stories we tell ourselves and the assumptions we make influence our behavior and the choices we make.

In the second chapter of Part One, Marvin tells the story of his own experience in his family business. "How I Learned to Manage by Managing" tells the story of his struggles working with employees to set up multi-skilled work teams that focused on the customer. Not only did this highly participative process work, increasing productivity, but also brought to the workforce a sense of dignity, meaning, and community. As you will read, the walls literally came tumbling down. It was this experience that propelled Marvin to venture out on a learning journey.

This book is the story of his travels, starting with Fredrick Taylor and pursuing the theories and experiments of those who strove to improve organizations. Marvin is constantly testing, moving back and forth from theory into practice and practice into theory. The book contains wonderful reflections on the work and insights of Fredrick Taylor, Kurt Lewin, Douglas McGregor, Eric Trist, and Fred Emery.

I want to call attention to Parts Three and Four in this book "Learning from Experience" and "Integrating the Past into the Present." Marvin highlights cases where he worked as a consultant searching to develop better organizations and workplaces, always testing theories and assumptions. What is remarkable about these sections is his return to these organizations, years after the work was completed, to find what had happened to the work they did together. How many consultants and managers dare go back to the sites where they have worked to learn what has occurred in the interim? It is a courageous thing to do! Many of us would rather live with the illusion that we made a difference and leave it at that!

The analyses of these cases is fascinating. Learning from experience is somewhat of a cliché, but as the reader enters Marvin's thoughtful insights and reflections the trip becomes an exciting journey.

Two important cases in this book are from the Sparrows Point plant of Bethlehem Steel and Atomic Energy of Canada's Medical Products Division (see Chapters Seventeen and Nineteen). These two cases offered a major opportunity for "involving everyone to improve the whole system," applying Marvin's core principles from his experience. Marvin also reminds us "sustainable change is an oxymoron" (see Chapter One). Organizations and our interventions often do not outlast the waves of tumultuous internal and external change: new managers, technologies, mergers, changes in the economy. However, those who are involved in participative organizational renewal processes report that they wouldn't have wanted to miss the experience. They carry the learning with them into the future.

Why, even when we get so fed up with bureaucratic and hierarchical systems, is it so hard to let go of old models? Could it be that early in our lives we are socialized into hierarchical systems—in family life, education, religious institutions, the military, and our early work experiences? Much as we disliked these systems, when push comes to shove we fall back on them, familiar and internalized. There is a wonderful examination of Douglas McGregor's Theories X and Y in this book. Marvin points out that the X and Y polarities are internal dialogues within the individual, not just a way of categorizing organizations and management styles. Marvin quotes Kurt Lewin, "We know more about autocracy than we know about democracy." In spite of the outstanding examples in this book, the act of working with these principles requires courage, daring to say "yes" to the dialogue within us.

I appreciated, throughout the book, the guidelines and principles that support the work of engaging everyone to improve the whole. I found myself noting many of the sage recommendations; guidelines for engaging the whole system, generic menus for work design, important insight in the use of team building, and, above all, always operating out of a clear set of values and principles, before worrying about methods and techniques.

Chapter Twenty-Six, the last chapter, has a wonderful closing section on "a life long agenda for managers and consultants." It contains suggestions for our journeying as we look to make a difference where we work and live. Marvin points out that all change—social, technical, economic—takes place one meeting at a time. Thus we have boundless opportunities to make constructive changes through the meetings we have each day.

There is a beach in the southern part of Chile that is strewn with stones marked with crisscrosses, tossed up by the waves. Legend has it that the

Southern Cross periodically scatters these stones. People collect them as a talisman. It is said that these stones bring mental clarity, wisdom, and wholeness. As you go through this book you will find ideas that resonate for you, underscoring your own experience. You will also discover fresh insights and new ways of taking action. Gather these treasures and take them with you. Bon Voyage!

Billie Alban

PREFACE: WELCOME TO *PRODUCTIVE WORKPLACES*, 25TH ANNIVERSARY EDITION

This is a book about people who have sought for 150 years to improve life at work. For the last fifty, that has included me. Starting as a manager in 1959, I spent a decade in business, more than twenty years as a consultant, and from the early 1990s have co-directed a global nonprofit. I spent several months refining this new edition. I especially sought to highlight the influence of the past on today's paradoxes. Although the world has changed exponentially since I first wrote PW, my key themes endure like granite. So do principles of productivity, even when confounded by technologies I could not imagine a quarter century ago.

In 1985, I sent an early draft of this book to Eric Trist, a key figure in my story. A few weeks later I flew to Florida, where he was retired, to review with him several cases in which I discerned an emerging new way to improve workplaces. Eric asked a few questions, then replied with a phrase I had never heard. "What you need," he said, "is a 'conceptual emboldening.'" That startled me. I had not known such an act was possible. I soon understood that he was asking me what conclusions I could draw from my cases. On a piece of scratch paper I sketched what I had lived through in my work during the previous quarter century. Such was the origin of "The Learning Curve" that ties together the chapters of this book.

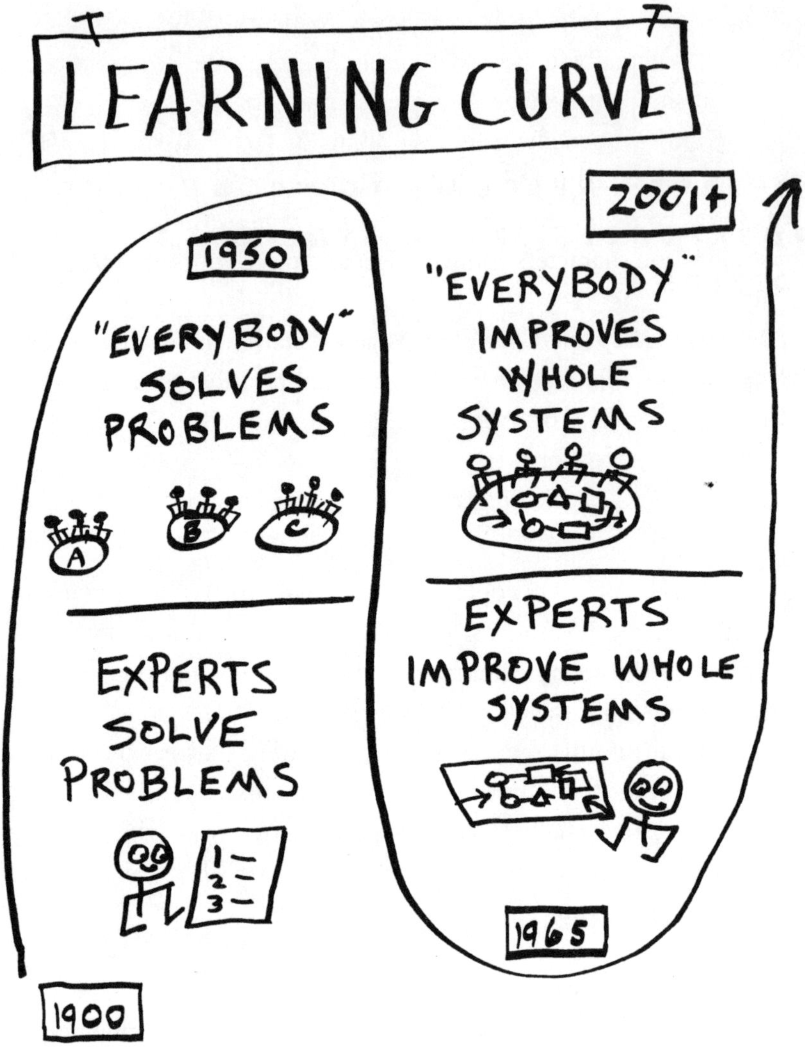

LEARNING CURVE

2001+

1950

"EVERYBODY" SOLVES PROBLEMS

A B C

EXPERTS SOLVE PROBLEMS

1— 2— 3—

1900

"EVERYBODY" IMPROVES WHOLE SYSTEMS

EXPERTS IMPROVE WHOLE SYSTEMS

1965

I will tell you in the pages that follow how experts solving problems morphed into everybody improving whole systems. You can see that these strategies are not mutually exclusive. Maybe you know them all. Indeed, what led me to this edition was that so many people had moved since 1987 toward "everybody improving whole systems." To my handful of past cases, I have the good fortune to bring you forty more examples from colleagues around the world who replicated my experience and added wrinkles of their own.

Thus, I am able to tell this story anew. While the four learning curve strategies co-exist, if you aspire to dignity, meaning and community, you won't be satisfied until you get everybody improving the whole. Not if you seek the economic benefits from ever-changing technologies. If you have read a past edition, you will find the original shortened, sharpened, and expanded. If you are reading this for the first time, you too may identify with some of the characters you will meet and place yourself in this never-ending story.

The Times Keep on Changing. When I started managing in 1959, nobody had cell phones, pagers, fax machines, personal computers, CDs, DVDs, PDAs, Google, or Wikipedia. The now obsolete Sony Walkman would not be invented for twenty years. My "personal digital assistant" was a little black book in which I wrote dates in pencil because they were sure to change. Blackberries were something you put on pancakes. To research a topic, I went to the library, looked up sources in a card catalogue, and made notes on 5 by 8–inch index cards. I wrote whole books on a typewriter. I backed up with carbon paper, something you may never have seen. I thanked my stars for these efficient technologies, wondering how Charles Dickens found time to write thousands of pages by hand.

I began a love/hate affair with computers in 1961. My company became one of its industry's earliest users, and I met my first expert systems improver who told me of a customer glitch I wanted to solve, "You can't do that. The program won't allow it." For decades I've been an early adopter, down to the iPad that contains drafts of this book. Without the Internet I could not have updated it. I have seen many life-changing technologies come and go—the linotype, monotype, key punches/verifiers, mimeograph machines, word processors, dot matrix printers, Polaroid cameras, and vinyl records. If you think Apple, Microsoft, and Amazon are the last word today, just wait until tomorrow. The thing to remember is that technology, like money, doesn't care what you do with it. Make life better, fritter it away. Your smart phone couldn't care less.

So, while I have a lot to tell you about effective human interaction, I have little to say about online conferencing, social networking, and technologies not yet invented. Fortunately, so many media cover those topics you are unlikely to miss them here. I believe you can apply the principles I advocate anywhere, including on the Internet. Until the day you can access a website and get back all that you would want from face-to-face meetings, what I shall tell you is worth pondering. Task-focused work has little in common with social networking. If your success requires collaborating with others, you'll still long at times to meet them up close and personal.

That life is speeding up is not a new observation. In the 1960s Eric Trist and his collaborator Fred Emery wrote a ground-breaking paper describing how outside events impacted organizations in ways that they could neither control nor ignore. Emery and Trist (1964) were the first to identify greater environmental uncertainty and interdependence among systems as conditions calling for responses few people knew how to make. What none of us appreciated in those years was that the *velocity* of change was accelerating at warp speed. The pace was outstripping our methods.

When I started consulting in 1969, business schools taught that big companies reorganized every seven years. They centralized in one cycle and decentralized in the next. For consulting firms this was a windfall. You took nine months to interview, diagnose, and write a report recommending to the client the structure they did not have, eighteen months to implement it, and had four plus years of stability before doing it again. The seven-year cycle became five years in the early 1970s, then three years, and by the 1980s reorganizations were as predictable as the seasons. Mergers, acquisitions, downsizings, globalizings, right-sizings. People were changing organization charts faster than they could photocopy them.

When I left the consulting business in 1992, the cycle was more like seven weeks. By the time you wrote a report, the scenario had changed. Companies and communities also were diversifying. Over the next twenty years I found myself helping people do strategic planning in many of the world's cultures. The meetings I ran grew more diverse with multiple ethnic groups speaking a Babel of languages, thrown together only by the task at hand, for example, improving economic conditions, extending health care, marketing new technologies, or reducing the risk of natural disasters. But what became of the stable old cultures that needed a jolt to unfreeze, move, and refreeze at some elusive higher level of functioning? One day I woke up and noticed I had restocked my tool kit.

I had worked by then in all kinds of systems with all sizes of groups. By the late 1980s I was certain my clients were infinitely more satisfied to the extent they could involve everyone in improving the whole. We are still learning how to do that. It takes everybody to maintain a satisfying equilibrium among economics, technology, and people. That, however, is only half the story. To sum up the rest of it, I paraphrase a wise teacher of traditional Chinese medicine, Dianne Connelly, to point out that this quest, online or off, will never be "a one-walk dog."

INTRODUCTION: GETTING THE MOST FROM *PRODUCTIVE WORKPLACES*

This edition brings up to date a practice theory for managing and consulting that I proposed in 1987 for a world spinning at warp speed. I call it "getting everybody improving whole systems." By "improving" I mean equal commitment to economic viability, and universal life values—dignity, meaning, and community. I came to that conclusion while rethinking methods I had used during a quarter of a century as a manager and consultant.

Processes for involving everyone have proliferated like wildflowers in the last quarter century. So too have assaults on dignity, meaning, and community. Few jobs are secure in the 21st Century. The march of technology and globalization is a mixed blessing if you seek techniques equal to your values. The challenges of the workplace have never been greater nor aspirations higher. Researchers for years have confirmed the economic benefits of attending equally to the needs of customers, employees, and shareholders (Kotter and Heskett, 1992), of maintaining community by optimizing people ahead of capital (de Geus, 1997), and of focusing on purpose and values before profits as a key to superior market performance (Collins and Porras, 1997). In the 21st Century you can add the tensions among work, personal health, and family life, exacerbated by technologies that encourage working at home or on vacation (Fisher and Fisher, 2011). The "systems" view I have adopted can be summed up simply this way:

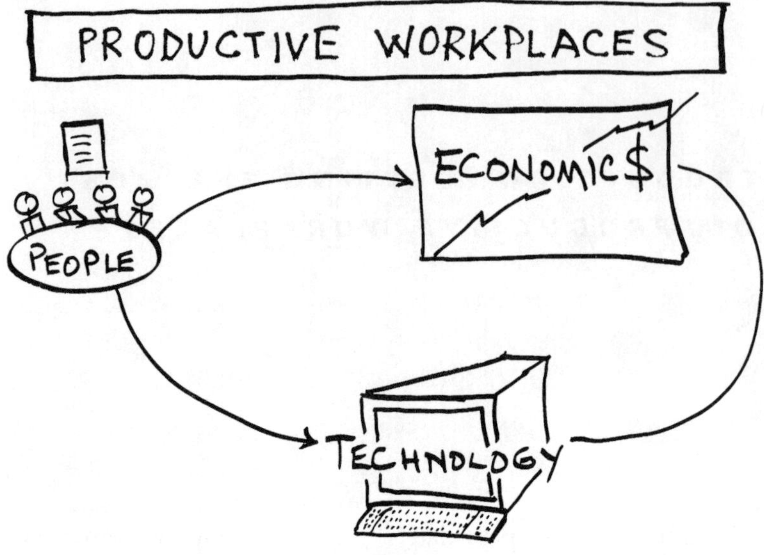

Purpose and Intent

In this book I present a history, principles, and successful methods for improving organizations caught up in nonstop change. I intend to show you that values matter more than techniques. I hope to encourage you to appreciate your own experience. This book summarizes what I have learned from mine.

I began thinking about these matters in the 1960s as executive vice president of a company in which conflict was so bad that people asked to have a wall built down the middle of a large, open office—a bit of Cold War Berlin in North Philadelphia. Into this hostile climate I introduced self-managing work teams. Output went down at first. Then it shot up like a rocket—40 percent—as the teams caught on to this new way of working.

My biggest surprise was the surge of energy and commitment among co-workers. Antagonists became friends. The psychic wall came down, followed by the real one. People built a community of interest around learning to care for customers. Absenteeism and turnover went to near zero. "I used to hate coming to work in the morning," said Anne, a veteran who hadn't smiled in years. "Now I can't wait." That's when I knew I was on the right path.

I saw self-managing teams as a way to increase business results by acting on my own values. I believed that autonomy and self-control were good for people. I had barely begun to connect productivity with dignity, meaning, community. Now, I have a serious case to make.

In 1987, the year this book first appeared, I took a leave of absence from my consulting company and joined Max Elden, an American professor, at the Norwegian Institute of Technology in Trondheim. Then I resumed consulting for four years, after which, tired of writing proposals and hiring staff, I called it quits. I thought of an exchange with my friend Gunnar Hjelholt, the late Danish social scientist, just after he gave up his company in Copenhagen for a 14th Century farmhouse in Jutland. Why did he quit? "Well," said Gunnar, "I was no longer lying awake at four in the morning worrying about the clients!" After more than twenty years of worrying, I too let go.

I had no plans other than to step off the merry-go-round. To this end, I joined with John Weir and Michael Merrill to offer several yearly "Men at Work" personal growth workshops. Interacting with a hundred men—executives, artists, consultants, businessmen, engineers, musicians, and teachers—I learned a lot about the theory and practice of personal change . I learned even more about myself.

In 1993, drawing on principles explicated here, Sandra Janoff and I started Future Search Network as a global nonprofit dedicated to service, colleagueship, and learning. While teaching "whole system" methods to thousands in subsequent years, I heard an oft-repeated theme: How can you be sure that people will carry out the action plans they make?

How Do You "Build In" Follow-Up?

I have pondered that question for years. I know one shopworn practice that doesn't work—external "coordination" by those not involved. I also can identify a guaranteed strategy with enormous benefits: interactive review meetings with "the whole system in the room." This book documents both polarities. I doubt that anybody can "build in" a technical insurance policy that trumps people's willingness to stay connected and revisit worthy goals. The key leadership policy I advocate is involving those who do the work in planning and coordinating the work. The best methods tend to be simple.

At the turn of the millennium I began wondering what became of the organizations whose case studies formed the core of my first edition. What could I learn about continuity in a turbulent world by seeking out former clients in organizations I once had sought to improve? What became of them during the fifteen to thirty years after I left? *Productive Workplaces Revisited* (2004), was the result of that inquiry. Everything I learned then you will find here.

For this edition, I added another question. What are readers of this book doing to advance the practice today? But for Future Search, I had no recent hands-on consulting experience, but perhaps I could get those who did to help me update the book. My query to friends and colleagues produced forty engaging new stories, bringing to life a future I could not have predicted in 1987.

Who Might Benefit from This Book?

For all these years my readers have been managers, consultants, students, researchers, and teachers. Having played all these roles too, I have suggestions for each.

I want to show managers that working toward dignity, meaning and community opens the door to quality and output far beyond what most organizations settle for.

To consultants I suggest that we are in the midst of a revolutionary revisioning of expertise. So much work cuts across multiple fields that no expert can do it all. Treating every consulting engagement as a potential step toward helping people collaborate to improve whole systems is a service desperately needed.

To researchers, students, and teachers I say that no further research is needed to prove the efficacy of task-focused participation in democratic societies. There are no technical alternatives to shared goals, cooperation, and personal responsibility. What's needed are more people who will stick their necks out. That means learning as much about ourselves—our impulses, noble and ignoble—as we learn about other important subjects. A "whole system" includes economics and technology, which exist only in and for us. I urge those engaged in studying organizations to see self-knowledge as integral to systems. Without us, there are no systems.

You might appreciate this book if you are . . .

- Looking for guidance in helping large, diverse groups pursue big purposes;
- Wondering what happens to "interventions" years later;
- Curious about what I learned during two decades of community and nonprofit service based on principles gleaned from three decades in businesses and medical schools; or
- Among those readers who asked me over the years to sign well-thumbed, annotated copies of earlier editions. I have got a great deal of job satisfaction from meeting you. You remind me of my life-changing encounter with Douglas McGregor's *Human Side of Enterprise* in 1966, enabling me years later to write this book.

Three Major Themes

Productive Workplaces has three themes woven into a counterpoint of history, case studies, criticism, and guidelines for action. One theme is that *people hunger for community in the workplace.* Those who find it are happier and more productive.

My second theme is that *the world is changing too fast for the short half-life of expert problem solving.* Involving people and experts together in improving the whole is the way to solve great handfuls of problems as they arise. Systems "thinking" lives only when people experience systems for themselves.

My third theme represents *a fresh interpretation of Douglas McGregor's (1960) dichotomy between Theories X and Y.* He called these assumptions about human nature, X grounded in laziness and incompetence, Y in self-motivation, achievement, and growth. After a hundred projects with thousands of people, I changed my mind in the 1980s about Theories X and Y. These are not polarized "management styles." They symbolize an inner dialogue we are having with ourselves—between parent and child, hard guy and soft guy, decisive self and passive self. Managing this dialogue—not techniques, strategies, or models—represents our main challenge in building more productive workplaces. Changing our workplaces is inevitably bound up with changing ourselves.

These themes mark my journey down a path as old as the Industrial Revolution. Elton Mayo (1945), founder of industrial human relations, noted how "science and industry put an end to the individual's feeling of identification with his group, of satisfaction in his work" (p. 6). But engineers had noticed the effects of alienation—accidents, low morale, low output—more than half a century before that. I write as a practitioner committed to involving people in continuously renewing their workplaces. I see myself on an endless road toward practices grounded in dignity, meaning, and community, central to economic success in a tsunami of global upheaval.

Overview of the Contents

Part One. Here you will find a chronicle of the way 19th Century methods gave way to 20th Century practices, preparing the ground for large-scale participation today. I retell stories from management history to support my contention that no good alternatives exist for worthy goals and employee involvement. I offer new interpretations of how the first consulting engineer, Frederick W. Taylor, and four social scientists, Douglas McGregor, Kurt Lewin, Fred Emery, and Eric Trist, translated values into action, I hope to convince you that building on their innovations is a critical 21st Century challenge.

I explore how Frederick Taylor's "scientific management" lost credibility as it metamorphosed into engineering solutions for what Taylor considered people problems. Organization development (OD), a social science of managing change derived from Kurt Lewin, took a similar turn whenever its advocates based solutions on feelings, human relations, and participation unconnected to markets and technology. Likewise, descendants of Emery and Trist—enamored of sociotechnical methods—sometimes lost sight of individual and group skills even as they designed work systems tied to consumer needs and technical flexibility.

Part Two. Here I take up my own evolution toward effective practices. I present six cases in which my colleagues and I helped to diagnose and resolve commonplace dilemmas—employee turnover, costs, production, staff-line cooperation—in the 1970s and early 1980s. I then critique this practice against a backdrop of accelerating change. Here I demonstrate my second theme—the inadequacy of expert management and consulting methods for coping with fast change. Through these cases I illustrate an evolution of practice from participative problem solving toward whole-systems improvement.

Part Three. Here I critique my cases and offer a "21st Century practice theory" for managing and consulting derived from the principles and practices in Parts One and Two. I outline simple criteria for assessing the potential for action—leadership, a business opportunity, and energized people. I propose three guidelines for success in high-risk projects: getting the whole system in the room, focusing on the future, and helping people do it themselves. I include cases from primary medical care and steel-making to illustrate how involving diverse parties in looking at the whole changed my approach toward consulting.

Part Four. Here I illustrate an attempt to apply the foregoing principles and methods to the year-long rescue of a Canadian medical products company.

Then I lay out three methods I found worth knowing—team building, participative work design, and strategic planning with Future Search. Since the early 1980s I have considered the latter a learning laboratory for large group processes, applicable to social, technological, and economic dilemmas today. Team building, a basic management mode for more than fifty years, ought to be in everybody's tool kit. Work design keeps evolving with permutations like process improvement and total quality management; techniques aside, nobody has a good substitute yet for involving the people who do the work.

Part Five. I have added a new chapter on choosing among "large group interventions," identifying these as evidence of a paradigm shift toward "getting the whole system in the room." You cannot hope for constructive change unless people experience themselves as part of a larger whole. Finally, I review what I learned from ten cases in earlier editions and the implications for practice today.

In a new concluding chapter, I tell my personal "aha," after all these decades, that the future never comes. The bottom line is ridiculously easy to say and ambiguously hard to implement: discover your own values and act on them every day.

What You Will NOT Find in This Edition

A decade ago, when Jossey-Bass asked practitioners and college teachers to suggest revisions to *Productive Workplaces*, some noted "dated references and outdated examples." I have remedied that here in part with the help of colleagues whose recent experiences appear throughout. Remember, though, that this fix lasts only a few eye blinks. I hope you still find the stories, cases, and research here relevant, and that you will join me in the possibility that values and principles have no "sell by" date. Various people suggested a long list of characters they wished I had included, from B.F. Skinner to W. Edwards Deming. One wanted more on Mary Parker Follett, a pioneer whose bold ideas I cite more than once.

Follett, a contemporary of Taylor's and Lewin's, wrote about the power of groups decades before "group dynamics" existed, of the integration of systems years before Ludwig von Bertlanffy's general systems theory, and of the value of diversity in organizations before most of us were born (Tonn, 2003). If you like history, you will find intellectual roots for team building, work design, and even Future Search in Follett's writings going back nearly a century!

That I have not put in more on Follett and the others is a choice, not an oversight. I wrote about people who directly influenced my work as I was doing it. This is an idiosyncratic, intensely personal book. This edition likewise reflects my experiences and passions with the notable addition of readers' stories.

Appreciating the Limits

If you decide the practice I describe fits for you, the formula is as plain as a Shaker table. Focus on worthy purposes. Get the right people in the room. Help people design and control their own work. Resolve to be a leader who does that or to work with those who do. Involving everyone, though, only succeeds under certain conditions. The money, in for-profit and nonprofit alike, has to come from somewhere. When society can no longer pay for goods and services, those who provide them must change what they do or look for other work.

If you want to walk easy in your skin, don't expect eternal life for your beloved methods, norms, and processes. The cosmos cares not one whit for people's struggles to get "change" accepted. All changes change. Anything you do today to enhance productivity in parallel with dignity, meaning, and community is existentially valuable. You cannot control what people do afterward. Perhaps this book will help you walk easy.

One of my favorite jazz pianists, Teddy Wilson, had a knack I have envied since my youth. He had an awesome left hand and could keep many improvised lines going without losing the melody. I have enjoyed weaving together themes from management history with my own practice in this fugue on productive workplaces. I also have found the lyrics extraordinarily hard to write. I am describing circles, wheels, and spirals in a medium that only permits straight lines. I hope that what comes through is the music and that you will find it natural to add your words to mine.

Marvin Weisbord
Wynnewood, Pennsylvania

May 2011

PART ONE Mythology and Managing

A baby has brains, but it doesn't know much. Experience is the only thing that brings knowledge, and the longer you are on earth the more experience you are sure to get.

—The Wizard of Oz to the Scarecrow,
Baum, 1900, 1958, pp. 113–114

I open this edition with two chapters that form the bookends for this volume. Chapter One summarizes ten myths I have revised after fifty years of managing, consulting, and running a nonprofit network. They constitute advice to myself for leading in an era of accelerating diversity and change. You may agree with me or not. You cannot escape acting on your assumptions.

Chapter Two describes how I first learned to manage, discovered self-managing teams, and began on this journey in the 1960s. Had I not been socialized to "bottom lines" for a decade, I could not have written this book.

In the remainder of the book, I will show how my encounters with key figures in management history influenced the way I managed and consulted, and how, working in corporations and medical schools, I came to devise a practice theory I thought better fit conditions of increasing diversity and nonstop change. I also describe how I and others have applied it with surprising results around the world.

chapter **ONE**

A Mythology of Organizational Change

Mythology—The body of stories associated with a culture, institution or person.

—The Visual Thesaurus

I begin this 25th Anniversary edition with ten stories I no longer believe. I gathered them during fifty years of working with businesses, medical schools, social agencies, and communities. Myths are real and they shape your behavior. I reframed mine over many years while interacting with students from computer science, criminal justice, education, engineering, finance, government, health care, marketing, manufacturing, and sales in Seattle University's Organization Systems Renewal master's program (formerly at Antioch/Seattle) and in Benedictine University's doctoral program in organization development (OD). Nearly all sought OD training because they wanted better myths for their lives and work. Several students have rewarded me with their stories for this anniversary edition.

Perhaps my description of the myths I have given up will help you put your own in perspective. Consider this a primer on how I would manage or consult today. Rather than save all my advice for later, I offer you "Alternative Stories" to whet your appetite for what follows.

Myth 1: Changes Are Sustainable

Sustainable change is an oxymoron. For years I believed I had a responsibility to "build in" follow-up mechanisms with organizations. These were intended to reinforce new leader behavior, solidify learning, make collaborative problem-solving instinctive, and promote a new culture as a "way of life." Hierarchies were to be flattened like pancakes. In the 1970s I learned to admire companies like Hewlett-Packard, whose founders had cooked up an attractive recipe. My follow-up practice was long on team meetings, task forces, training, coordinators, and coaches. It fell short on longevity. Half the organizations I consulted with in the 1970s and 1980s no longer exist. Nor does H-P in the form I once admired. No organization lasts, no matter how dazzling your "interventions." Of the thirty companies that became the modern Dow Jones Industrial Average in 1928, only General Electric is still listed. If you invest your life force in sustaining change, the only thing you are likely to sustain is a bruised ego and impaired idealism.

Alternative Story. I recommend seeing whether you can sustain new practices from one meeting to the next. Organizations change one meeting at a time. Their destinies entwine in a maelstrom of markets, technology, and world events that nobody controls. Your best strategy will always be to help people do the best they can now with what they have. If you seek a new "culture," make every meeting congruent with the culture you seek. You can have it all now. Not the outcomes, but surely the processes you advocate. The goal of all projects ought to be giving *these* people, in *this room*, at *this moment*, opportunities they never had before. That's structural change. It's controllable. Keep doing this, and *you* will be sustainable, no matter what happens after the meeting. If you work at "building in" sustainable behavior in turbulent workplaces, you may burn out before the organization does.

Myth 2: Training Will Fix It

In the 1970s I believed with multitudes of colleagues that training everybody transforms organizations. We trained tens of thousands to supervise, manage, appraise, cooperate, set goals, give feedback, and participate in decisions. Such training took place in peer groups, lest people embarrass themselves with those above or below. Training was intended to help people change the way their companies operated. We kept getting people ready to do what they never did. Indeed, many people transformed their relationships with spouses, children, and co-workers. Their companies—a tangled maze of policy, procedure, programs, controls, and technologies—went on doing whatever they did before. Individuals receive enormous benefits from training in leader behavior, self-awareness, cultural sensitivity, and personal skills. Organizations should offer all they can afford. Do not mistake training for organizational change.

Alternative Story. All people already have skills and knowledge they cannot use at work. They are blocked by job descriptions, their place in the pecking order, the location of their desks, the size of their turf, restricted information, and limited influence over working conditions. These structural issues cannot be altered through skills and awareness training. People improve organizations using what they already know to influence policies, procedures, systems, and structures. People motivate themselves doing projects that have consequences for the whole. Paradoxically, when you empower people to act together on business tasks, they often change their behavior. Measurable outcomes follow employees' influence in the design, control, and coordination of their work. Then training can be of enormous benefit. Fix structures first. Then watch how many people "straighten up and fly right."

Myth 3: Profit Rules

If making money were a rational motivator, than everybody would do participative work redesign and Future Searches (Chapters Twenty and Twenty-Two). That's where the big gains lie. For many executives the bottom line is power and control. Keeping control is much more comfortable than opening a system to who-knows-what, even to make more money, especially if you can keep shareholders happy with modest gains. For many executives, the perceived risks and uncertainty of broad involvement outweigh the evidence of significant financial benefits.

Alternative Story. An organization builds infinitely more economic strength empowering people to cooperate in keeping costs down and productivity up. Indeed, some firms embrace a "triple bottom line" that includes not only money but social capital and benefits to society. They invest a percentage of profits in developing their people and supporting their communities. Which strategy attracts you? Watch yourself around people whose stated motivation is money alone. Nearly always they are the same people whose control needs are so great they cannot do what creates value in the long run. I did my most productive work with those who could imagine bottom lines beyond net profit. They used capital to benefit everyone.

Myth 4: Fortune 500s Are Forever

The Fortune 500s ought to be good places for organizational innovation. Consultants love claiming them as clients. Indeed, in the 1970s and 1980s they were good to me and my colleagues. Big corporations put organization development on the map. They paid well, changed fast, and needed lots of help. They enabled us to put our kids through college. In the 1970s many "personnel departments" adopted OD and experiential training. They became conduits for OD consultants at all levels. They were great places to practice the consulting art.

Over time, many of us came to realize Fortune 500s were among the least auspicious places for OD. I suggest three reasons. First, good OD requires continuity in leadership. Our projects rarely outlasted the managers who sponsored them. Two, good OD seeks systems integration. Even visionary executives are stuck with one department running technology, another cost control, a third human resources. Good execs know that the way to fix chronic coordination deficit is to put all parties into the same room. That many cannot do this stems from the "faster, shorter, cheaper" virus infecting public companies.

Alternative Story. It's hard to make long-term improvements in firms that (a) are publicly traded, (b) pay quarterly dividends, and (c) churn executives at the top. If the quarterly dividend comes in a few cents below some analyst's prediction, the stock price goes down. Billie Alban, who wrote the foreword to this book, once asked a multi-national CEO what he would do with a magic wand. "I would buy back the company's stock," he said without hesitation, "so I could invest for the long term and not have to dance each quarter to Wall Street's pipes!" This is not to say you can't do good OD in such firms. Only be aware that you are building for today, not for the ages.

It's worth noting an extraordinary exception. "Our long-term focus may be the wrong business strategy," warned the founders of Google, when they took public in 2004 one of the most successful start-ups in history. They proceeded to invest in robot autos and off-shore wind farms that might not pay off for decades (Liedtke, 2010). It's no coincidence that I did my most impactful strategic conferences with Berrett-Koehler Publishers, Haworth, IKEA, Resources for Human Development, and Whole Foods Market (Weisbord and Janoff, 2010). What had they in common? All had decades of continuity at the top and all save Whole Foods, which went public and 1992 and paid no dividends until 2003, were private corporations.

Myth 5: Organizations Learn

Organizations don't learn. *People* learn. Organizations have Alzheimer's. They have a hard time retaining experience. I believe this holds too for the "double loop" (learning how to learn) and "triple loop" (learning how to learn how to learn) variety. These concepts make engaging workshops with little long-term systemic impact (Bounds, 2009). This conclusion has led me to drop "Learning Organization" from the title of Chapter Six on Kurt Lewin's legacy. Lewin's priceless idea was not just learning by doing, but also "doing by learning." He saw workplaces as laboratories for collaborative "action research," a practice of systematic inquiry, on which I built a career. Inquiry may have been a way of life for many consultants, but not the clients. It is hard to institutionalize new norms amidst the turbulence. Norms—the unwritten rules of behavior—follow the leader. If organizations learned, Chrysler and Daimler-Benz might not have merged. If organizations learned, People Express Airlines, Bethlehem Steel, Digital Equipment, and Scott Paper would still be leaders instead of no more. If organizations learned, those who lived through Vietnam might not have taken on Iraq.

Alternative Story. I believe an organization's memory is no longer than the tenures of those in charge. I have spent years helping managers build great learning organizations that their successors took apart in months. I never met a new manager who said, "This place runs like a Swiss watch. I think I'll leave it alone." They all set out to improve what they inherit, even if they make things worse. Do not imagine—whether you manage or consult—that any processes you establish will survive a change in leadership. My advice is to put away your illusions if you work in a place you cannot control. Today is the future. You cannot flatten pyramids for the ages or "build in" honest communication. Do your best to help people learn today with no expectations for next year. One benefit of Future Search (Chapter Twenty) is that those responsible for the present revisit the past together, reminding each other of where they have been. They also interpret their experience in light of world events. This sets the stage for systemic action—if those in charge choose to take it.

Myth 6: Layoffs Improve Bottom Lines

Wall Street loves layoffs. Costs go down, and the stock's price goes up. Alas, the fix turns out worse than the problem. Rensis Likert (1967) called layoffs "liquidating human assets"—trading skills, experience, future capability, and competitive advantage for short-term cash. In earlier editions of this book I made a strong case against layoffs, especially in Chapter Nineteen on the rescue of AECL Medical Products. When I started working on this edition, during the worst recession since the 1930s, I reconciled myself to the ugly idea that secure employment, like fossil fuels, had no future. Some argued, for example, that job security and loyalty are artifacts of an old paradigm. A hopeful new one would focus on helping people keep marketable skills, stay mobile, and value what they do (Noer, 2009). I prepared to backpedal on my naïve idealism.

My mood changed when I read a *Newsweek* cover story by Stanford professor Jeffrey Pfeffer (2010). He noted that every airline save one laid off people after 9/11. The outlier was Southwest, the largest U.S. domestic carrier, with a market value greater than all its competitors combined. It had never in its history opted for an involuntary layoff. (It's co-founder, the legendary Herb Kelleher, led the company for thirty-seven years, enabling it to avoid Wall Street madness.) Pfeffer cited study after study to bolster the case that layoffs incur hidden costs, hurt people, undermine the future, injure a company's reputation, diminish its capacity to act, and reduce shareholder returns over time. "The facts seem clear," he concluded. "Layoffs are mostly bad for companies, harmful for the economy, and devastating for employees." Pfeffer calls downsizing "copycat behavior," a kind of contagion that infects companies. You can resist if you control your business. My father made it a policy for thirty-five years in good times and bad never to lay anybody off. You can see where I get my bias.

Alternative Story. If I were in a cost crunch now, I would take the AECL Medical approach—involve everybody in rethinking markets, products, services, and systems. I would push for across-the-board pay cuts to keep everybody employed. In this scenario, nobody loses jobs, health care, and homes nor ends up in a welfare line. All tighten their belts until the turnaround, when my company gains market share, increases profits, restores pay cuts, pays bonuses, and is the hub of a vibrant business community. Layoffs would be the last resort, when nothing else could save the company. Imagine a society built on that myth.

Myth 7: Hard Data Motivates Skeptics

Pfeffer mobilizes persuasive data in his case against layoffs. I detect little impact on businesses. I began compiling positive statistics when I noticed a 40 percent jump in productivity by the multi-skilled teams I started in the 1960s (Chapter Two). This book contains many more examples. Anybody who ever tried to influence skeptics with hard data knows how futile it is. If managers were rational, all companies would have employees designing their own work. Such involvement has been known for decades to produce gains of 20 to 40 percent in higher output and lower costs. Why "prove" that yet again in this book? I do it to reassure myself and other believers that we are not crazy. Never underestimate the psychic benefits of positive reinforcement. You can always test this proposition for yourself. Involve people and measure the results. That's an experiment that skeptics, locked into self-fulfilling prophecies, are loath to do.

Alternative Story. There is a "shadow" side to the data myth. That is the fact that you can assemble statistics to prove whatever you please. You can find scientific studies for and against what you eat, how you heat your house, the way you get to work, and the toothbrush you use. (Electrics work best, but if you make and/or use them you increase global warming.) Pollsters frame political questions to obtain whatever answers they seek.

"Do you believe taxes are too high?" Resounding yes. "Would you support a tax cut if it meant poorer education for your children and more potholes on your street?" No, no, no. In the end, which data you choose to believe becomes an act of faith.

Myth 8: Diagnosis Solves the Problem

Many organizations rely on experts to diagnose situations and prescribe changes. Diagnosis means finding gaps between what is and what should be. Some experts will tell you how to close the gaps; others leave it to you. There are economic fixes, technological fixes, and people fixes aimed at every human failing. Sometimes closing one gap opens up another, for example, the computer system that saved nanoseconds while driving its users crazy.

Here's a short diagnosis of the diagnosis myth by one who wrote an organizational diagnosis textbook still in use (Weisbord, 1978b). The first law of diagnosis is what you look for is what you find. Everything is there all the time. The second law is that there are more categories for things you can find than stars in the galaxy. If "resistance" is your hobby horse, for example, look no further than the next proposal for change. Costs are always too high, systems are always failing, and few people behave the way they should. Those who seek to remedy these situations by imposing programs invented elsewhere are sure to stir up resistance. The cure worsens the disease.

Alternative Story. Diagnosis, like "hard data," is a trap for the unwary. While the problems you turn up may be real, fixing them may not make an organization better. If you want people to collaborate while they compete for bonuses, forget it. If you expect creativity in a hierarchy with seven levels of management, forget it. Only you can decide which categories require immediate action and which you can live with. A diagnostic model—for example, what categories will yield the best results with the least effort—is backed only by the experience of people authorized to apply it.

Labeling people "change resisters" or "in denial" is sure to evoke the behavior it predicts. "Isms" are everywhere. Learning to contain ourselves and act responsibly is a lifelong project. Interestingly, when people work together to fix economic and technological problems that affect everybody, they often change their attitudes and relationships. If you seek to fix all diagnosable shortcomings before people can do good work, they will never do any work. Perhaps the most liberating thing I did for myself was to cut "defensiveness" and "resistance" from my vocabulary. I decided to work with people the way they are, not the way I wish they would be. The only proven strategy to workable implementation of anything is involving people in their own diagnosis and action planning.

Myth 9: The Technology-Saves-Time Myth

Human ingenuity is limitless. Creativity abounds. Inspiration may strike in an instant. Time, like old man river, just keeps rolling. Time is the world's least renewable resource. When it's gone, it's gone. The shadow side of technology is that it fragments time. The more "labor-saving" technology you have, the harder you work overall. You end up doing more than you used to, in shorter and shorter time frames, at the expense of anything else that matters. PDAs go to the supermarket, out to dinner, to the golf course, and to the beach. I have an IN-BOX of emails daily, each calling for me to answer now, look at pictures, read a document, make a new friend, visit a website, or endorse a book that I have no time to read. "People sit in meetings," noted an ex-partner of mine who was a corporate OD director, "balancing the art of listening with reading and sending messages on their BlackBerries and laptops. During breaks they attack their cell phones. Facebook. LinkedIn. Twittering. Texting. The meetings become secondary. They are merely the place to gather as everyone becomes more and more adept at juggling priorities at a frenetic pace" (Dupre, 2010).

Alternative Story. You cannot make a meeting longer without borrowing from whatever comes after. You cannot get back the days, weeks, or months spent on plans you can't implement. Many of us run from one fruitless meeting to another, month after month, when three solid days spent with those who matter most to our work could simplify everything. The only way to check the validity of what I say is to try a three-day meeting instead of a new computer app when you want an implementable strategic plan. Discover how to do it shorter, faster, and cheaper without cutting corners or driving everybody crazy. If you have the time, Chapter Twenty-Two will tell you how and why.

Myth 10: Meetings Undermine Work

The first thing I learned when I started consulting was the endemic cynicism people dump on meetings. Meeting jokes and cartoons abound. Q: "What's the best way to avoid working?" A: "Call a meeting!" One reason you have so many meetings is that a lot of them really do waste your time. Meetings, like techniques, could care less how you use them. To what extent is your meeting fatigue traceable to PowerPoints nobody cares about? All major change projects, for better or worse, proceed via the reviled, maligned, and unavoidable meetings that everyone loves to hate.

Alternative Story. Meetings are the best shot you will ever have at making an organization better. Meetings of the right kind, that is. I'm advocating purposeful meetings, interactive meetings, meetings that matter, meetings where people solve problems and influence decisions. Whether you hold them live or online, you will be interacting with others for all your days in the workplace. My last bit of advice, like my first bit, is to make every encounter worth the time you put in. I'll close with a short commercial. If you want to run productive meetings, check out *Don't Just Do Something, Stand There!* (Weisbord and Janoff, 2007).

■ ■ ■

"THE PUBLIC SECTOR IS UNDER PRESSURE..."

KOLDING, DENMARK—Some twenty years ago I was in a transition from working as a field biologist with marine systems to social psychology and counseling. My education was influenced by the Scandinavian tradition pioneered by Gunnar Hjelholt, the Danish applied social scientist (see page 109). I have since worked mostly within the public sector in Denmark as internal consultant on the basic education of new managers while supporting a network of experienced managers. I also have worked in my own praxis as a consultant and trainer in Denmark and abroad; as a T-group trainer (University of Graz, Austria); and as a steering committee member at the Philosophical Institute, University of Aarhus, Denmark, for the master's program in Organizational Philosophy and the Ethic of Professional Work.

I also serve on the examining committee for the "Diploma in Leadership"—a bachelor-level certificate for Danish managers. Most are adult business school students working as in-job managers. Reading their work and exams, I have noticed some basic assumptions that seldom are explored in class:

- Everything is changing and is changing faster than before;
- Modern employees are self-managing and of a quite different sort than employees earlier in time;
- Leadership and management in the past were totally detail- and control-oriented, that is, management by fear;
- The solution to almost every problem today is innovation, with self-governing teams managed by dialogue and value-based leadership; and
- We have no time to work with what's really needed.

The last statement above has become a standard comment from managers. "Something needs to be changed, but we can (will) not take the time needed—because of 'the very fast-moving world' we live in." This perception, especially about social systems, is to me pure imagination; yet the assumption of stress strongly affects my clients. The public sector in Denmark is under pressure. I can understand their dilemma. Everyone wants something more from public workers. Their perceptions correspond with the working conditions. This does not help, of course, because we are working with human beings—even in groups and organizations—so taking the required time is important in some situations. I think that the students, who also are managers, don't always realize that being in a rush can be a nice way to avoid analyzing what's going on.

Moreover, for years I have read in older books all the statements about what's needed. It strikes me that the student introduction to change literature today mostly includes only the "newest" books, often with a short (if any) summary of relevant themes other authors have explored earlier. At the same time I sometimes feel pressure from my clients to present something *new.* I can understand why. But in order to be professional, I will have to be both critical and helpful to relate in a meaningful way to my clients and students. It takes time to change one's perceptions. If my point has validity, then we and our management education schools are in some danger in not introducing basic works of the past to the next generations. In this respect *Productive Workplaces* is a great guide for reflection on what is actually happening today in my work.

—Henrik Simmelkjær, consultant, former secretary of the European Institute for Transnational Studies in Group and Organizational Development (eit)

chapter
TWO

How I Learned to Manage by Managing

Behavior speaks louder than words.

—*The Selected Wisdom of New Jersey*,
Clapp and others, 1975, no. 99

In the 1960s, before I had the concepts and methods that became this book, I was executive vice president of a direct mail printing company. My father founded the business on the eve of World War II. Like all entrepreneurs, he managed everything, hiring "pairs of hands" to print, keep books, write ad copy, and ship orders. In the 1950s cheap methods for interleaving business forms with carbon paper and crash-printing names and addresses led to an explosion of new markets. Expensive multi-copy forms became mass consumer items anyone could afford.

For many years my dad had worked in a staid Philadelphia brokerage firm, earning a finance degree from the Wharton School at night. Now, in his own business, he could indulge his inordinate, even naïve, faith in modern technology. It would make life better, he felt certain, which meant easier, more cost-effective, and above all Depression-proof. This suited my experimental nature perfectly. We quarreled over many decisions, but never whether something new was worth trying.

Long before equal employment opportunity became the law of the land, for example, we accepted the tensions associated with hiring blacks into our office. From lily white in 1959, our workforce became by 1966 one-third minority. We also retained an industrial engineer to do a new plant layout based on the inventory required by rapid growth. We hired an advertising agency as many new competitors entered a market our firm had pioneered.

We were among the early computer users in our industry. Our first service bureau in 1962 was the Franklin Institute, a Philadelphia science museum that had an ancient Univac, direct offspring of ENIAC, the first computer, developed in the 1940s at the nearby University of Pennsylvania. Its massive vacuum tubes required a room the size of a tennis court and forty tons of air conditioning. But it organized our mailing lists and spit out reports that told us a great deal that we did not know about customers' buying habits. That it had less computing capability than a cell phone astonishes me. It also had the frustrating tendency to shape business policy. Among my indelible memories is the first time a system analyst said of a customer decision I wished to make, "You can't do that. The machine isn't programmed to handle it."

Crisis Management. Despite favorable economics, we had a full platter of social and technological problems. Trained as a journalist, I had never attended a workshop or read a management book. My energy focused on crisis, what my father called "going to war every day." Would the truckers strike and interrupt our supply lines? Would employees start a guerrilla operation in the shipping department? Would paper company negotiations break down, causing chaos in the pressroom? Would Congress raise postal rates?

I fought my war as a series of daily skirmishes, all tactics, no strategy. By osmosis I had assimilated what social scientists David Bradford and Allan Cohen called "the heroic style" of management. "Middle and upper managers," they wrote in a passage that knocked me back twenty years, "are almost invariably preoccupied with control" (1984, p. 28).

In those days I knew nothing about the human relations movement washing like a tidal wave over U.S. industry. The T-group phenomenon was the subject of intense involvement and research in such companies as TRW Systems, Esso Research and Engineering, and Union Carbide. Thousands of managers were learning in these groups to listen more effectively, take initiative, cooperate, and modify their behavior. They also found that improving self-awareness and personal skill could not alter the policies, procedures, systems, and norms at their work sites. Years later I would discover how this research had stimulated team building, intergroup problem solving, and other applications of training theory more closely attuned to organizational goals and structures, the foundations of organization development. (See Chapter Seven.)

None of this did I know in the early 1960s. My teachers were salespeople, trade journals, competitors, suppliers, my father, who was full of practical wisdom, and our employees, some of whom were mechanical wizards. Jimmie Lee Jones, for example. One day Jimmie Lee showed up on our doorstep, diploma neatly folded in his back pocket from a segregated black high school in North Carolina, looking for a job, any job. I hired him to wrap packages. Within a year, he was training on printing equipment. Within two years he had suggested a modification to the vaunted Jet Press that the manufacturer declared would not work. I insisted the change be made, promising to relieve their engineers of responsibility. The manufacturer, without a nod to Jimmie Lee, incorporated his fix on future models because it significantly improved output and quality.

Taylor's Legacy. Engineering prejudice against hourly workers goes back to the turn of the century and Frederick W. Taylor, "the father of scientific management." Taylor's system called for trained industrial engineers to figure out the one best way to do things. All others—even managers and supervisors—were to keep their hands off (Chapters Three and Four).

Newer principles that confounded some of Taylor's notions already existed then but were not widely known until U.S. industry discovered Japanese methods in the 1970s. In the 1960s I was learning to up productivity the same way Jimmie Lee did—by doing. On a particular day significant for my later career, my dad asked me to investigate piecework pay that would motivate machine operators to run more jobs each day. I called my friend Don Kirchhoffer, a compensation specialist at RCA, and asked him how they got people to produce more.

Introduction to Theory Y

Hourly workers, Don said, tend to level off production at a rate comfortable for the majority. "We have lots of plans," said Don, "but even the best individual incentives rarely increased overall output." Don referred me to William E. Whyte's research (1955) showing that, if you want all that's possible, you have to consider the operators' needs in addition to money, such as good relations with one another. So saying, he handed me Douglas McGregor's *The Human Side of Enterprise* (1960), the "Theory X, Theory Y" book. I devoured it in one weekend. To use language I did not know then but would learn soon enough, it blew my mind.

Management's assumptions, said McGregor, determine management's behavior. Theory X assumes that most people are lazy, irresponsible, passive, and dependent. They require work broken into tiny pieces and tightly supervised lest they make a mess. This was the theory that "Taylorism" had reinforced for decades. McGregor suggested alternative assumptions derived from recent behavioral research—that, if given a chance, most people will take responsibility, care about their jobs, wish to grow and achieve, and do excellent work. This he called Theory Y.

From the first chapter I knew which side I was on. Yet when I looked, I saw Theory X everywhere: time clocks, narrow work rules, jobs so subdivided even an idiot would be bored, grown people treated like children, never let in on decisions, having little knowledge of the business or even their own work, expected to deliver in return for a $5 raise every six months, a turkey at Christmas, and a chance, if they didn't die of boredom, to become supervisors. The title, I observed, gave people who had been treated like children the license to treat others that way.

The Wall. I had inherited "Taylorism" without knowing it. Now, stimulated by McGregor, I started listening and soliciting ideas. The supervisors, encouraged by my new accessibility, came with a request—that a wall be built down the center of the order processing area, a huge bull pen in which five groups worked in their own areas.

"A what?" I asked, wondering if I'd heard right.

"A wall," one of them said, "between order entry and billing."

"Why?" I asked.

"The groups fight a lot. They defend their turf. Bad feelings are building up. If they don't have to look at each other, they won't fight. We supervisors get along, but the people distract each other."

By now I was Theory Y all the way. If people needed a wall, they would get a wall. I called in the carpenters. Next morning an eight-foot-high partition divided the room, with space at each end to walk around. The place was quiet, people bent over their desks in a miasma of depression.

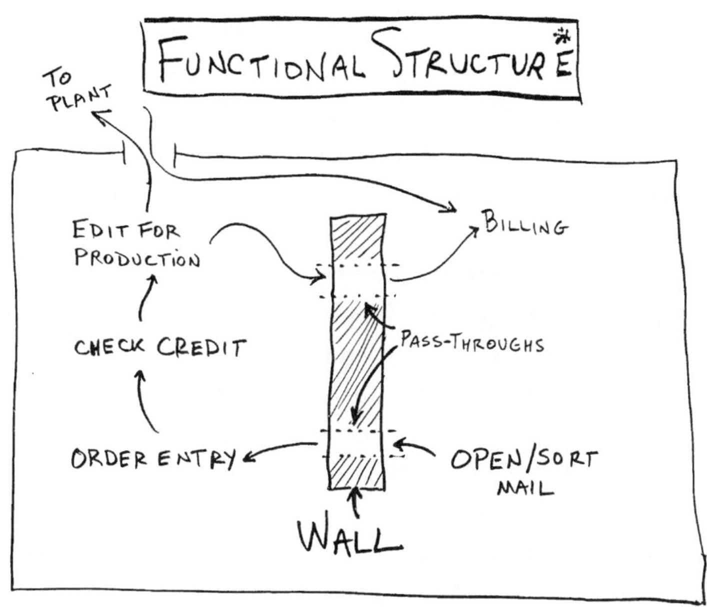

*ORGANIZED BY NARROW TASKS

The supervisors were waiting for me. "There's a small detail," one said. "We need pass-throughs so work can go from one group to the other." The carpenters cut openings in the wall, below eye level to minimize contact. The "Functional Structure" sketch shows how the wall was intended to reduce conflict in order processing.

Despite a nagging uneasiness, I believed the wall was a good example of my new management style. It was the supervisors' idea, not mine. People no longer fought openly. They just flashed hostile glances across the continent that divided them, a vast psychological distance it would take me years to appreciate.

The wall was a tangible symbol for the separation of functional specialties, the pass-throughs a necessity for integrating functions while avoiding contact. In their "differentiation/integration" studies, Harvard Business School's Paul Lawrence and Jay Lorsch (1967) highlighted the subtle ways in which structure influences behavior. They showed, for example, how avoiding conflict hurts output. I would soon learn how our considerable absenteeism and turnover were connected to the narrow jobs, status differences, and lack of trust built into our policies, procedures, and control systems.

Narrow jobs diminish all workers, including those sentenced to supervise them. Nobody can discover their capabilities. My experience also revealed the paradoxes inherent in systems change. I had upgraded my "management style" with a decision that worsened the problem. Had I been more sophisticated at OD I might have sought to build trust by getting both sides to put their grievances on the table. Fortunately, my ignorance freed me to make an important discovery: how bad structures fracture relationships. This was not a psychological time bomb to be defused through "feedback." I was managing an alienating, unproductive work system.

Hiring Consultants. I turned to Don Kirchhoffer, who had given me McGregor's book. He and Bob Maddocks, an RCA training specialist, met with me on Saturday mornings on how to implement Theory Y. The next several months became the most intense learning laboratory of my life. Maddocks introduced me to systems thinking. He suggested I stop building discreet problem lists and instead imagine myself managing three related systems, a "Human System," "Work System," and "Reward System." When solving a problem, consider the consequences for each. (I did not know it then, but I had here the seeds for "the six-box model" for organizational diagnosis that I would put into a book in 1978.)

This introduction to conceptual thinking enormously expanded my ability to manage. For the first time I could see which technical problems I could solve with, say, a new factory conveyor system, and which human problems I might encounter. The capital cost was a management decision. Operating costs were entirely in the employees' hands. They needed to be in on the decision from the start.

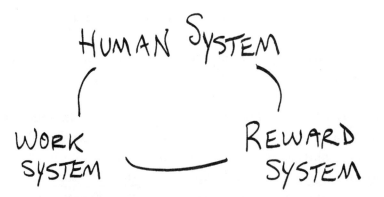

HUMAN SYSTEM

WORK SYSTEM

REWARD SYSTEM

The Initial Project: Multi-Skilled Teams

Our major bottleneck, I decided, was the department with the wall. Picture this situation: four or five people staffed each of five narrow functions through which orders flowed. One group sorted mail and sent out samples. Another entered data, a third checked credit, a fourth wrote production orders. A fifth typed and mailed invoices and matched incoming checks with unpaid bills. Each person had a few simple tasks and little discretion.

Up to three hundred orders arrived each day by mail or phone. One absentee in any function put the system down 20 percent. Two people absent from, say, order entry, cut order flow nearly in half, even though 90 percent of the workforce was present! This cost overtime dollars and hurt morale because people hate to fall behind.

Reading McGregor on teamwork, talking with Don and Bob, I had an insight. I could reorganize order processing into teams that included all specialties. Each could have its own customers. People could acquire many skills. Teams could set their own goals and priorities, based on total workload. A few absentees would hardly matter. The entire workforce would develop greater flexibility and become more productive. How much more would prove extraordinary—40 percent, it turned out (a number not unusual, I later learned, in sociotechnical design projects).

But how to do it? My friend Don, after twenty years with an international giant, was excited at the prospect of total systems change in a small company. He quit his HR job and joined us as operations head. Determined to institute work teams, we sought to enlist the supervisors. Two out of five were enthusiastic, two thought it wouldn't work, and one was neutral. We charged ahead. We formed new teams of people from each of the five functions. The enthusiastic supervisors became floating coordinators, teaching procedures, linking with production, buying supplies, interviewing potential new-hires. The reluctant ones chose working on a team together.

Our model was Non-Linear Systems, a California maker of electronic voltmeters noted by McGregor (McGregor, Bennis, and McGregor, 1967). At Non-Linear, teams made the entire product and team members put their names on it—so a customer could call them if something went wrong. In our adaptation, each team managed 17,000 customers, arranged by region.

They had their own desks, typewriters, and telephones. My instructions encompassed everything I knew about training. "Teach each other your jobs," I said.

Endless Problems. It soon became apparent this simple dictate wasn't enough. We had endless problems. Team A didn't know what to do when Carrier B shipped to the wrong city. Team D misunderstood the production order sequence. Team C's new samples person didn't know all the products. I was appalled at how many problems had been solved only by supervisors or, more frequently, me.

I realized that crises flowed to my desk because most employees didn't have the whole picture. For years we had played "blind men and the elephant." Each of us saw a tiny piece of the puzzle—a payment record to be checked, a number to be corrected. Few could connect quality products and fast service to business success.

What the Boss Doesn't Know

What I experienced accidentally in the 1960s has since been studied systematically. Max Elden (1983a, 1983b), in his participative research projects in Norway, showed that people at the bottom have a much deeper appreciation of operating problems than do middle or upper managers. In a bank where a new online computer system was being installed, top management thought its peak load problem was an uneven workload and too few backup people. Employees lower down pointed out organizational structure and practice—overload on the vice president, centralized decisions, and too little worker flexibility. In work-design projects today, this is a predictable phenomenon. When top managers sit on a design team with workers, they are taken aback at their own ignorance of how much people know that they are not allowed to use.

I was blind, too. I talked with customers, but I hadn't the least inkling why it was so hard to reduce errors and improve service. None of us was stupid. We were just ignorant of how impossible it is for any one person to track the many moving parts of a complex business. There was a great deal that could go wrong, and it did. Early on we made a decision to fix errors before investigating the cause. When customers complained, we would do whatever they asked, even replacing an order at no charge. No more "I'll investigate and get back to you." This proved to save a lot of time and money.

The Meetings. At Don's urging, we began a radical practice—meetings. Large corporations, Don assured me, held meetings all the time. How, I asked naïvely, did people make up the enormous time lost? They didn't, Don said soothingly; meetings were built into the job. Each team would save up its problems and rotate its members into a weekly meeting. The problems piled up and poured out. The meetings dragged on interminably. I could not believe that so many people, myself included, knew so little about the impact of their work. The supervisors, now eliminated, had been making all decisions, all that is, except those they delegated upward to me.

We treated employees as extensions of their phones, typewriters, and copy machines. They didn't have the capacity to solve the endless parade of problems. After four weeks I concluded the work team experiment had fizzled. Theory Y was okay in principle, but not in practice. Maybe psychologists could implement these far-out notions. Not me. I had a war to win. Don was disappointed. Give it more time, he pleaded. Frustrated, we held our fifth and, as I planned to reveal, final meeting. I sat at one end of the table, palms cold and wet. Don sat at the other end. The troops filed in and sat down. I still recall that scene: the square office, the small rectangular table with the walnut-grain laminate top, the high ceilings, the tiny windows at one end of the room, the eerie white fluorescent bulbs throwing a shadowless pallor over a depressing tableau. "Where," I asked, halfheartedly, "are the problems?" My voice wavered at the thought of the speech I must deliver, that the work teams were not time-efficient. We had blown it.

"We don't have any problems this week," one woman said sheepishly.

"What do you mean you don't have any?" I asked impatiently.

"Well," said another, "nothing new came up." She looked crestfallen, as if wondering what sort of screw-up that could be.

"We knew how to handle all the problems from our other meetings."

From our other meetings! Those long, unproductive, time-wasting meetings? I could hardly believe my ears. Suddenly I thought of the words of flight instructor Wolfgang Langewiesche (1944), whose writings had comforted me when, as a fledgling pilot, I had convinced myself I would never master three-point landings. "When you really understand something," he wrote, "a little spark jumps. Watch for it!" In that moment, in the fifth meeting, a little spark jumped for me.

Discovering Learning. I understood, really understood, that the essence of effective organization was learning, not coercing and controlling output. I realized that learning took time; required real problems to be solved; involved trial, error, give, take, and experimentation. Above all, it generated tremendous anxiety. I also had my first hint of what good managers do instinctively: involve people in setting important goals, structure the chance to learn, offer feedback and support, provide tools and ideas, and stay out of the way.

With a shock I realized that the way we had run our business was anti-learning. I wanted everything done right the first time, including solving problems nobody had faced before. Naturally, only I could handle such problems. Only I knew what a fraud I was, appearing to be the only one who knew the right answers. I did not understand the subtle connections among learning, self-esteem, and productivity. I thought the work team was simply another "solution." Team members were learning by doing it how to be self-correcting. But until they knew that was what they had learned, it was not really usable knowledge. In short, we had stumbled on a process—the periodic problem review—essential to the success of our structure. When people were encouraged to learn, grow, achieve, when mistakes become okay, when teams coordinated their own work, there was a great deal more control in the system. It's called self-control, the strongest kind; and it can't be bought or legislated.

When I attended my first T-group a few years later and heard the expression "learning how to learn," I understood it because of the work teams. I also learned the extent to which I liked to do it all myself—and how this kept others dependent, blind, and unskilled, outcomes which were far from my intentions. Without Don and Bob's help I could not have conceived the notion of stopping the movie in the middle to ask, "Now what did we learn from that?" Instead of dropping the work teams, we decided teams could call meetings any time they believed something affected the whole department.

Within a week an ad hoc meeting was called. "We want the wall taken down," said one person.

"Why?" I asked.

"Easy," replied another. "We don't need it anymore. We like talking to each other."

Back came the carpenters; down came the wall. (Although I did not know it, I was on my way to a new career, helping people take down walls.)

Successes

Pay for Knowledge. "Team Structure" shows our new department layout with the wall gone. All team members could learn every job. Teams began to interview and hire new members. Inevitably, compensation came up. How would we administer wages when people were no longer functional specialists? A committee, helped by Don, a former compensation expert, convened to recommend a new pay scheme. They came up with a matrix. "Pay for Skills" illustrates the plan.

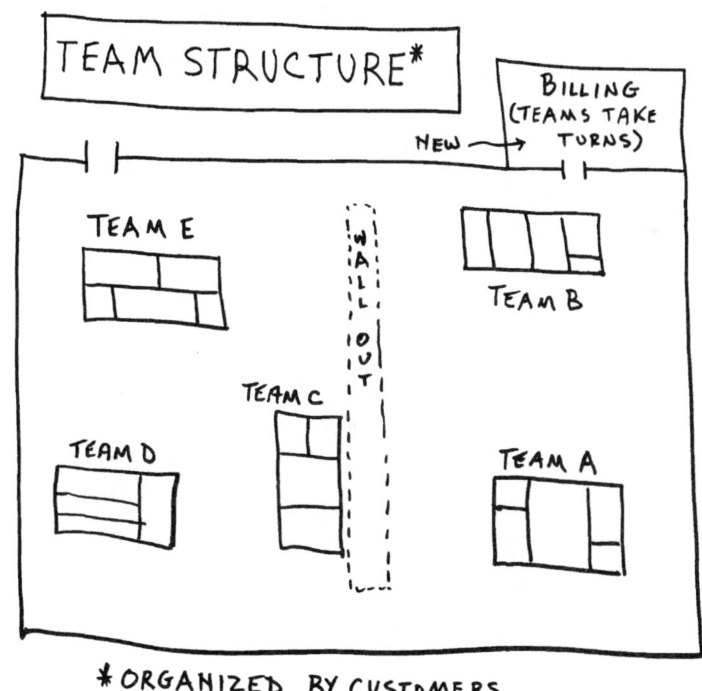

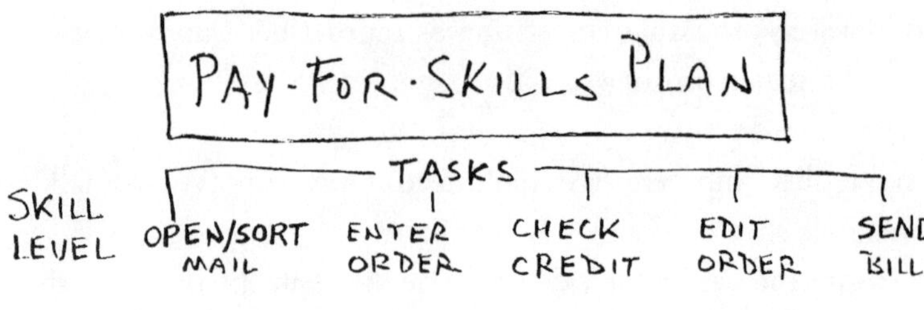

They noted skills required at each level in each function. Raises, they said, could be granted for increasing broad knowledge across functions, or in-depth knowledge of any one. The highest-paid people could be those who could do everything. "You mean," I said, a bit taken aback, "that if everybody learns all the skills, everybody gets the highest rate?"

"Right," said a committee member.

"How can we afford that?"

"We figure when we all know how to do everything we can handle a lot more work without adding people."

Nowadays, it's called a pay-for-knowledge plan. In the early 1970s the former General Foods pet food plant at Topeka, Kansas, installed a widely publicized example with help from Harvard Business School. Reading that tickled me because I knew the scheme was dreamed up with a handful of high school graduates in a North Philadelphia printing plant in 1967. Who knows how it got to Harvard? (Later I found out. It came by way of Norway, where it was first used in the pioneer design of Norsk Hydro's new fertilizer plant in the early 1960s.)

For equitable compensation, you can't beat pay for knowledge where multiskilling is feasible. Yet relatively few managers have been willing to try it. It strongly contradicts traditional schemes. Of course, as the lady said, when everybody does everything, you don't need so many people—including direct supervisors, middle managers, and staff specialists.

In his seminal writings on sociotechnical design, Fred Emery (1967) pointed out that there are essentially two work-design strategies: redundant parts or redundant skills. In the first strategy, people are treated as interchangeable cogs, in the second as capable learners. This astounding breakthrough in human thought had gone from Norway to Non-Linear Systems to McGregor to me. I did not realize at the time that I was implementing an idea literally inconceivable only a few years earlier. Individuals earn more when they are more productive and require less supervision because they generate more money than when they are spare parts.

Good News and Bad News. Another task force took on the computer. Working with a systems analyst, they revised order processing procedures, integrating a new computer billing machine run by volunteer team members. We had changed the office structure significantly. What surprised me most were the dramatic changes in behavior. Spontaneous parties sprang up at lunch and after work. People began celebrating co-workers' birthdays during coffee breaks. They started visiting one another's homes. We had become productive. Now we were becoming a community.

We were not without casualties. Two former supervisors stuck it out for three months, complaining bitterly that "this system will never work." Meanwhile, not fifteen feet away, another team, all doing jobs it might have taken years to learn under direct supervision, were putting out more orders than the most driven supervisor ever imagined.

The reluctant ex-supervisors left for traditional places they could understand. At the time I hated that outcome. Now I know it was unavoidable. Both morality and practicality dictate that those whose work must change be offered jobs at their former pay. What cannot be preserved are jobs that are no longer needed. I also believe strongly in a point made by Marshall Sashkin (1984). It is irresponsible for managers to knowingly maintain work systems that punish, diminish, and perhaps injure workers simply to preserve status and perks for a handful who often don't get much job satisfaction either.

Nor could I get much going in the shipping department. Our best shipper, Sidney, a world-class miracle of distribution, had as much interest in participation as a gourmet chef in fast food. Sid liked time clocks. "I don't want more responsibility," he said. "Why can't I just pack orders?" Sid made it clear that he had advanced as far as he wanted. He never missed a day, and as long as I had my job, his was secure too. I thought I would find a way to reach him. I never did.

A High-Performing System. Our order processing operation, however, boomed. The literature called it high commitment. McGregor, I decided, was a pretty sharp fellow after all. Without any team training or social technology except chart pads, we had obtained remarkable results. Our "throughput" increased 40 percent. Absenteeism and turnover, with the exceptions noted, went nearly to zero. Teams finished work early and prowled the office looking for new things to do. We accepted a free offer from the telephone company to coach people in collecting overdue accounts, our first ever formal training. This led to reductions in past-due receivables and bad debts. It also meant higher self-esteem for former "clerks," who found they could make significant contributions to the business. (It's hard to overrate the symbolism. In the old days, only my father could call up large past-due accounts. He hated to let the job go—until he saw the checks roll in.)

The Transformation of a Family Enterprise (2003)

I left the business in 1968, having decided that I needed to be on my own. Rare is a family enterprise passed on smoothly down the generations. Fathers and sons have conflicting agendas, one desperately wanting power, the other desperately holding onto it. Four years later my dad invited me to lunch and announced that he was selling his business. He offered it first to me, a gesture of reconciliation that earned my respect and gratitude. By then I had a solid consulting practice and said "no."

In 1972 a venture capital group bought the business, which grew tenfold under its new owners. They, in turn, sold it in the 1990s to a mail order conglomerate making forms, greeting cards, stationery, and work clothes. In 2000 I found the phone number from a website and called a vice president, who sent me the latest catalogs. The collective businesses now filled more than 100,000 orders a week for 2.5 million customers. What had been a thirty-two-page business forms catalog in 1968 was now a 148-page wish book of office specialties. Buried inside I found a few business forms that I had designed forty years earlier!

I arranged for a tour and soon found myself in a rental car with my son Dano in rural Massachusetts. I was curious to see how customer service functioned all these years later after a computer revolution. What had become of the work teams with the skills to do the whole job? We were ushered into a large, brightly lit space in which perhaps 150 people sat in personal cubicles. Greenery hung in baskets from the ceiling and filled planters near the door. Each cubicle reflected its owner with family photos, children's art, or favorite cartoons. Employees interacted more with customers than with each other.

Most orders now came in by phone, fax, or the Internet, rather than by mail. I met Bill, a service rep, who pulled a second chair up to his desk, gave me headphones, and patched me into his line. He pointed out a large display board hanging high over the middle of the room. It showed the number of incoming calls and the longest wait time. A light flashed and the numbers changed with each call.

With access to the same database, any service person could serve any customer. Bill took the next call. As the incoming phone number appeared on his screen, he hit a button. Instantly, he had the customer's buying history. It was a small retailer in Baton Rouge, Louisiana. When he picked up and heard a woman's voice on the phone, he said, "Hi, this is Bill. Am I speaking to Marie?" For a second there was silence, then a laugh, followed by "Yes! And I need to reorder invoices."

Bill went on to review with Marie her buying practices, offer her savings on larger quantities, check to see whether she needed envelopes, and remind her to fax the exact wording for her imprint. He checked her billing address and credit history. Then he thanked her for the business. The exchange took ten minutes. I looked up at the board. There were six calls in the queue, the longest on hold for less than a minute.

From Work Team to Team of One

I was impressed by Bill's product knowledge and phone presence. He was at once salesperson, order taker, credit checker, customer relations manager, and database updater. I was watching a one-person multi-skilled work team. “How long have you been doing this?” I asked, expecting a six-month learning cycle. “About a month,” said Bill. “It took a couple of weeks to learn the system. Now it’s a piece of cake.” This was technology undreamed of in the 1960s, friendly to employees and customers alike.

People were organized in teams, Bill said, that met mainly to share information. Each person did the whole job. Supervisors were available for troubleshooting and training. Customer service reps spent their time on the phone. What had changed from the 1960s? The most obvious thing was that paperwork was largely a thing of the past. The keyboard was king, the terminal a form of empowerment nonexistent during my tenure. I also noted that the company still promised it would do whatever you wanted if you weren’t satisfied with an order.

In the 21st Century the customers were royalty, and “delighting” royalty become an inviolable norm for direct marketing firms. The forms company office seemed to me relaxed, orderly, and effective, a good place to work. Computers gave people feedback so they could control their work. In electronic sweatshops I had seen computers used to monitor bathroom breaks, personal phone calls, and emails. Here I saw computers in service of employees and customers rather than the other way around. Old cynic that I had become, I felt reassured that my father’s legacy was in good hands.

Those years in the forms business, I realize, had put me on an unending learning trip. Without my dad’s technology bug and Don Kirchoffer’s interest in humane work structures and Jimmie Lee Jones’s mechanical aptitude and Bob Maddock’s three systems and the incredible adventure with the wall, I would not appreciate the utter simplicity and astonishing economic benefits of involving employees in designing their own work. Nor would I appreciate how much patience and hard work it takes. Even Sidney the shipper taught me a valuable lesson: every management theory has its limits; not one of them fits everybody.

■ ■ ■

"I CHANGED MY LIFE DRAMATICALLY..."

SEATTLE, WA—For twenty-seven years I served in general management and marketing roles at Weyerhaeuser, then a Fortune 500 forest products company. I set up the company’s first sales training programs in the 1960s, became a national sales manager, a division general manager, and then international sales and marketing director. Traveling the world in the 1980s, I became interested in my customers' organizations. I was having dinner one evening with a customer in Aarhus, Denmark, who said, "What you do now, doesn't it get boring ?" That got me thinking.

In 1979, Don Swartz, Weyerhaeuser's former training and development head, started the master's degree program in organization systems renewal (OSR) at Antioch University/Seattle. My wife entered the program. Although I had an MBA, I studied vicariously along with her. At work I was engaged in a major paper machine rebuild. But my heart was with OSR, and in 1986 I too started the program.

In my second year, I joined a "Knowledge Component Team" whose task was to teach fellow students sociotechnical systems, joined by a visiting faculty member. That turned out to be Marv Weisbord. I soon got my first copy of *Productive Workplaces* in that session, signed, "To Bob—Glad I ran into you in Seattle!" Marv and I became friends that weekend and have been close colleagues since.

Toward the end of OSR, my life changed dramatically. My desire to change my organization and my time focusing on OSR resulted in more and more pushback. After some unsettling times, I became an internal consultant for my last four years with the company. I was teaching total quality concepts, putting theories I had learned into action. The challenge was to teach people who already were experts how to more effectively use their expertise.

In 1992, encouraged by Marv, I established my own consulting practice. In 1994 Don Swartz asked me to succeed him as a faculty member and leader of the OSR program. At OSR I did the most satisfying work of my life. I was able to encourage many mid-life students to stretch further than they thought they could, just as I had done. I also joined Marv and Sandra Janoff for a workshop in Point Reyes, California, became a Future Search Network member, and co-conducted fifteen Future Searches for clients as diverse as religious organizations, insurance companies, and government agencies. The work enabled me to integrate everything I had learned.

Bonnie Olson and I, for example, teamed up to lead an economic development Future Search in semi-rural Mason County, in Washington State. The sponsors had at first imagined inviting developers, businesses, and investors only. During the planning, they decided to invite the "whole system"—some eighty-one participants, including educators, health care providers, environmentalists, politicians, interested citizens, and young people. The local port commissioners supported the effort, which took almost a year to plan, pending the major rebuild completion of a new resort, Alderbrook on Hood Canal, that would be both our meeting revenue and a symbol of the county's economic growth. The long ramp-up worked to our advantage, as stakeholders on the planning group became fully committed to the process.

The Future Search produced nine initiatives for infrastructure, business development, tourism, health and safety, trust in government, celebration of the county's heritage, culture and history, education/workforce development, the environment, and affordable housing. Six years later all were still alive. In 2010 the main focus was providing sewer and water infrastructure for three urban growth areas that could not move forward without them. Annual tourism events like "Shellfish Day," participation in an Olympic Peninsula culinary network, and a local heritage day were ongoing reminders of Mason County's renewal.

—Bob Woodruff, The Woodruff Group and the Institute for Systemic Learning. Former program manager and faculty, OSR.

PART TWO Searching for Productive Workplaces

You have plenty of courage, I am sure. All you need is confidence in yourself. There is no living thing that is not afraid when it faces danger. True courage is in facing danger when you are afraid.

—The Wizard of Oz to the Cowardly Lion, Baum, 1900, 1958, p. 114

In this part of the book I reinterpret the stories of courageous innovators who influenced me—an industrial engineer and four social scientists. Frederick W. Taylor, the "father of scientific management," started a new profession in 1893—"consulting engineer"—because he saw that captains of industry, caught in a swirl of change, did not know how to untangle cost, productivity, and motivational problems. Taylor was among the first to realize that workplace problems are best solved together, not piecemeal. He intended to reduce labor/management conflict by eliminating authoritarian supervision. I know this because eighty years after he consulted to Bethlehem Steel Corporation, I helped the company untangle from problems traceable to his early solutions. I tell his story, with my own twist on his dicey reputation, in Chapters Three and Four.

Kurt Lewin, a legendary social scientist, is my second exemplar. He provided the concepts for bringing change to workplaces in ways both practical and ethical. Applying Lewin's insights to industries influenced by Taylor, I discovered many commonalities between technically and socially based change efforts. Lewinian thinking underlies successful large-scale efforts, no matter which experts are involved. In Chapters Five and Six I tell about Lewin, his interest in Taylor, and his major contributions to managing. I have added a new Chapter Seven to give you an inside look at the T-group, a significant milestone in experienced-based management education traceable to Lewin.

Douglas McGregor (1960), a gifted professor, wrote *The Human Side of Enterprise* and changed the way managers view their assumptions. From his writings I learned how I acted to reinforce the conditions I disliked. That insight put me on the path to this book. In Chapter Eight, I describe McGregor's influence on the organization development profession, and in Chapter Nine I show how similar his values were to Taylor's and how their ideas were misused in roughly the same way.

Eric Trist, a British social scientist, friend of Lewin and McGregor, spiritual progenitor of quality of working life (QWL), and Fred Emery, an Australian disciple of Lewin, achieved the conceptual breakthroughs needed to bring systems thinking to the workplace. Their work on "sociotechnical systems" remains an inspiration the world over to those who would give working people a chance to use the brains they were born with.

I had the good fortune to know Emery and Trist, and to benefit from their support. In Chapters Ten and Eleven I tell of their intellectual exploits and liken their achievement in rethinking work after observing coal miners to the Wright brothers cracking the mystery of flight by watching birds.

chapter THREE

Scientific Management: A Tale of Two Taylors

The relations between employers and men form without question the most important part of this art.

—F. W. Taylor, *Shop Management,* 1911, p. 21

If ever a reformer fought for labor-management cooperation, it was the engineer Frederick Winslow Taylor, "the father of scientific management." Taylor stimulated all the social scientists I shall profile. I became aware of his pervasive influence in 1981 while consulting to the Bethlehem Steel Corporation, where more than a century ago Taylor installed the most highly rationalized incentive wage schemes industry had ever seen. When the imperious financier Charles M. Schwab bought Bethlehem in 1901, he went on a cost-cutting spree and threw out Taylorism.

Within a month, output in perhaps the world's most productive machine shop fell 50 percent. To stem the losses, a conscientious manager secretly set up a skunk-works of slide rules and time-study manuals in a kitchen Schwab never visited. When the kitchen burned years later, the paraphernalia and records were lost. Production fell so much that Schwab fired the shop managers. His subordinates finally told him the truth. Time study thereafter was practiced openly at Bethlehem Steel (Copley, 1923, Vol. 2). When Tony Petrella and I showed up eighty years later, there were 3,400 wage incentive plans and four hundred industrial engineers setting rates in plants across the United States. Jobs were so narrow it took enormous staffs to support them. Incentive bonuses were paid for good steel and bad.

The U.S. steel industry in the 1980s yielded about 70 percent good steel compared to Japan, which, helped by modern technology, got 95 percent. Taylor's solutions had now become a serious problem. Bethlehem was losing $80 million a month. Its leaders decided only labor-management cooperation could save it.

■ ■ ■

"THE ANCHOR FOR WHAT I LEARNED AND DID..."

CHICAGO, IL—In the mid-1980s I moved into change management at Bethlehem Steel Corporation not long after Marv Weisbord began working there. So I had the great good fortune to be involved in that significant transition from an autocratic to a participative organization. I got to see first-hand how to manage a significant organizational change, the impact it had on people, and the energy and expertise required to do it right.

Fast-forward a few years. I began doctoral studies at Benedictine University. One of the first books we read was *Productive Workplaces.* The book described everything I had learned in my years at Bethlehem Steel. and of the many, many books I read in graduate school, PW was the anchor for all that I learned and did. After Bethlehem Steel, I spent a dozen years in change management roles with AG Communication Systems, International Truck and Engine, and U.S. Cellular and then took a full-time graduate faculty position. One of my goals is helping students with little real-world experience understand the wisdom that lies in knowing the history of our field. They like my teaching because I bring in all of my experience and make textbooks like *Productive Workplaces* come to life for them.

—Connie S. Fuller, Ph.D., associate chair and assistant professor, Business Psychology, The Chicago School of Professional Psychology, co-author, *Bridging the Boomer-Xer Gap: Creating Authentic Teams for High Performance at Work* (2002)

I started reading Taylor's scientific management book and had hardly got past the introduction when I made a startling discovery. It is first and foremost a treatise on human resource management. "We can see our forests vanishing," he wrote, "our water-powers going to waste, our soil being carried by floods into the sea; and the end of our coal and our iron is in sight. But our larger wastes of human effort, which go on every day through such of our acts as are blundering, ill-directed, or inefficient . . . are but vaguely appreciated" (1915, p. 5). Taylor's overriding objective was productive labor-management cooperation—the same objective that had brought Block Petrella Weisbord to Bethlehem (Chapter Seventeen).

Today Taylor's name conjures up dehumanized, inefficient, and conflicted work methods. His purposes were exactly the reverse. No consultant has ever had so much impact on the workplace. I determined to learn as much as I could from his experience. My search took me back one hundred years, to Taylor's writings, biographies old and new, scholarly studies, research papers, strident attacks, passionate defenses. Few men ever were such powerful magnets for both admiration and revulsion. There exist, I discovered, two Taylors. One is a mechanistic engineer, dedicated to counting, rigid control, and the rationalization of work, an unfeeling authoritarian who turned his own neurosis into repressive methods anathema to working people. The other was a humanitarian social reformer who believed workers could produce more with less stress, achieve greater equity in their output, and cooperate with management for the good of society. This Taylor has hardly been recognized since 1925.

The first Taylor, obsessed with self-control, invented a harness at age twelve to keep himself sleeping on his back, hoping to avoid recurrent nightmares (Copley, 1923, Vol. 1). This Taylor, a compulsive systematizer, also was a brilliant inventor, holder of many patents, and discoverer, through thousands of experiments, of high-speed steel, a major 20th Century innovation. The second Taylor was a devoted husband who put his wife's severe illness ahead of his own fame, who adopted three children late in life, who identified with working people and invited them to his home.

One historian labeled Taylor a reactionary, "indifferent, even ruthless, in his relations with workers" (Nelson, 1980, p. x). His biographer noted that retirees who had worked for Taylor described him "with admiration and affection running on into reverence and worship"; many kept his photograph on the mantelpiece (Copley, 1923, Vol. 2, p. 170). By all reports Taylor was an abrasive cuss, honest, plainspoken, stubborn as hell. But his scorn was directed mainly at financiers and managers. On the shop floor he was a sympathetic listener who tempered his perfectionism with "a touch of human nature and feeling," encouraging workers to unburden their personal problems. He was quick to admit his shortcomings. "I never saw a man," said one of his former employees, "who had a greater courage of his convictions . . . willing to rise or fall by his own actions and not blame any mistakes on other people" (Copley, 1923, Vol. 1, p. 176).

Although many rank-and-file workers liked Taylor's system, early union leaders denounced it as exploitive. They hounded him to the end of his life, sparking an acrimonious congressional investigation that debilitated his spirit. Organized labor's jaundiced viewpoint, "a myth . . . of popular magazine writers" (Mathewson, 1931, p. 151), is favored today in human resource management circles. When I pointed out similarities between Taylor and psychologist Douglas McGregor to an executive conference, a veteran HR staffer angrily accused me of "de-Stalinizing Taylor," whom he dubbed a "first-class p—" (impolite epithet).

That was not what his liberal contemporaries saw. Muckraking journalist Ida Tarbell (1925) and social reformer Stuart Chase (1925) supported Taylor's attempts to create rational, humane management systems. Taylorism became a cornerstone of the Harvard Business School when it was founded in 1908 and of the Amos Tuck Business School at Dartmouth in 1910. Uninterested in politics, Taylor was adopted by the Progressive political movement. *The Principles of Scientific Management* (1915) was greeted with critical acclaim by the liberal thinkers of his day. The title was coined by social activist Louis Brandeis, later a Supreme Court justice, who used Taylor's work to argue against a rate increase for inefficiently run railroads. The case catapulted Taylor into a public figure, in demand as a speaker, adviser, and university lecturer. In his later years he metamorphosed into a social philosopher, espousing ideas, theories, and practices more idealistic and comprehensive than those he actually implemented (Nelson, 1980).

The myth continues today. Academic detectives discredited Taylor as a fraud and a cheat who plagiarized or made up much of his great book (Wrege and Perroni, 1974; Wrege and Stotka, 1978). Another scholar concluded that "most of his insights are still valid" and his practices widely accepted now (Locke, 1982, p. 23). Peter Drucker (1976), the late management philosopher, ranked Taylor with Marx and Freud for his impact on the modern world. Taylor above all, said Drucker, deserves to be called a humanist. A recent *New Yorker* article said Taylor was probably a "shameless fraud," who "fudged his data, lied to his clients, and inflated the record of his success" (Lepore, 2009).

I find Taylor a perfect projection screen for the dialogue in each of us between social and technological impulses, external control and self-control, freedom and constraint, authority and dependency—the tension that Douglas McGregor vividly immortalized as Theories X and Y. Indeed, so similar were Taylor's values to Douglas McGregor's that many of their sentences cannot be told apart. (If you doubt this, see Chapter Nine.) Taylor's story deserves to be better known by those who aspire to productive workplaces—a cautionary tale for all who believe they have the answer.

Taylor's career can be divided into three phases: his years as worker, engineer, and manager (1878–1893); his stint as consulting engineer (1893–1901), a new profession he invented because he believed entrepreneurs did not understand how to use capital and people productively; and a stormy period as proselytizer for scientific management, when, during his final fourteen years, he refused money, even travel expenses, for his services.

Throughout, he was the experimenter, tinkerer, and inventor. Henry Gantt, of Gantt Chart fame, a major figure in the democratization of work, and Frank Gilbreth, hero of the film *Cheaper by the Dozen*, were among his disciples. Taylor's principles have affected the lives of practically every person in the industrial world.

Quaker Pacifist: Social Consciousness and Wealth

Taylor was born on March 20, 1856, into a liberal, upper-class Philadelphia Quaker family. His father, a Princeton graduate and lawyer, earned a good living from mortgages and served—noblesse oblige—as trustee for a retarded children's school. His mother, a spirited abolitionist, feminist, and friend of Lucretia Mott, was rumored to have run an Underground Railroad station for runaway slaves.

True to their roots, the Taylors espoused plain living and high thinking. In the Taylor household children were seen, not heard, and family members addressed each other with "thee" and "thy." Taylor learned self-control at an early age. He internalized pacifist values, hated war games, and sought to avoid or resolve conflicts among his playmates. He also was a compulsive kid, always measuring, counting, figuring out better ways to do things. Other croquet players lined up their shots and smacked away; Taylor plotted the angles. Others daydreamed while walking; Taylor counted steps to find the most efficient stride. When the Taylors toured Europe from 1869 to 1872 to expose their children to art and culture, their son tolerated the experience without enthusiasm (Copley, 1923, Vol. 1). Fred excelled at sports and math, graduated from exclusive Phillips Exeter Academy in 1874, and easily passed the Harvard entrance exams. Pleading severe eyestrain, he begged off and apprenticed as a pattern maker and machinist at the Enterprise Hydraulic Works in Philadelphia.

Blue-Collar Aristocrat. From the start there were two Taylors. On weekdays he worked a noisy ten-hour shift at Enterprise, inhaling the stink of oil fumes and burning metal. A nonsmoker and nondrinker, he cultivated a salty vocabulary to accentuate his egalitarianism. Yet he could not hide his origins. "Mr. Taylor," said the journalist Ida Tarbell, "never seemed more of a gentleman to me than when he was swearing" (Copley, 1923, Vol. 1, p. 91). On weekends he played tennis at the Young America Cricket Club, sang with a choral society, and sported a wig and long gown playing female roles in amateur theater. He became a superb tennis player, a sparkling social companion, and a skilled machinist—Philadelphia's most sophisticated blue collar worker.

After his apprenticeship he used family connections to become a common laborer at the Midvale Steel Company. William Sellers, Midvale's president, a scholarly ex-machinist and inventor, believed in methodical experimentation. He had enormous influence on Taylor. When other workers made fun of Taylor's zeal, calling him "Speedy" or "Monkey Mind," Sellers's support sustained him (Copley, 1923, Vol. 1, p. 130). Taylor rose rapidly to shop clerk, machinist, gang boss, foreman, maintenance foreman, and chief draftsman. Within six years he was research director, then chief engineer.

Earning an Engineering Degree. At age twenty-five Taylor enrolled in Stevens Institute of Technology in Hoboken, New Jersey, showing up mainly for exams. Given his elite education, he easily passed tests in French, German, and history. He is the only Stevens student ever to earn an engineering degree in two years while holding a full-time job. He also became a star athlete, using his own patented spoon-shaped racket to win, with his brother-in-law, the U.S. Lawn Tennis Association doubles championship in 1881.

Frederick Winslow Taylor as a Stevens Institute of Technology graduate, 1873.

Source: Williams Library, Stevens Institute of Technology

Taylor's graduation picture shows a long, unsmiling face framed by short straight hair parted just right of center, a firm, dimpled chin, a straight, full-lipped mouth topped by a wispy moustache, prominent nose and eyes set deep under a high forehead. He looks off into the distance (in control, I fancy), oblivious of the photographer. Shortly after this picture was taken, he married socialite Louise Spooner, who became his lifelong companion.

At Midvale Steel the wasted effort, exhausting work, long hours, petty dictators, arbitrary rules, inefficient methods, and goofing off appalled the young Taylor. He understood, having been one, why skilled workers rarely gave their best. Still, when he became a supervisor, he sought to dictate compliance, using traditional "driving" methods.

Taylor abhorred conflict and now had more than his share. He was ambivalent about authority. Alone among his peers, he owned up to an obvious conclusion: driving was ineffective with workers who practiced the exquisite subtleties of passive resistance. "It's a horrid life for any man to live," he would write, "not being able to look any workman in the face without seeing hostility there, and a feeling that every man around you is your virtual enemy" (Kakar, 1970, p. 62). Long before McGregor, Taylor decided that coercion was a waste of time.

Unprecedented Management Problems of the 1880s

It is useful to view Taylor's career against a backdrop of dramatic industrial change after the Civil War. Small factories became large plants. Local trades—glass, steel, textiles, shoes—became national industries. Mass production meant enormous wealth for the owners of capital. Workers, in comparison, received a trickle. Machines also deprived craftspeople of manual skills and forced alien work patterns on ex-farmers and immigrant peasants. The widely discussed "labor problem"—increasing conflict between owners and workers—sparked the rise of unionism.

Employers had no remedy for inefficiencies and accidents save arbitrary supervision. One obvious symptom was soldiering—worker foot-dragging—on the job. It was widely observed that workers resisted producing as much as they could. They were thought lazy at best, uncooperative at worst, dumb in any case.

Steel Industry Innovation

A great deal of Taylor's 19th-Century vision was embodied in a trailblazing agreement between National Steel Corporation and the United Steel Workers of America (1986). Union and management agreed to cooperate in reorganizing the steel mills, reducing the labor force, merging jobs and functions, and jointly planning production. To protect labor's central interest and gain commitment, National guaranteed employment security for the existing workforce. Labor costs would be reduced through attrition, retraining, and voluntary termination rather than layoffs. The company guaranteed workers a share of profits. The latter guarantee could not mitigate the economic decline of the 1990s. In 2002 National filed for bankruptcy and voluntary reorganization, the twenty-fifth steel company to do so since 1997. Employment guarantees, however, remained in place.

The first to recognize the labor problem were 19th-Century engineers installing new technology in factories. The American Society of Mechanical Engineers, founded in 1880 at Stevens Institute, worked out the first factory incentive wage schemes long before personnel staffs existed. Labor has continually defeated these schemes. "We have a good understanding with management," a unionist once told me. "They pretend they pay well, and we pretend we're working."

Taylor, the ex-machinist, knew that incentive bonuses were futile unless all parties benefited. Workers could make more money and management could cut costs dramatically only if they cooperated on goals, work methods, and quality. The work had to be redesigned to remove oppressive supervision. The concept remains a contemporary challenge; see "Steel Industry Innovation."

Innovating at Midvale

Taylor's thinking evolved rapidly after he became Midvale's machine shop foreman. He concluded that incentive wages would work only when coupled with efficient, easily learned tasks. Engineers would specify the tasks and the best way to do them, selecting those Taylor called "first-class men." The right pace was something a first-class man could keep up month after month without stress. The secret of productivity was paying each person well for increased output. Management would support workers with tools, equipment, and training. This was what Taylor called cooperation.

The supervisory equivalent of a first-class man was the well-rounded foreman. The latter had more attributes than an Eagle Scout: brains, education, technical knowledge, strength, manual dexterity, tact, energy, grit, honesty, common sense, and good health. Taylor (1911, p. 96) could not imagine all these traits in one person. So he chopped the supervisory role into eight discrete roles, and invented functional foremanship. He first implemented it in Midvale's machine shop in 1882. A gang boss set up jobs and kept material flowing; a speed boss picked cutting tools and machine speeds; a quality control inspector set standards; a repair boss maintained equipment; an order-of-work and route clerk wrote out production lists; an instruction card clerk tracked job specs and rates; a time and cost clerk kept score; and a disciplinarian handled insolence.

Because he believed specialists learned faster and were more careful, Taylor did something contrary to what many people believe. He systematically undercut centralized, authoritarian supervision. He did it by contradicting a central tenet of bureaucracy: one person, one boss. In his system bosses became "servants of the workmen." They did not order people around. They implemented a rational system, based on discovering the one best way to work. Mary Parker Follett, an early-day humanizer of bureaucratic systems, would later call it "the law of the situation." Its great virtue was that "it tends to depersonalize orders" (Metcalf and Urwick, 1940, p. 59).

Taylor and T-Groups. Breaking supervision into small pieces as well, Taylor reduced the lead time for hiring and training super-bosses. His system was based on the authority of knowledge, not position. He saw no conflict in each functional foreman taking leadership. I am amused to note that group dynamics pioneers discovered this principle in quite another way (Chapter Seven). Human relations group trainers began in the 1950s as leaders who refused to lead, creating a vacuum to be filled by group members. Once members confronted their unrealistic dependency on the leaders, they made an interesting discovery: a leaderless group could rotate leadership based on relevant skills and knowledge, a structure efficient and functional in the absence of hierarchy. Where Taylor relied on external motivation and control, the T-group shifted control to its members.

To promote harmony, Taylor, the erstwhile pacifist, set up over-foremen to coach and resolve disputes among bosses or, as a last resort, to call in the assistant superintendent, guardian of the unwritten shop rules. In modern jargon he set up conflict management procedures. He advocated four modes of discipline: lowering wages, temporary layoff, fines, and "bad marks" leading to the other remedies. He preferred fines, insisting they be impartial and that every cent be returned to the workers' mutual benefit fund. At Midvale he demonstrated impartiality by fining himself.

Rethinking Wage Incentives. In the 1880s many engineers proposed bonus plans to split gains between workers and management. Taylor shrewdly observed three factors that led these schemes to fail. One, people work first for themselves, not the general welfare (a conclusion McGregor later shared). Two, people respond to immediate feedback, not "a profit six months or a year away." Three, only costs and output are controllable by workers. Both profit and loss "may be due in great part to causes entirely beyond their influence or control, and to which they do not contribute" (Copley, 1923, Vol. 1, p. 407). Today this concept is the key to successful gain-sharing plans—group bonuses of a kind Taylor opposed. Finally, Taylor held in contempt management's tendency to cut incentive rates each time people increased their daily output—a practice that made the worker, in Irving Fisher's words, "a donkey following an ever receding bundle of hay" (1925, p. 55). Under these conditions, said Taylor, workers "become imbued with a grim determination to have no more cuts if soldiering can prevent it" (Taylor, 1915, p. 23).

Paying the Person, Not the Job. Taylor improved on a method so old the Egyptians had used it to build the pyramids: breaking tasks into their smallest components. His cornerstone was a novel incentive wage system. He set daily production quotas based on time study. Workers received an instruction card each morning. Those who made the daily goal received 60 to 100 percent more pay than under an hourly wage. Those failing received much lower pay. If workers failed after repeated coaching, they were assigned other work. Those considered able but unwilling were fired.

In short, Taylor paid the person, not the job. At Midvale Steel in the 1880s Taylor doubled productivity using functional foremanship, time study, and his new wage scheme (Drury, 1915).

A Failed General Manager

Taylor left Midvale in 1890 to become general manager of Manufacturing Investment Company (MIC), a firm set up to capitalize on a new paper-making process. Through time study and piecework, he cut cost per ton to less than half and doubled production in one plant. To his chagrin, he ran into problems he could not control: weak patent protection, poor plant location, flaws in mill design, and finally the Panic of 1893. Pressured for a quick fix, Taylor short-circuited his systems, quarreled with the financiers, and finally quit, losing $25,000 of his own capital.

The experience was not a total loss. He had been impressed while at MIC by a former railroad accountant who reduced paperwork and provided quick feedback on results through financial controls. Realizing how neatly these procedures dovetailed with his, Taylor hired the accountant to integrate cost controls into his system (Wren, 1979). (Some years later a Chicago University professor named James O. McKinsey picked up on Taylor's notion that accounting information could be a management tool, not a score sheet. The consulting company that bears his name is testimony to the power of that idea.)

In 1893, at age thirty-seven, during a business turndown, with little money and no prospects, Taylor quit his job and printed up a business card:

FRED W. TAYLOR, M.E.
Ross Street, Germantown, Philadelphia
Consulting Engineer
Systematizing Shop Management and
Manufacturing Costs a Specialty

His assets were fifteen years in factories, contacts from his Midvale days, and a personal vision for integrating standardized tools, tasks, financial controls, wage incentives, and labor-management cooperation. "I believe," Taylor later wrote, "I was the first man in this country to undertake this work as a profession" (Copley, 1923, Vol. 2, p. 345).

Taylor the Pioneer Consultant

Taylor's core procedure was time and motion study, supported by piece-rate wages, cost and inventory controls, functional foremen, and training. Taylor was inventing a professional practice neither he nor his clients quite understood. He quickly found no correlation between his elegant solutions and their probable implementation. The issues have changed, but not the dilemmas of putting them into action.

Consulting Dilemmas

Taylor knew enough to get total support at the top. He spoke the workers' language and was patient with those at the bottom. He was shrewd about how long change takes. He understood the need for experimenting. His consultancy came apart on two issues that persist to this day. He was baffled by resistance from middle managers and supervisors, the ones most threatened by his system. He also was single-mindedly focused on cutting production costs, even when survival called for new products and customers. When all else failed, managers were used to firing those who opposed them. Taylor sought to retain that prerogative as a consultant. He often would take over and operate a client's factory, threatening to leave if management balked at implementing whatever he wished.

Taylor's clients were personal contacts from his Midvale and Manufacturing Investment days and family ties to old-line Philadelphia Quakers. Between 1893 and 1901—his entire paid career—he installed systems in such firms as William Deering & Company, Northern Electrical Company, the Steel Motor Works division of the Johnson Company, Cramp's Shipyard, and Simonds Roller Bearing Company, which had given him stock for his forging patent in the 1880s.

He took charge of the Simonds plant in 1896 and increased output from five million to seventeen million balls a month. Over workers' protests, he cut the inspection department workday from ten and a half to eight and a half hours, physically separated people, inserted four breaks to provide for socializing, and raised wages more than 80 percent with piece rates. Accuracy and speed improved dramatically.

He added clerks, teachers, time-study experts, and supervisors. The cost was trivial, though, because thirty-five women, selected for "quick perception," now did the work of 120 (Taylor, 1915). One critic used Simonds to argue that Taylor "took a harsh, often ruthless approach" to chopping heads rather than saving jobs (Nelson, 1980, p. 75). Simonds' problem turned out to be environmental. Bicycle makers sprouted like weeds in the 1890s, eroding the company's market share. Ball-bearing prices fell from $3 to $.75 per thousand in less than a year. Reducing the workforce could not stave off disaster. Simonds shut down in the summer of 1898, a victim of market conditions productivity could not cure.

Taylor Appreciated Unions. In 1895, Taylor challenged the common view that unions hurt everybody, noting that they "have rendered a great service not only to their members, but to the world, in shortening the hours of labor and in modifying the hardships and improving the conditions of wage workers" (Copley, 1923, Vol. 1, p. 406). Workers were driven to collective bargaining by mismanagement, argued Taylor. Unions would be unnecessary if employers subscribed "to the plan of stimulating each workman's ambition by paying him according to his individual worth, and without limiting him to the rate of work or pay of the average of his class" (Copley, 1923, Vol. 1, p. 406).

Both labor and management, said Taylor, assumed that wages came from a fixed pie. He believed that the pie could be enlarged by greater efficiencies. Thus the paradox of high wages and low costs was resolved by finding the one best way to do the job. First-class men would attain the high rate without extra effort. The ideal rate would be one that a first-class man "can keep up for a long term of years without injury to his health. It is a pace under which men become happier and thrive" (Wren, 1979, p. 131). Taylor was sure his scheme would make unions redundant. He never understood group solidarity and the divisiveness of incentive wage differentials among co-workers. He could not see that unions fulfilled a powerful communal need.

Taylor's Consulting Methods. Taylor expected top management's total backing. "Before starting to make any radical changes," he said, "it is desirable, and for ultimate success in most cases necessary, that the directors and the important owners understand what is involved in the change." He insisted on a vote of support before entering. Once in, he expected resistance. "I have found that any improvement is not only opposed but aggressively and bitterly opposed by the majority of men," he later reflected, "and the reformer must usually tread a thorny path." If management can't wait "two to four years, they had better leave things just as they are, since a change of system involves a change in the ideas, point of view and habits of many men with strong convictions and prejudices." Moreover, "they should be prepared to lose some of their valuable men who cannot stand the change and also for the continued indignant protest of many of their old and trusted employees who can see nothing but extravagance in the new ways and ruin ahead" (Copley, 1923, Vol. 1, p. 416).

Sometimes Taylor engineered the demotion or removal of opponents, a risky tactic that contributed to his downfall at Bethlehem Steel. He did not understand that the way to get past resistance was to encourage its expression. "I always personally insist," he wrote, "that in all essential matters . . . management . . . must do as I tell them, and the only way . . . to enforce this is that I hold myself free to withdraw from the work at any time." Thus he contracted only for two or three months at a time (Copley, 1923, Vol. 1, p. 417). He also shared the risks, offering to reimburse clients for economic losses resulting from his unilateral decisions.

He was at his best with hourly workers, winning converts with his empathic swearing, his mastery of materials, and his hands-on machine skills. He recruited volunteers, studying jobs one at a time, upping the wage, allowing one person to experience success, then moving to the next one. He stressed quality standards and careful inspection, observing that more output usually meant lower quality, a lesson rediscovered in the United States as a result of Japanese competition. Workers, Taylor said, must come to see that the previously antagonistic management is now working alongside them to upgrade quality, reduce conflict, cut costs, and raise wages.

Systematizing Bethlehem Steel

Taylor's most important client was Bethlehem Iron Company renamed, in the wake of Navy contracts for all-steel ships in 1899, Bethlehem Steel. The president, Robert Linderman, wanted costs cut in the company's biggest bottleneck, Machine Shop Number 2. Bethlehem manager Russell Davenport, Taylor's former boss at Midvale, brought him in. The necessary steps, Taylor wrote Linderman, "will undoubtedly be strenuously opposed by the workmen . . . , and probably also by most of your foremen and superintendents" (Copley, 1923, Vol. 2, p. 12). To succeed, he required:

- A shop head who believed in piece work and had the authority to reverse or fire those who would not cooperate;
- A promotions policy based on merit, not "whose friend a man may be or what influence he has"; and
- Wage rate increases up to 50 percent for increased production.

The job would take nine months to two years, depending on "the tractability of your men and upon the energy of the foreman and assistants" (Copley, 1923, Vol. 2, p. 12). Joseph Wharton, company chairman, soon to endow a famous business school, balked at higher wages until Taylor convinced him how much higher output would be. Taylor fully discussed his approach with Bethlehem managers, superintendents, and foremen. When they made him welcome, he rented a house in town and went to work full time.

The honeymoon ended within a year. Taylor forced the removal of the general superintendent's brother as head of Machine Shop Number 2 and split the top plant job in half, giving manufacturing to the loyal Davenport (a sort of reverse nepotism). Using Henry Gantt, another Stevens graduate, he installed functional foremanship, production planning, and differential piece rates in 1899, making Machine Shop Number 2 by 1901 "the world's most modern factory and potentially a prototype for manufacturers and engineers in other industries" (Nelson, 1980, p. 85).

Early Participative Management. Indeed, the real innovator at Bethlehem might have been Gantt who, with his assistant, C. H. Buckley, straightened out the disorderly shop. Today Gantt's name stands for a planning chart. He also is one of the more interesting figures in the history of participative management. At Bethlehem, for example, he used instruction cards, a Taylor innovation, coupled with a bonus. "The next and most obvious step," he wrote, "is to make it to the interest of the men to learn more than their cards can teach them." He allowed workers to ignore the cards and attempt to improve the way the assigned tasks were done. If they succeeded, the cards were revised—an early example of workers gaining influence over their jobs.

Gantt also instituted a foreman bonus if all workers in a team made individual bonuses. It was for the foreman's "bringing the inferior workmen

Henry Gantt, developer of the Gantt Chart and early advocate of learning and democratic work methods.

Source: Williams Library, Stevens Institute of Technology

up to the standard" and for "having him devote his energies to those men who most needed them." It is probably the first recorded effort to reward management for teaching people the right way to do things. "Whatever we do," wrote Gantt, "must be in accord with human nature. We cannot drive people; we must direct their development" (Wren, 1979, p. 162).

Gantt believed that autocratic management threatened free enterprise. "In order to resume our advance toward the development of an unconquerable democratic civilization," he wrote, "we must purge our economic system of all autocratic practices . . . and return to the democratic principle of rendering service, which was the basis of its wonderful growth" (Wren, 1979, pp. 167–168).

The Pig-Iron Loading Experiments. The Bethlehem experiments Taylor exploited, however, were related not to technology but rather heavy yard work like shoveling ore and loading iron. In later years his basic speech featured "Schmidt," a prodigious pig-iron loader whose tale became the most memorable, and curiously damaging, example of Taylorism.

For years Taylor had sought to find the law governing hard physical labor. There was no connection between human energy expended and output.

Shortly after he arrived in Bethlehem, the firm sold a large quantity of pig iron, which had to be hand-loaded onto railway cars. Taylor seized the opportunity to continue his heavy labor studies. An iron "pig" weighed ninety-two pounds. The loader picked it up, walked an inclined plank, and deposited it on a rail car. The job required strong leg, arm, and back muscles. An average man was moving twelve and a half tons a day. Taylor's theory was that physical stress caused deterioration of the muscles, which needed recovery time. Using a stopwatch and varying loading times, researchers decided a first-class man could load forty-five tons a day as long as he was paced properly (Copley, 1923, Vol. 2).

Volunteers were offered $1.68 a day if they hit this goal, against the old rate of $1.15, a 46 percent increase. This much is roughly supported by the evidence, although there is doubt about how scientific the rate setting was. (Wages, Taylor readily admitted, were set through trial and error at an amount high enough to encourage productivity but not so high as to support frequent absences. The figure had to be rediscovered in each new situation—exactly the practice now; not science exactly, but not haphazard either.)

Recruiting "Schmidt." In Taylor's oft-told story, the Spanish-American War presented Bethlehem a chance to sell 80,000 tons of pig iron rusting in the yard. A hardworking Pennsylvania Dutchman he called Schmidt, whose dialect he mimicked, was recruited to prove the standard could be obtained. Taylor's version of the discussion is embarrassing to read.

"Schmidt, are you a high-priced man?"

"Vell, I don't know vat you mean."

"Oh, come now, you answer my questions. What I want to find out is whether you are a high-priced man or one of those cheap fellows here . . . whether you want to earn $1.85 a day or . . . are satisfied with $1.15, just the same as all those cheap fellows."

"Did I vant $1.85 a day? Vos dot a high-priced man? Vell, yes, I vas a high-priced man."

"Oh, you're aggravating me. Of course you want $1.85 . . . everyone wants it. You know perfectly well that has little to do with your being a high-priced man. . . . Now come over here. You see that pile of pig iron?"

"Yes."

"You see that car?"

"Yes."

"Well, if you are a high-priced man, you will load that pig iron on that car tomorrow for $1.85. Now do wake up and answer my question. . . . Tell me whether you are a high-priced man or not."

Schmidt decided that he was indeed high-priced and would walk, lift, rest on cue, and not answer back. Such rough talk, noted Taylor, "is appropriate and not unkind," for it fixes attention on high wages "and away from what . . . he probably would consider impossibly hard work" (Copley, 1923, Vol. 2, p. 45). So motivated, Schmidt, the John Henry of pig-iron handlers, proceeded to load forty-seven and a half tons a day. Only one in eight—"a man of the type of the ox"—was capable of such sustained work, said Taylor. Schmidt he characterized, with unconscious bigotry, as little more than an "intelligent gorilla."

What Really Happened. In point of fact there were only 10,000 tons of pig iron to load, not 80,000. The lot was sold in 1899, some months after the war with Spain ended. Taylor's recruiting dialogue with Schmidt was imaginary. The offer was made to the whole work crew, most of whom resisted piece rates, even high ones. Taylor had the rate wrong; it was $1.68, not $1.85. One gang, mostly Hungarian, threatened to strike and were initially discharged. The remaining men, Irish and Pennsylvania Dutch, were told that if they fell below the goal they would be given easier work until they were rested enough to return. Seven volunteered, two lasting only a day. Others came and went, including some of the recalcitrant Hungarians. Only three first-class men, able to load forty-five tons a day for days on end, turned up. About ten others earned more than the old day rate by averaging about thirty tons.

Bethlehem records show that Schmidt, whose real name was Henry Noll, far from an ox, was five feet seven and weighed 135 pounds—the smallest man on the crew. Yet he had extraordinary strength and endurance. He was the only one who showed up daily for two months, running to and from work, using the found money to build a new house on nights and weekends. During one two-week period Noll averaged 49.9 tons a day, 2.4 more than in Taylor's story.

But two workers exceeded him. One named Conrad averaged 55.1 tons, lifting an incredible 70.9 on one occasion, earning more than twice the old wage (233 percent) for more than six times the output (Wrege and

Perroni, 1974). This prompted the socialist Upton Sinclair to point out the discrepancy between increased output and wages under Taylorism. Taylor countered that a person could earn more only because management had invested in figuring out and teaching workers how to do it, a social benefit leading to higher wages, lower costs, higher profits, and lower consumer prices. This outcome would not occur under Sinclair's proposal that workers "take possession . . . of the means of production" (Copley, 1923, Vol. 2, pp. 50–51).

Why Fake It? Why would Taylor embellish facts and understate tonnages that would make his story even more persuasive? A plausible answer is that he recited it from memory to illustrate his principles, not his practice. It is a fact that much of *Scientific Management* was based on transcripts of talks Taylor gave at his estate years after he stopped working for money. It reflects evangelism more than facts. Hardly a public speaker ever lived who was above embellishing a good story to make a point.

There is a contemporary explanation for this phenomenon that I like very much. Harrison Owen, writing of transforming organizations, says, "From the point of view of the function of mythos it makes little difference when something happened, where something happened, or indeed if it ever happened at all. The single important factor is the existence of the myth in the culture and the way that myth functions by itself and in concert with all other present myths to create the field of meaning which images the spirit and guides its activity" (1984, p. 318).

The Inadvertent Myth. There is a second, related question that I find, from the standpoint of "mythos," even more intriguing. Why would Taylor report with pride a phony dialogue that makes him sound like a slave driver and a bigot? We can only speculate that he didn't see it that way, nor did his progressive friends. Racism in Taylor's factories was vastly more accepted than now. Rivalries among Hungarians, Irish, Poles, and Pennsylvania Dutch in the steel mills were intense. Managers played immigrant groups against one another, as the pig-iron story shows. Taylor never discussed this facet of factory life. It's a good bet that the workers he invited to dinner were skilled machinists, not yard laborers.

Taylor's own contribution to his tarnished reputation, I'm convinced, stems from his constant repetition of a story that reveals elitist prejudice, offending modern sensibilities. In 1911 even progressive liberals accepted

Taylor's apocryphal dialogue and mimicked accent in another spirit. Few true-blue Americans saw anything wrong with calling muscular immigrants who spoke broken English oxen and gorillas.

Today it is difficult to infer from this example the cooperative spirit between management and labor that Taylor valued. He was oblivious to the myth he was creating for posterity. It is hard to stomach Taylor's public bigotry now because it surfaces universal feelings we are seeking to resolve in more constructive ways. I would rather not look at that side of Taylor because I wish to restrain it in me. Each of us, I suspect, regardless of ethnicity, race, creed, or gender, has a "them" buried somewhere, unconsciously experienced as odd, scary, or inferior.

After Noll retired, Taylor's detractors spread rumors that he had been worked to death at Bethlehem. Taylor dispatched two old friends to pose for a picture with a mustachioed "Schmidt" standing between them in a bowler hat and overcoat, tie and rounded collar. He outlived Taylor by almost a decade. Anybody can view him today in *The Stevens Indicator* (Spring 1980), alumni magazine of Taylor's alma mater.

Taylor's Swan Song

By 1901 Taylor had given Bethlehem a modern cost accounting system, a real-time analysis of daily output and costs. He had doubled stamping mill production, reduced yard workers' ranks from 500 to 140, and lowered cost per ton of materials handled from eight cents to four cents, even after adding clerks, time-study engineers, teachers, a telephone system, labor office, implement room, supervision, and staff support.

He had raised hourly wages by 60 percent and the company was saving $78,000 a year in 1901 dollars (more than $2 million today). He and Manusel White also discovered high-speed tool steel, building on Taylor's Midvale work. They found that tools made from steel heated 300 to 400 degrees higher than recommended performed at twice the speed of conventional tools. Bethlehem paid the inventors $50,000 and licensed the process around the world. This discovery, after twenty-five years of dogged experiments, probably advanced Taylor's international reputation most of all.

Despite impressive achievements, he made enemies. His reduction in the yard force, said some managers who also were landlords, would "depopulate South Bethlehem" (Nelson, 1980, p. 97). That, said Taylor, is essentially what they had hired him to do. His critics replied that they did not expect he would actually do it—a sobering reminder to modern consultants to mistrust their own too-ready acceptance by any client. In fact, given Bethlehem's growth rate, displaced workers were moved to other jobs and did not lose employment.

By 1899, demoted executives were thwarting Taylor's plans by delaying changes requiring a new plant layout. Taylor repeatedly went over their heads. However, when he sought more people for his staff and higher pay for others, President Linderman drew the line. In May 1901 he forced Taylor out. Taylor's self-esteem was injured, but not his pocketbook. His response to this setback was to adopt three orphaned children, concentrate on his home and his hobbies, and begin a missionary campaign that would make scientific management a worldwide phenomenon. He had been born rich, and his investments plus patent royalties made him richer. After leaving Bethlehem Steel he never worked for money again.

The "other" Taylor, a family man, with wife, Louise, and the three children they adopted in 1901.

Source: Williams Library, Stevens Institute of Technology

■ ■ ■

"THE HARD-BITTEN UNIONISTS WERE CONVINCED THIS PROCESS HAD INTEGRITY..."

SYDNEY, AUSTRALIA—I began working in the mid-1950s in an Australian textile company as a methods engineer—a "Taylorizer" of work. Fifteen years later, doing post-graduate research in a transport company on managers' attitudes and workers' orientations, I read the industrial humanists like Likert, McGregor, Argyris, and Maslow and discovered systems thinking and the sociotechnical (STS) approach to organizational change. Shortly after that Fred Emery became my intellectual mentor.

By the time I met Marv Weisbord at the Einar Thorsrud Memorial Conference in Norway in 1987, I had my STS consulting career well underway. On the plane back to Melbourne, I read, with growing excitement, a draft Marv had given me of his "Third Wave Managing and Consulting" chapter, soon to be in *Productive Workplaces.*

It both captured my experience and sent shafts of insight into it. I was quite experienced in work redesign and Search Conferencing. To see these modes presented as "getting everybody improving whole systems" transformed my understanding of what was required in designing and implementing change processes.

I loved the idea of checking whether potential clients had "an itch they wanted to scratch," of looking for a business opportunity instead of the "people problems," that we are all subject to anxiety and craziness under stress, and that these might be signs of readiness to learn. I especially loved this quote: "The seeds of success are sown in Confusion and sprout in Renewal." Reading PW in the cocoon of a long plane trip, I determined to be more ambitious and demanding of myself and my clients as we searched for the best way to work together.

All of this, and it was only one chapter!

When the book was published, I gained a view of Taylor both sympathetic and appreciative to balance the ogre image popular among work reformers. I loved the description of my mentor Fred Emery as "a born protagonist" who "thrives on opposition," which captured perfectly the behavior I had seen so often. I knew also that Fred had a gentle, generous, helping side for those without pretension whom he sensed were eager to learn.

After reading *Productive Workplaces*, I commenced a long association with a manufacturing plant in a provincial town. Working with Tony Richardson, I introduced many ideas from PW. It became one of my most successful consulting relationships. Here, Tony and I first used Bill Lytle's wonderful "Flying Starship Factory" simulation that I learned about from Marv. We found it a brilliant tool for enabling participants to "get" the paradigm shift from bureaucratic to democratic workplaces.

In the late 1990s, inspired by Dick and Emily Axelrod's conference approach, Kate Nash and I involved hundreds of workers and managers from the Australian Postal Service in creating a whole system plan for operating their systems with new technologies. We brought to bear all we had learned since 1987 to enable highly productive workplaces at Post.

My last project came after attending a Weisbord/Janoff workshop in Australia with managers and unionists from a Sydney Oil Refinery. Normally suspicious of "management maneuvers," the hard-bitten unionists, experiencing the training simulation, chose Future Search to reenergize what had become a moribund, fractured workplace. They were convinced that the process had such integrity it could not be manipulated.

I am working now on re-creating "Workplace Australia," an organization that Marv knew from his first visit here in 1991. We see the need to build again a body dedicated to promoting sustainable, innovative and productive workplaces based on participation by all.

—Neil Watson, independent sociotechnical systems consultant

chapter
FOUR

Taylor Invents a New Profession

It would seem to me a farce to devote one's whole life and money merely to secure an increase in dividends for a whole lot of manufacturing companies.

—Frederick Taylor, in F. B. Copley, 1923, Vol. 2, p. 238

Between 1880 and 1910 the United States "underwent the most rapid economic expansion of any industrialized country for a comparable period of time" (Bendix, 1956, p. 254). Management theory and methods always reflect their time and place. Getting rich from new technologies, cheap labor, and untaxed capital was dignified by a new term, social Darwinism, meaning that only the fittest survived the jungles of commerce. Taylor, the erstwhile factory hand, realized that European immigrants, many of them ex-farmers, would be unlikely to understand new technology. Taylor blamed management for unmotivated workers. It controlled the playing field. But workers controlled quality, quantity, and costs. Taylor proved that immigrants working the repetitive jobs they did best would produce if they received higher wages in return. His system enabled tens of thousands of semiskilled newcomers to become productive while assimilating into American society.

Preaching cooperation between labor and capital, Taylor helped bury social Darwinism. He also undermined the arbitrary use of authority in factories. Taylor said what everybody knew but could not articulate: people who have power don't necessarily know what to do with it. Only trained experts could bring reason, order, high output, and high wages to industry. It was not a message to warm managerial hearts. If Taylor was right, what were managers for? Taylor did not see technology as the fix, just one factor in an equation. Machines could be speeded up without achieving gains. "A good organization with a poor plant," he wrote in words that might come from any modern theorist, "will give better results than the best plant with a poor organization" (Taylor, 1915, p. 62).

Taylor made expert industrial engineers the drivers of his system. They would collect the data, gain agreement on easier methods, higher output, and higher pay, and then install and teach the system. Managers were there just to see that it ran right. It was the way reasonable people would want to solve problems and make money, better than fighting, better than forcing. Remember that Taylor disliked conflict and sought to depersonalize it. He put the work itself, not labor-management conflict, at the center of his analysis. That the work did not always stay put is more a commentary on human fallibility than Taylor's values.

Extending Taylorism

From 1901 on Taylor tirelessly advocated his system. He wrote books and papers, delivered speeches, and presided over the American Society of Mechanical Engineers (ASME). He developed a cadre of disciples whose services he sold in a unique way. He would regularly invite potential clients to Boxly, his Germantown estate. They would hear a two-hour lecture (always including "Schmidt"), then tour the Link Belt Company or Tabor Manufacturing, two local firms run on the Taylor system.

Those who liked what they saw were introduced to trained consultants like Gantt or Morris Cooke, a brilliant young engineer who had worked at ASME. Taylor "supplied advice and moral support to both the employer and disciple, acted as conciliator in the event of disputes, and, above all, guaranteed the expert's competence and professionalism" (Nelson, 1980,

p. 124). At first Taylor was an absolutist—his ideas had to be used in toto or not at all. He softened his message when Cooke, whom he respected, pointed out that many businessmen were not ready to grant consultants authority to do whatever they wished.

Cooke became Taylor's alter ego. He transcribed the Boxly lecture and used much of it in an unpublished manuscript called "Industrial Management," begun in 1907. By mutual agreement this later became a major segment of the book *Scientific Management* (Wrege and Stotka, 1978). One biographer, disparaging Taylor's speeches, said that "no more than 10 percent of the businessmen who listened to the lecture subsequently employed one of Taylor's select corps of scientific management practitioners" (Nelson, 1980, p. 124). That would mean two new clients from every twenty-person seminar, the consultant's equivalent to a baseball players having "only" three hits for each ten times at bat.

Unpaid Consultant

Taylor performed his brokerage and monitoring services free. He acted as unpaid consultant to the U.S. Army ordnance department and Navy shipyards and to business and engineering schools. He became a popular speaker on college campuses—Toronto, Penn State, Penn, Dartmouth, Wisconsin, Chicago, and, of course, Harvard. Yet he became increasingly anti-academic, criticizing business schools for not imposing more discipline on their curricula and urging that every student be made to work six months in a factory. He thought the best scientific management consultants would be ordinary working people, not college graduates.

Many opportunistic Taylor imitators did not meet his standards. A typical trial for him was Harrington Emerson, an ex-professor of modern languages, who set up the Emerson Company in 1907 and had as a client the Union Pacific Railroad. Emerson, a promoter and salesman, lacked system, methods, or sequence of work. He did whatever the client would pay for, using associates less competent than Taylor's. Like most consultants of the time, Emerson admired Taylor, writing to him, "I would rather have your approval of what I am trying to do than any other man living or dead" (Kakar, 1970, p. 179). His was love unrequited. Taylor thought Emerson's work tainted scientific management.

Union Troubles

The Railroad Rates Case. Taylor first achieved public notoriety through a lawsuit brought by Louis Brandeis on behalf of manufacturing trade associations fighting a railroad rate increase. Brandeis argued that more efficient work methods would cut costs $1 million a day. He called Emerson, Gilbreth, and Gantt as witnesses. Taylor declined to appear, saying that he knew too little about railroads. His work was cited so often, however, that Ray Stannard Baker, editor of the *American Magazine*, offered to serialize *The Principles of Scientific Management.*

It was during the rate case planning sessions that Brandeis coined the term "scientific management." That is how Taylor came to be identified with Progressive politics. Progressives loved the idea that rationalizing work could make it more humane and eliminate class conflict. Taylor's philosophy fit their faith that science would improve every area of society. Taylor "made efficiency synonymous with morality and social order," an industrial complement to Progressive reforms like women's suffrage, direct election of senators, workman's compensation, a minimum wage, aid to low-income people, and the income tax (Wren, 1979, p. 284).

Trouble at Watertown. The installation of Taylor's system by a disciple at Watertown Arsenal in Massachusetts in 1911 finally stirred up organized labor. Taylor had insisted that worker sentiment be checked in every department before starting time studies. At Watertown his disciple neither consulted molders nor briefed them on time study's benefits. In a test of power, one molder, following union orders, refused to participate and was fired. The others walked out. The workers did not oppose time study and bonuses, but rather the method of introducing the change (Nadworny, 1955, p. 80).

When Renault workers similarly struck in France in 1913, Taylor wrote, "If a man deliberately goes against the experience of men who know what they are talking about, and refuses to follow advice given in a kind but unmistakable way, it seems to me that he deserves to get into trouble" (Nelson, 1980, p. 179). Indeed, at the Frankford Arsenal in Philadelphia, where Taylor's system had been installed smoothly, several hundred rank-and-file unionists petitioned to continue it against their own leaders' advice (Drury, 1915).

One contemporary study performed in response to the hubbub showed that by 1912 there were sixty Taylor and two hundred Emerson systems in use, that production went up 100 percent at Midvale, 50 to 75 percent at Bethlehem and on the Santa Fe Railroad, 250 percent at Tabor, and 200 percent at Link Belt. All this happened without widespread turmoil or displaced workers and was seen as beneficial by management and labor alike (Drury, 1915).

Congressional Hearings. Nevertheless, Taylorism became a lightning rod for one of the great social struggles of all time. The Watertown strike attracted so much attention that Congress in 1911 ordered an investigation of charges that workers were mistreated under scientific management. Union leaders badgered Taylor mercilessly during his four days as a witness. The pro-union committee chairman refused to let him define what he meant by first-class man, insisting on the implication that only a few exceptional people could ever hold jobs under his system.

The panel concluded that there was no evidence that Taylor's system abused workers. It added that it was too soon to evaluate effects on health, pay, and labor costs. It proposed no legislation. Still, anti-Taylor forces used the hearings as a lever to prohibit the Army or Navy from spending money

Portrait of Taylor late in life, after many battles.

Source: Williams Library, Stevens Institute of Technology

on systematizing. Thus ended the first attempt, successful until then, to make government agencies more efficient (Wren, 1979).

In his running battle with labor leaders, Taylor repeatedly invited Samuel Gompers, president of the American Federation of Labor (AFL), and John Mitchell of the United Mine Workers to talk with workers in plants operating under his system. Both refused. Gompers denied the existence of soldiering. Unions observed an informal truce during World War I and did an about-face during the 1920s, when a recession thinned their ranks. Both clothing workers and railroad unions adopted joint committees to address work issues. The AFL under William Green hired its own consulting engineer, and other unions did research on job design. Union acceptance of Taylorism lasted until 1932 when, at the bottom of the Depression, the AFL gave up on cooperation and started lobbying for survival (Wren, 1979). Eventually, unions institutionalized the subdivision of jobs as a way to protect employment, and workers continued to find ingenious ways to defeat time-and-motion studies.

The Bitter End

Taylor's last years were marked by bitterness and resignation. A portrait painted about this time has him staring at the artist, self-possessed, belligerent, hair and moustache gone gray, face fuller than in his college graduation picture, straight mouth thinner and more tight-lipped. He is unsmiling, challenging. Widely admired by political reformers, still he felt misunderstood by zealous unionists and quick-fix managers and wronged by consultant-imitators. More, his energy was drained by constant attention to his wife's periodic illnesses. The Taylors moved regularly—Atlantic City, the Poconos, New England, Europe, Philadelphia—seeking quiet, a pleasant climate, a change of scenery that would lift Louise Taylor's spirits.

On a speaking tour in the Midwest early in 1915, an exhausted Taylor contracted influenza. He entered a hospital in Philadelphia, where on March 20 he celebrated his fifty-ninth birthday. The next morning a nurse heard him winding his elegant Swiss watch somewhat earlier than usual. When she looked in at 5:00 a.m., he was dead.

■ ■ ■

"NOW I FEEL EMPOWERED WITH THE TOOLS I NEED..."

CHICAGO, IL—I read *Productive Workplaces* as a student and thought this was a typical required college text that I would likely never use. To my surprise, I found everything in the book purposeful and could relate to a lot of the concepts and theories presented. Having grown up in a small town dominated by industrial plants, having worked in one for a summer, I particularly appreciated Frederick Taylor's challenges and ideas.

Suddenly, I was seeing organizations in a different perspective. Their complexities, I saw, were not challenges but opportunities to bring out the best of what an organization could offer. Now a consultant for financial institutions in trying times, I feel empowered with the mental tools to help with job redesigns, addressing anxiety, management training, evaluating stakeholder investments and so on. I now look at institutions from the point of organization development and how it can impact, influence, and possibly save an institution from itself. These challenges I now look upon as possibilities for many potential organization development projects.

—Gina Lowdermilk, CRCM, CAMS, and Ph.D. student, Benedictine University

Learning from Taylorism

I have been a long time arriving at an appreciation of Frederick Taylor that makes sense today. His is a sort of wall-sized projection screen on which every scenario comes across larger than life. It is not generally appreciated how modern Frederick Taylor's core values were. He knew the importance of productive workplaces. He was working on the right problems—social, technical, economic—even when he did not have the right solutions. The tension between the two Taylors is the tug of war in all of us between what we believe and what we do. We have a great deal to learn from Taylor's story.

The Every-New-Idea-Has-Nomenclature-Problems Department

What Scientific Management Is Not . . . (1912)

"Not an efficiency device . . . not a device of any kind for securing efficiency . . . nor any bunch or group of efficiency devices . . . not a system of figuring costs . . . not a new scheme of paying men . . . not a bonus system . . . not a premium system . . . not a stopwatch on a man and writing things down about him . . . not time study . . . not motion study or an analysis of the movements of men . . . not divided foremanship or functional foremanship . . . not any of the devices which the average man calls to mind when scientific management is spoken of.

"In essence, scientific management involves a complete mental revolution on the part of the working men—and on the part of those on the management side, the foreman, the superintendent, the owner of the business, the board of directors—as to their duties toward their fellow workers in the management, toward their workmen and toward all of their problems."

—Frederick W. Taylor, testimony to a special committee, U.S. House of Representatives, January 25–30, 1912, Washington, D.C.

What Quality of Work Life Is Not . . . (1978)

"Not a single, specific notion . . . not a soft, touchy-feely approach to working . . . not a vague, imprecise kind of notion . . . not a threat to power—management's or union's . . . not quick . . . not easy . . . not a panacea . . . not a closed system, not an end . . . not job enrichment, not a productivity gimmick . . . not imposable . . . not manipulative . . . not an ideology . . . not a passing fad . . . not elitist.

"The cluster of notions it sucks into itself combine to suggest something simple, operationally feasible, intensely human and even more intensely cost-effective. . . . That something is to provide people at work (managers, supervisors, rank-and-file workers) with structured opportunities to become actively involved in a new interpersonal process of problem solving toward both a better way of working and a more efficient work organization, the payoff from which includes the best interests of employees and employers in equal measure."

—Ted Mills, director, American Center for the Quality of Worklife, speech entitled "The Name That Isn't There," to Centre international de Recherches et d'Etudes en Management, June 8, 1978, Montreal, Canada.

He was not an "open systems" thinker by any stretch. More than anyone, he believed every effect had a cause. At the same time he had an intuitive appreciation for how things fit together that went far beyond most people in his day. He created a unique role—the industrial engineer—as a sort of third-party facilitator to bring reason and impartiality to labor-management relations.

Today many productivity programs rely on third-party facilitation for the same reasons. Unionized places (some auto and steel plants are typical) pair facilitators, one from labor, one from management. Instead of a stopwatch, their main tools are patience, trust, and group problem-solving techniques derived from Kurt Lewin. They seek to bring about, from a much wider perspective, the sort of cooperation between management and labor that Taylor envisioned. Still, the methods are widely mistaken for the goals—the psychological dilemma of the Industrial Revolution. The quotes in "Every New Idea" are a sobering reminder of how mixed up we become between form and substance when we try to program a new way of looking at things.

Resistance from middle managers cut out of the action is as pervasive today as it once was to scientific management. The reasons are the same. How can you claim to make life at work better if you exclude a significant segment of the workforce? We have a hard time accepting and using policies and procedures we did not help to select or invent. It does not matter how good they are.

Taylor's Contemporary Values

Disdaining Taylor's contributions, human resource experts embraced his core values: labor-management cooperation, higher output, improved quality, lower costs, higher wages, the rule of reason, questioning old habits, experimentation, clear tasks and goals, feedback, training, mutual help and support, stress reduction, and careful selection and development of people. Taylor thought people could be trained to succeed, not thrown into the water to sink or swim. He standardized tools and equipment to match human capability. What is now called ergonomics was an integral part of Taylorism. He was the first to consider a systematic study of the interactions among job requirements, methods, tools, and human skill, to fit people to jobs both physically and psychologically, and to let facts and data do the talking rather than prejudice, opinions, or egomania.

Taylor saw restriction of output as a consequence of poor management, not worker inferiority—a radical idea in his day. He believed in giving people feedback on their performance, a central tenet of participative management. He thought that labor strife was not inevitable—extraordinary in light of the bitter, sometimes murderous relations between employers and employees at the time. He argued that raising output and cutting costs would make possible higher wages, a view embodied in labor-management cooperation in many industries now. He was sure that money was the major motivator, certainly true in 19th-Century factories and still true for many people low down on the economic ladder—a conclusion Abraham Maslow would applaud.

Considering the time and place, Taylor's version of applied science was not so different from our own. There was a great deal of judgment in time study. Taylor, like every consultant, did not look only at "what is." He searched for the gap between "what is" and "what ought to be." The ought is a statement of future intent, not prediction or probability, but aspiration based on reasonable judgment derived from existing data, tempered by social values. Scientific time study for Taylor was the discovery of how a job should be done. When jobs were broken down into their smallest parts, it was possible to discard wasted motions and, through trial, error, and observation, to find out what worked best—meaning most accurately, most efficiently, with the least stress.

In summary, Taylor wanted a more humane and sensible solution to the degradation of work, which, like smog and pollution, was an early byproduct of the Industrial Revolution. We were not a society of innocent artisans before Taylor. We were a society of growing inequity, sweatshops, brutal working conditions; and he wanted, with all the tools of science and engineering, to do something about it.

Despite resistance, Taylor's ideas, embraced at last by organized labor, spread after his death to the public sector, office management, even marketing. Germany, Sweden, Great Britain, and the Soviet Union adopted scientific management in the 1920s. Lenin called it, with exquisite ambivalence, "a combination of the refined brutality of bourgeois exploitation and a number of the greatest scientific achievements. . . . We must organize in Russia the study and teaching of the Taylor system and systematically try it out and adapt it to our ends" (Simmons and Mares, 1983, p. 26). Hugo Munsterberg, called the father of industrial psychology, built directly on Taylor, seeking to discover "the men whose mental qualities make them best fitted for the work which they have to do." He too asked "under what psychological conditions we can secure the greatest and most satisfactory output from every man." He sought through psychological means to "produce most completely the influences on human minds which are desired in the interest of business" (Wren, 1979, p. 212).

The field of human resource management is directly traceable to the integration between industrial social work, once called welfare, which Taylor disdained, and scientific management. "No man in the history of American industry," wrote Ida Tarbell, "has made a larger contribution to genuine cooperation and just human relations than did Frederick Winslow Taylor. . . . He is one of the few—very few—creative geniuses of our times" (1925, p. 81). No wonder Peter Drucker credited Taylor with as much influence on the modern world as Karl Marx or Sigmund Freud.

Lessons to Remember

But that is not the whole story of Fred Taylor. So attractive were his ideas, so dramatic his results, that his descendants simply divorced his values and married his techniques. Greedy managers coveted the quick fix of time study without staff-line cooperation, and without paying workers a fair share of the gains. A modern analogy might be reducing the larger notion of a new corporate culture to task forces, attitude surveys, or flex time while leaving narrow jobs and hierarchical structures intact. Taylor hated that his integrated system was trivialized by 1912 into measured piecework, the wage differential treated as a rate to be cut each time previous output goals were exceeded.

Lessons for Management. In time Taylorism became synonymous with speedups, employer insensitivity, people turned into robots, and doing more work for the same pay. This last gasp of social Darwinism fanned the flames of unionism. Between 1897 and 1904 American trade unionists increased from 487,000 to more than 2,000,000. Technocratic engineers mastered the method and forgot the intent.

"The stopwatch and time study are baseball bats to clobber workers to get more," said industrial engineer Mitchell Fein at a seminar I once attended. "I'm a high priest of time study. It won't work anymore." Gain-sharing plans like the Scanlon Plan and Fein's Improshare symbolized a constructive return to Taylor's original intent: to give workers equity in increased productivity. These plans were based on a design principle that turned Taylorism upside down—to promote group control of results, a form of accountability unimaginable in 1911.

Lessons for Labor. Organized labor by 1930 largely accepted Taylorism. In the Depression unions turned toward bread-and-butter issues, especially job security, which narrow specialization could enhance. Many unions made a deal with the devil: jobs might be dumb but they would be safe. Each specialty would protect its own turf with restrictive work rules.

Decades later Chrysler's manufacturing vice president described what happened when an engine block angled out of place on the assembly line. The line stopped. A foreman came from the other end of the plant and called in a toolmaker assistant, who straightened the block. When he noticed a bent switch, he called an electrician. Half an hour of production was lost. In Japan, he noted, workers fixed similar problems in a minute or two. "We have a stock chaser and a stock counter and a high-low man who moves the stock. Why can't the man who moves the stock be the chaser or the counter?" (Flint, 1984, p. 94).

Perhaps the most historic clause in the 1984 agreement between General Motors and the United Auto Workers was the provision to protect employment in return for job flexibility. Without job security there is as much resistance to dismantling Taylorism as there was to installing it. "None of GM's ambitious plans to automate factories will be worth much," noted one writer, "if in the 21st Century plants are run under systems rooted in the 19th Century. Like other American manufacturers, GM has to overcome inefficient practices built up by both management and labor that stand in the way of high output and high quality" (Flax, 1984, p. 228).

Lessons for Operations. For Taylor, subdividing tasks was an essential but minor part of a grander integrating scheme. Unfortunately, the form survived without the spirit or substance. Companies have staff experts for anything you can think of—pay, benefits, safety, hours, forms design, machinery, plant layout, diversity, schedules, inventory, quality control, public relations, law, maintenance, planning, safety, training, organization development—you name it. None of it guarantees anything except overhead. You can't simply break jobs down indefinitely without spending pots of money to put everything back together. So more line managers and supervisors are needed to integrate the system—the reason Bethlehem Steel reached fourteen layers of management in the 1970s. "Who should I listen to?" asks a manager. "Me first!" answers every staff specialist within earshot. Managers drown in a sea of conflicting staff pressures. Because they are not visible like a pile of pig iron, these pressures—the intangibles that determine whether people will cooperate—cannot be managed according to scientific principles.

What were Taylor's "scientific principles" anyway? They are so simple as to be laughable: simplify each task; reduce conflict; cooperate; increase output; develop people to their highest capabilities. Who could argue with any of that? See Taylor's own words below:

Scientific Principles

- Science, not rule of thumb.
- Harmony, not discord.
- Cooperation, not individualism.
- Maximum output, not restricted output.
- Development of each man to his greatest efficiency and prosperity.

—Taylor, 1915, p. 140

Taylor Mythology

There are other reasons why Taylor became an ogre and a bogeyman. One is that his "scientific" task simplification violates social systems thinking and psychological knowledge. One Taylor precept was that "brainwork" should be taken from the shop floor and put in the planning department, where staff roles became repositories of enormous technical skill and conflicting objectives as they sought to tread the fine line between being cops and being coaches.

Another Taylor dogma was to gather "all of the great masses of traditional knowledge, which in the past has been in the heads of the workmen, and in the physical skill and knack of the workmen," and reduce it "to rules, laws, and formulae" (Copley, 1923, Vol. 1, p. 13). His intent was to institutionalize "best practices."

Yet we know now that optimum productivity and human satisfaction can't be reduced to rules and formulas, whether from economics, engineering, or human relations. Indeed, high-quality work requires a creative interaction of all three perspectives. In successful workplaces, workers, managers, and staff specialists achieve a partnership, learning together, bringing skills, expertise, information, and mutual support to economic and technical problems. Workers, specialists, and managers, facing uncertainty, all have "real-time" information and expertise that can be accessed only through joint discussion and learning.

Taylor insisted late in life that his main goal was a degree of "intimate, friendly cooperation" between workers and managers impossible under the management practices of his day (Copley, 1923, Vol. 1, p. 18). What he could not envision were the more dramatic forms such cooperation might take—work teams without supervisors, management through self-control, multiple skills in each person.

New technologies, more than anything, made Taylorism obsolete. Ironically, in de-skilling individual jobs Taylor removed skill and discretion from managers, supervisors, and staff people too. Industrial engineers, whose job it became, found it difficult to introduce new knowledge into a system. The "law of the situation," as Mary Parker Follett called it, became the law of past precedent. It could not regulate continuous process plants, microchip technologies, automation, robotics, computer-based systems—even when PERT-charted to the last detail.

Taylor was not interested in democratizing work. He stood for rational control, not shared influence. He opposed group tasks and group incentives, arguing that, unlike solo tasks, they reduced accountability. He had no concept of the power of multi-skilled work teams, joint decision making, or worker participation. Such matters would not be studied systematically for decades. No theories existed in 1900 for harnessing the unpredictable synergy of well-motivated workers. Even today no one knows enough to make a science of the complex interdependencies among people, economics, and technology. We do know, though, that, given a chance, people can work out excellent solutions for themselves.

We come at last to the inadvertent myth. What obscures Taylor's values more than anything, I think, like mists swirling across a dark road at night, are shadows of "Schmidt" and harnesses used to control nightmares, battles with organized labor, battles with middle managers, battles with the owners of capital, battles with the government, battles with the university, battles with other consultants who could not meet his standards. Taylor, like many pacifists, fought endlessly for a more rational, objective way to manage agreement. If his results fell short of his aspirations, that is more a commentary on human limitation than on what he stood for and what he accomplished.

Taylor's Main Contributions

Taylor made three kinds of contributions. First, he was an enormously creative technical engineer in the spirit of Thomas Edison. His forty-plus patents alone assure him enduring fame. Second, he pioneered concepts of organization and management—the integration of methods, policies, planning, people—that were light-years ahead of his time. Finally, he spoke eloquently for labor-management cooperation—an ideal that his techniques could not support. A letter written just ten days before his death—and reproduced here—leaves no doubt of his sentiments.

Management accepted Taylor's organizing principles to a much greater degree than is generally recognized today. But neither operating managers nor factory workers have been entirely happy with the results. "What is resisted and criticized," wrote Peter Drucker, "is a misapplication of work analysis rather than work analysis itself. . . . The fact remains that scientific management or industrial engineering has been content to stop where Taylor stopped" (1974, p. 202).

FREDERICK W. TAYLOR
CONSULTING ENGINEER
NEAR
HIGHLAND STATION
CHESTNUT HILL
PHILADELPHIA

Hotel Brighton, Atlantic City, N.J.

March 11th, 1915.
(Dictated March 9th)

R.A.T.

Mr. Richard A. Feiss,
c/o Clothcraft Shops,
Cleveland, Ohio.

My dear Richard:

I am still thinking of the two most delightful and instructive days that I spent in your shops. What you have accomplished there is certainly magnificient and I am sure is destined to be even better yet. You can hardly improve, however, on your main feature, i.e. the fine relations which exist between the management and the working people.

I wish that every honest trade unionist in the country would go there and stay long enough to fully appreciate what you are doing so that it may be borne home to him that true co-operation and friendship is better than war.

Will you not knidly remember me to all of the friends at the shop who were so attentive to me.

Please tell Mrs Feiss that I regret exceedingly not having see her.

I succeededing in staving off the grippe until after my address at Youngstown. The following morning, however, I was so hoarse with a bronchial cough that I was almost unable to speak and the fever and grippe still continue. I consider this a great piece of luck.

With kindest regards, believe me,

Very sincerely yours,

Fred. W. Taylor
M.

(Williams Library, Stevens Institute of Technology.)

Taylor cannot be blamed for that development. Companies are learning, just as mine did in the 1960s, that they can get along with a great deal less management and supervision when workers help design their own work. This changes the system in an exponential way, making possible product quality and productivity previously thought impossible. The important thing to see is that three realities—social, technical, and economic—must be simultaneously worked with if we wish to achieve productive workplaces. More, none of the three bailiwicks can be left to experts. Information from and about all three must be freely available to everybody, so that an organization develops through mutual influence, knowledge, and commitment, rather than coercion, whimsy, or unilateral action.

Lessons for Consultants

Taylor understood the inevitability of resistance, the virtue of support and experimentation. Yet he did not know how to act as constructively as he would have liked. He tried out his total system in no more than two or three factories and never implemented the whole exactly as conceived. Not only was Taylorism complicated, but it worked against the development of management generalists, people who could see a meaningful whole. The system Taylor described in his famous book was a composite of everything he had learned from trying bits and pieces in many companies. I find this oddly reassuring. Taylor did what he could in each situation, fitting as much of his thinking as he could to his client's motives and problems. That, by and large, is what consultants do now. We can conceptualize processes—large systems change, cultural change, transformation—far beyond our capacity to implement them. Social, technical, or economic progress seems a lot less rational and programmable in practice than our models of it—an entirely appropriate phenomenon, which in no way depreciates the models.

Out of many projects have come grand designs for planned change, cultural change, organization development, corporate excellence, total quality control, and transformation. Pinpointing cases—the megabuck, all-out, everybody-in-it-until-the-job-is-done, honest-to-goodness, full commitment, synergistic, use-everything-we-know, culture change effort—is a lot like hoping to meet somebody who has rowed across the Atlantic Ocean. I know for a fact that it has been done, but you probably don't know anybody who did it.

The "Other" Taylor—Take Your Pick

Those who think this way about change—that the job can be done once and for all with a particular program—share the least universal aspects of Taylor's thinking: that every effect has a cause; every problem has a solution; big problems have big solutions; organizational change is largely a matter of the right program or the right expert. That is one form of contemporary Taylorism. It is also one side of the dialogue in all of us, the yearning for control, the wish to be seen as competent and successful, the desire to influence others, the fear that we are too lazy, too irresponsible, too incompetent, too humorless, or too frivolous, too unworthy, too . . . (fill in your own most pessimistic worry) to ever measure up.

In his first Harvard lecture, Taylor attributed the withholding of output to two sources. One was the "natural" tendency to laziness, which only money could overcome. Another, more systemic cause, which presaged Kurt Lewin's work, was a form of social collusion, "association with other men, with the deliberate object of keeping their employers ignorant of how fast work can be done" (Simmons and Mares, 1983, p. 26). That was a shrewd observation of what is now called a "group norm." What Taylor could not see was the social need behind the norm.

Yet, in his efforts to integrate and manage his own inner dialogue, Taylor was more holistic than either his direct descendants, the efficiency experts, or the human relations experts who disowned him. Turn the prism just a little bit and it is not so hard to view Taylor as the original QWL pioneer. He was the first person in history to make a systematic attempt to improve both output and work life in factories. He argued, as McGregor would sixty years later, that the big gains would come through the development of effective human systems.

Taylor erred in believing his system was the only game in town. "Throughout his life," wrote his admiring official biographer, "he was inclined to take too much upon himself, to assume and to feel too great a responsibility. He did not leave enough up to God" (Copley, 1923, Vol. 2, p. 438).

It remained for a later mental revolution to implement Taylor's more radical values. What new technologies have made essential has become possible only because of a new social science. To understand that, we have to investigate action research and Kurt Lewin.

■ ■ ■

"WHAT'S WORKING, AND HOW CAN I HELP?"

SEATTLE, WA—Transformational work in my large corporation is not considered mainstream. I have been fortunate in having had a few managers who value my way of working to improve a whole system, not just solve the problems. I have heard people say, "This problem is too big or complex. There is nothing I can do!" Understanding how systems work, I look for small pockets of interested people who see a bigger picture. My guiding question is, "As a change agent, where can I have the most influence?"

In 1995, studying in the Organization Systems Renewal Program (OSR) at Antioch Seattle, I met Marv Weisbord. He made a comment that shaped my work ever since. "Working in organizations," he said, "I would ask about 'what's broken and what will fix it.' Now, I go in asking, 'What's working and how can I help?'" That question has sustained my passion during my thirteen+ year career in whole systems design.

In 1996, I began a new chapter as an internal consultant in The Boeing Company on a four-person team called Quantum Shift Learning. We were charged with transforming a large information technology (IT) group into a learning organization. In 1997, Boeing purchased McDonnell Douglas and undertook to merge two large organizations. My department faced a Herculean task—creating a single IT infrastructure for our global network. The IT group knew the technical side; the cultural side begged for attention. My colleague N'Shama Sterling and I were tapped to bring our expertise in applying systemic thinking.

We met with the IT director, the program manager, and their organizational design consultant to find out what was working and how we could help. We learned that they had a visionary leader and looked upon the infrastructure project as a developmental journey, not just a technical one. They were willing to invest the time required to make systemic changes to reporting relationships, competing processes and tools, reward systems, and mental models.

We helped create a forum in which they might get past their biases and longstanding competitive behaviors, bringing a cross-section of the "whole system" into the room to tell their stories. We helped them use a method for mapping the dynamics of their behavior to discover a rich store of mental models that highlighted what was getting in the way of merging two computing infrastructures. All were shocked when the people from both sides identified each other as the "the evil empire." Each blamed the other for impeding the success of the project. As these feelings and resentments came out in the open, we noticed a major shift. People became aware that they weren't arguing the technical aspects of the change. What stopped them were their biases and assumptions about the others. Years later the director told us our work with them was key to aligning the infrastructure.

Their success could be measured in intangible and tangible outcomes. Cooperation increased as the lines that had been drawn slowly dissolved. In operational terms, some of the "ca-ching!" results could be measured in the increasing number of transactions the system could handle, and the decreasing cost of each one. The merged infrastructure became stronger, gaining capacity to manage centralized and distributed operations. Resource sharing led to significant cost savings To this day, that key question, "What's working and how can I help?" resonates in me. I find much more power in moving toward the future than in trying to fix the past.

—Albie Merrill, MA, Whole Systems Design,
learning organization consultant

chapter FIVE

Action Research: Lewin Revises Taylorism

When the intellectual history of the 20th Century is written, Kurt Lewin will surely be counted as one of those few men whose work changed fundamentally the course of social science.

—Dorwin Cartwright, editor, introduction to Lewin, *Field Theory in Social Science*, 1951, p. vii

I first heard Kurt Lewin's name at a workshop in 1969 when Bill Dyer, later dean of Brigham Young University's Marriott School of Management, echoed Lewin's famous line, "There's nothing so practical as a good theory." Dyer went on to prove it by demonstrating force field analysis, Lewin's unique problem-solving tool. (See Chapter Seven for more on Dyer.) Lewin's organizational change theories enormously attracted me after my experiences as a manager. And "action research" soon formed the core of my consulting practice.

I also undertook a systematic inquiry into Lewin and my professional roots. I devoured Alfred Marrow's biography (1969), and I began hounding colleagues who had known Lewin—notably Ronald Lippitt and Eric Trist. In the library I found a curious parallel between Lewin and Taylor. In 1912 the American Society of Mechanical Engineers had observed that

Taylor's revolution was built on "an attitude of questioning, of research, of careful investigation . . . seeking for exact knowledge and then shaping action on discovered facts" (Nelson, 1980, p. 198). That describes Lewin's approach exactly if you add one radical enhancement: full participation of the research subjects.

Lewin's Contributions to Management

Lewin's life, like Taylor's, was marked by a passion for experimentation. Taylor sought to rid workplaces of authoritarianism and conflict through scientific management. Lewin strove to free the world from prejudice, ignorance, and self-hate through social science. In Part Three, I propose that to honor Lewin's values today is to update his theory in practice. That requires an appreciation of how important his contributions are to modern management.

What struck me first about Lewin's legacy is how rarely his pervasive influence is acknowledged. Peter Drucker, in his "classic management book" (1974), for example, does not mention Kurt Lewin at all. Neither does Edward Lawler in his thorough review of participative practices (1986), nor Peter Senge (2006) in his notable treatise on management disciplines except in a cross-reference to the work you are reading. Yet Lewin's stamp is everywhere in contemporary organizations: running meetings, work design, training, team development, systems change, cultural change, leadership styles, participative methods, race relations, survey feedback methods, consultation skills.

Lewin conceived a novel form of problem solving that might be called "doing by learning." I was tickled to find that one of Lewin's early research interests was scientific management, a fact known only to Lewin scholars and (now) you and me. Lewin wed scientific thinking to democratic values and gave birth to participative management. And he did much more. He taught that to understand a system you must seek to change it. This led to one of the key managerial insights of the last century: Diagnosis does not mean just finding the problem, but doing it in such a way as to build commitment for action.

His was an unprecedented idea. While solving a problem, you could study your own process and thereby refine the theory and practice of change. In contrast to Taylor, who believed only a trained engineer could improve work, Lewin believed any well-motivated person could "learn how to learn" from everyday situations, improving general as well as specific skills. Hardly a corporate training department exists that does not build on his ideas. Lewin's twin emphases on science and democracy form the philosophical base for effective participation everywhere.

He also pointed the way toward collaborative consultation—a radical departure from the mode pioneered by Taylor in 1893. Lewin showed that even technical and economic problems have social consequences that include people's feelings, perceptions of reality, sense of self-worth, motivation, and commitment. It is not given to consultants to sow the seeds for change (a screwy notion that spells trouble), but to discover what seeds are present and whether they can be grown. We owe that priceless insight to Lewin. If he were better understood, fewer consulting reports would be filed in bottom drawers. The practice of organization development—adopted by corporations, government agencies, schools, universities, hospitals, and nonprofit institutions—was Lewin's living monument. "I have come to believe," wrote Warren Bennis, a major shaper of OD practice, "that we have so carefully disguised our identification to ourselves that we forget we are all Lewinians" (Marrow, 1969, p. 234).

An experimental social psychologist, Kurt Lewin's career overlapped both Taylor's and Freud's. He lived on the fringes of academic psychology, an odd duck, trained in Germany by class-conscious "Herr Professors." Unlike them, he was egalitarian with students, an eager collaborator, an inspired teacher and loyal friend. He lived and breathed psychology, often losing track of time, forgetting to eat. Instead of specializing, he studied everything—child behavior, industrial psychology, social services, war research, education, community development. Instead of guarding his concepts, he freely offered them to all.

Psychologist Edward C. Tolman linked Lewin, the great experimentalist, with Freud, the great clinician, "the two men whose names will stand out before all others in the history of our psychological era. For it is their contrasting but complementary insights which first made psychology a science applicable to real human beings and to real human society" (Marrow, 1969, p. ix). Lewin saw unsolved problems frozen in a field of forces—people, institutions, motives, perceptions, wishes—that pushed toward and away from good solutions. In Lewin's youth that notion was considered kooky psychology, a pseudoscience of factors nobody could see or touch. Its tangibility now is a tribute to Lewin's faith that science could advance only outside the laboratory, that real-time experiments were required to make breakthroughs in theory and practice.

Lewin aspired to make psychology a science based on formal principles that account for human behavior. He knew that psychology could never be as precise as physical science. Yet, like Taylor, he had faith in experimental procedures and believed they could bring more predictability to human affairs. Lewin "was singular in that he . . . could transpose a life problem into controllable experimental form," wrote Alfred Marrow (1969, p. x). Taylor's passion was work measurement. Lewin's was accurately measuring psychological forces. For thirty years he used a mathematical system, "topological psychology," based on a geometry of relationships rather than sizes or shapes. He applied it to any human problem. The "Topological

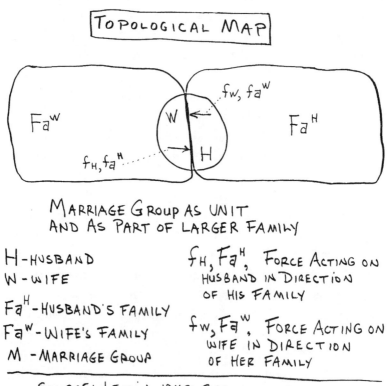

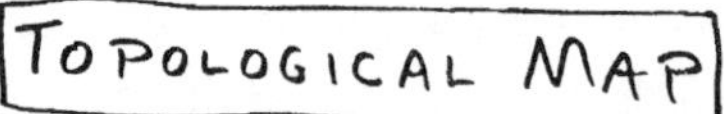

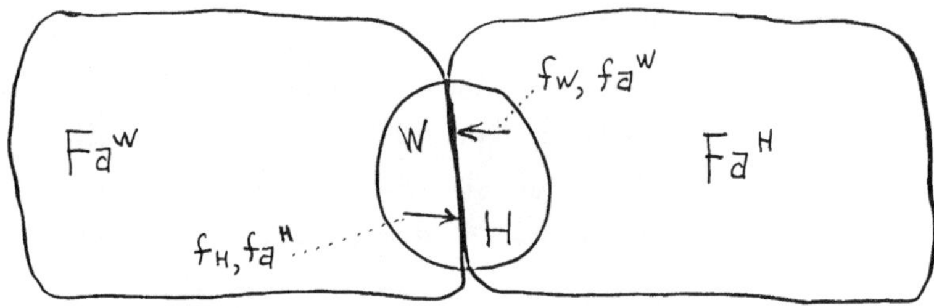

MARRIAGE GROUP AS UNIT
AND AS PART OF LARGER FAMILY

H - HUSBAND
W - WIFE
Fa^H - HUSBAND'S FAMILY
Fa^W - WIFE'S FAMILY
M - MARRIAGE GROUP

f_H, Fa^H, FORCE ACTING ON HUSBAND IN DIRECTION OF HIS FAMILY

f_W, Fa^W, FORCE ACTING ON WIFE IN DIRECTION OF HER FAMILY

SOURCE: LEWIN, 1948, P. 99

Map" is an example. The circle in the middle represents the marriage space. Each partner's family of origin—the large ovals—affects the marriage. Lewin believed that forces holding the pair together and pushing them apart could be delineated in a force field analysis.

"The drawings," said psychologist Norman Maier, "convinced me that Lewin and his students were trying to communicate concepts that were entirely new, and they suggested the need to explore forces that went beyond psychological processes" (Marrow, 1969, p. 37). Maier based his famous group exercises emphasizing both quality solutions and commitment on this insight. Always a nonconformist, Lewin agitated people to question assumptions, use common sense, and find out what works by trying it. Lewin's thinking made possible the evolution of an orderly method for dealing with events that are irrational, unmanageable, and—but for this way of doing things—out of control.

From East Prussia to Iowa

Kurt Lewin was born, the second of four children, into a close-knit, middle-class Jewish family in the Prussian province of Posen (now in Poland) on September 9, 1890. (In that year, thirty-four-year-old Frederick Taylor left Midvale Steel to manage a wood pulp business.) Lewin's parents ran a general store. His mother had high aspirations for her son. When he was fifteen she moved the family to Berlin where he could receive a classical education and become a physician. Instead, at age twenty Lewin enrolled in Berlin University to study an offshoot of philosophy called psychology. He was sociable, popular, a good dancer, a lover of the outdoors, whose conversation tended toward topics like "democratizing Germany and liberating women from the conventional restrictions of their freedom" (Marrow, 1969, p. 6).

His psychological interests were equally radical. He wanted to study human will, emotions, and sentiments, considered in 1910 the stuff of poetry. Who could see a motivation or measure a feeling? Lewin was an alien in academia. He joked that he felt like the little boy in the fairy tale shouting that the emperor had no clothes. Still, he set his heart on college teaching, a bold choice considering the anti-Semitism in Kaiser Wilhelm's Germany.

Lewin volunteered for the German Army in World War I, advanced from private to lieutenant, sustained battle wounds, and won the Iron Cross. Convalescing, he wrote an article on "The War Landscape," observing that soldiers' reality depends on whether they are behind the lines or in battle, when everyday objects—a haystack, for example—become survival tools (Marrow, 1969). He made the interplay between environment and behavior a central focus of his life's work.

Lewin married while on furlough in 1917. When the war ended he and his wife, also a teacher, settled down to academic life in Berlin. He was greatly attracted to the psychology of work. In 1919 he wrote a paper contrasting farm and factory labor, driven, his daughter speculated, by a "romantic attachment to the small farm his parents owned" (Papanek, 1973, p. 318). Farm work, unlike mill labor, he pointed out, was not specialized. It required the whole person. Shrewdly, he speculated that new farm technology meant new problems. Written decades ago, this paper contains the seeds of open-systems thinking and the first glimmers of what he would call "action research." Nothing could have seemed more far-fetched in German academia than Lewin's proposal that psychologists leave the laboratory and team up with farmers to improve work methods. Starting with a simple tool like the hoe, he wrote, they could devise systematic experiments to find less strenuous procedures for all tools and tasks.

Lewin Discovers Taylor

If these ideas sound familiar, Lewin's follow-up essay (1920) leaves little doubt of their origin. In "Humanization of the Taylor System: An Inquiry into the Fundamental Psychology of Work and Vocation," Lewin accepted that scientific management raised output, cut costs, increased wages, and reduced stress and working hours. But that was not the whole story. Work, he insisted, had "life value." It gave meaning to a person's existence. To the extent that Taylor's methods reinforced boredom and reduced learning, they exacted a cost in life value.

"The worker," wrote Lewin, "wants his work to be rich, wide, and protean, not crippling and narrow. Work should not limit personal potential but develop it. Work can involve love, beauty, and the soaring joy of creating. Progress . . . does not mean shortening the work day, but an increase in the human value of work." Commented his second wife, Gertrud Lewin, after his death, "You cannot help realizing that this is how Lewin actually felt about his own chosen work and how he lived" (Papanek, 1973, p. 318).

Among the Berlin psychologists who established the Gestalt school, Lewin alone had an interest in industrial management. Taylor knew before 1900 that less stress and more equity were critical to improved labor-management relations, more humane workplaces, and higher output. By 1920 Lewin was advocating that psychologists team with efficiency experts to enhance both productivity and job satisfaction.

Lewin's psychology differed radically from beliefs that all behavior is motivated by past influences (Freud) or future goals (Skinner). Lewin saw motivation as an interaction of a specific person in a specific situation, like the soldier in battle. Lewin's field theory holds that we act to resolve tensions that impinge upon our life space—unfulfilled desires, for example, or unfinished activities. Invisible they might be, yet measurable as precisely as weighing a stone. Lewin translated this insight into a formula. Behavior (B) is a function (f) of person (p) and environment (e), or $B = f(p,e)$.

This formula underpins force field analysis, which allows you to act more confidently on problems you cannot measure in ordinary ways. In the simplified "Force Field Analysis" drawing, for example, the behavior (B) of the smoker (p) results from all the forces (f) both in the environment (e) and the smoker (p). Briefly, the forces driving toward and those restraining problem resolution reach an equilibrium, the status quo line. Arrow length indicates the intensity of forces. Adding driving forces attracts resistance. Cutting restraints permits existing drives to prevail.

Lewin combined abstract thinking with great personal warmth. He had an unusual knack for turning everyday events and observations into useful theories. Like a benevolent sponge, he sucked people into his pet projects. His biographer Alfred Marrow (1969), for example, while a graduate student, first visited Lewin in the early 1930s. They became lifelong friends, and Marrow's family business, Harwood Manufacturing Company, sponsored the first industrial action-research projects in the United States.

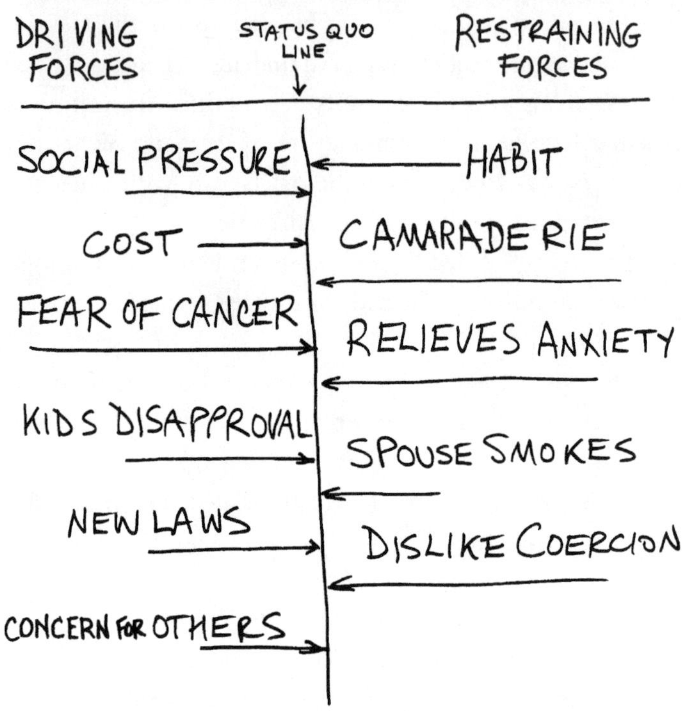

1920s Origins of Management Practices

Lewin's influence goes further still. As a young professor in the 1920s, he attracted a legion of mavericks to Berlin. Their novel research significantly affected management practices decades later. Strikingly, most were women in a field dominated by men. Tamara Dembo, for example, had read Taylor in her native Russia and became interested in "making machines more suitable to human beings" (Marrow, 1969, p. 21). Her Berlin experiments confirmed that reactions to frustration—working harder, running away, fighting the researcher—were a function of the situation, not just individual styles. She coined the term "level of aspiration" to describe a person's assessment of the difficulty of reaching a goal—the basis for the concept of "stretch" in setting business objectives.

Bluma Zeigarnik, also Russian, discovered a phenomenon that now bears her name. She was among the students Lewin met regularly at a Berlin coffeehouse. The waiter tracked the bill accurately in his head for hours. One day Lewin, after paying, asked for another rundown of the total. The waiter sad he could not remember it because the bill had been paid. Lewin instantly formed a new hypothesis: the waiter's memory was erased by completion. Zeigarnik went on to prove experimentally that people tend to remember interrupted tasks better than completed ones—the famous Zeigarnik effect.

Another Russian student, Maria Ovsiankina, showed that interrupted tasks are almost always resumed. Unfinished business cries out for completion. These discoveries underlie conference design today. Merrelyn Emery (1983), a veteran meeting manager, advocates starting a long meeting with a group task after dinner, results to be reported next morning, as a sure way to keep momentum. Anybody who has struggled to start a new task at 8:30 a.m. can appreciate the Zeigarnik effect.

Another student, Anita Karsten, proved that simple tasks, repeated until a subject tired and stopped (called "satiation") would be picked up easily later only if seen as part of some larger, personally meaningful whole. That discovery was the forerunner of job enrichment and a central tenet of work redesign. When Ford assembly-line workers called car buyers at night to ask them how they liked their cars, they were enacting Karsten's discovery—a quantum leap beyond Taylor's concept of what workers needed to know. One reason the psychoanalytically oriented Tavistock Institute (see Chapter Ten) later adopted Lewin's ideas was his experimental proof that people continued to deal with unresolved issues—a demonstration of the theory that childhood conflicts carry over into adult life.

By 1928, Lewin was deeply into the development of field theory. He studied the "life space" of Silesian textile workers, noting that the successful ones organized their total work flow to cope with disruptions like broken threads and empty spools. It was not just dexterity but a feeling for the whole—systems thinking, we call it now—that allowed them to be effective. Even Lewin's procedure foreshadowed "sociotechnical" systems: one researcher followed the machines, another the people (Papanek, 1973, p. 319).

Lewin's finding that manual dexterity tests for mill workers were not relevant to total job demands was a significant revision of Taylor's

Kurt Lewin, a primary shaper of ideas and methods for democratic leadership and social change.

Source: Miriam Lewin

scientific selection based on narrow competence. In these early explorations, Lewin, like Taylor, still focused on individuals. It remained for his American colleagues—notably Ronald Lippitt—to draw his attention to the power of groups.

Lewin in America

By 1930 Lewin's work was known throughout the psychological world. Yet, being Jewish, he could not obtain a permanent teaching job. In 1933, when Hitler became chancellor, Lewin resigned from Berlin University, declaring he would not teach where his children could not study. He took a two-year appointment at the Cornell University Home Economics School and never returned to Germany. On his way to the United States, he stopped in Cambridge, England, and was given a sightseeing tour by a young graduate student named Eric Trist. In the chapel of Trinity College, standing in front of Isaac Newton's statue, Lewin gestured wildly at the swirls in the ceiling and told Trist they reminded him of the topological diagrams in a book he was writing. Trist was so taken with Lewin's thinking, he told me in 1987, that he reoriented his career from literature to psychology and later became Lewin's leading exponent in Great Britain.

In the United States, Lewin held a string of non-tenured jobs in American outposts of psychology. (He Americanized the sound of his name, but many who knew him still said "La-VEEN.") In 1935 he became a child psychologist at the University of Iowa's Child Welfare Research Station. There began his most fertile period, as he shifted interests toward the use of the social sciences to solve social problems.

Photos taken about this time show a slender man of forty-five, on the short side, balding in front, straight black hair combed back from a high-domed forehead. Large rimless glasses, set firm on a long, broad nose, frame intense dark eyes with laugh wrinkles in the corners. He is clean-shaven, with a straight mouth, thin upper lip set back on a broad lower one, above a large, square jaw. He looks pleasant, not smiling exactly but benevolent; and there is something else, a tenseness, like a coiled spring.

Studying Groups

Lewin was the quintessential collaborator. He had the rare gift to seed new ideas with warm enthusiasm and dispassionate critique. "It was a common experience," wrote Dorwin Cartwright, "when coming to him with some vaguely conceived notion to have him react enthusiastically, and then to discover that from the conversation a new view of the problem had emerged, hardly recognizable as the original notion but incomparably better" (1947, p. 97). Nowhere was this unique alchemy more evident than in his relationship with Ronald Lippitt, a former Boy Scout leader and recreation major from Springfield College, who came to Iowa City as a graduate student in the fall of 1938.

In college Lippitt had led and studied neighborhood youth street clubs. When he saw the word "group" on Professor Lewin's suggested theses list, Lippitt told me in 1982, he went to visit "this funny little man with the German accent." He proposed to research his observation that the way leaders managed camping trips and hikes affected a group's experience and success. Lewin immediately saw the implications: that leader behavior could shape culture. He had already perceived grim echoes of Nazism in American colleges that had Jewish quota systems and resort hotels that banned Jews. His attraction to Lippitt's ideas was intensely personal. Together they conceived a comparative study of how autocratic and democratic leadership affected children's groups.

In early dialogues between Lewin and Lippitt, the term *group dynamics*, used by Lewin in a 1939 article, was coined. Ironically, Lewin's group theories were triggered by a misunderstanding. Years later he confided that until that first conversation with Lippitt he had seen "group" in topological terms—an interaction between parts of any system, rather than interdependent people who develop unwritten rules for their behavior.

Discovering Management Styles

Lippitt, with fellow student Ralph White, designed experiments with volunteer boys' clubs doing typical activities like arts and crafts. Each led a group democratically for six sessions, then autocratically for six more. As authoritarians, White or Lippitt dominated, set goals, issued instructions, interrupted, made all decisions, and criticized the work. Group members argued more, showed more hostility, fought, damaged play materials, lost initiative, became restless, showed no concern for group goals or others' interests. They picked on weaker members (an analogue to Hitler's Germany not lost on the researchers). Then, as democratic leaders, the researchers encouraged groups to set goals, make decisions, and mutually critique one another's work. These groups stuck to the task and developed more friendliness, group spirit, and cooperation.

Lewin, running a movie camera behind a screen, soon observed White, an inexperienced group leader, using a third variation: letting the boys do what they wanted. The team called this style "laissez-faire" and made it part of the experiment (Marrow, 1969). Groups led in laissez-faire style showed less task focus than either of the others. Lack of direction frustrated the boys, who felt vaguely inadequate and blamed their unhappiness on less able members. Climate and results followed style, no matter which leader exhibited it. The extraordinary thing was how fast group behavior changed when leaders changed their styles. The chart "Aggression in Boys' Groups" plots these changes over time.

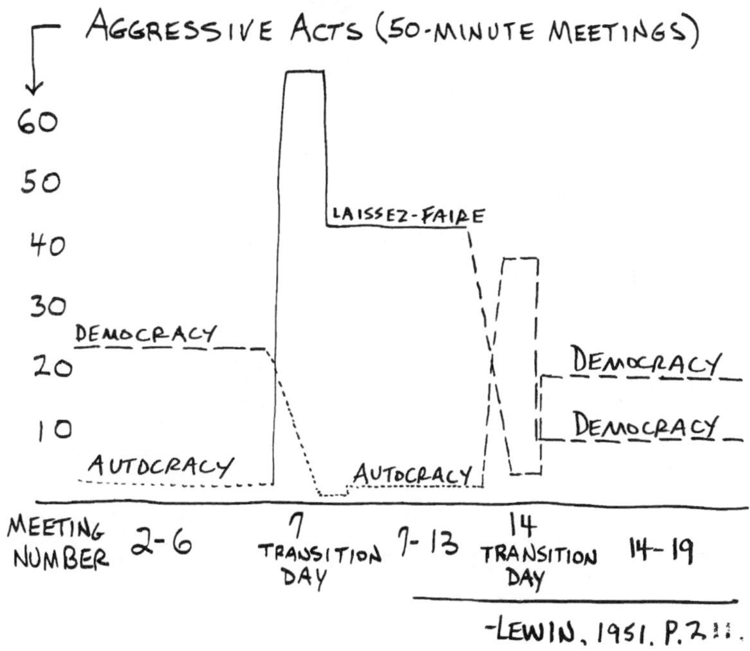

Watching Lewin's film in my office. I was struck by the marked differences in behavior when the leader deliberately left the room. In the autocratic mode, the boys bullied weaker members, goofed off, even destroyed their work. In the democratic group, the boys hardly noticed the leader's absence and kept right on working. In laissez-faire, boredom quickly surfaced. Some boys quit doing anything and wandered around the room.

The last one reminded me of a company where I had consulted. The boss, a self-professed democrat, allowed people to do what they wanted. His people, hungry for leadership, wandered around uncertain of what to do, while the boss seethed silently at their "childish" behavior. "I thought that's how democratic leaders get results," he said. He did not know that democracy has always required goal focus and active leadership.

"I think there is ample proof," wrote Lewin, "that the difference in behavior . . . is not a result of differences in individuals. There have been few experiences for me as impressive as seeing the expression on children's faces during the first day under an autocratic leader. The group that had formerly been friendly, open, cooperative, and full of life became within a short half-hour a rather apathetic-looking gathering without initiative" (1948, pp. 81–82). It took groups much longer to adjust from autocratic to democratic leadership. Lewin's inference will be instantly recognized by those who have sought to modify their management styles. "Autocracy is imposed on the individual," he wrote (pp. 81–82). "Democracy he has to learn!" Thus unfolded in a 1938 student project on child behavior the impact of management styles on climate and output in work groups, a core technology of leader development to this day.

Change Efforts Are Group-Based

The researchers were now on the verge of discoveries that would usher in a new applied social science. "In our discussions with Margaret Mead," Lippitt told me of those days, "the importance of the small face-to-face group as the linker between person and 'macro' system became a basic rationale for group dynamics." The group, Lewin would assert, was a powerful shaper of individual behavior. From this practical theory came a central tenet of organization development: A group's behavior changes with the conditions operating in and upon it. Nowhere is this more evident than in the leader's behavior. If you want to be an effective leader, you need to do more than study group dynamics. You need to learn more about yourself.

Reading Lewin, I suddenly had a new appreciation of the "personal style" exercises so important to my own training in the early 1970s: paper-and-pencil instruments like Atkin's and Katcher's Life Interpersonal Orientation Survey (LIFO), Strength Deployment Inventory, Will Schutz's FIRO-B, the Myers-Briggs Type Indicator, and so on. Each highlighted aspects of my behavior, attitudes, and preferred actions under different conditions. They taught me how my style augments or conflicts with other people's styles, how I help myself or dig my own hole deeper.

Personal styles were only part of the story. Lewin's field theory suggested that my style and yours interact in a particular way, depending on the situation. We might behave differently with different others or in different groups. For that reason, in each situation dialoging anew on our own and others' styles could be a powerful form of team development. Validating diverse styles could lead to acceptance and commitment to build on one another's strengths and to minimize weaknesses.

Positive group experiences, based on mutual tasks, could alter peoples' attitudes and actions more quickly than personal awareness exercises alone. There are solid reasons, then, why groups, rather than individuals, became the focus for change strategies. Many aspects of behavior simply cannot be understood or modified in any other way. (During World War II Wilfred R. Bion, of the Tavistock Institute, initiated a group dynamics tradition based on similar insights; see Chapter Ten. In Part Four, I trace how Lewin and Bion converged in current practice.)

American individualism abhors herd behavior. A group can be a pressure cooker for mindless action. It can also promote personal identity and lead to acceptance of diversity. Unless they grew up playing team sports, most people acquire group skills (if ever) only as adults. Few schools or colleges offer training in meeting skills. Many people remain suspicious of group problem solving and teamwork. That is too bad, because only in groups can you learn that each member makes unique contributions. Moreover, we are more likely to modify our behavior with group support than without it. Not just any groups. Only in democratically led groups can you learn the considerable skills needed to resist group pressure to conform.

If it is possible to have too much of a good thing, from ice cream to football, we Americans manage to have it. In the 1950s and 1960s consultants sprouted like dandelions in the meadows of group dynamics. Applied social scientists, like engineers enamored of piece rates, packaged Lewin's insights in every conceivable format—books, instruments, tapes, and films. Group exercises, committees, and task forces came to be prescribed for everything that ails you, from low morale to lower back pain. That is no fault of Kurt Lewin. It is an example of a universal phenomenon. Some of Lewin's descendants mistook techniques for values the same way Taylor's did.

■ ■ ■

"THE GAP BETWEEN THE REALITY AND IDEAL GNAWED AWAY AT ME..."

AUCKLAND, NEW ZEALAND—I decided early on that I wanted to be a lawyer, thinking I would be able to help people change their circumstances for the better. The gap between the reality of practicing law and this ideal soon started to gnaw away at me. Having been so certain for so long that being a lawyer was what I wanted to do, I thought changing my client base might help me close the gap. So I moved from a private practice, with a focus on general litigation, to a non-governmental organization providing human rights litigation.

Then I discovered mediation and realized that this gap—my disillusionment with the reality of legal practice and my aspirations as a change agent—had more to do with the adversarial approach on which traditional legal practice is founded than with my client base. With this discovery of a dispute resolution process based on joint problem solving rather than the zero sum process of litigation, I started to close this gap and began working as a mediator of labor disputes. While I loved the process of dispute resolution, it dawned on me that in much of my practice I was addressing effects rather than causes. This led me to seek out roles in which I might be more influential in shaping the culture and processes of workplaces, and unionized workplaces in particular.

I started reading *PW Revisited* after a consultant friend mentioned how useful he'd found the book, and a colleague sent me a number of papers he was writing in which he had cited the book. Pretty much every page of my copy is now marked, scribbled on, and underlined. The book gave me a large conceptual framework for thinking about organizational transformation—the idea that there are two broad approaches to improving organizational effectiveness and employee well-being. The one, based on learning to do things to/for others that started in the 19th Century, the other "learning to do things with others" that is a function of Kurt Lewin's work in the 20th Century. This crisp distinction has become an important "diving rod" for me in my labor-management work.

I currently work for a unit located in the New Zealand Department of Labour, the Partnership Resource Centre, helping businesses and unions identify long-term mutual interests and put in place programs that ensure that both the business and the people who work there thrive. Starting in 2005, we have collaborated with more than thirty-five unionized workplaces, large and small, public and private, across a variety of sectors, including transport, health, infrastructure, and utilities. One of our recent projects helped a public mental health service and the union that organizes the majority of its staff to build a "workplace partnership"—or as we define it "an active interest in each other's success." This involved helping them develop the necessary relational infrastructure, processes, and practices as well as supporting them in introducing a high performance work system aimed at improving organizational effectiveness as well as employee well-being.

—Alex Twigg, practice manager, Partnership Resource Centre, New Zealand Department of Labour

---

chapter
SIX

Lewin's Legacy to Management

Today, more than ever before, democracy depends upon the development of efficient forms of democratic social management and upon the spreading of the skill in such management to the common man.

—Kurt Lewin, "Frontiers in Group Dynamics," 1947b, p. 153

Lewin's action research studies of group behavior rank with the 20th-Century's great social science innovations. In addition to leadership styles, he planted the seeds for participative management working with Iowa housewives during World War II. His collaborator was anthropologist Margaret Mead, their objective to free up rationed foods like prime beef for the armed forces. Lewin's research strategy was to reduce resisting forces by involving the "gatekeepers" who control the change. In this situation, said Mead, the homemakers, who bought, prepared, and served the food, would determine whether their families could live with "variety" meats like Spam in place of pot roast. In the control groups, an expert nutritionist lectured volunteer homemakers on nutrition, scarcity, and patriotism. Women in experimental groups heard the same lecture, then discussed with each other what to do. It's easy to guess the result. Groups that reached consensus through discussion changed their food habits much more than those only given expert advice.

The Power of Participation

Lewin had found the core principle of participation: we are more likely to carry out decisions we have helped make. "Kurt's special gift for understanding American ideals of democracy," said Margaret Mead, "led him to include in these first research plans his clear recognition that you cannot do things to people but only with them" ([1954] 1983, p. 164). Lewin's gatekeeper theory showed that he understood "stakeholders" long before the word was coined. He never advocated participation as an end in itself.

After the war the Iowans extended action research to industry. When Harwood Manufacturing, Alfred Marrow's garment company, opened a pajama factory in rural Virginia, local women at first produced only half as much as Northerners. Alex Bevalas, an Iowa graduate student, sought to involve the women in determining their own goals and methods. He discovered again a fact on which Taylor had based his system—that people did the same job many ways. Instead of engineering "one best way," however, Bevalas conducted weekly discussions between high and low producers on the pros and cons of various techniques.

One group, for instance, voted to go from seventy-five to eighty-seven units a day within five days—once an unimaginable goal. They then raised output to ninety units, greatly increasing piecework wages over what they would have earned had industrial engineers set the rates. No other groups increased at all (Marrow, 1969). Harwood produced the first experimental evidence that group decision making, self-management, and democratic leadership training could up output far beyond time and motion study.

The Motivational Force Field. Lewin compared social change to altering a river's channel rather than building a dam. Discussion alone did not raise production. Motivation was closely tied to people's direct influence on results. One force suppressing production at Harwood was the stress of hard, fast work. Increasing pay would not reduce it. "There is an upper ceiling for human activity," observed Lewin. "The common belief views the desire to make more money as the most important force toward higher production levels" (1947a, p. 25). Rural women, earning more than ever at

Harwood, however, had upped their living standards enough, and would not work harder."

Thus Lewin reinforced Taylor's observation that there is an optimum wage rate that encourages production. Set the rate too high or too low, and forces enter the field to cancel out potential gains. Again, he added a crucial social factor opaque to Taylor: "general living standards of the group." Pressures of stress, fatigue, aggressiveness, anxiety, and variation in output resulted in part from group norms, not just individual capacity. Lewin suggested self-management to optimize results. This practical theory today underpins innovative labor-management cooperation in hundreds of U.S. and European firms. Force field analysis is one of many widely used tools.

Extending Harwood. Personnel manager Lester Coch and social scientist John R. P. French (1948) extended Bavelas's pioneering work to Harwood's managers and supervisors. They used role plays, feedback, and group problem solving to build confidence in democratic supervision. French broke new ground in his efforts to reduce manager stereotyping of workers. Harwood supervisors refused to hire women over thirty for machine jobs, insisting they were less productive. French knew from the food studies that "just the facts" would not change their minds. He suggested that they test their assumptions and find out how much it cost to keep older women on the payroll. Supervisors chose to measure output, turnover, absenteeism, and learning speed. They found that women older than thirty did as well as or better than younger ones on all measures. Imagine their chagrin when upper management, the gatekeepers not involved in the study, refused to change hiring practices despite the evidence. Old myths die hard.

No research finding in management history was ever more relevant. Directly involving gatekeepers is a principle, not a technique.

Reducing Resistance to Change

Coch and French tested the principle another way at Harwood. As pajama-making jobs changed with seasons and styles, people's output always went down. Although an industrial engineer set new piece rates, the usual outcomes were more absenteeism, grievances, and turnover. The researchers tested the usual procedure against two strategies: (1) work group representatives discussing change-overs with management and (2) the work group recommending and planning its own transitions.

In a comparative experiment, the control group's output dropped 20 percent as usual and never came back; morale was low and one in ten quit. The represented group recovered output in two weeks. The direct involvement group did something extraordinary. They regained productivity in two days and steadily increased to 14 percent above old levels (Marrow, 1969). Lewin thought production figures exactly calibrated the strength of driving forces for output. External job changes increased restraints. Direct participation removed them, allowing workers to break through to higher productivity. Resistance dissolved when you "got through the gate."

W. Edwards Deming (1982), the statistical guru who introduced quality circles into Japan, went further, showing that emphasizing quality instead of setting production targets leads to much higher output. This is one of the most startling insights in management history. It is part of a new mental revolution that I believe started with Lewin. It is a mistake to assume we know any system's productive capacity before we involve people in pushing the limits.

Harwood and Hawthorne: A Modern Perspective. To understand what really happened at Harwood, contrast that research with the controversial Hawthorne studies (Roethlisberger and Dickson, 1939). The latter varied conditions like light levels to find the effects of environment on output. Researchers planned and made the changes. The famous "Hawthorne effect" was discovered by accident: output went up regardless of changes, a result attributed to special attention paid to the people. That had nothing to do with participative problem solving.

The Harwood experiments from 1940 through 1947 involved researchers and subjects in joint action research, intended both to solve problems and to create useful knowledge about change processes. Coch and French brought to life Lewin's vision when, as a young man in Germany, he had proposed that psychologists and farmers improve hay loading jointly. The Harwood pajama factory, as best I can tell, represents the first recorded attempts at participative systems change.

The method had worked for Lippitt and White, wearing their "democratic leader" hats with the Iowa boys' clubs. It worked in the wartime

Lewin-Mead food habits experiments. Only direct participation led to effective changes at Harwood. It is one of the best-researched practices, and one of the least used. Most managers think they do it already. Only a handful know what "it" looks like—a serious effort to maintain community by involving people in the economics and technology of the business. It means high stakes, high anxiety, and high payoff.

Yet Kurt Lewin saw no panacea in participation. "Managers rushing into a factory to raise production by group decisions," he wrote, "are likely to encounter failure. There are no patent medicines, and each case demands careful diagnosis" (1947a, p. 36). No two force fields are ever the same, no two solutions identical. Involving people was not a "technique." It was the bedrock of social learning, requiring goal focus, feedback, leadership, and participation by all the relevant actors.

"Unfreezing" as a Key to Change. From many such studies, Lewin (1946) conceptualized his famous three-phase process: "unfreezing, moving, and refreezing." Unfreezing meant reducing the negative forces through new or disconfirming information—nutrition for Iowa housewives, productivity for Virginia factory workers. That was the function of diagnosis. Moving meant changes in attitude, values, structure, feelings, behaviors—what happens when people discuss and plan new actions. Refreezing meant reaching a new status quo with support mechanisms to maintain the desired behavior.

From this formulation came an action-research model of consultation, which I describe in Chapter Twelve. Briefly, it involved contracting for joint study, diagnosis, and action. The consultant's role was to collect the data that would unfreeze the system, reduce the resisting forces, and alter the status quo. Of all Lewin's ideas, I find this the one most in need of revision today. The concept falls apart as the rate of change in markets and technologies becomes a state of perpetual transition, rather than the "quasi-stationary equilibrium" Lewin described. The cycles tumble on so fast that "changes" last only weeks instead of years. Hence the growing realization that the future is shaped by present responses, that we make our future dreams come true now by acting on our values. In Part Three I propose a new theory for doing that in places where "moving" has become a way of life.

Action Research Today

Lewin's standing offer was to trade help with the solution in exchange for the advancement of knowledge. He embraced applied social science, insisting ("the emperor has no clothes") that laboratory experiments are not enough. In real life you cannot control all the variables, especially other people, so you do the scientific thing—you involve them in doing the experiment. That's the hardest principle to master if you have been trained as an "expert." Low tech or high, it does not matter what a machine is rated to do. It does only what those who run it are willing for it to do.

There are no failsafe technologies, as we will see in Chapter Eleven. The best insurance policy is having all workers involved. It takes wisdom to see that no one person knows enough to do it all and courage to involve those who have the information and control the change. Note how similar Lewin's and Taylor's goals were: raise output, reduce stress, improve labor-management relations, increase wages. But Lewin added a new value as old as the American experiment: democracy. That called for novel and, for managers, anxiety-provoking, techniques. This enlarged view of "scientific" called for considering workers' entire life spaces, not simply their relationship to tools and tasks.

Taylor was ambivalent about lecturing business students. He believed that education short of experience was futile. So did Lewin. Neither mistook methods for values. Reading Lewin, I realized that he had devised experiments proving what Taylor had intuited: that the authoritarian in all of us is ineffectual when faced with modern technology and skilled coworkers. Taylor hated conflict so much, yet had so much need to control, that he devised impersonal, technical systems to humanize industry.

Lewin, abhorring Nazism and fearful of democracy's shadow side too, added social systems to Taylor's thinking. He expanded the concept of workplace to include the life space of each person, and the unwritten rules governing action. Lewin helped develop the knowledge needed to break through the frustrating paradox faced by every expert: knowing the right answer and not able to persuade others to act on it. "Lewinian methods," wrote Marrow, "helped shift the focus of industrial management from mechanistic engineering approaches to social-psychological concepts. The great interest in recent years in the humanization of industry stems in large

Lewin's Practical Theories

Theory	Management Implications
You can understand behavior only in relation to all forces acting on a person at a given moment.	To change a system, take into account economics and technology by involving all stakeholders.
The best way to advance knowledge is having experts and workers study together the relations among person, tools, job, and situation.	Successful work design requires teams of engineers, managers, supervisors, and workers starting together from scratch.
Only freely chosen work has the meaning and life value needed to motivate high performance.	People should have as much elbow room as possible in doing their own jobs.
Democratic leadership leads to higher achievement and better relationships than authoritarian OR hands-off behavior.	Leading people to set goals, choose methods, and make decisions is learned. Nobody is born knowing participative management.
It is easier to change behavior in a group than one-on-one because norms (unwritten rules) strongly affect individual actions.	Talking over important decisions in groups before implementation leads to higher commitment to change.
People are more committed to solutions they have helped to design than to carrying out "expert" advice.	It is better to give people a few boundary conditions and let them solve the problem than to hand them ready-made solutions.
Every unsolved problem represents forces pushing for and against resolution. Solutions come easier by reducing restraints rather than adding pressure.	Force field analysis is effective as a group exercise because it helps people see all at once restraints to reduce, and it builds group support for follow-through.
No two force fields or problem diagnoses are ever the same. Every situation is different.	The solution, package, design, policy, or system that worked for someone else may not work for you.

measure from Lewin's emphasis on the dynamics of groups at work" (1969, pp. 151–152). "Lewin's Practical Theories" demonstrates the accuracy of that assessment.

From Research to Real Life

By 1945 Kurt Lewin had determined to use social science to alter systems, not just to describe them. He saw changing individual behavior as a weak, even futile strategy for intractable social problems. Managing participation required skilled leadership. Someone had to fertilize the soil for effective groups to take root. Developing such group leaders called for an applied social science far outside academic psychology.

A New Kind of Research Center

Lewin's ideas attracted Douglas McGregor, a young psychology professor at the Massachusetts Institute of Technology (MIT). McGregor, whose story I tell in Chapters Eight and Nine, had spent the war years as an industrial relations manager. He believed that Lewinian thinking could solve many labor-management problems. In 1946 McGregor helped Lewin launch the Research Center for Group Dynamics (RCGD) at MIT. (By establishing the new center at an engineering school, Lewin preserved his unblemished record for avoiding the mainstream of academic psychology.) Thus began a revolution—still in progress. The center sought to do something wholly new: train leaders to become skilled at improving group relations and managing change. Group experiments, insisted Lewin, must be governed by a code of ethics—no manipulation, only honest, above-board objectives and socially acceptable procedures. Involving research subjects as partners was a bedrock principle.

Decades later even practitioners would criticize group methods as "soft" on power. Lewin had no illusions. Leaders must learn to see themselves as part of both the problem and the solution. "There is no individual," he wrote, "who does not try to influence his family, friends, occupational group. . . . We have to realize that power itself is an essential aspect of any and every group. Not the least service which social research can do for society is to attain better insight into the legitimate and non-legitimate aspects of power" (Marrow, 1969, p. 172).

Nor did he stop there. Having suffered anti-Semitism since childhood, he envisioned using action research to reduce bigotry, which he considered an aberration of democracy. In 1946, backed by the American Jewish Congress, Lewin started the Commission on Community Interrelations (CCI). (Another founder was Supreme Court Justice Louis Brandeis, Frederick Taylor's advocate decades earlier.) In the late 1940s CCI did fifty community-based action-research projects, studying prejudice against black store clerks, vandalism of synagogues, and juvenile gang wars. CCI staffers developed an action-research repertoire that later would be adapted to the managerial problems of large organizations (Marrow, 1969).

■ ■ ■

"WE START BY SECURING LEADERS' COMMITMENT..."

ALBANY, NY—For many years we have built our practice on helping organizations move from hierarchy, fear, information control, and silos to an environment in which people have a voice and do the right work at the right time in the best way they know how. We call our method "Inclusion as the HOW^{sm} and advocate twelve "inclusive behaviors" to transform a culture—everything from saying an authentic "hello" to listening, mutual support, problem solving of disagreements, and the seeking out of all voices.

We start by securing leaders' active commitment, collecting data and hearing from the people, a variation on Lewinian action research as described in *Productive Workplaces*. We then use this "snapshot" in educational sessions to help leaders understand and practice new behaviors. The leaders empower a core group from all levels and functions, who model new behavior with their peers. People collaborate to break down silos between departments, becoming more energized and productive.

One manufacturing client, for example, reduced product errors by 50 percent. A plant group experienced a 40 percent improvement in environmental monitoring tests. Union and management partnered in another company to reduce waste by 40 percent.

And a regional Chamber of Commerce won a national award after including people's voices in clarifying their mission and strategy.

—Frederick A. Miller and Judith H. Katz, The Kaleel Jamison Consulting Group, Inc., authors of *The Inclusion Breakthrough: Unleashing the Real Power of Diversity*

Origins of NTL Institute

Lewin also was central to the founding of a world-famous adult education organization, National Training Laboratories (NTL Institute). NTL pioneered the T-group, a generic name for a human relations training group that studies its own "here and now" behavior. The T in T-group was short for BST or basic skills training. The method grew out of a Lewinian action-research project in which the researchers found more than they were looking for. In 1946 the Connecticut State Inter-Racial Commission sought Lewin's help in training leaders to combat racial and religious prejudice. He tapped Lippitt, now at MIT, as project director, and Lippitt recruited Lee Bradford of the National Education Association and Kenneth Benne of Boston University. They planned a training event to observe and measure how people transfer leadership skills from workshop to workplace—to what my erstwhile partner Peter Block called "realife" (as in, "Yeah, that's fine for a workshop, but what happens if you try it in realife?"). The forty-one participants, mainly teachers and social workers, about half of them black or Jewish, wanted more skill in understanding prejudice, changing attitudes, and dealing with resistance to change. They would learn by studying themselves, using group techniques like role playing and problem solving.

Discovering the Power of Feedback. This 1946 conference became an educational milestone. Training groups were observed by researchers, who reviewed interactions with the staff each night. One evening three trainees asked to sit in. "Some time during the evening," Lippitt recalled, "an observer made some remarks about the behavior of one of the three. For a while there was quite an active dialogue between the research observer, the trainer, and the trainee about the interpretation of the event, with Kurt an active prober, obviously enjoying the different source of data that had to be coped with and integrated" (Marrow, 1969, p. 212).

Next night half the group showed up. Bradford recalled "a tremendous electric charge as people reacted to data about their own behavior" (Marrow, 1969, p. 212). The interchange on what "really" happened proved to be the most exciting session. None had fully appreciated the learning potential of feedback until that summer evening in 1946. People became aware that we always attend, in my late colleague Jim Maselko's words, "the same different meeting together." The discovery created anxiety and enormous energy for learning as groups noted changes in their daytime productivity. A set of effective feedback rules evolved: be specific, nonjudgmental, express your feelings, don't "psych out" the other person, don't give advice. Such premises today underlie performance reviews, goal setting, even the praises and reprimands of one-minute managers (Blanchard and Johnson, 2003).

Pioneering New Technology: The Chart Pad

The 1946 conference marked the first use of newsprint, antecedent of chart pads, traceable to Lewin's habit of drawing topological force fields on butcher paper taped to the wall. That summer Lippitt secured newsprint from the end of the press rolls at a local newspaper; it was cut into manageable pieces and everybody started using it. For decades afterward NTL bought newsprint from local papers for its Bethel workshops. When I served as overall dean in 1982, groups ran out of newsprint, a technology failure akin to losing the Internet. People used the reverse sides of discarded sheets until a fresh supply could be rushed in.

Transferring Skills. Follow-up interviews confirmed Lewin's hypothesis. About 75 percent of attendees said they had gained group skills, become more optimistic, and worked better with others. The research also revealed that teams of two or more were more likely than individuals to use what they learned. This important finding was lost in the enthusiasm to spread T-groups everywhere. It took many years to prove what was suspected from the start: individual training, no matter how powerful, cannot by itself be a strategy for organizational change.

Supporting the Use of New Knowledge. Despite this knowledge, many people still put extraordinary faith in training individuals as an OD strategy uncoupled from structures, policies, procedures, and rewards. Organizational voodoo abounds in seminars where people hear all the right noises about dealing with resistance to change and why employee participation builds more commitment than "kicking ass." People are cynical about programs that do not include action. They rightfully feel conned in classes full of good ideas they cannot apply to alter policies, procedures, strategies, goal setting, and work design. This is an abuse of Lewin's work as egregious as abusing Taylor's efforts to give workers more equity in output by raising quotas each time they succeed. It is using Lewin's words divorced from his music, which can be heard only when we seek to involve people in pushing beyond a system's assumed design limits.

The Road to Bethel and NTL

In 1947 Lewin obtained a grant from the Office of Naval Research to establish summer workshops at a private boarding school in Bethel, Maine. It was a "cultural island" (translation: small town, hard to reach), picked because it was thought people would unfreeze faster outside the office. T-groups opened a new window on human consciousness. We take organizational structures for granted. Substitute an unfamiliar form and we shake up perceptions of reality. The trainer does little leading, and people are asked to find their own way in "the here and now." People find themselves puzzled, anxious, excited, vying for leadership—behaving in ways we rarely stop to examine. The T-group made possible the study of phenomena latent in all meetings that cannot be studied in any other way. It also delivered on Robert Burns' longing "to see ourselves as others see us," a valuable gift not always pleasant to receive. (For an insider's view, see the next chapter describing my first-ever learning group experience in 1969.)

Tens of thousands have attended NTL laboratories in group processes, personal growth, consulting skills, organizational change. Hundreds of training and consulting organizations adapted experience-based methods. "Sensitivity training," wrote Carl Rogers, "is perhaps the most significant social invention of this century" (Marrow, 1969, p. 214). NTL's founders, Benne, Bradford, and Lippitt, were influenced by many others, such as John Dewey, the philosopher of education, and Mary Parker Follett, one of the most interesting figures in management history. Jacob Moreno, the innovator who created sociodrama and psychodrama, was the source of the role-playing techniques used at Harwood and in NTL.

Experience-based learning and social systems thinking have been put to ingenious uses. To cite one example, the Danish social psychologist, my late friend Gunnar Hjelholt, who had worked in Bethel in 1958, adapted T-group methods to the outfitting of new Danish merchant ships. In parallel with early sociotechnical projects, Hjelholt organized conferences of officers, engineers, mates, stewards, administrators, and ship owners. Together they integrated new technologies and made innovative decisions about food service, location of quarters, leisure time, and use of alcohol. They reconfigured the ship for a crew of forty-two rather than sixty, giving more influence to mid-level officers and hands. The training led to significantly more crew involvement, fewer disciplinary problems, and less sickness and accidents. After a year at sea, the once-skeptical captain said, “It’s the best ship I ever had—and I mean the crew” (Hjelholt, 1968, p. 16).

Limits of Sensitivity Training

Lewin’s insights, like Taylor’s, also were diverted early on by some disciples swept up in the headiness of group encounter. Organizational life, enthusiasts concluded, reinforced the (mainly male) tendency to repress feelings. The T-group became a laboratory for the recognition and expression of feelings—joy, sadness, confidence, anxiety, fear, anger, appreciation, guilt, excitement. Because T-groups engendered intimacy and support—“together this group can lick the world”—many concluded that organizations could be transformed using in-house T-groups. Business firms testing this proposition in the 1960s learned that the impulse to be open sometimes backfired. Trust might lead to embarrassing self-revelation. An authoritarian norm also could evolve in which people were pressured to express feelings about one another that they would later regret doing. Still, many people had remarkably positive experiences. Unfortunately, to appreciate them you would have to have been there, as participants could not describe them very well. More importantly, people gained little leverage on company goals, tasks, policies, and procedures—a proposition supported by extensive research (Dunnette, 1969). This disappointment had an up side. It stimulated more practical innovations like team building (see Chapter Twenty).

Lewin did not live to see NTL Institute born. In his last years he was like a top, spinning faster and faster, driven, like Taylor, to extend his ideas widely. He felt compelled to accelerate social science, as he wrote, "to that level of practical usefulness which society needs for winning the race against the destructive capacities set free by man's use of the natural sciences" (1947b, p. 5). Lewin organized a research fund to aid residents of World War II displaced persons' camps. He grew deeply worried about black-white relations, believing that "every minority problem is, in fact, a majority problem." He saw democracy threatened by self-rejection and advocated positive group experiences to alter negative black self-image, which, he inferred from anti-Semitism, could damage a person as much as prejudice could. An important source of self-esteem was strong group identity, an insight on which consciousness-raising and black-power groups later were built.

Ronald Lippitt, a pioneer of leadership theories, group dynamics, and future-oriented planning.

Source: Peggy Lippitt

In 1946 Lewin joined Eric Trist (Chapters Ten and Eleven), of the Tavistock Institute of Human Relations in London, to found a distinguished journal, *Human Relations.* His planned sabbatical at Tavistock never materialized. "Something profound and extraordinary would have happened had Lewin come to us that year," lamented Trist, who had known and admired Lewin since the early 1930s (interview with author, February 19, 1985).

Toward the end of his life Lewin focused on conflict, tension, crises, and change. If action-research projects have seemed overly focused on group tensions, the reason is easy to locate. The originator of this major organization development strategy was motivated, like Taylor before him, to alleviate, with all the tools that science and good sense could muster, humankind's self-made travail. In that respect, he was very much in the tradition of his adopted land. After a hectic February day in 1947, Lewin, then fifty-six, spent a quiet evening with his wife. That night he died unexpectedly of a heart attack.

"Lewin," said psychologist Donald MacKinnon of his former teacher, "took on much more than any human being should have taken on; he was too generous of his time and energy, too busy, too involved with too many projects, too many people. It is almost surprising that he lived as long as he did" (Marrow, 1969, p. 225).

On the last day of his life Lewin talked by phone with Ronald Lippitt about how unfortunate was "the American cultural ideal of the 'self-made man' and everyone 'standing on his own feet,' " a notion "as tragic as the initiative-destroying dependence on a benevolent despot." To Lippitt he said what might be a benediction for leaders everywhere, especially in a time of fast change and dramatic new technologies. "We all need continuous help from each other. Interdependence is the greatest challenge" (Marrow, 1969, p. 226).

■ ■ ■

"A NEW DYNAMIC AT *CITY PAPER*..."

PHILADELPHIA, PA—I was introduced to *Productive Workplaces Revisited* by Tom Gilmore, vice president of the Center for Applied

Research (CFAR), after asking his advice on MindShare, a discussion series I had convened with local thought-leaders who assist one another with their personal and professional goals. The meetings fostered collaborations both thrilling and unexpected. An industrial designer joined a high-level city official to design a transportation concourse, a graphic designer created the pocket guide for a citywide design festival. People discussed financing plans to connect Amtrak to Philadelphia International Airport.

Tom suggested that Future Search, in particular, might provide a broader context for what I was developing. I concluded that facilitating major change using the methodology described in Marv's book would not require a Ph.D., only the ability to create an open environment, an understanding of self-organizing, and the confidence to step into the unknown. Days after reading PWR, I introduced a new dynamic at *City Paper.* I told the staff that, instead of limiting key decisions to the management team, we would open the dialogue and surface the collective wisdom of all. I asked people to imagine themselves as one big brain, reminding them that the knowledge in the room was more profound than what any outside consultant could impart.

I invited everyone to share beliefs about our paper's editorial mission. We listened to each other passionately express ideas. The conversations went on for weeks in the office, over lunch, and over beers at a nearby bar. It was the start of a new, more open process that profoundly energized our staff. For me, it was tangible evidence of the power behind the core principles I was beginning to master.

—Paul Curci, founder, Re:Generation; former publisher, *Philadelphia City Paper*

chapter
SEVEN

The Transition to Experiential Learning

In the fall of 1968, while freelance writing after leaving the family business, I got a call from my friend Bernard Asbell, an education writer, asking if I'd join him in consulting to the Ford Foundation's Division of Education and Research.

"Why me?" I said. "I don't know anything about consulting."

"All we do is interview people and write a report," he said. "What you do all the time. Besides, they pay $100 a day." That convinced me. We spent several days talking with educators at Ford's glass-and-steel monument to philanthropy in New York. I had by then written three books. One evening over dinner, I told Bernie that I was casting about for another book topic.

"Hey," he said, "all you talk about are the work teams in your business. Why don't you write about that?" I decided to explore the topic with a series of magazine articles. So it was that in 1969 I discovered T-groups, pioneered in the 1940s by NTL Institute. I secured an assignment from the *New York Times Magazine,* called NTL and asked Lee Bradford, the president and co-founder, if I could attend a group run by an outstanding trainer. Bradford invited me to lunch with him and Charlie Seashore, then an NTL staffer. After grilling me on my management background and magazine credits, they accepted that I was competent, albeit a bit naïve.

That spring I went to Aspen, Colorado, and met Bill Dyer. Of the many pieces I wrote back then, the article that follows—vagaries of magazine writing—was not published until now. If you've never been in a T-group, here is an intimate look into an all-but-extinct 20th-Century format that has influenced all executive education since. Dyer was integrating group and personal growth dynamics for managers at a fertile moment in the evolution of experiential learning.

That was my first training laboratory. I empathized with the trainees and with Bill Dyer. More, I learned how much I knew about managing that I did not know I knew. I had been through a ten-year management lab without any reflection. Now I began conceptualizing what I had done. As a result of the Ford work, I had by then acquired two more clients and launched a new career. Nearly twenty years later I put my experiences from those years into the original edition of *Productive Workplaces.* Below is the first workplace-related article I ever wrote. Although T-group training did not change workplaces, it enabled many people to acquire self-knowledge they could not get any other way. It became a significant transitional phenomenon influencing leadership training to this day.

A WEEK IN A T-GROUP WITH TRAINER BILL DYER

By Marvin R. Weisbord

Dr. William G. (Bill) Dyer, sociology professor, sits sipping a ginger ale at the bar, adrift on a sea of soft lights, music, pretzels, booze, mini-skirted waitresses, and corporate executives incognito in sports shirts and slacks. It is the last night of a Key Executive Conference or T-group ("training laboratory") for upper-level managers. The men, strangers six days ago, have reached a plateau of intimacy unattainable on liquor alone. Now they are drinking it up to friendship.

Dyer, the T-group's "trainer," a stocky red-head with sideburns, china blue eyes, a long Irish nose, and a chin like Kirk Douglas, has been strictly business most of the week. Now, cold sober, he is tossing off stories with a gusto uncharacteristic of a devout Mormon who neither smokes nor drinks: the one about the guy with the wood eye and the girl with the club foot; the one about the guy who falls off a cliff, hangs on for life to a bush, hears the Lord intone, "Trust me. Let go and I'll catch you," and replies with an epithet signifying disbelief.

Trust has been one of the week's major themes. "The thing I keep coming back to about T-groups," Dyer says, "is what I call the 'Camelot phenomenon,' that 'one brief shining moment' of what close contact is *really* like. Most guys, if you lecture them about trust, or interdependence, or openness, all shake their heads yes. My guess is very few of them have ever experienced any of it. They're just words.

"They don't know what trust is really like, or openness, or what real sharing and real collaboration mean. The lab lets them feel what it's *really* like. If they could achieve it back home, that's what it would *really* be like." One of the executives, tipsy with sentiment, throws an arm around Dyer's shoulder. "Let's drink," he says, hoisting his glass, "to trust and openness!" Dyer picks up his ginger ale.

From Human Relations to Management Training

The T-group—variously named sensitivity lab, encounter group, marathon—is called by its advocates "a social invention for the purpose of learning." It evolved shortly after World War II from the work of a group of social psychologists connected with the late Kurt Lewin, "the father of group dynamics," who discovered nothing could change a person's behavior faster than hearing its impact described (or "fed back") by others. Feedback is a T-group's essential building block. To engage in feedback, you describe as honestly as you can what you see, feel, think, or believe about a situation, person, or action unfolding in front of you. Effective feedback results when you report rather than evaluate. For example:

Evaluation: "Only an idiot would talk like that."

Feedback: "I get annoyed at the language you use."

T-group values reflect a blend of science, democracy, the Golden Rule, openness, trust, shared feelings, experimentation, freedom to err, and consensus. As anyone over the age of twelve knows, these virtues are often praised but seldom practiced where profit is king. Nevertheless, despite a flurry of interest by schools and churches, the T-group's most enthusiastic boosters were, and are, large corporations. For fifteen years T-grouping has grown steadily as a form of management development.

The first executive T-groups were held in the mid-1950s by what is now the NTL Institute for Applied Behavioral Science, a Washington-based affiliate of the National Education Association. More than ten thousand managers have attended NTL groups, scheduled year-round, usually at resorts or country clubs. An impressive list of firms—General Foods, RCA, American Airlines, Procter & Gamble, Union Carbide, Lever Brothers, Polaroid, Dow Chemical, Bankers Trust, and TRW Systems, to name a handful—run their own T-groups or send executives to NTL's or both.

One company, Syntex Corporation, reported recently an experiment in which laboratory-trained groups increased their gross sales by two to four times over groups without lab training. More research has been done on what happens in T-groups than on any other form of management training. Oddly enough, despite the Syntex example, little is known or understood about the "back home" value of such training.

Do T-groups equip you to be a better business manager? The answer is that it depends on a long list of factors. Perhaps the central one is the trainer. Trainers, by their action or inaction, can make or break T-groups. Yet there is no research at all on the impact trainers have. Unlike doctors or lawyers, nobody licenses sensitivity trainers. Only the trainees can say whether a group experience helped them.

What does a good trainer do? Why? What pressures is he or she under? There is considerable misunderstanding on this point, even among enthusiasts. Trainers rarely make explicit, except to each other, why they perform in certain ways. Recently I had the opportunity to spend a week watching and talking with Bill Dyer as he went about the demanding business of training a T-group. Dyer is considered among the best. As a "fellow" in the NTL Network, he is one of fifty or so professionals who enjoy the highest status and prestige among NTL's roughly four hundred staff trainers.* He is also on the NTL Board of Directors and a consultant to corporations, universities, and state governments. In twelve years, Dyer has trained more than 150 groups, among them the one I attended last spring at a secluded resort in Aspen, CO.

Sunday Afternoon

Bill Dyer, in old khakis and a polo shirt, sits in his motel room. He had arrived the day before to design the program with psychologists Douglas Bunker and William Eddy, who will work with one group while he handles a second. "We still don't know which training activities produce the best results," says Dyer. "Executives come to a lab to find out how they function with each other and how to use their resources to do it better. One of my goals is to help each guy get clear feedback on this. At the same time, I try to teach them about group issues: climate, leadership, power, decision making. I'm working on two levels all the time."

Half an hour later Dyer faces the trainees for the first time in the resort's lounge. They range in age from thirty to sixty, all men. They have come from both coasts and the Midwest on company time, their firms having paid $2,500 each [about $15,000 in today's dollars] plus expenses for the week. They listen politely while Dyer explains that they will learn on three levels—how you affect others and vice versa; what makes work teams effective; how you use group skills back on the job.

They break into two groups. Dyer's contingent, eleven strong, file into a nearby motel room and take seats in a circle. Following T-group protocol, Dyer tells them there is no agenda or leader. What happens is up to them. He'll help them examine what's going on, but he won't be chairman or anything like that.

Silence.

Everybody waits for something to happen. Nothing does. Seconds tick off. "What are we here for?" one man asks at last. A frustrating first session has begun. For two-and-a-half hours

**Author's Note:* NTL, now based in Arlington, VA, left the NEA in 1967. It did away with the member hierarchy in 1975.

the men struggle to organize something, anything, appoint a chairman, pick a topic, set an agenda, take turns saying why they have come. Each pushes his own idea, to the exclusion of everybody else's.

"This is a hell of a way to run a meeting," someone mumbles. The action soon swirls around a tall redhead who manages to alienate everybody. Fred at age forty is vice president of a small industrial firm making plastic coatings. He is aggressive, articulate, and quickly establishes that he has been in T-groups before. "It'll get there," he says smugly. "Just watch. We really came to talk about each other."

When Paul, a young Ivy League MBA with a high-pressure marketing job, says his toughest problem is selling management's goals to his people, Fred explodes: "You're hung up! I think you get screwed if you don't have a hand in setting goals. You work for a lousy company." A minute later, he hauls off on Tal, an engineer born in India, who has described his high standards, driving style, strict deadlines, tight schedules, "You're rigid," Fred says emphatically. 'You don't know how to motivate people." He then offers his own company's approach to management—loose, free-swinging, lots of group decision making. Why, somebody asks, if his firm is so far ahead, has Fred come out here?

"I've got to learn to listen," Fred replies defensively. "People say I 'send' too strong. That's bad if it inhibits others." The comment, self-evidently true, has the effect of inhibiting everybody. No one knows how to give Fred feedback. Dyer demonstrates. "Fred," he says evenly, "I have mixed feelings about you. I like what you say, and you irritate the hell out of me. You ridicule and third-degree people. How can they ever see your point of view?"

Fred looks thoughtful, but says nothing. Dyer turns his attention to the group. "Let's forget the schedules and supervisors back home," he says." We don't *know* anything about that stuff. Look what's happening *here* in this room. It's the only accurate data we have."

It is near 11 p.m. when a tired bunch of businessmen sans chairman, sans agenda, sans discussion topic, stagger out of the room, some to the bar and some to bed. Dyer seems tired too, but unaccountably happy. "There are two or three things I feel good about," he explains. "One, we have lots of what I call 'verbal aggressives,' guys willing to get in there and mix it up. I always live in terror that I'm going to have a group that doesn't have anybody like that. You've got to have them to be successful.

"Second, they don't seem too dependent on me. They don't sit there asking me all the time, 'What should we do now?' Finally, we've got lots of interaction: people in conflict, people making decisions, people getting ignored, people getting chopped up. We've generated a whole series of issues for the group to process out."

Monday

Monday morning, the first full day, Dyer gives a short theory lecture, offering some perspective on the previous night's frustrations. "The T-group," he explains, "is *not* a way to run a staff meeting. Here, we deliberately remove norms like leadership, agendas, procedures, and create a vacuum so that people can move in and supply the missing ingredients. When we begin to interact, we can start learning."

The basic data, "feedback," he explains, reduces the "filters," or the gaps people experience between what they intend to do or say and how others interpret it. One sure way to get feedback, says Dyer, is to ask for it. Invite others to tell you what they think, not in general, but quite specifically in those areas where you're most unsure of yourself."

The first to catch on is Tal, the Indian engineer. Shortly after the T-group resumes, he becomes involved in an argument with Fred over motivation. Tal insists that "people work best under pressure, not when they're happy." Several men oppose him. Tal lowers his eyes.

Suddenly, he explodes. "Why do people build filters against me?" he pleads. "I'm hard-working and conscientious. But I rub people the wrong way. Is it the way I speak? My nationality? Skin color? What is it?"

For ten seconds nobody answers. Then the dam breaks. Tal is inundated in a flood of feedback.

Vic: You don't let the other guy's ideas sink in. You form opinions without listening.

Fred: You're good in a structured situation, but emotions and people confound you.

Phil: You're too concerned with recognition here. You keep pushing us to accept your ideas.

Ralph: It's not your skin color, it's your attitude toward us."

The vacuum has begun to fill. Dyer slips his shoes off, looks around, and says slowly, "I want to point out how Tal set it up to get feedback. He described his own behavior, which he sees getting him in trouble. That opened the door to a tremendous amount of data." The point is made. The group has learned something about feedback.

But Dyer sees a chance to do more—to teach something about feelings too. "You described yourself as an introvert, Tal," he says. "I feel you have a lot of warmth that doesn't come out. Do you feel good about anybody here?"

"Yes," Tal says, looking around, then at Dyer.

"Do you have good feelings toward me?

"Very much."

"Will you try an experiment? Can you show me how you feel about me without talking?"

Tal looks stricken. Slowly, he gets up and crosses the room, wondering what to do. In his bewilderment he reaches out to shake Dyer's hand. "Bill," he starts to say, "I like you very. . . ."

"No talking," cautions Dyer. The room falls silent. Gingerly, Tal slips an arm around Dyer's shoulder. Dyer stares into the darker man's face. Suddenly, both men relax and hug each other. "Good," Dyer says at last. "I get the message."

Glassy-eyed, Tal returns to his seat. The room hums. "I could never do that," one man says, "hug another guy." Tal sits dazed while the group ruminates on what keeps men from showing affection for each other. At last, snapping to, Tal glances over at Dyer. "I have a real feeling of gratitude," he says excitedly. "I don't know whether I should cry or not, but . . . thank you."

Tuesday

By Tuesday Dyer has formed opinions about every man in the group. Fred, the one who elicits so much antagonism, is "pretty strong, open, willing to engage, a good man to have." Paul, the Ivy Leaguer, has "moved into a dominant role." There's a leadership battle shaping up between Paul and Fred. George wants more structure and is "dying to get some feedback, but no one will oblige." Vic, ex-football player and a district sales manager, is nervous about himself. "He's big, handsome, powerful," Dyer notes, "so people don't see how sensitive and easily hurt he is."

Ralph, older, dignified, a scientist, is "an unknown quantity. He's holding back, and I'd like to flush him out, find out where he stands." Phil, a college professor like Dyer, "seems like a second trainer, always trying to point out what's going on, but seldom giving direct feedback. Tal has had his moment in the sun, and he's satisfied for now." Herman, who jumps in and out of the discussion, and Pete, whose hands twitch nervously when he talks, "both ache for feedback but are too wary to solicit it."

Ernie and Hank are "quiet guys." Ernie, a taciturn sort from a small town, seems put off by talkative people. "He needs to become more aware of how threatening his silence can be," says Dyer. Hank, a round-faced man with light wavy hair, has smoked a cigar silently for two days. "I think he's kind of lost," Dyer says, "the sort of guy who could just float through and never really understand what we're up to. I feel I've got to work with Hank, get him to see what the learning process is."

It's dinner time. Dyer joins a table with Ralph, Tal, and a couple of others. The businessmen order lobster. Dyer, mindful of his ulcer, a legacy of graduate school, settles for cottage-cheese salad. "What about Hank 's never saying anything?" Ralph asks. "How can we help him?"

"Start giving him feedback," says Dyer.

"Do you think we ought to play God?"

"Sharing data, giving feedback, isn't playing God. For me to tell you how your behavior affects me is not the same as telling you how you ought to behave. I'm just giving you data. What you do with it is up to you."

"My feelings," Dyer says later, "are 'data.' I want them to know that. My ideas, my thinking, my experience—all data. I want to share that. I think we tend to withhold feeling data. We're a feeling-deprived culture. People don't know what to do with negative, hostile reactions. So they gloss over them, hide them, bury them. I think we need to help people learn to deal with their feelings in productive ways. People are afraid if they let others know how they really feel, they're going to create enemies or problems. Oddly enough, we have more trouble expressing good feelings than bad ones. If we could learn to express *all* feelings, good or bad, we'd be richer, happier, more resourceful people."

Wednesday Morning

Next day, Dyer starts on group skills, especially leadership. There is no scientific support for the common belief that great leaders possess certain character traits like self-confidence. The evidence suggests leadership is best defined by effective behavior rather than personality type. This becomes quite apparent in a T-group. Without a formal leader, the group can't reach decisions until it redefines leadership. This group begins to develop a new leadership norm during an argument about management styles.

"I see a form of one of Eric Berne's *Games People Play* going on here," Dyer observes. "'Now I've Got You, You SOB.' I see us trapping the other guy with his own arguments, then pouncing on him—but still no clues about using the time productively." Everybody seems upset. What Is Dyer driving at?

Suddenly Vic smacks one huge fist in his palm. "I'm playing 'Gotcha,' " he reports. He turns to Fred with whom he's been arguing. "What I should have told you sooner is that I'm frustrated and bored with your comments," he says. "And I'm *really* upset now," he adds, as if he's made a mess he doesn't know how to clean up.

No one has tackled Fred head on so directly before. His leadership bid had been opposed from the start by several others. Now, like a wolf pack scenting fresh meat, the group moves in on Fred, letting him know he is considered bright but, as one puts it, "a great pontificator." At last, Dyer cuts off the barrage. "Fred," he says, "is probably the strongest guy in the group. Do you always let a guy like that carry the ball, then search out his weaknesses? You want him to shut up? Or learn how to use his resources, and yours?"

"Maybe that should be our agenda item," says George, who has been competing with Fred for influence. He walks to the newsprint easel at one end of the room, picks up a felt marker, and writes: "HOW DO YOU DEAL WITH A STRONG MAN?"

Before anyone can respond, Paul is up writing. Then Bill Dyer, whose contribution reads: "HOW DO WE LEARN TO WORK TOGETHER?"

"I see a power struggle shaping up between the three guys who wrote," Vic says excitedly. "Each of you has the courage to say, 'Hey, I'm the one!' "

"How about Bill?" Phil says. "He *claims* he doesn't want to be a leader."

"I've got to be free to use my resources in the group my way, too," Dyer responds. "When I feel moved, I try to act on it."

The conversation returns to Fred. Is he helping, or has he pulled a "power play?" Fred responds with more barbs. "Okay," Dyer says at last, "Fred, you're *always* in confrontation. You've got so much to offer, but people continually fight you instead of using your resources. Instead of fighting back, why not try asking how you could be more helpful?"

"That's pontifical," Fred says facetiously.

"No, no," several others shout, "It's helpful."

"At the point where you start a fight," Dyer continues, "let's stop and ask why."

"How about the newsprint incident?" asks George. "Fred accused me of trying to dominate the group, then he took the marker and put his problem up too." Fred straightens up and begins to argue.

"You're starting a fight," says Dyer. "Why not ask him, 'George, how could I have been more helpful?' "

Fred looks sheepish. He smiles. "Okay," he says. "George, how could I have. . . ."

■ ■ ■

"I've been through 150 groups," Dyer tells me afterward. "I'm being paid to be the trainer. So it's ridiculous for anyone to imagine I'm just another group member. But in the sense that they look at me as a person with resources and capabilities, and weaknesses too, I do become one of the group. I don't have to be perfect. That's one of the major leadership issues. Does a leader have to play a role and always be right? Or can he be himself, right or wrong? It's a very freeing thing for me to get to the point where the group can say, 'Gee, that's interesting, Bill, but it sounds like a lot of bs.'"

■ ■ ■

Bill Dyer became a trainer largely under the influence of his half-brother, Jack Gibb, a psychologist. Born and reared in Portland., Oregon, Dyer, forty-five, served a hitch as an Air Force navigator in World War II, earned a Ph.D. at Wisconsin, and began teaching sociology in 1953.

"My brother Jack was interested in group dynamics and became associated with NTL," Dyer recalls. "So I began to read up on that stuff, met some people, got invited to a few labs. I liked it." By 1959 Dyer was a summer intern with NTL and that fall joined its Washington staff as a full-time training consultant. "For a year-and-a-half all I did was design, set up, and run training labs," Dyer says. "In those days the theory was that the trainer ought to be impassive, non-involved, a blank figure, so that you wouldn't hang the group up on the authority issue. You sat there, never smiled, never responded, never did anything. It was about as phony a way of behaving as you can imagine.

"But other guys were much freer, and I was intrigued. I began to modify my style, and I think I've been more effective in recent years, trying to be more open, more spontaneous, more myself. Now, if they become dependent on me it's because they have a dependency problem. If they fight me, it's because they really don't like what I am. Not because I'm some sort of phony."

Although he now teaches sociology full-time at Brigham Young University, Dyer still manages to do five or six labs a year. "I couldn't do more than that," he says. "I remember one guy who does full-time training. Somebody said he was all 'labbed out.' Going through the motions, but no real feeling. I don't ever want to get like that."

Wednesday—Late Afternoon

By mid-week Dyer's group, deprived of formal authority, picking up the trainer's cues, despite disparities in age, education, jobs, and values, literally have invented a social form, evolved unspoken ground rules, and found a way to share leadership. Paul, impatient at the group's bickering, picks up the marker and says, "Look, we'll never get anything done if we don't get to work."

The others, Fred and George included, help him define the next steps for the group. They stick to the subject. Next day, it's Ralph, the dignified scientist, who offers to carry the ball for a planned presentation to the other T-group. Later Fred takes over the task of inviting ideas for using the final days productively. By now, most of the antipathy toward Fred has waned, testimony to the power of positive feedback. Paul tests him anyway.

"Why do you want to write it?" he asks. "Couldn't we just remember it?"

Fred keeps his cool. "Just so we won't forget it and have to keep repeating it," he says matter-of-factly.

"Can we examine this process for a minute?" says Vic. "Yesterday I made a judgment about Fred. He bored me. He wasn't credible. But, getting emotion out of the way, I hear him. He's interesting. He's got a lot to contribute."

"Do I really come on as such a threat?" Fred asks, reaching out for feedback.

Thursday and Friday

By Thursday good feelings are rampant in the group, but one problem nags at them. Nobody can figure out how to get the "quiet guys" to participate. Neither Hank nor Ernie has given the group enough data to elicit any feedback. Should they? Is it reasonable for the group to pressure a naturally quiet person into talking? That night Dyer purposely raises the issue. He asks Hank and Ernie if they feel under pressure to participate. "Quiet guys," he says, "often don't realize what a threat they pose, especially to talkative guys like Fred. Can you learn to share your concerns with the group too?"

This comment, although Dyer had not intended it, smokes out Hank, who has been sitting silently on a couch, staring at the floor. Suddenly, in an articulate burst, Hank begins to release several days of stored up feeling. "I realize, sitting here," he says softly, "that I run a dictatorship—in my business, in my family. I don't expect people to follow my values. I *demand* it. I set the tone. I take all the responsibility. I make all the decisions. And I don't like it."

His voice falters. "I've learned more in this room in four days than in the last ten years in business. I'm torn up." By now every man has frozen in place. "I have a serious problem. I care about people, I really do. But I draw and pull and don't give to others. It really hit me today, the talk about Phil's education and know-how. I left home at seventeen, and I'm self -made. Here I am sitting in the same room with a guy like that, and I feel I don't belong.

"I'm like a stage-player. My whole damn life is a mask. I wondered why I was here, but after two days I knew. In my field I'm highly regarded for my technical skills. But I don't know how to make the jump from professional expert to professional manager." He adds that he has never opened up before to anybody—really been himself. "I laid awake all night last night wondering if this would help me or destroy me," he confesses. "If you have feedback"—he looks at the others for the first time—"I'd be damned happy to hear it."

Cries of support fill the room. "You can do it, Hank," one man says. Another, fighting tears, calls out, "Hank, you're highly regarded *here*!"

"No, I'm not," Hank replies bitterly.

Dyer decides things have gone far enough. He looks Hank full in the face. "Hank," he says gently, "I see this all the time. 'If people only knew what a dud I really am.' But the fact is, when you do what you just did, people really like you. There's something in all of us that responds to honesty and humanity in others. I know my feelings about you have changed. I don't know what your home situation is, but it seems to me that if you level with people back there the way you just did with us, chances are they'll respond positively to you too. That's the best data I can give you."

Several heads nod assent. Dyer sits back, obviously relieved. Hank, sorting out his feelings, is beginning to quiver with the euphoria that can follow the release of blocked emotions. "I've noticed a fantastic thing," he says, breaking into laughter. "I'm a guy who always goes on first impressions. I look around this room, and I see that Sunday night I wasn't batting 20 percent. It's amazing how much you've all changed in four days!"

■ ■ ■

Back in his motel room, Dyer looks tired, but too wound up to sleep. "Even after twelve years and hundreds of groups," he says, "there's always an element of uncertainty. You *think* everybody will get his feedback, but I really was beginning to believe Hank would just ride it out all week. Never open up. Never reach anybody or be reached.

"And then, all of a sudden, he's letting it all out—honestly, openly, really exposing his authentic self, which he's *never* done before—and it's *okay.* No damage. No hostility. Just sympathy and support. The commonest criticism of T-groups is that they tear away people's defenses, leave them devastated, hurt, damaged. I don't buy that at all.

"My experience is much closer to this—that the group is sensitive about what happens to a vulnerable guy. Of course, there's a danger here the trainer has to guard against. A guy feels trust, confidence, and begins to unburden himself. People respond. The man says, 'Gee these guys care about me.' It's awfully easy, at that point, for him to unload all sorts of personal problems. Some trainers get sucked into the process and let them go on.

"That's not my style. I try to stay with the here and now. I try to discourage personal problems, marital problems, sexual problems. They can move into a group very quickly. But I want the guys to learn how to give and receive feedback, and how to be effective in a group. I'm dealing with their behavior, not trying to solve their personal problems.

"The thing I liked about Hank is that his here-and-now data turned around the way he was feeling in that group, listening to better-educated and more articulate guys sound off. And then he related those feelings back to his job and his behavior. To open all that up for himself in four days is truly amazing. He's got the insight now. He's motivated. Still, I guess the biggest problem we have is transfer of learning. Good things happen, but they're hard to measure. I just don't know what will happen to him when he goes home."

■ ■ ■

Friday night finds a tired Bill Dyer sitting in the bar, engulfed in waves of camaraderie, sipping his ginger ale. It's been a pretty good lab, no surprises, no major traumas, some high points, some good solid learning. Dyer begins winding down, anticipating. "One problem of being a trainer is being away from home a lot, and the strain on your family life," he says. "The lab is very rewarding. You get a lot of positive regard, develop a lot of emotional affect. You want to go home and be more open and trusting, implement in your family all the values you talk about here.

"So you get off the plane, in the house, and your wife has been alone for a week with nobody to talk to. You say, 'How are things going?' and for the next hour and a half she unloads on you: The furnace is broken, the kids aren't helping, strange bills arrived, all while you've been off eating good meals in some plush place. So now, instead of being loving and responsive, you've got some tough interpersonal work to reduce her hostility. It's much more basic than simply coming home and being more loving.

"My wife and I resolved this with an agreement that for the first hour or so she'll just let me hook into the family at a good level, kind of pick up where I left off, and then let the problems come in later, instead of dumping them all at once. . . ."

A participant comes over to say goodbye. He looks almost as tired as Dyer. "Great lab!" he says. Dyer grabs the extended hand in both of his and stares into the man's face. "Nice having you in the group." he says. Both are reluctant to part.

"Well, Bill," the man says at last, "I hope I'll see you sometime."

"Yeh," Dyer replies, "I hope so."

Then the man is gone. "It's a hard thing, terminating," Dyer says. "You really get locked in with these guys, appreciate them, feel deeply about them, and suddenly, it's cut off. We just go our own ways. I never see them again."

He shrugs. "There's a haunting theme about training. It's exemplified by an essay I read once. A seventeen-year-old girl ran a head-start program for ghetto kids. Somehow she managed to reach a tight, withdrawn four-year-old. The child began to open up, laugh, enjoy things.

"Then the funds ran out. So here's the older girl watching the child go back to the streets, wondering if the experience was for nothing—opening this whole new world for the little kid, then sending her back to a painful reality. When guys come for a one-shot lab, I'm never sure what happens when they go home. It bothers me. I see these guys beginning to make modifications, changes, in a week, but I don't know what becomes of them. I get letters sometimes, saying they did this, or they did that, but I'm never sure.

"Of course, the flip side of that is the 'Camelot phenomenon'—that one brief shinning moment. That's the idealism of it for me. But . . ." Bill Dyer stares into the darkness, toward the laughing faces, clinking glasses, and the orange glow of lights around the bar, suddenly receding, moving back, tucked away, half gone already. "I never know what happens to them," he says softly, "when they go home."

Epilogue 2010

I sent Bill Dyer the above draft in 1969. "I feel that you have truly caught the essence of what I was trying to accomplish in a training group," he wrote back. "I'm especially pleased that you are able to inject a great deal of training theory into the article without reducing the readability. Perhaps I am biased because you have written about me, but I think you have written the best article so far describing the real aims and goals of a training group."

Bill's response confirmed my growing sense that I was on the verge of a new career. We saw each other at conferences for years after. I last met him when he had become dean of Brigham Young's Marriott School of Management. Margaret Wheatley, who was teaching there then, invited me to keynote a conference in the late 1980s. I remember Bill sitting in the front row, beaming as I recalled how timely had been my meeting him at a critical turning point in my life.

■ ■ ■

"I RESOLVED TO EXPLORE BETTER WAYS FOR ENGAGING PEOPLE..."

CHICAGO, IL—My teammates and I at the Ball Foundation in Chicago had been working in 2007 with Sandra Janoff, co-director with Marv of Future Search Network. Ball partnered with urban school districts to create "whole systems change" as a way to improve literacy and learning for all students. We were doing organization development in school districts, the "bottom line" being student achievement.

Sandra offered to help us apply the concepts from *Productive Workplaces* to our work. Over the next eighteen months, we delved into the book. I had just completed an organizational assessment involving hundreds of people in two school districts. The process, using a powerful learning tool, still did not yield the outcomes I had expected, an effective action plan owned by the stakeholders.

As we progressed from Taylor to Lewin to McGregor in PW, I started realizing where I had been right and wrong in my assumptions about organizational change. One powerful moment for me was reading how Lewin's work had led to "one of the key managerial insights of the last century: diagnosis does not mean just finding the problem, but doing it in such a way as to build commitment for action" (p. 122).

I resolved to explore better ways for engaging people, allowing them to take ownership, so that momentum for action was built at each step along the way. One way I tried to do this with clients was to create cross-functional work teams that included people with authority, resources, expertise, information, and need (Weisbord and Janoff, Ch. 1, 2007).

During our book study, I got an opportunity to facilitate the organizational redesign of a school district during an unprecedented budget crisis. This was a chance for me to put into practice what I had been learning about holding the duality of "task and process," using "link pins" to coordinate among work groups, and the metaphors of "movie-making" and "snap-shooting." The role of a consultant as a "stage manager" began to resonate more and more in me as I grew in my understanding of what it takes to move organizations. When up against the wall, I could always take comfort in Marv's insight that "not everybody is ready to be helped, nor every culture amenable to remodeling."

In 2010, I took a position with a national nonprofit focused on giving new teachers and administrators the intensive support they need in their early years to succeed. My task was to create a coherent, systemic, organization-wide effort to better understand, measure, and maximize impact of the organization's work on teachers, administrators, and students. As I moved from external school district consultant to internal consultant for a national nonprofit, I found myself going back to the lessons of *Productive Workplaces.* One of my first initiatives was to propose an organization-wide convening as a way for people to experience, understand, and think about the whole system. In this way I could continue to learn and grow my skills for systems change—standing on the shoulders of the giants described in this book.

—Srikanth Gopalakrishnan, director of Impact,
New Teacher Center

chapter
EIGHT

McGregor and the Roots of Organization Development

The essence of [McGregor's] message is that people react not to an objective world, but to . . . their own perceptions, assumptions, and theories about what the world is like. McGregor wished passionately to release all of us from this trap, by getting us to be aware of how each of our worlds is of our own making. Once we become aware we can choose—and it was the process of free choice that we believe was Doug's ultimate value.

—Edgar Schein, quoted in McGregor, Bennis, and McGregor, *The Professional Manager*, 1967, p. xii

It was Douglas McGregor, author of the management classic that changed my life, who brought Kurt Lewin to MIT in 1946. I have used Lewin's story to illustrate my second theme: that the world is changing too fast for experts. Now I will give you my interpretation of McGregor's work to illustrate my third theme: how and why social change starts deep inside each of us, and what the implications for action are.

To do that I must draw connections between the "two Taylors" and McGregor's controversial Theories X and Y, which stirred up generations of managers. I described X and Y in Chapter Two. In the next chapter I will tell why I believe that X and Y, rather than opposing views of human nature, represent an internal dialogue we are having with ourselves. For X and Y each can have positive and negative aspects. Accepting all the parts in ourselves and in others may be a critical discipline for improving life at work.

McGregor and Taylor

Paging through *The Human Side of Enterprise* some years ago, I came across a sentence about doubling productivity that reminded me of *The Principles of Scientific Management.* Comparing the books, I made a startling discovery. Half a century apart, the Harvard psychologist and the industrial engineer had drawn remarkably similar conclusions (see "Management According to Taylor and McGregor," page 135). I was struck by their shared passion for rational problem solving, dislike of authoritarianism, and faith in science. Both Taylor and McGregor were dedicated to labor-management cooperation, more satisfying work, and greater equity for all—the bedrock of productive workplaces.

Given so many shared values, how did people come to associate Taylor with negative Theory X assumptions and McGregor with a benevolent Theory Y? Theory X seems to originate from a punitive, judgmental measuring rod built into some human psyches. It is not hard to imagine Taylor's external work measurements embodying that assumption. Theory Y seems rooted in a faith that each person has the potential for unlimited creativity, learning, self-development, and responsibility. I think both exist in each of us—in you, me, Taylor, and McGregor too. In McGregor's life story I found many clues as to why he saw the polarity between people rather than within.

A Family with a Mission

McGregor was born into a strict Scotch Presbyterian family in Detroit, Michigan, on September 16, 1906. (That year Kurt Lewin was a sixteen-year-old philosophy student in Berlin and the University of Pennsylvania gave Frederick Taylor an honorary doctorate.) Ministry and mission were McGregor's heritage. His great-grandfather was a preacher. His grandfather, a piano and organ vender, started McGregor Institute, a shelter for homeless

Management According to Taylor and McGregor

Taylor (1915)	McGregor (1960)
"The best management is a true science, resting upon clearly defined laws, rules, and principles as a foundation" (p. 7).	"Progress in any profession is associated with the ability to predict and control, and this is true also of industrial management. To insist that management is an art is . . . a denial of the relevance of systematic, tested knowledge" (pp. 3, 8).
"The general adoption of scientific management would readily in the future double the productivity of the average man in industrial work" (p. 142).	"Many managers would agree that the effectiveness of their organizations would be at least doubled if they could discover how to tap the unrealized potential present in their human resources" (p. 4).
"The time is fast going by for the great personal or individual achievement of any one man alone without the help of those around him" (p. 140).	"We cannot hope much longer to operate the complex, interdependent, collaborative enterprise which is the modern industrial company on the completely unrealistic premise that it consists of individual relationships" (p. 42).
"The universal prejudice in favor of the management of 'initiative and incentive' is so strong that no mere theoretical advantages which can be pointed out will be likely to convince the average manager that any other system is better" (p. 35).	"The philosophy of management by direction and control—whether it is hard or soft—is inadequate to motivate because the human needs on which this approach relies are relatively unimportant motivators of behavior in our society today" (p. 42).
"The first object of any good system must be that of developing first-class men. No great man can hope to compete with a number of ordinary men who have been properly organized so as efficiently to cooperate" (pp. 6–7)."	"Management should have as a goal the development of the unique capacities and potentialities of each individual rather than common objectives for all participants" (p. 187).

laborers in Detroit; he died of pneumonia contracted while digging the foundations. Douglas's father, a Bible scholar and lay preacher, became the shelter's director in 1915.

The mission once fed and housed seven hundred men. They were, in the words of Douglas's wife, Caroline, "low on the totem pole of human dignity" (McGregor, Bennis, and McGregor, 1967, p. xi). The elder McGregor conducted daily services and played the organ behind his wife's hymns. Young Doug worked in the office after school and became an accomplished gospel pianist. Management professor Jerry Harvey, a graduate student in the 1950s, once recalled for me a meeting of social scientists where, during the break, "all the biggies like Argyris, Likert, and Blake suddenly disappeared. I peeked through the door to the next room and saw them huddled around the piano singing gospel songs, accompanied by Doug McGregor."

Like Taylor, McGregor had a strong, energetic mother, deeply imbued with the Protestant ethic. She was forthright and optimistic in her belief in the salvation of productive work. His father, by contrast, was weighed down by the social pathology of the men he sought to save. Douglas shared his father's compassion while rejecting his gloomy outlook. He often pointed out how many of those the McGregors befriended later repaid them, prima facie proof of Theory Y.

McGregor drifted as a young man. After two years at Detroit City College, he spent a semester at Oberlin College, thinking to become a minister. Ambivalent about that career, he answered an ad in 1927 for a gas station manager in Buffalo, New York, and at age twenty-one took his first management job. The following year he married Caroline Ferris, moved with her back to Detroit, reentered college, and worked nights in the mission to finance his education.

In 1932, at age twenty-six, he decided on graduate training in psychology, choosing his school by tossing a coin. When it came up Stanford (heads), he decided that Harvard (tails) was what he really wanted. Most tough decisions, he told his friends, could be made that way; the heart's desire emerged the moment the coin landed. With financial help from his wealthy Uncle Tracy, McGregor earned a doctorate in social psychology in 1935 and became a Harvard instructor. When he asked professor Gordon Allport for advice, Allport suggested he stop jingling keys and coins in his pockets and keep his feet off the lecture desk. He also observed that "the trouble you will have next year is to get a theoretical framework into which to put things" (McGregor, Bennis, and McGregor, 1967, p. xiii).

Two years later McGregor went to the Massachusetts Institute of Technology, where he helped found its noted Industrial Relations Section. In the 1930s and 1940s he also did research and consulting in labor-management relations. After 1948 he put many of his theories into action as president of Antioch College. Except for six years at Antioch, he taught at MIT from 1937 until his death in 1964.

McGregor's Influence

McGregor had an enormous impact on those he met. Eric Trist, my friend and mentor (see Chapter Ten), was a frequent visitor to McGregor's country home in Acton, Massachusetts. "He was one of the most wonderful people I've ever known," Trist told me. "He had the art of being both gentle and confrontational at the same time. He was a maternal person, a nurturer, and it's characteristic of him that when he became famous he went to live in the country where he could tend his garden and reflect on his basic ideas without being imposed upon as he was while living near MIT" (February 25, 1985, interview). He wrote *The Human Side of Enterprise* sitting in a chaise lounge beside the garden pond.

Organization development professionals owe McGregor thanks not only for his ideas and exemplary practice but for the people he encouraged and inspired. He helped Kurt Lewin found the Research Center for Group Dynamics at MIT. He recruited the extraordinary MIT organization group—Richard Beckhard, Warren Bennis, Mason Haire, Joseph Scanlon, Edgar Schein—who played major roles in setting the boundaries, practices, and values behind systematic organizational change. Applying Lewin's ideas, he encouraged the Antioch College community to use itself as a learning laboratory in democratic education and self-management.

Edith Whitfield Seashore, consultant and former president of NTL Institute, recalled McGregor's inaugural address as Antioch's president when she was a student in 1949. "Two minutes before he started to speak," she told me, "I had no idea what I wanted to do with my life. At the end of his talk, I knew" (August 11, 1985, interview). Seashore, at McGregor's urging, attended NTL Institute and became a trailblazing woman in what had been a wholly male profession.

McGregor encouraged Richard Beckhard, among this generation's most influential consultants. The two became lifelong friends. "When I started in the management consulting field in the early 1950s," Beckhard told me, "he helped me learn to use the knowledge from the behavioral sciences as a way of working with clients" (interview August 11, 1985). Later McGregor recruited Beckhard for the MIT faculty, one of a few social science professors back then to come from practice to academia . "Doug was a gardener with people," Beckhard said. "He just grew people the way he grew plants. He was the most meaningful person in my life." Consulting together at General Mills in the 1950s, the two coined the term organization development (OD) to describe an innovative change effort that fit no traditional categories.

Pioneer Consultant. McGregor was perhaps the first psychologist to emphasize the strategic importance of personnel policies, such as congruent values, cultures, procedures, systems, and training. Bell of Pennsylvania, Standard Oil of New Jersey, and ICI in Great Britain were among his clients. He built deep personal relationships with clients, often visiting and inviting them to his home. He acted like a concerned friend more than an expert or professor. "If you walked in the middle, you couldn't tell the players without a program," said Beckhard. "He was gentle in his criticism. But he could also be very piercing. And he was a great integrator."

Change at Union Carbide. Stories abound of the way McGregor influenced large systems-change projects when the idea was quite novel. In the early 1960s, for example, Union Carbide's industrial relations manager, John Paul Jones, building on McGregor's prediction that an organization's full human potential would stand or fall on people's ability to work in groups, set up a pioneer OD department,. He introduced team management, based on "leveling" and collaborative problem solving, into what had been a disunited company. "Organization development's group programs offer no panacea," reported *Fortune* magazine. "You can't make a town meeting out of a stock-option plan [and] some executives are still indifferent or skeptical. But . . . if it never took on another job [OD's] residual influence would be immense. Practically everybody of consequence in the company is tolerably familiar with Jones's ideas" (Burck, 1965, p. 149).

Douglas McGregor, author of a major management book on how assumptions affect behavior.

Source: The MIT Museum

Affectionate Memories. People found McGregor engaging and attractive. He had large features and a high forehead topped by a burr haircut. His brow was furrowed by worry lines, deepened, his friend Warren Bennis (1972) would speculate, by a persistent guilt that he could never measure up to his own ideals. He often sported just the trace of a moustache. "He had an enormously interesting face," recalled Seashore. "It was a mobile face, very warm and boyish." Trist described a tall, slightly bent figure, with a long "bloodhound face, a hanging face," relaxed, soft-spoken, with a wry wit likely to pop up at any moment. Once Trist asked him what he was doing in England with a large corporation. "Cleaning up after—," said McGregor with a laugh, mentioning a well-known consulting firm whose proposals had led to "regressions to an older, authoritarian, bureaucratic culture." Lack of trust at all levels had curtailed innovation and market opportunities.

The assignment deeply upset McGregor, who still could laugh at the absurdity. "McGregor," Trist told me in 1985, "reversed this disastrous trend."

McGregor's sudden death of a heart attack on October 13, 1964, was a shock to his family and friends; at age fifty-eight he seemed in good health and good spirits. Edith Seashore was astonished at hearing the news by telephone. "I remember standing there in the kitchen, saying, 'That's not possible. He didn't say goodbye. Doug would never leave that way, he wouldn't be that inconsiderate.'" In a memorial service a colleague said he would always "remember Doug bending over slightly, a quizzical look in his eyes, followed by a probing question in a soft voice . . . always designed to make the other person grow." His friend Warren Bennis missed "his warmth, directness, immediacy, and spontaneity," others his responsiveness and sense of fun. An outpouring of calls, wires, commentary, reminiscence, admiration, respect, love, affection, and, above all, loss, followed his death ("Memorial to Douglas McGregor," 1964, p. 2).

Theories X and Y

For years McGregor and his father exchanged letters on their philosophies of life. In them could be seen opposing theories of human behavior, each informed by compassion, one based on essential sinfulness, the other in the potential goodness of each person (Bennis, 1966). No wonder I had found McGregor's writings contrasting Theories X and Y so confirming in the 1960s. The dialogue Bennis described is one I had had with my own father when I was experimenting with self-managing work teams. The emotional hook in me was a wish to stand on my own feet. I also heard a nagging inner voice saying, "Suppose the old man is right?" X and Y were descriptions of my own struggle for independence.

So I was not surprised to learn that McGregor told Trist that he thought Theory Y might be "an avoidance mechanism" for his own rebellion. Trist pointed out to McGregor that he sounded a lot like the late Wilfred Lord Brown, whose problems using managerial authority had led to the famous Glacier Project in a company he controlled (Jaques, 1951). Whatever its source, McGregor used his personal dilemma creatively to illuminate a central dilemma of the Industrial Revolution. He put into a boss-subordinate context the age-old struggle between authority and dependency, master and servant, father and son. He converted a philosophical, and at bottom a religious, issue into a metaphor for managing large organizations.

In so doing he reached an audience hungry to find alternatives to bureaucracy, authoritarianism, alienation, and the mechanical relationships that went with the mechanization of work. It was not simply ideology. For me it was an expression of life's purposes—affirming dignity in every person, finding meaning in valued work, achieving community through mutual support and accomplishment.

By which assumptions, McGregor asked, are large industrial enterprises managed? He could as well have asked by which assumptions is a homeless laborers' shelter run, or is a life best lived. X and Y were metaphors for what Trist called "a profound cultural diagnosis of our time." (See "Trist on McGregor" on the next page.) McGregor's ability to express this universal theme in managerial language accounts for the great success of *The Human Side of Enterprise.*

McGregor's contrasting assumptions still resonate. The specter of unemployment haunts us even in high-tech industries. My guess is that McGregor believed that if he could reach people whose hands moved the levers of power, he could change conditions that led to degrading unemployment, the lot of those who sought shelter in his family's mission. A sympathetic psychologist has observed that an important appeal for executives in McGregor's message was "the subtle way it addresses itself to the underlying guilt which plagues men who exercise power in modern organizations" (Zaleznik, 1967, p. 68).

McGregor refined his ideas in papers and speeches between 1937 and 1949. From his earliest writings we see him note the same phenomena Taylor did, often in similar words, then apply psychological knowledge to new solutions. In a paper with his friend Irving Knickerbocker, he speculated on ways to enhance labor-management cooperation and achieve "superefficient production" during World War II (Knickerbocker and McGregor, 1942). The pair criticized traditional labor relations as based on "conflicting opinions and unverified beliefs" (p. 50), a charge McGregor later leveled at management in general. Like Taylor, they also held management responsible for worker resistance to change.

Trist on McGregor

"The last time I saw Douglas was on a golden September afternoon sauntering in the London sunlight down the narrow side street leading from the Strand to the Savoy, on an embankment overlooking the Thames. I had just driven him in from my house after several hours of absorbing discussion. When he got out of the car, I just sat and watched, unwilling to turn away. Eight days later he was dead. I don't think we'd heard the last of him. We'd only heard the first.

"X and Y were a profound cultural diagnosis of our times. McGregor understood that a far-reaching reversal was taking place in contemporary values—a reversal of superior-subordinate relationship, not only in bureaucracies but deeper in Western and other cultures as well. This contemporary shifting of values was also necessary, in his view, for the effective management of large, complex organizations. He was a profoundly democratic man. I talked with him far into the night the last time I stayed with him in Acton. His concern was that modern industry was on the wrong path and that there has got to be a very profound change in relationships throughout organizations to permit participation and learning" [conversation with the author, February 19, 1985].

"It is not the fact of change but the method of bringing it about which is important if we are going to achieve a greater degree of cooperation," the authors wrote (pp. 53–54). (Taylor said something similar, though probably less printable, after his associate rushed things at Watertown Arsenal and brought down the wrath of organized labor.) Like Taylor, the authors traced resistance to reorganizing production methods without consulting or even informing workers. Unlike Taylor, they had money as a limited motivator. Once wages are adequate, other things matter more: equity, recognition, a chance to contribute. "Factory workers would strive less desperately to express their uniqueness and importance if this expression were not denied them by the increasing regimentation of industrial life" (p. 54).

A New Prescription

McGregor's prescriptions came from research on group norms and personal needs. Taylor understood groups only as restrictors of output. He did not consider that group solidarity, emotional support, and the self-esteem inherent in belonging might add productivity. (Unions later embraced narrow jobs, time study, and work measurement as a way of increasing wages and protecting jobs—exactly Taylor's intent—without, however, that spirit of "friendly cooperation" he believed would follow.) "We want to develop the morale of the working force," wrote Knickerbocker and McGregor (1941, p. 57). "We want to encourage enthusiastic cooperative effort; we want to increase efficiency to the utmost. These things we can accomplish only if the changes which are made in technical processes are perceived as necessary and reasonable by those whom the changes affect."

The authors, to dissolve resistance to change, advocated talking with foremen and shop stewards and using counselors to sound out employee sentiment. In the 1940s they could not yet invoke participative group decision making, for it was only then being discovered by Lewin and Mead with Iowa housewives. Still, they were shrewd in identifying excellent first-line supervision as the key to good union relations. Such is still the case except in those innovative places that substitute self-regulation for supervision.

Becoming More Practical. Knickerbocker and McGregor (1942) also proposed a three-stage map of the rocky road to mature union-management relations. The first stage was usually aggressive antagonism during union organizing. Then followed a period of bureaucratic bargaining and contract enforcement. In rare cases there emerged mature, mutual problem solving. Management and labor differ in key ways. Unions, for example, are run by elected officials. Members think short range, want specific gains, are quick to grieve and slow to forgive. Union members need to express past resentments and be heard before they can let go of them. The union's toughest problem was that the rank and file tended to support rebellious leaders at first, while mature relations awaited the election of confident, steady people. Even so, the union rank and file "always lags behind their leaders in understanding and in willingness to accept broad policies and long-range aims" (1942, p. 528).

Management had to change too. "Many firms have faced a real problem in the re-education of 'unenlightened' old line foremen after a union has been organized in the plant," they pointed out (Knickerbocker and McGregor, 1942, p. 528). Union members tend to judge management's intention from their experiences with foremen, who need training in building trust and close cooperation. (This was exactly what took me to Bethlehem Steel decades later, an adventure I detail in Chapter Seventeen.)

Using the Past in the Present. What struck me forcefully in 1985 about this 1942 concept was its relevance to a then current project of mine. "We can't get too far ahead of our people," a union local president confided to me, "even when they're wrong." The day I read the McGregor-Knickerbocker article I was called to an emergency meeting: two union officials had walked out on a joint committee, having decided that differences of opinion proved that "management is not serious about participation."

McGregor and Knickerbocker also proposed group gain-sharing plans and intangible rewards like prestige, recognition, and job security. They argued that workers and managers want to be treated the same way. That was radical stuff in the 1940s. A half century later egalitarian practices like open parking, a single cafeteria, informal dress codes, and identical offices regardless of rank were features of "new design" Honda and GM auto plants and Union Carbide's corporate headquarters. (I wrote this chapter when 20 percent of the U.S. workforce was unionized. Today the number is 12 percent. Now even unorganized workers, thanks to McGregor, are much less likely to run into ignorant managers.)

■ ■ ■

"WHERE TODAY'S MANAGEMENT FASHIONS ORIGINATED..."

MALIBU, CA—I have assigned *Productive Workplaces* in both MBA and MSOD programs. Students like the pragmatic applications of the concepts. All of them have worked in business and learned through the world of hard knocks. They haven't been able to make much sense of their experiences without paradigms and models through which to interpret them.

Exposing mid-career managers to an in-depth analysis of these theorists prepares them to understand where today's management fashions originated. It also protects them from unscrupulous at worst, or ignorant at best, professionals who want to sell them expensive copycats as newly inventive ideas. It also gives them a host of practical ideas on ways of implementing change.

For example, we are developing cross-cultural skills and OD in different parts of the world. During the twenty-four-month program we have classes abroad where we interact with local communities. In Lyon, France, for instance, we conduct research into various industries, assess joint venture opportunities, and benchmark practices in sustainability or technology. In Costa Rica we have worked with different stakeholders to build houses and upgrade a community. In China we have continued for several years to assemble multiple stakeholder networks for water conservation.

The book is priceless for helping students develop a personal view of how complex systems work. It takes the mystery out of some management approaches and makes them actionable and practical. I see more of my students now coming to understand their role in creating and sustaining a culture of quality and learning.

—Miriam Y. Lacey, Ph.D., academic director and professor, MSOD Program, Graziadio School of Business and Management, Pepperdine University

---

Labor Relations Manager: Dewey and Almy

During World War II McGregor had a rare chance to enact his theories. He became temporary labor relations manager at Dewey and Almy Chemical Company, a firm founded in 1919 on a bedrock of benevolent paternalism. It employed 1,500 people in two plants making container sealants, shoe cement, football bladders, and organic chemicals (McGregor and Scanlon, 1948, p. 42).

An idealistic president accepted unionization in 1939 because he trusted the American Federation of Labor's regional director. Yet paternalism persisted, as he personally handled contracts and grievances. When he left for war work in Washington, he hired McGregor, the firm's consultant, to manage labor relations.

McGregor later wrote a primer on participation with Joseph Scanlon, a former union organizer, who, in the late 1930s, had conceived a cost-reduction-sharing plan to save an on-the-skids steel company. McGregor brought him to MIT as a teacher and gave the Scanlon Plan worldwide visibility in his book. Scanlon Plans were still a viable form of gain-sharing in 2010, touted on the Internet for "reduced tensions in labor-management relations and increased productivity and profit."

Involving Middle Management. McGregor realized the futility of buying labor peace while alienating middle managers. So he redefined the personnel function as advisory, establishing a principle now widely recognized if not always practiced. He required that operating managers be involved in negotiating and carrying out the contract. He installed human relations training for foremen, and transferred or forced out those judged unfair or inept.

Line managers took over personnel functions—weekly policy and company/union meetings, a loose-leaf labor policy manual based on joint discussions, and union consultation on non-bargaining issues like job evaluations and promotions.

Cooperation applied only to personnel policies. Despite a desperate need for wartime production, it was impossible to get joint action on key decisions involving methods, systems, and plant problems. The pioneering 1943 attempt at Dewey and Almy to involve union members in technical matters "failed miserably, quite probably because the management representatives . . . were defensive and somewhat antagonistic. Worker suggestions were accepted but not carried out. Committee meetings involved a great deal of petty bickering" (McGregor and Scanlon, 1948, p. 42). Manager prejudice against worker competence, subtly reinforced by decades of Taylorism, was too strong to overcome.

Early Visions of QWL Principles. McGregor's early attempts at creative personnel work anticipated by more than thirty years the quality of working life (QWL) movement. He and Scanlon summed up the contributing factors. First (then, now, always) was leadership—a president who "believed in the possibilities of successful union-management relations" (McGregor and Scanlon, 1948, p. 42). Next was acceptance by middle managers and supervisors of their unique responsibility for labor relations and their willingness to learn how to become good at it. A third was good communication within and between management and the union.

Finally, the union local's capacity to stand on its own feet as a secure, independent bargaining force was essential. Today these principles still underlie union-management cooperation in those few industries where unions remain strong.

■ ■ ■

"I APPLY THE KEY PRINCIPLES DAILY..."

SEATTLE, WA—After seven years as HR director in a suburban city government, I was in turmoil at age forty-three, yearning for more creative and life-affirming work. I ached for fresh thinking on how to address my management challenges. The path forward eluded me. Then, in a consultant newsletter, I discovered *Productive Workplaces* (PW). Suddenly, the door swung open for me to the prospect of bringing life, energy, and fresh thinking to the world of work.

Learning OD's antecedents, the power of participation, Kurt Lewin's ingenuity, and Douglas McGregor's ability to empower others, I owe to PW. The book helped me find my latent creativity. About the same time, I read Margaret Wheatley's *Leadership and the New Science* (1992), whose metaphors also opened new pathways for me. I was by then attending an OD discussion group that alerted me to a graduate program in organization systems renewal at Antioch/Seattle. When I learned that both Marvin and Margaret were visiting faculty, I had to go.

I've since facilitated strategic planning events, retreats, and workshops on four continents, twice in languages I don't speak, with participants from a dozen countries. For a time, I served as an internal OD consultant in a global NGO. My clients were in far-flung places—France, Burkina Faso, South Africa, Kenya, India,

Tanzania. Participative processes, I learned, worked in all these settings.

Now, at fifty-nine, I am an HR director again, for a global health center. This time my approach is fully informed by an OD practice based on principles from PW that I apply almost daily in my work, for example, "get the whole system in the room, focus on the future, and give people tasks they can do themselves."

—Richard Wilkinson, HR director, International Training and Education Center for Health (I-TECH) a partnership of the University of Washington and University of California–San Francisco

---

chapter **NINE**

Theories X and Y for a New Generation

I believed . . . that a leader could operate successfully as a kind of adviser to his organization. I thought I could avoid being a "boss." Unconsciously, I suspect, I hoped to duck the unpleasant necessity of making difficult decisions, of taking the responsibility . . . , of making mistakes and taking the consequences. I thought that maybe I could operate so that everyone would like me. . . . I couldn't have been more wrong. . . . I finally began to realize that a leader cannot avoid the exercise of authority any more than he can avoid responsibility for what happens to his organization.

—Douglas McGregor, "On Leadership," 1954, pp. 2–3

McGregor had most of *The Human Side of Enterprise* thought out before going to Antioch. Had he written it then, it would have been a good book. His six years as a college president gave him leadership insights that led him to write a great one. Reading it as an uneducated manager in the 1960s, I felt from page one that this man had been there and knew what he was talking about. I experienced awe, empathy, support, challenge, anxiety, and excitement that I have gained from no other nonfiction work. McGregor expressed ideas I did not know it was possible to think. The book touched thousands of others the same way. Published in 1960, it became one of the all-time business classics.

McGregor at Antioch

In 1948 McGregor was asked to recommend candidates for the presidency of Antioch, a unique Ohio college where students divided each year between studies and paid employment. He showed so much enthusiasm for Antioch's goals that he was offered the job. Antioch's faculty were skeptical of this "human relations expert," an alien from the engineering and business worlds. His insisting on his friend Irving Knickerbocker as chief assistant, rather than an Antioch veteran, didn't help. In fact he needed Knickerbocker's toughness and political judgment to counterbalance his own deep wish to be liked.

Influenced by Lewin, McGregor visualized Antioch as a learning laboratory for "a genuine program of research, with ourselves as subjects." His objective was to "discover why the things we try work, or why they fail . . . to resolve the major paradox of our culture by making educational institutions a democratic way of living, rather than a democratic way of talking" (1949, p. 7).

A Learning Laboratory. McGregor started an "Antioch Goals Discussion," involving secretaries and janitors with students and faculty. Some faculty called the goals exercise "Madison Avenue manipulations." The criticism stung. In a typical response, McGregor wrote of his loneliness and nostalgia for MIT when he felt insecure in this unfamiliar and challenging job (McGregor, 1949). Skeptical teachers said that Antioch already was a model democracy. It had students on admissions, curriculum, and discipline committees—a great rarity in the 1940s. Representative democracy, McGregor insisted, was not enough. Everybody must help explore the college's future. "We know pathetically little about how to make democracy work," he insisted. "The list is long of problems that baffle us and frustrate us" (McGregor, 1950, p. 4).

Persistence paid off. Eventually "his warmth and gift of laughter and respect for the convictions of others" won over many critics, recalled Antioch's dean of faculty ("Memorial to Douglas McGregor," 1964). A consensus emerged for a smaller student body, a revised curriculum, greater integration across fields of study, new methods of teaching and learning, closer connections between academia and the workplace. "Skeptics," said the dean, "were soon amazed at the new sense of purpose that resulted" ("Memorial to Douglas McGregor," 1964).

By his second year, McGregor had facilitated major changes. Students chose their own newspaper editors, managed the publications budget, ran the fire company, and oriented freshmen. An honor system was implemented. In student meetings "he was likely to be found sitting on the floor as an alert listener and participant," said Dean Keeton. "He never lost sight of a college's primary function—the education of young people. For him the way to do this was to be with them in person" ("Memorial to Douglas McGregor," 1964). When a rich donor cut off Antioch because of "malicious rumors," McGregor invited him to come see for himself. The man "became Douglas McGregor's admirer for life." At the height of the McCarthy hearings in the early 1950s, when superpatriots cast suspicion on academics, McGregor took the offensive in a speech to the Cleveland Rotary Club, defying charges that his faculty were anything but loyal Americans.

An Exciting Place to Be. McGregor and Knickerbocker became campus fixtures. Their Christmas shopping foray was a legendary afternoon of drinking, followed by a splurge on gifts for family and friends. Indeed, Knickerbocker was McGregor's alter ego. Edith Whitfield Seashore, student community manager in 1950, recalled for me the first time Knickerbocker sat in on her meetings. "Knick began to make comments that were, I thought, enormously disruptive—but terribly interesting and insightful—about what was going on. I didn't have the foggiest idea about process. 'I'm coming in to sabotage your meetings,' he told me, 'because you're running very bad meetings and don't know what's going on in the room.' I said, 'This is the most fascinating thing that's ever happened to me in my whole college career' " (August 11, 1985, interview).

Some students began meeting regularly with Knickerbocker to study group dynamics. One was a twenty-two-year-old freshman named Warren Bennis, recently discharged from the Army. Later he would join McGregor at MIT, become his close friend and confidant, and achieve prominence as a management professor, college president, and leadership authority. Another was Matt Miles, destined to be a noted writer, teacher, researcher, and consultant on social change. Antioch students also took up race relations

Irving Knickerbocker, McGregor's unsung collaborator and alter ego at Antioch.

Source: The MIT Museum

and invited the director of the Lewin-founded Committee on Community Interrelations to consult with them. They put on an exhibit of what they had learned from their action research on participation in campus governance.

Antioch, in short, was an exciting place to be in the 1950s, a spawning ground for what would later be called organization development. "We are pioneering a method about which nobody knows very much," wrote McGregor and Whitfield in a joint report. "Widespread participation in setting direction and determining organizational policies is rare, and we have a lot to learn" (1950, p. 15).

After six years McGregor grew weary of administration. He disliked a role that put him at odds with the faculty. He wanted everyone to like him, impossible for an effective college president. He told Keeton that he "preferred the role of colleague and student to the role of boss." With typical candor he wrote in his valedictory (quoted at this chapter's start) that he had changed his mind about leadership, that its essence was the courage to decide.

Creating a Classic

McGregor wrote *The Human Side of Enterprise* in the late 1950s, targeting it for those who manage "the production and sale of goods and services at a profit." His theme was that managers base their actions on theory, conscious or not. He attributed the failure of "stick and carrot" methods to faulty assumptions about human nature. External controls demotivate, inducing the behavior they predict. Many organizational practices seem based on the belief that people dislike work and "must be coerced, controlled, directed, threatened" to produce (McGregor, 1960, p. 34). Indeed, many would rather be directed, since a worker's main motivation is security, not growth.

Look behind that stuff about "our people" in the annual report, said McGregor (1960), at what is actually done—time clocks, work rules, goals and reorganizations dictated from the top, asking opinions on decisions already made to "make people feel involved," one-way performance appraisal. All this, he wrote, "could only have been derived from assumptions such as those of Theory X" (1960, p. 35).

Taylor and Theory X

Taylor's practices too looked as if they derived from Theory X, although he started with different assumptions. He believed in workers' initiative, "their hard work, their good will, and their ingenuity" (1915, p. 36) when treated fairly. He wanted all persons in jobs tapping their highest abilities. Workers were not lazy. They were ignorant of the best methods. So was management. Taylor's remedy for ignorance was breaking jobs into small pieces, enforcing uniformity through rigid procedures and high wages.

Peter Drucker (1976) argued that Taylor expressed Theory Y assumptions when he held that every person was "first class" at something. I think this stretches Taylor too far. He believed workers should work to the limit of their ability; but also that no worker could ever define tools, tasks, goals, systems, methods, and procedures. Who could imagine a century ago that higher productivity would one day result from individuals performing all the tasks Taylor had fragmented. The concept of multiple skills, conceptualized by Emery and Trist in the 1950s (see Chapter Ten), turned Taylorism upside down. It became the modern solution—at a new level of technology—to the problems Taylor set out to solve a century ago.

Moreover, Taylor's view of teamwork meant a rigid division of labor among staff experts, managers, and workers, all doing tasks that engineers had defined. Taylorism proved McGregor's self-fulfilling prophecy. Assuming workers' ignorance, scientific managers set up systems to keep them that way. Taylor rejected social workers in industry for their lack of appreciation for productivity, contending that the right work system would take care of social pathology. He was right in one way, as well as narrow-minded about what the "right" system meant. Like many reformers, he could not see that his system had limits. Where markets, technologies, and systems change rapidly, people must interact across levels and functions constantly to do anything right.

One curious result of Taylorism was the splitting off of personnel from engineering. As Taylor's system went global, labor reformers successfully established "the human side" as a specialty. Hardly had the engineers wrested job descriptions, people selection, and pay plans from management than a new breed of "employment managers" stole them from engineering. By 1920 there were between four thousand and five thousand personnel professionals.

"The last bastion of the 19th Century foreman's power had been breached, and a new relationship, based on managerial control of the worker, became the basis of personnel work" (Nelson, 1980, p. 201). This was the staff role McGregor had played and abandoned at Dewey and Almy in the 1940s. *The Human Side of Enterprise* argued that expert staff specialization was a mistake, that first-line supervisors, armed with 20th Century human relations skills, were the right people to select, train, and evaluate workers.

Theory Y

McGregor's thinking matured in parallel with a burst of creativity in the social and behavioral sciences. Kurt Lewin, whom he brought to MIT,

A Comparison of Theory Y and Scientific Management

Theory Y Assumptions	Taylor's Assumptions
1. Work is as natural as play. People like or dislike it based on conditions management can control.	Soldiering on the job is management's fault, not the fault of lazy workers. Management is arbitrary as long as nobody has figured out the best tools, methods, incentives, and required talents for each job.
2. External control is not the only way to achieve organizational goals. People will exercise self-control toward objectives they feel committed to.	People will be committed to methods that clearly have been found, through trial and error, to be the best, least stressful, most productive, and most suitable for them. The incentive is greater success, higher pay, easier work, and less conflict.
3. Commitment comes from rewards based on satisfying people's needs for status, recognition, and growth.	*No Taylor analogy*. He believed in feedback, but did not understand social needs like status, recognition, and community.
4. Under the right conditions the average person will seek and accept responsibility rather than avoid it.	All workers, supervisors, and staff experts have a role to play in making a workplace successful, and all will readily do it if they believe the system is the best possible and they are paid well for their efforts.
5. Many people have the ingenuity and creativity needed to solve organizational problems. These qualities are not the rare province of a gifted few.	*No Taylor analogy*. He believed the contrary: only those trained in specific functions would be allowed to carry them out.
6. Modern industry uses only a part of the ability, talent, and potential brainpower of the average person.	The best work system is one where every job is filled by the person for whom first-class performance represents that person's highest level of functioning.

had by the late 1950s influenced a generation with his "practical theories." Abraham Maslow recently had described his famous "needs hierarchy," theorizing that when security and safety needs are satisfied, we require intangible rewards—status, recognition, responsibility—to perform at our best (Maslow and Murphy, 1954). Frederick Herzberg, studying accountants and engineers, discovered that job "satisfiers"—pay, benefits, working conditions—don't motivate. They only dissatisfy when inadequate. "Motivators"—recognition, achievement, responsibility—must be built into the work itself (Herzberg, Mausner, and Snyderman, 1959).

McGregor, building on Maslow and Herzberg, pinpointed the source of bad quality years before Japan raised our consciousness. Separating producing and inspecting, he observed, encourages workers knowingly to pass mistakes down the line to those whose job is to find them. High quality could be achieved only by making quality everybody's business. Curiously, of Theory Y's six assumptions, four incorporate echoes of Taylor; only numbers 3 and 5, based on a changed society and modern psychology, directly challenge scientific management. See "A Comparison of Theory Y and Scientific Management."

A New View of Staff-Line Relations. In the decades between Taylor and McGregor, staff expertise flowered. After World War II corporations scrambled to build state-of-the-art planning, engineering, finance, personnel, information, and training departments. Too many CEOs, noted McGregor, delegated control, but not responsibility. They built big staffs to monitor exceptions, driving line managers to become as ingenious as hourly workers in defeating home-office policies. Paradoxically, the more in-depth knowledge a staff person has, the harder it is to transfer. Every form of expertise tugs against every other, competing for manager attention. So McGregor came to a paradoxical conclusion: for staff expertise to be fully used, it can't be mandated.

Effective Staff Work. Staff, said McGregor, could be coaches, not cops, giving managers data for controlling themselves. They could consult on managerial problems, not coerce compliance with corporate directives. Staff could "devote a great deal of time to exploring 'client' needs directly, and to helping the client find solutions which satisfy him. Often the most effective strategy . . . is one in which the client develops his own solution with professional help" (McGregor, 1960, p. 169). My erstwhile partner

Peter Block, in *Flawless Consulting* (2011), embodied this concept in his groundbreaking manual on how technical experts, lacking formal authority, can transfer their knowledge.

Leadership and Teamwork. McGregor also contradicted Taylor's concept of "the one best way." No one style of managing satisfies every situation. Successful managers tend to have a clear sense of direction and a flexible repertoire of behavior. They can listen, delegate, and involve and also know how to decide and direct. These are not opposing behaviors. Managers need a full tool kit the same way carpenters need hammers and saws.

McGregor also made a compelling case for teamwork. The astonishing potential of groups for high creativity, good ideas, and fast implementation upends a sacred American myth: the manager as Lone Ranger, heroically doing it all. Most management "teams," McGregor observed, were really groups of individuals vying for the boss's favor. Managers misused groups because they had low expectations and took too much on themselves. Properly used, groups could improve decision making and problem solving. Effective teamwork required give and take, openness, frank criticism, shared responsibility and self-examination. These skills are best learned, he thought, through team building, which I take up in Chapter Twenty. McGregor emphasized that "groups" and "participation" are not synonymous. Those who think Theory Y means "everybody participates in everything" obviously have not read his work.

McGregor also rejected fitting people to jobs. He thought the best HR strategy "is to provide a heterogeneous supply of human resources from which individuals can be selected to fill a variety of unpredictable needs" (McGregor, 1960, p. 76). No one can tell what a firm will need tomorrow. Therefore, we do best encouraging diversity and human resource systems that give people control over their own career moves.

Theory Y assumptions, McGregor wrote, surely will be revised by new knowledge. Meantime, people would do well to abandon practices that don't work "so that future inventions with respect to the human side of enterprise will be more than minor changes in already obsolescent conceptions of organized human effort" (1960, p. 245). Perhaps the most far-reaching difference between Taylor and McGregor was their views of control. Taylor, who made a harness for himself as a youth to prevent nightmares, sought to located controls outside the work system. McGregor, the missionary who believed that even the worst among us were capable of growing, taught that the best control is self-control. That radical idea has caused a managerial revolution for those who apply it. The bottom-line performance of systems that place coordination and control with the people who do the work is incalculable (Chapter Ten).

Worldwide Acclaim

The Human Side of Enterprise was met by a worldwide outpouring of praise, letters, reviews, awards, and invitations to speak. McGregor had married Lewin's work to Maslow's and created personnel, labor relations, performance appraisal, goal setting, and compensation methods for a post-industrial age. He also accented the big if: leader behavior. He gave many analogies and cited compelling examples from his experiences as manager and consultant. Criticism came mainly from fellow academics, grumbling, harumphh . . . that McGregor, uh . . . er . . . did not cite specific research to support his ideas. Indeed, the book's great weakness is lack of an index and bibliography. Yet McGregor wanted a book managers would read, understand, and identify with, as little like a textbook as possible. Academic quibbling only highlighted how well he had succeeded.

The most direct challenge to the book came from those who said Theory X—embodied in paying well and "kicking ass"—is the only sensible way to motivate people. A second charge, more sorrowful than angry, came from people who shared McGregor's values but saw Theory Y as idealistic, impractical, and futile. Notable among these was the same Abraham Maslow whose theories underpinned McGregor's. Maslow, during his year as a scholarly gadfly-in-residence at Non-Linear Systems (the firm on whose self-managing work teams I had modeled my own in the 1960s), repeatedly questioned the application of Theory Y (Maslow, 1965). There was, he said, too little evidence, including his own, for this view of human potential. It required hothouse conditions and astute selection of rare, self-motivated people. It "assumes good conditions, good luck, and good fortune" (Picker, 1968, p. 51).

Indeed, Maslow wished to believe. Yet, as a psychologist who had studied human pathology, he doubted—like Douglas McGregor's real father—that the darker forces of human nature could be overcome. Another sympathetic critic saw too much zero-sum conflict (if you win, I lose), too few shared goals, too many power differences, and too much boring, routine work negating Theory Y assumptions. "In sum," he wrote, "there do not appear to be enough influential advocates for the redesign of work according to 'theory y' principles to stimulate the allocation of scarce resources to this goal" (Nord, 1978, p. 65).

The statement illustrates one of McGregor's major themes: how an assumption leads to a belief that "the facts" support it. My own contrary evidence comes from countless projects, some described in Part Three, to which many corporations, medical centers, hospitals, and government agencies had allocated enormous resources since 1969. Indeed, one of the positive outcomes of the 1980s recession was the investment by General Motors (Saturn auto plant), Nissan (Smyrna, Tennessee, truck plant), Diversified Printing (Attie, Tennessee, printing plant), and a hundred others in "new design" factories in which Theory Y assumptions played a central role. In 2010, I noted, the Saturn plant, like so many others, was no more, a victim of business strategy, not its work system. It is no surprise, though, that many 21st Century high-tech businesses were largely built on platforms of human capability.

Systems, Not Formulas

McGregor could not always specify management practices embodying all his ideals. It must have hurt him that his many vivid analogies, examples, and illustrations did not satisfy critics who demanded more "how-to" stuff. McGregor was busily writing it into *The Professional Manager* when he died. In that posthumous book, he strongly argued that no single technique could ever embody the philosophical implications of a manager's mental map of reality. Systems change involved "costs and risks," might take "three to five years," and required as much investment as new product research and development. Anything less, said McGregor, left managers with "recipes, fads, and other 'instant cures' " (McGregor, Bennis, and McGregor, 1967, pp. 95–96). Nobody criticized, and few even observed, the central theme of McGregor's life and work: that efficient, humane management was not a function of any particular formula. McGregor above all advocated an experimental style of change, finding out what works in each new situation.

His pragmatism was grounded in a faith in democracy and human potential, which Western science has linked to effective management through the medium of open systems thinking (see Chapter Eleven).

Taylor had engineers find one best way to do anything, McGregor advocated involving everybody. One paradox is that Taylor's motivation formula—concrete goals, tied to a bonus—has been shown to increase output in routine jobs 40 percent or more in studies cited by Edwin Locke (1982). It is equally true that work systems embodying principles McGregor advocated also have improved output up to 40 percent over traditional systems. My own case from the 1960s (Chapter Two) is one of many examples. Such systems have also registered important social gains—better jobs, less absenteeism and turnover, more mutual support, personal growth, and higher morale. They also have cut overhead by moving supervision and staff expertise outside and skills and knowledge inside of work teams (Lawler, 1986). That, I'm convinced, is what makes managers and supervisors so skeptical. If people can plan and ensure their own output, why do they need supervision? McGregor's vision threatened middle-manager status and power.

More, there is an organizational version of "Gresham's Law" (bad money drives out good), which says that technology tends to drive out other values in the workplace. Narrow tasks and expert control proved attractive to managers holding Theory X assumptions, although few embraced Taylor's value that workers should share productivity gains. McGregor believed that X assumptions were dated by education, experience, and social science. For a good part of the population they were false—but when acted upon could be made to come true.

A New Look at X and Y: Two Selves in Each of Us

Here's the rub with X and Y. From Jungian psychology comes a profound possibility McGregor's writings elude. That is the presence in each of us of *both* X and Y assumptions—a polarity of the human spirit within, not just between, persons. But there is more. Here is the possibility that boggles me: X and Y each have positive and negative aspects.

To tell you why I believe that requires a short digression. Some years ago in Sweden, through my friend Jan Boström, I met social psychologist Claes Janssen (1982, 2011a, b), who had worked out a powerful group exercise to surface our projections on others. (A projection is seeing in someone else traits we admire or deny in ourselves.) He created a twenty-four-item yes/no questionnaire. Those answering most questions "yes" he called "yes-answerers"; those answering most "no" were "no-answerers." If you ask these two groups to write adjectives about themselves and the other group, you get the chart in "Yes/No Observations"—a result I have repeated many times.

NO+ (ABOUT SELVES)	YES+ (ABOUT SELVES)
CALM, RELAXED	SINCERE, OPEN
SURE OF SELF	SENSITIVE, IMAGINATIVE
REALISTIC	ARTISTIC
GOOD MIXER	INDEPENDENT
WELL ADJUSTED	SEEKER: OPEN TO CHANGE
RELIABLE	NON CONFORMIST
COOPERATIVE	INQUISITIVE
SATISFIED	CHILDLIKE
ACCEPTS GROUP DISCIPLINE	CREATIVE
NO− (SEEN BY "YES")	**YES− (SEEN BY "NO")**
REPRESSED, UNAWARE	DIFFERENT
AFRAID OF SELF	LONELY
BORING	OUT OF TOUCH
RESISTS CHANGE	SELF-ABSORBED
INSENSITIVE	UNHAPPY SOUL
AUTHORITARIAN	WANTS TO BE NOTICED
CYNICAL	HARD TO RELATE TO
CENSORING	ANXIOUS
DIFFICULT	ANARCHIST

"Yes-answerers" see themselves through a Theory Y lens—optimistic, creative, independent. They give "no-answerers" Theory X traits—repressive, authoritarian, fearful. "No-answerers," on the contrary, cite their own positive traits—dependability, loyalty, and cooperativeness. They see "yes-answerers" as confused, anxious, and self-centered.

Projecting Our Own "Shadows." Janssen's theory is that each list represents a projection of what we value and fear in ourselves. The feared side—our "shadow," the human impulses we disown—may appear on the Yes or No adjective list. More, he shows that in any life crises we are likely—each one of us—to move through the four positions, experiencing (or running from) all the states described. (In Chapter Eighteen I show how Janssen's Four Rooms of Change theory also can be used to assess an organization's potential for change.)

The reason McGregor's Theories X and Y stirred such strong feelings, I believe, is that he unintentionally set up a good guys/bad guys scenario that left people in an uncomfortable box. I can't change my assumptions the way I change my socks. To do that is to surrender part of my identity. McGregor—the passionate optimist of human potential—was tuned in on the negative aspects of his No side, which came through strongly in his father, and on the positive aspects of his own Yes.

Yet both sides exist in each of us. Edwin C. Nevis, a consultant and applier of Gestalt theories to organizations, surveyed five thousand managers between 1970 and 1979. Consistently, they opted on the average for 56 percent of the Theory X statements on the survey and 67 percent of those based on Theory Y (personal memo to author, January 1987).

So I know I am not alone. I was propelled by McGregor's vision to initiate change in the 1960s because of my urgent need for an outside voice granting relief from the incongruities I experienced. I was out to change company policy and procedure. I soon learned that the hardest work would be changing myself. As a manager, I wanted constant (although unconscious) control in a striving for unattainable perfection.

To act on constructive assumptions—X or Y—is to accept that not everybody wants to grow, and that we ought not take it personally when our good intentions fall short. Most of all it means accepting our own tendency, when we are denied what we had hoped for, to jump to the negative Theory X conclusion that people are no damn good. Shocked at our primitive impulse, we may (like McGregor) repress the feelings, thus deepening our own anguish. I believe now that I need both sides of my X and Y, to hear my inner dialogue as a creative but not always harmonious discourse on my own growth and learning.

One critic imagined that McGregor intended for his theme to relieve the guilty consciences of people in authority. "It is as though leaders listen for the voices outside themselves," wrote psychoanalyst Abraham Zaleznik, "which will testify to their humanity in opposition to the disquieting inner voices that disapprove, depreciate, accuse" (1967, p. 67). That describes part of my experience.

But there is more. Years ago, his close friend Warren Bennis observed that McGregor's conception of Theory Y also created an intolerable burden for leaders—accepting responsibility for the growth, nurturance, and success of subordinates. "When," asked Bennis, "do the boss's needs, growth, defenses, distortions, 'hang-ups,' disappointments, narcissism, sufferings, come into play?" (1972, p. 142). Unless we accept good/bad X and good/bad Y in ourselves, we cannot become fully human.

■ ■ ■

"FROM BUS COMPANY TO MULTI-MODAL TRANSIT AGENCY..."

SALT LAKE CITY, UT—I discovered the Four Rooms of Change theory and model in 1990 while reading *Productive Workplaces.* Marv had described two ways the concepts could be helpful. One explains what happens when we look at the X and Y in our projections and ourselves. Another was how Claes Janssen's theory could be used to assess an organization's potential for change, depending upon which position people take at any particular time. This knowledge helped me as an internal consultant supporting the management team of a manufacturing plant during a major redesign. Applying the Four Rooms model and theory, the managers moved themselves from Self-Censorship and Denial, through Confusion and Conflict, into Inspiration and Renewal, then to Contentment. In the redesign, they created a more efficient plant based on self-directed and semi-autonomous work teams.

In 1997, I joined Utah Transit Authority (UTA) as its internal organization development consultant. I introduced the Four Rooms of Change to the labor relations and union executive committee in a workshop where they were seeking to improve their relations. Not long after, I learned that there were tools associated with Janssen's theory. I became certified and started using the theory, model, and tools along with Future Search at UTA with the board, senior leadership, and employee groups throughout the company. People adopted a common language for understanding Self-Censorship and Denial, Conflict and Confusion, and how to move themselves into Inspiration and Renewal, then Contentment. Adopting principles derived from *Productive Workplaces*, Future Search, and the Four Rooms of Change, UTA transformed itself from a bus company into a multimodal transit agency, among the most progressive in this hemisphere.

—Drusilla Copeland, partner, Ander & Lindstrom AB

Values Over Techniques. Taylor lamented that managers embraced his methods, not his principles. He was furious with greedy employers who raised quotas instead of sharing gains and with ignorant consultants who put in systems without proving their value to workers. McGregor was disappointed that so many managers thought he wrote a Theory Y cookbook when his intent was more ambitious: to show that wrong assumptions lead to ineffective management. We must resist the temptation, then, to value Taylor or McGregor for pioneering techniques . If ever two polar opposites had a common objective, it was the application of science, the spirit of experimentation, to the workplace.

Every technique described by Taylor or McGregor has worked. And—this is why social science can never be a science—every technique has failed. We can specify the right conditions until the moon becomes an Earth colony. Unlike high school chemistry, we cannot repeat one another's experiments. The fact is that Hewlett and Packard started working side by side in a garage with certain values of human dignity. As their company grew, they invented policies and methods to embody their values. They did not, could not, "create a culture" that was not already indigenous to their lives; they would consider it ridiculous even to try.

If you wish to find out what works for you, start with your own values and situation. Management is best conceived as acting in ways to make happen what you most believe in. It is at bottom an exercise of moral imagination. I fancy Taylor, Lewin, and McGregor would have agreed to that.

chapter TEN

Emery and Trist Redefine the Workplace

Information technologies, especially those concerned with the microprocessor and telecommunication, give immense scope for solving many current problems—if the right value choices can be made.

—Eric Trist, *The Evolution of Socio-Technical Systems*, 1981, p. 59

Douglas McGregor was writing a how-to book, *The Professional Manager* (McGregor, Bennis, and McGregor, 1967), when he died suddenly in 1964. I derived my multi-skilled work teams from McGregor's account of Non-Linear Systems. It was not until the early 1980s, investigating management history for this book, that I came to appreciate the origins of my experiment. I can trace it to a revolutionary discovery in a British coal mine in 1949.

Sociotechnical Systems: Choice, Not Chance

I owe my enriched understanding of what I did in the 1960s to the work of two remarkable social scientists, Eric Trist, an Englishman, and his frequent collaborator, the Australian Fred Emery. Trist coined the phrase *sociotechnical system* to underscore that the interaction of people (a social system) with tools and techniques (a technical system) results from choice, not chance. Emery enlarged the concept, creating the practice theories necessary to contemporary work redesign. Sociotechnical systems (STS) design revolutionized the division of labor among managers, workers, and experts. It leapfrogged both Taylorism and participative management.

Trist, an unpretentious man in his late sixties when first we met, had a lean, benevolent face, thinning hair, and a small moustache still showing traces of red. His dark eyes, somewhere between blue and brown, peered out from silver-rimmed bifocals. He disdained photographs, and the severe portrait here gives no hint of the engaging pixie smile that often lighted his face. Small-boned, physically delicate, tough in mind and spirit, Trist influenced two generations of practitioners to value learning, caring, and collaboration as quintessential ingredients of social change. William Westley, former head of McGill University's Quality of Work Life Centre, once said in a meeting I attended that "Trist is to QWL what Sigmund Freud was to psychoanalysis." What made Trist an innovator was the way he derived organizational choices and showed, in social, technical, and environmental terms, the consequences of each. He also organized early field studies that led to new work designs, and he inspired major change efforts in cities and communities.

Trist was born, "totally a Celt," to a Cornish father and Highland Scottish mother near the white cliffs of Dover in Kent, England, on September 11, 1909. A sea captain's son, he was the first male in his line since Elizabethan times to turn down a life at sea. Instead, he studied English literature and psychology at Cambridge and moved decisively toward the latter after meeting Kurt Lewin. He attended Yale on a fellowship, mentored by anthropologist Edward Sapir. After World War II he was a founder of the Tavistock Institute of Human Relations. After 1967 Trist lived mainly in the United States, teaching at the University of California, Los Angeles, the Wharton School of the University of Pennsylvania, and at York University in Ontario, Canada, and directing or consulting to some of the more ambitious change projects of our time.

Emery, younger than his sometime-collaborator, was a lanky, rawboned, sandy-haired Australian, with blue eyes set in a lined, world-weary face.

Eric Trist, a shaper of modern thought and action for improving work and community life.

Source: Beulah Trist

Antiauthoritarian in the extreme, he disliked sitting at the head table in a seminar or being introduced as an expert. His erudition and extraordinary ability to synthesize obscure sources, research, theories, and practical experience into new concepts and methods made him a leading social innovator of this or any era. His concept (1967), for example, that developing "redundant skills" in each person irrevocably transforms work systems, was, in Trist's words, "a major breakthrough that has affected everything that has happened since in the enlightened practice of sociotechnical theory" (memo to author, December 3, 1986). Hans van Beinum, director of the Ontario Quality of Work Life Centre, characterized Emery as "someone who is inclined to go for the dark corners," those parts of social reality "which are a bit foggy, misty; the twilight areas" (1985).

Emery was born on August 27, 1925, into a working-class family (his father was a sheep shearer and drover) in Narrogin, a tiny town in the rugged outback of Western Australia. A "wild, independent bush kid" (his wife's words), he quit school at fourteen, went back later to night school, finished Fremantle Boys High School, and had two degrees from the University of Western Australia by age twenty-one. In 1953 he earned a doctorate in psychology from the University of Melbourne, where he became a senior lecturer (associate professor) while still in his twenties.

Emery met Trist at the Tavistock Institute in London while on a UNESCO research fellowship in 1951–1952. For a decade starting in 1958, Emery was a senior Tavistock staff member, doing projects in England and Norway. He worked mainly from Australia after 1969, traveling the world as an independent researcher and consultant, except for two years at the Center for Advanced Study in the Behavioral Sciences at Palo Alto, and two as a visiting professor at the University of Pennsylvania. For many years he also was connected with the Centre for Continuing Education in the Australian National University in Canberra.

Tavistock Institute

For the full story of Taylorism's undoing, we must turn back the clock to visit London's Tavistock Institute of Human Relations just after World War II. The institute was incorporated separately from its parent, the Tavistock Clinic, a mental health treatment and training facility, when the clinic joined Britain's National Health Service. The institute's purpose was teaming with client-sponsors to use social science knowledge for a wide spectrum of human problems, intending along the way to make new theories about what works (Gray, 1970).

If these twin goals—solve the problem and learn to solve future ones—sounds Lewinian, the reason is not far to seek. Trist had avidly read Lewin's Berlin experiments since the early 1930s. As a graduate student he became noticeably excited over a Lewin paper in the Cambridge library and "received a bad mark for that, because no Briton should be guilty of enthusiasm" (Sashkin, 1980, p. 145). When Lewin visited Cambridge on his flight from Germany, Trist, the starry-eyed student, showed him around. They remained friends until Lewin's death. As Lewin had read Taylor, the better to use psychology in the workplace, so Trist would read Lewin, the better to undo Taylorism and give Taylor's values—labor-management cooperation, optimum use of each person's talents—a new lease on life.

Like Lewin in the United States, Tavistock's founders sharpened their ideas through wartime action projects. Trist, for example, had worked as a clinical psychologist in the Maudsley Hospital, Britain's premier psychiatric facility. He quickly realized the futility of one-at-a-time treatment compared with the enormous wartime need, finding it impossible to accept that only the hour with the doctor could be therapeutic. Imbued with Lewinian thinking, he sought support for the idea that the social institution, the hospital community, could be a powerful rehabilitator.

Bion's Group Theory

His search led him to Major Wilfred R. Bion, a much-decorated World War I tank commander. Trist was immediately attracted to this physically imposing "psychiatrist who looked like a general" (Trist, 1985b, p. 6). He especially liked Bion's private memorandum on using everyday hospital events and relationships as treatment—the first notion of a therapeutic community (later applied in a British military hospital and in the resettlement of repatriated war prisoners). Trist became an Army psychologist in 1942, rose to lieutenant-colonel, and won the Order of the British Empire. He also joined Bion and his colleague J.D. Sutherland in a collaboration that would have far-reaching consequences for the workplace. Among their first challenges was devising a field officer selection process as veteran officers were killed in early battles.

Bion proposed putting candidates into leaderless groups to solve field problems. He faced the soldiers with the dilemma of competing to pass a test that required cooperation. Bion observed that tension between cooperation and self-interest under stress was the officer's core battle dilemma. Selection became a therapeutic learning experience for soldiers and psychologists both, increasing the military's confidence in its ability to pick good officers. It was based on the concept of "handing back power from the technical to the military side," a tenet of later consultancy (Trist, 1985b, p. 9).

From experiments like these, Bion, a psychoanalyst, evolved another version of group dynamics in parallel with Lewin's. He imagined a group's dilemmas as an interplay between the task (its stated purposes) and the process, contained in three unconscious basic assumptions people make to contain anxiety. One, "fight-flight," is the tendency to battle others or withdraw. A second, "dependency," is the predilection to let the leader do everything. A third, "pairing," describes the inclination to find a partner in the group. Bion (1961) thought that exclusive pairs symbolized the unborn leader or messiah who guaranteed group survival, and also raised others' defensiveness. Each assumption required different leader behavior.

In 1957 Tavistock Institute devised a form of laboratory education on Bion's ideas. The "Tavi" groups emphasized structure, boundaries, and collective behavior when presented with responsibility for self-learning by an impassive authority. In contrast to NTL Institute's T-groups, Tavistock trainers refused interaction with group members. Instead, they delivered infrequent, impersonal, and sometimes cryptic analytic interpretations. ("This consultant believes that the group collectively avoids action and refuses to know that is what it does." Period. End quote. What did that mean? No comment.) People projected on the trainer every feeling they ever had about parents, teachers, or bosses. Acting as if the trainer really were these other characters, they lived out Bion's basic assumptions in the meeting room. Tavistock groups, like those of NTL Institute, became rich learning laboratories. (Later they were developed in the United States by the A. K. Rice Institute.)

You can see obvious analogies between these learning groups and workplaces. Conflicts, passivity, demoralization, and withdrawal are traceable to group feelings about authority. When people fight, run away from the task, pair up defensively, or depend on a leader to solve their problems, they become childish, immature, and unable to create or collaborate.

Keeping people working on mutual tasks and seeking to reduce dependency on experts or bosses are major consultant objectives with clients buffeted by high-anxiety change. They are at least as important as the "right answer." When people run away, fight, abdicate, or wait for a new leader to be born, they cannot act on right answers. This knowledge became a cornerstone of sociotechnical work design based on having people think for themselves.

Wilfred R. Bion, a pioneer of leadership and group behavior and a major force in the Tavistock Institute of Human Relations.

Source: Francesca Bion

Industrial Action Research in a Yorkshire Coal Mine

Like the T-group a few years earlier, sociotechnical practice was discovered in real time, and later turned into concepts and methods that could be used by others. More, it was stimulated—like group dynamics in both the United States and Britain—by a social crisis. At the end of World War II Britain had no investment capital. So Tavistock researchers devised an industrial action research program to find examples of quantum leaps in output based on human skill and brainpower rather than money.

In 1949 Tavistock student Kenneth Bamforth, a former coal miner and trade unionist, visited the South Yorkshire colliery where he had once worked. He was startled to discover self-regulating work teams sharing jobs, shifts, and responsibilities in a new seam. Excited, he returned to London and in Trist's living room described what he had seen. Trist went down into the mine with Bamforth. "I came up a different man," he said (Sashkin, 1980, p. 151). Later he wrote Fred Emery, "It was both moving and exciting to talk to the men about the value they placed on their experience in the newly formed autonomous groups. The older miners remembered the very small self-regulating groups of pre-mechanized days and how these had been broken up, with bad consequences for them when semi-mechanized long-walls had come in" (Emery, 1978, p. 6). In the long-wall system, each miner specialized. One shift blasted the rock, a second shift transported it out of the mine, and a third shift shored up the roof. If any shift stalled, subsequent shifts sat idle.

Improved roof control had made feasible short-wall mining in a rich coal seam not accessible by long-wall methods. To complement the new roof-control methods, miners on each shift undertook all three tasks, making possible continuous mining. "I was certain that the things I observed were of major significance as I experienced the two methods in parallel," Trist recalled. "It was the same sort of discovery that we had made with Bion in studying leaderless groups. All of the work on therapeutic communities . . . [and] all of Lewin's work on group dynamics came together in my mind as I was seeing it happen" (Sashkin, 1980, p. 151).

Two features struck Trist. First, the catalyst for change was a new technology. Long-wall miners underground had done one narrow task, under close supervision—an ugly way to make a living. Imagine a factory, damp, dark, and dangerous, in which workers move their machines daily, extract an ever-changing raw material, move supplies, equipment, and product through two narrow tunnels, and spend much of each day keeping the walls and ceiling from falling in. Add repetitious, stressful jobs—drilling, cutting, hewing, and building roof supports—and a coercive supervisor: voila, you have a workforce marked by 20 percent absenteeism, high attrition, frequent accidents, and low productivity.

In pick-and-shovel days the miners' fathers had worked in small, mutually supportive teams. Each team did whole groups of tasks, its members conscious of their dependence on one another for safety and output. In 1949 advanced roof-control technology had led a new generation back to the teamwork and self-control lost years before. Trist and colleagues (1963) titled their landmark study of coal mining *Organizational Choice: The Loss, Re-discovery, and Transformation of a Work Tradition.*

The second important feature, not fully appreciated at first, was where the teams came from. The general manager and miners, with union support, had jointly carried out the change. The miners showed they could make wise decisions about their own work. Bamforth and Trist called it "responsible autonomy." Extraordinary consequences followed. "In marked contrast to most mines," Trist wrote, "cooperation between task groups was everywhere in evidence; personal commitment was obvious, absenteeism low, accidents infrequent, productivity high" (1981, p. 8).

Although experimental sites were hard to come by, Trist and A.T.M. Wilson ([1951] 1983) found a general manager of an area with twenty collieries that had more advanced equipment. The manager had created "a new basic pattern" of continuous mining without being fully aware of the great social importance of what he had done.

Sad to say, the initial innovations ended when they ran afoul of Coal Board politics. But the cat was out of the bag. Another way of working was possible, one that defied beliefs about the primacy of technology. This way depended on finding what Trist called "the best match" among customer needs, the producers, and their equipment. Separate attempts to improve human relations alone fell short because they left the work structure intact. A new unit of analysis was needed that included both technology and people.

The researchers soon found another mine in the north of England using the group method (called "composite" mining) with long-wall technology, a feat mining experts had assured them was impossible. Now they could do a meticulous comparison of identical mines with different work organizations. They showed the decisive superiority of composite methods in output, costs, absenteeism, turnover, health, and safety. Tavistock confirmed the benefits of teamwork in several field studies in other industries undergoing technological change in the 1950s.

A Paradigm Shift

What was learned from these studies between 1949 and 1958 Trist and Emery later called a "paradigm shift," a wholly new view of workplace reality. "I never would have seen the old paradigm for what it was," Trist wrote Emery, "had I not experienced the reality of the new" (1977, p. 6). That this was a perceptual breakthrough can be seen in an early chart drawn by Trist for use by A.T.M. Wilson ([1951] 1983) in the first public presentation of their organizational studies when the Tavistock Group won the Kurt Lewin Memorial Award; see "Comparing Mining Methods."

The new systems, based on values similar to Frederick Taylor's, differed in every particular. Taylor sought to rationalize jobs, using a

COMPARING MINING METHODS

	LONGWALL	CONTINUOUS
WORK ROLES	FIXED	INTERCHANGEABLE
TASK ORDER	RIGID	FLEXIBLE
INDIVIDUAL SKILLS	SPECIALIZED	ALL-ROUND
RESPONSIBILITIES	OWN TASK	GROUP TASK
STATUS	DIFFERENCES	EQUAL
PAYMENT	PIECE-RATE	FLAT-RATE
SUPERVISION	EXTERNAL INSPECTION	INTERNAL LEADERSHIP
INTRA-SHIFT STRUCTURE	SEGMENTED	INTEGRATED
INTER-SHIFT RELATIONS	DEPENDENT	INDEPENDENT
COMMUNITY EFFORT	SPLITTING	COHESIVE

—A.T.M. WILSON, 1951

primitive stick-and-carrot psychology. Using a stopwatch, he broke jobs into tiny pieces—scoop a shovel full of coal, swing it in an arc, dump it in a car—each motion timed to be done as quickly as humanly (and, he believed, humanely) possible. Taylor offered the ablest people the carrot of a large bonus for higher output. He also removed all discretion from jobs. Engineers designed the tasks. Supervisors enforced standards and discipline. Workers did as instructed. Old paradigm mining came straight from Taylor.

Turning Taylor Upside Down. As students of Freud and colleagues of Bion, the Tavistock researchers brought a sophisticated view of individual and group dynamics into the mines. They understood technology in a way not possible a half-century earlier. Still, they started where Taylor did—with an analysis of the work itself. As Trist later wrote, "appropriate structural settings had to be created before desirable social climates and positive interpersonal relations would develop" (1981, p. 23).

There was a significant difference between Taylor's concept of structure and Tavistock's. Taylor reduced discretion at each step, reasoning that scientifically designed jobs would be learned fast and carried out accurately. This led to "dumber" jobs at every level, including, ironically, managers and specialists. Taylor's system evolved to deprive everybody of a whole view of what they were doing together. Engineers rationalized task efficiency, ignoring the customer. Supervisors enforced output, but had no criteria to judge whether engineers had done the job right. And workers, who knew a great deal that could not be put on a slide rule, were considered too ignorant to be consulted. So they passed mistakes down the line, investing creative energy in beating the rate system without being caught.

Sociotechnical designers put the fragmented jobs back together. They treated the work system, rather than discrete tasks, as the unit of analysis. The work group, not each person, became the focus for change. Sociotechnical principles called for internal regulation, each person monitoring and helping achieve group goals. It's obvious why McGregor saw participation as exemplary Theory Y in action.

Now the Tavistock researchers made a complementary discovery. Autonomous work groups could develop a capacity for self-regulation far beyond the best supervisor's powers of control. Both Lewin and Bion had caught the essence of processes as old as the species. Groups could be self-regulating if dedicated to a common task. What Taylor conceived as an adversarial herd instinct might also be a constructive force. The question was not whether such behavior was possible; that had been proved conclusively. The tantalizing question—we still ask it—was under what conditions it would happen.

People as Skilled Resources, Not Spare Parts. There were clues in the mines. Each miner learned several skills. They could cover for each other if somebody took sick. If work backlogged in one spot, they could unblock it quickly by putting more people on it. The group in a sense stored excess capacity.

Taylor's system relied on excess bodies—people not needed just now were standing around or making mischief. However—get this—too much work in process could idle people too. A blockage at one end of the line stemmed the flow. None of the other "spare parts" had anything to do until those before them completed their tasks. Everybody took a mini-holiday, even though under failure conditions there was more work to do than when things went smoothly.

Instead of one person/one task, the new principle became one person/many skills. That enormously increased team flexibility. (I started work teams in the 1960s out of frustration that two absentees in a twenty-five-person department could cut output 40 percent because nobody else knew how to do their simple tasks.) Taylor improved productivity by squeezing out of jobs human variability, managerial whim, and personal control. By reducing variability he increased safety, output, quality, and wages.

The world moved. Markets shifted, technologies evolved, workers became better educated, and management information improved. Yet Taylor's descendants had hardly passed "Go." Fifty years later the short-wall miners put the discretion back into jobs. Why? To restore the balance between technology and people that Taylor had sought to improve by removing discretion in the first place! The miners organized around the need to make frequent independent decisions that could not be captured in job descriptions. They discovered a design principle more suited to fast-changing technologies and unpredictable market pressures: increased variety for each person and department. The miners made a technical breakthrough. They enormously stepped up system control and flexibility. Imagine a system so versatile that at a moment's notice it can do any job required of it—a huge economic breakthrough. They reduced costs not controllable by technical means—absenteeism, turnover, safety, and quality. Most of all they achieved a social breakthrough, validating the enormous power of cooperation for personal and mutual benefit.

The miners not only found a superior way to dig coal. They conjured up an opposing organizational philosophy to scientific management. They enacted values of learning, social cooperation, and self-control in their methods. No wonder McGregor quickly picked up on this example. He was a frequent visitor to Tavistock in the 1950s, comparing notes on consultation and change projects. "He became part of the Tavistock tradition," Trist recalled. "We made connections between Theory X and the Taylor tradition going back to the 1890s—all that parent-child stuff" (December 23, 1986, interview). The coal studies vividly illustrated McGregor's belief that the most effective control systems were self-induced and knowledge-based. They were found where you'd least expect them—inside all people caught up in their own work and committed to a common task.

Enter Emery and Open Systems

The person who developed the vast potential of the mining discoveries was Fred Emery, an assertive young activist who came to Tavistock in 1951. Two men could hardly differ more in temperament and demeanor than the small, patient, diffident Trist and the tall, brusque, supremely confident Emery. Trist constantly questioned his own ideas, listening closely, receptive to input, seeking the nub of the other person's reality. Emery was output-focused, deeply committed to opinions about which he had given a lot of thought. He conversed through a barrage of citations—of theories, studies, concepts, and experiences—and would ignore questions he did not like. A born protagonist, he thrived on opposition.

Still, the two developed an affinity for one another. At age twenty-six, Emery found Trist, fifteen years his senior, a willing mentor. "Fred had a vast, incredible erudition," Trist recalled. "None of us had time for reading during the war. Fred had read and digested everything" (December 23, 1986, interview). To Trist's delight, Emery also was an avid student of Kurt Lewin's work. Later Emery would say that Trist was the first person who fully recognized his ability. And Emery, growing up among working people, having labored in an Australian mine, gravitated toward the British

Fred Emery, voracious reader, writer, conceptualizer, and translator of theory into democratic practices.

Source: Merrelyn Emery

coal mine studies. He wanted to change social systems, not simply observe them. So intertwined did the two names become that when they were invited to a conference in the United States in the 1960s, one confused young participant asked, "Which one of you is really Emery Trist?"

Emery introduced into Tavistock a new concept that would influence all subsequent work—the "open systems" thinking of biologist Ludwig yon Bertalanffy (1950). Emery, Trist told me, "was the first social scientist who fully appreciated the significance of von Bertalanffy's ideas for psychology and the social sciences" (December 23, 1986, interview). The open systems idea, simple to state but radical if acted on, is that all things somehow link up and influence one another. Cause and effect is not the only possible relationship between force and object. Indeed, the effect might be the cause. An amusing example is the observation that psychologists don't train pigeons to ring bells by giving them food. Instead pigeons, by ringing bells, train psychologists to feed them. The pigeon reinforces the researcher. Cause and effect become an illusion of linear thinking.

Taylor assumed that any system could be isolated, rationalized, and its living parts taught their unvarying responses. That led him to "systematize" a ball-bearing company even while its market was drying up (see Chapter Three). He had no concept of environment as a source of renewal. The Tavistock researchers noted that closed systems are cut off from the energy they need for survival, let alone renewal. The people in them cannot learn anything new.

Emery and Trist posed a more workable description of reality: systems import stuff—ideas, raw materials, money—convert them, and export goods, services, and ideas back to whoever will pay for them. All those who touch the process add value, making possible income, jobs, and security. The exchange renews a system, for it provides feedback on effects.

It's not enough to know how the technology works. It's not enough to know what makes people tick. It's not enough to understand sales, manufacturing, and cost accounting. To make a system hum, you need feedback from customers, suppliers, regulators, local communities—outsiders who make demands for service, products, compliance, support. They spark innovation and change. Lewin had said that you only can understand a person's behavior in the context of the here-and-now situation. In an open system, traffic flows both ways. Everything counts.

The most deceptive of all open systems notions was von Bertalanffy's concept of "equifinality," meaning equal paths to the same place or, roughly speaking, lots of ways to skin a cat. So profoundly simple is the idea that I could not grasp equifinality until I read a symposium in a woodworking magazine on how to sharpen chisels. Some twenty experts swore by water stones or oil stones, artificial or natural, from the quarries of Arkansas or the factories of Japan. One expert said rub the chisel back and forth on the stone, another said side to side, a third in small arcs, a fourth in large circles, a fifth in figure eights.

"This is no help at all," I said to my wife, Dorothy, a ceramic sculptor. "Every one of these guys says his way is the only right way. I still don't know what I should do."

"The answer is obvious," she said. "They all work."

Equifinality! Nature arrives at the same place from many directions, and people, being part of nature, can do the same thing. That scientific observation never occurred to "one best way" Taylor. In the mid-1950s in one field experiment and many descriptive studies, the Tavistock researchers documented many variations on composite mining teams that obtained roughly the same results. The signs all pointed the same way. "Equifinality," Trist told me, "was the end of the one best way. The full implications are still not grasped" (December 23, 1986, interview).

After the 1950s, any person who internalized the ideas posed by Trist and enlarged by Emery could never again make sense out of workplaces conceived in Taylor's terms.

■ ■ ■

"I'VE USED SOCIOTECHNICAL SYSTEMS IN MANY PLANT START-UPS..."

ATLANTIC BEACH, NY—Eric Trist and Fred Emery found in the 1950s that, by studying coal miners work team innovations, they could enhance the effectiveness of other systems. They created sociotechnical systems (STS), and it was to this practice that I became attracted in the mid-1990s. I helped in redesigning the work system in a toothpaste factory (one of two worldwide) of a major consumer products company. The plant had aging equipment and an "old school" mentality toward supervising workers. The plant manager and his team had grown up in the business with little managerial training or leadership development. The journeymen and foremen, however, owned their own work. They were increasingly frustrated with the lack of management support for improving the plant.

We spent eighteen months with employees, analyzing the work, identifying variances, and developing scenarios for an ideal work environment. As a result, new equipment was purchased, and a slow integration of self-managed work teams began. Teams planned and developed their own work schedules, managed budgets, made decisions about hiring and their own development. The plant's managers, following the work teams' success, had to relearn their roles and responsibilities. The entire plant worked together to focus on the future and improve its performance. In a few years, the people transformed their culture, embarking on a multiyear process of continuous improvement.

I have since used sociotechnical principles in many plant start-ups. Take, for example, two warehousing facilities for the GAP retailer when they founded their Old Navy Stores. They developed a new warehousing concept and wanted a new way to operate it. We devised multi-skilled teams around the new equipment and built in responsibility for cross-training and the self-management of scheduling, communication, and planning. I also worked as an internal consultant to the start-up of a Johnson & Johnson medical supplies facility in Mexico. The important sociotechnical principle—working in self-managed teams—meant that the plant was designed so that team members could see each other. We also built in job rotation within teams so that from day to day people could learn new skills and share responsibility for the overall production.

In 2008 I consulted to the VP of production at *The New York Times* in closing their printing plant and resizing their facility in College Point Queens, New York. They needed to decrease the size of the workforce while maintaining productivity and employee engagement. I worked with six unions, labor relations, and *Times* leadership to plan and manage the selection and assessment of the workforce and the team building that was needed to start up the resized operation. We developed the vision, values, and success profiles, communicating with and engaging the workforce continuously. We developed role descriptions and helped each employee understand the new requirements that included behavioral competencies and new goals. Subsequent activities included team building and leadership development for everyone. The social system focus enabled individuals to transition out of the company or into new roles in a caring way.

—Marianne Tracy, MSOD, Pepperdine University,
Tavistock Leadership Coach

chapter ELEVEN

Learning to Work in a New Paradigm

If we survey the various fields of modern science, we note a dramatic and amazing evolution. Similar conceptions and principles have arisen in quite different realms . . . and the workers in the individual fields are hardly aware of the common trend. Thus, the principles of wholeness, or organization, and of the dynamic conception of reality become apparent in all fields of science.

—Ludwig von Bertalanffy, *Problems of Life*, 1952, p. 176

I trace my first lesson in systems thinking to a clear winter day on the beach at Kitty Hawk, North Carolina. As an amateur pilot, I was living out a Walter Mitty fantasy of the first powered airplane flight sixty years earlier. Surely you've seen the famous 1903 photo of the brothers Wright dressed as if for a formal picnic, with coats, ties, and peaked caps, Orville lying prone over the "flyer's" lower wing, Wilbur leaning into the wind.

Aviation pioneers—notably Otto Lilienthal, on whose calculations the science of flight rested in 1900—had figured out how to get planes into the air. They did not know how to control them. Lilienthal died flying a glider that he got aloft but could not steer. The Wrights, self-taught bicycle mechanics, took a different tack. Birds do it, bees do it, even fleas do it; why couldn't engineers do it?

In 1900 Wilbur, the philosophical brother, wrote to his mentor Octave Chanute, "What is chiefly needed is skill rather than machinery. It is possible to fly without motors, but not without knowledge and skill. This I conceive to be fortunate, for man, by reason of his greater intellect, can more reasonably hope to equal birds in knowledge, than to equal nature in the perfection of her machinery" (McFarland, 1953, Vol. 1, p. 15).

How did two young tinkerers from Ohio succeed where better-educated contemporaries had failed? You can find the answer in the Kitty Hawk museum. They alone were systems thinkers. They alone identified three interconnected facts of flight demonstrated by birds without motors. To hang wings on a bicycle and ride it through the sky, you had to figure out how to:

1. Get it into the air.
2. Keep it in the air.
3. Make it go where you want.

Not a bad management model, huh?

The Wrights tried out Lilienthal's calculations in a primitive wind tunnel and reached a startling conclusion. The whole "science" of flight was wrong! You could get killed flying a wing designed on Lilienthal's principles, a hypothesis that brave pioneer already had proved. (He may have been the prototype for my flight instructor's admonition, "There are old pilots and bold pilots but no old, bold pilots.") Watching birds twist their wing tips to control direction, the Wrights figured out the aileron. Next time you sit over a wing, notice the slight movement of one segment of the trailing edge each time the plane turns. That is how we humans, lacking perfect machinery, apply knowledge to imitate birds.

The Wrights turned to the other problems: an engine light enough to lift a wing, powerful enough to overcome gravity, durable enough to run a long time between overhauls. Then there was engine torque, the tendency of a prop turning in one direction to push the nose in the other. For smooth control they had to counteract the tail's wanting to skid in a turn, which meant coordinating aileron and rudder. They worked that one out by leaning the craft like a bicycle, instead of steering it like a car.

The flyer was an unstable machine in an unstable medium. Brute force made no difference; the birds flew effortlessly. To maintain control required exquisite balance among the system's many elements. Eventually the Wrights threw out all the "scientific" knowledge of aviation (Westcott and Degen, 1983). To fly like birds, they worked out how each part of the system affected the other parts. They invented their own wing, elevator, rudder, engine, and propeller. They used wires to hold the plane together and to link the controls. The first flight lasted twelve seconds. Within two years they could keep their flyer aloft for half an hour. After that even a natural dodo bird like me could become an eagle in ten hours, and in 1953 I actually did.

Work As a Systems Problem

What Eric Trist and Fred Emery did with work design after studying coal miners ranks with the Wrights' rethinking of flight from observing buzzards. Taylor's old solution was like Lilienthal's, incomplete and unscientific. The Tavistock researchers set out to discover whether their new systemic principles—notably adaptation to technology through unspecialized teamwork—were applicable elsewhere. They had repeated the South Yorkshire results in one field experiment and had observed viable variations elsewhere (Trist and others, 1963). Were these early results a fluke? To be valid, a new paradigm had to be repeatable in diverse workplaces.

Indian Loom Sheds. In the 1950s an important work-redesign opportunity emerged in the loom sheds of the Calico Mills at Ahmedabad in India. Trist happened to sit next to the owner, husband of a Tavistock student, at a party and heard his complaints about installing new machinery. Trist proposed the services of A. K. Rice, a former manager, personnel executive, and colonial service officer.

Rice went to India in 1953. Through a translator he suggested to workers, supervisors, and the manager that individual specialties be replaced by worker groups responsible for all tasks. His proposal derived from all that was then known, especially Lewin's and Bion's group concepts, von Bertalanffy's open systems thinking, and the coal-mine studies. The workers came back next day with an action plan that they and the managers implemented. Rice had used his expertise to be a catalyst, not a designer. It was a dramatic shift in the use of specialized knowledge.

Backed up by phone calls to Trist in London, Rice stimulated benchmark changes in supervision. Taylor was on the right track seeking to cut out authoritarian behavior. The British miners did it by decentralizing, broadening skills, and practicing self-regulation. Rice's adaptation made supervisors resources to worker teams operating the loom sheds. They became teachers and managed links with other departments rather than the actual work. As predicted, output, quality, and job satisfaction improved (Rice, 1958).

This adaptation of Lewinian thinking from the 1930s—manage the boundaries and help people learn self-correction—has proved durable to this day. Case studies of new design worksites all show that productivity rises when managers and supervisors guard the goals, values, and inputs, while workers manage the output. To reinforce self-control inside a system, the leaders must stay outside, working on it, not in it. Staff experts seek continually to transfer what they know. Where this does not happen, we get high error rates, unexplainable failures, dissatisfied customers, and a demoralized workforce. (I happened to be present at a seminar in the early 1980s when somebody asked Fred Emery, for the umpteenth time, to define "quality of working life." Said he with a snort, "It means get the foreman out of the system!")

In India Rice also built upon Bion's concept of group task. Every work system, said Rice, has a "primary task," its central purpose or core mission (Miller, 1975). If people can define their primary task, and study its social, technical, and economic assumptions, they can invent flexible, adaptable, dynamic, and self-renewing work systems. To get it into the air, you need a primary task. To keep it in the air, you need a new form of first-line leadership. To make it go where you want, you need self-control, based on feedback from those who use the outputs.

Norwegian Industrial Democracy Projects. Now there were two examples from two industries in two cultures. The next great leap came in Norway, an egalitarian nation with traditions of stable labor relations, social welfare, and work reform. A joint national committee of trade union and business leaders had been formed to shore up a flagging economy with democratic initiatives. Its members had fought together in the World War II underground. Now they set up a research institute at the Technical University in Trondheim. Their sparkplug was a former Resistance fighter and social scientist, Einar Thorsrud, a regular visitor to Tavistock in the 1950s. In 1962 he invited Emery and Trist to help discover how to "change work itself in such a way that new economic, technological, and social needs are met" (Thorsrud, 1984, p. 344).

Together they undertook four work redesigns—in a wire-drawing plant, a pulp and paper mill, a panel heater assembly operation, and a fertilizer plant. In each case productivity and quality increased at first. But the researchers soon learned how intertwined were history, economics, technology, and politics in starting and sustaining change. Trust was a long time building among workers, management, and the researchers. It took significant political skill to maintain public support. Changes in the work itself threatened supervisors and engineers. "Specialists were shocked to see how their models and measurements were inadequate or even irrelevant when workers were given a chance to use something more than their hands," wrote Thorsrud. "The very concept of controlled experimentation was open to doubt" (1984, p. 346).

Deep anxieties surfaced as status differences among supervisors, industrial engineers, and workers blurred. Self-managing teams were vulnerable unless managers at the top and middle appreciated how a simple principle—multiple skills—irrevocably altered their roles. Even when results could be shown beyond doubt, other departments and companies, as in British mining, did not adopt the new methods. There was something deep in the human psyche that clung to familiar patterns, even obsolescent ones. Curiously, the Norwegian results had significant impact in Sweden, where hundreds of adaptations occurred in the 1970s, including the famous Volvo project (Trist, 1971).

Norwegians associated with Oslo's Work Research Institutes kept the research tradition going for decades after. In the mid-1980s significant new labor-management initiatives were underway in several industries to put methods of inquiry, search, and democratic dialogue into the equation for creating more productive workplaces (Gustavsen, 1985). That work continues to this day.

Major New Concepts

Kurt Lewin said that if you want to understand a system, you have to change it. Now Emery, his close student, produced from the change efforts in Norway a series of conceptual "aha's." Social and technical systems, Emery observed, follow different logics, one derived from physics, the other from social relations. Either system maximized alone might reduce the output of the whole. Thus the requirements for each must be considered together whenever work is redesigned, what he called "joint optimization."

Emery's insight was widely ignored. It became common for consultants, after engineers had the "one best" technological solution, to be asked to graft on an "ideal" social system. Yet quality of output and work life both required involving people in rethinking the whole process, giving rise to a fallacy that sociotechnical design "takes too long." (In 2004, Sandra Janoff and I helped IKEA employees plan the restructuring of their global distribution system for ten thousand products in one three day meeting. See Chapter Twenty-Two.)

The Second Design Principle. Emery (1967) also contributed the insight that workers with multiple skills embody a design principle refuting Taylor's. Every work system requires redundancy—a way of storing excess capacity to cover fluctuating demands for goods or services. Taylor advocated redundant people—one person, one task, all interchangeable within specialties, but not between them. From sociotechnical studies we derive redundant functions—multiple skills for all, allowing flexible workloads within and between. Only redundant functions allow people to deal quickly with rapid shifts in markets, technologies, lifestyles, and jobs. Emery, an antiauthoritarian like Taylor, saw multi-skilled teamwork as the key to undoing parent-child style supervision.

Key Factors for Designing Work. At last Emery and Trist proposed a framework for work design. They drew on their own work and that of Louis E. Davis, a mechanical engineer who spent a year at Tavistock in the mid-1950s. Davis had shown that "scientific" engineers routinely impoverished job content, reducing motivation. Personnel people then sought to motivate people by improving working conditions, selection, training, and wage incentives—none of which added control, growth, or social meaning (Davis, Canter, and Hoffman, 1955). Personnel was mistaking satisfiers, to use Herzberg's term (Herzberg, Mausner, and Snyderman, 1959), for the motivators the engineers had taken away. Emery (1964) listed six intrinsic factors that make work motivating and six satisfiers that were necessary though not sufficient for high output.

Motivators

1. Variety and challenge
2. Elbow room for decision making
3. Feedback and learning
4. Mutual support and respect
5. Wholeness and meaning
6. Room to grow

Satisfiers

1. Fair and adequate pay
2. Job security
3. Benefits
4. Safety
5. Health
6. Due process

Of the motivators, variety, elbow room, and feedback should be optimal—not too much, which adds stress, nor too little, which produces tedium. On the other hand, people need as much respect, growth, and wholeness as technology and the environment will allow (Emery, 1959). Satisfiers, by contrast, are extrinsic conditions, necessary but not sufficient to motivate high output.

Emery (1978) and his wife later created simple do-it-yourself methods for creating jobs on the twelve dimensions. Their model replaces Taylor's as a core job design concept today. It is worth noting that the satisfiers are what unions always fought for, while motivators are central to management's wish for quality and output. Only in workplaces embodying both can people realize the century-old dreams of labor-management cooperation.

An Ethical Imperative. Researchers regularly find evidence to support these principles. Studies of Swedish and American men, for example, show that the more influence people have over their jobs, the less prone they are to heart disease (Sashkin, 1984). Marshall Sashkin has argued that low control of their work hurts people physically and emotionally (p. 4). Therefore, ethical managers would not knowingly reduce people's control by excluding them from matters that affect them. Others have considered participation and work design optional techniques rather than a new paradigm for

EFFECTIVE ORGANIZATIONS

OLD PARADIGM [EARLY 20TH CENTURY]	NEW PARADIGM [LATE 20TH CENTURY]
• TECHNOLOGY FIRST	• SOCIAL/TECHNICAL SYSTEMS OPTIMIZED TOGETHER
• PEOPLE AS MACHINE EXTENSION	• PEOPLE COMPLEMENT MACHINE
• PEOPLE AS SPARE PARTS	• PEOPLE AS SCARCE RESOURCES
• NARROW TASKS, SIMPLE SKILLS	• MULTIPLE, BROAD SKILLS
• EXTERNAL CONTROL: PROCEDURES BOOK	• SELF-CONTROL: TEAMS AND DEPARTMENTS
• MANY LEVELS, AUTOCRATIC STYLE	• FLAT ORGANIZATION PARTICIPATIVE STYLE
• COMPETITIVE	• COOPERATIVE
• ORGANIZATION'S PURPOSES ONLY	• INDIVIDUAL AND SOCIAL PURPOSES INCLUDED
• ALIENATION: "IT'S ONLY A JOB"	• COMMITMENT: "IT'S <u>MY</u> JOB"
• LOW RISK-TAKING	• INNOVATION

—ADAPTED FROM ERIC TRIST, 1978, p. 17

fast-changing societies. Not everyone appreciates how worker participation in work design alters all past concepts of effectiveness. Some simply consider it an optional technique (Locke, 1986). I believe it is by far the most successful option to Taylorism. Note how the modern version, described in "Effective Organizations," expands upon Wilson's coal-mine example in Chapter Ten.

Representation vs. Involvement. Sociotechnical design extends democratic and humane values in the workplace. Many European nations took a bolder step: worker or union participation on boards of directors and in national policymaking. Both modes embody democratic values. However, representation in management is not the same as fixing structural problems associated with mindless jobs and tight supervision. Norwegian researchers, for example, tracked what happened in five government-owned companies required by law to have workers on their boards. Contrary to expectation, neither rank-and-file participation nor productivity went up, and worker alienation did not decline.

Only when sociotechnical design principles were applied did major changes show up. In the wire-drawing plant redesign, for example, production went up so much that its workers took home more money than skilled people in other operations, and the union withdrew because of members' pay differentials. This is perhaps the most puzzling aspect of new-paradigm change. Taylor was right when he said the pie could be made larger. He was wrong in thinking that is what labor leaders, or managers, always want. See "Economic Paradox in the Workplace" on the next page for a contemporary example.

The early Norwegian experience showed how hard it is to untangle long-standing work cultures and rewards. This discovery showed how much old and new paradigms were in conflict. Unless a whole system could be switched over, innovation was bound to be swallowed up. Old norms are so deeply entrenched that they could not be changed incrementally. That's one reason pilot projects don't spread.

Is it ignorance or the "shadow" side of our natures that keeps us from making and sharing more? We still have a great deal to learn about the politics of effective work systems. The game is deeply rooted in our own inner dialogues about freedom and control, initiative and dependence.

> **Economic Paradox in the Workplace**
>
> Firms still reduce good economic results to control employees' ability to share more of the fruits of their efforts, a phenomenon that threatens free enterprise and democracy now, just as it did in Taylor's time. I know of a company that was acquired in the 1970s by a conglomerate. Its managers allocated workloads between plants to achieve maximum profits on each job. Because all shared in bonuses, there was no competition for profitable jobs. One plant, by design, showed higher profits than the others, but all managers shared a third of total net profits as bonuses. The parent firm considered this sum too high, even though the company was two and a half times more profitable than its competition.
>
> First the parent (apt term) reduced the total bonus pot, then put a cap on individual bonuses. Next it sought to allocate bonuses by plant instead of companywide, insisting that fragmented incentives would make all plants as profitable as the top one. Since the managers knew this was impossible, they were demoralized, cynical, and "resistant to change." It's this version of capitalism that keeps Marxism alive.

To become more aware of these dialogues is to stop saying "bottom line" as if systems generate money apart from the willingness of people to produce. The bottom line on bottom lines is dignity, meaning, and community. It delights me that W. Edwards Deming (1982), the quality expert, made quantum leaps in productivity by removing production goals and substituting an orientation toward quality. Top executives as interested in money as they are reported to be might take that idea more seriously. That many don't is a commentary on the human need to keep control.

The Knowledge Revolution

Two notable changes have occurred in industry since people started thinking open systems. First, the march of technology has taken workers outside the technology. In Taylor's factories, workers were extensions of machines. Now, machines do physical work better and faster than people do. However, people have to be smarter about using them. Instead of adding energy, factory workers increasingly add intelligence and judgment.

Second, knowledge work jobs are growing faster than physical work. The "output" of an airline reservations system is information and customer satisfaction. The worker, Trist pointed out, had became "a fact-finder, interpreter, diagnostician, judge, adjuster, and change agent; whatever else he does is secondary" (1981, p. 88). In fact, workers do many tasks once reserved for managers, exercising judgment and discretion exactly of the sort Taylor identified as dysfunctional. When knowledge workers don't have responsibility, we face serious accidents, foul-ups, poor service, high costs—all the things Taylor sought to eliminate.

In modern industrial plants, ideas like time and motion study, individual incentives, and piece rates become irrelevant. Control systems are based on constant feedback and course correction. Work means hand, eye, brain. Workers control the controls, not the machines. They must make decisions based on understanding the whole process.

In a powerful book, Larry Hirschhorn dissected the Three Mile Island nuclear accident to prove his point that "machine systems eventually fail, given the realities of materials and human behavior" (1984, p. 86). Nuclear power workers misread their gauges, making wrong assumptions taught to them by engineers who had anticipated all emergencies except the one that occurred. The workers turned off vibrating pumps, for example, although the vibration meant the pumps had never gone on. Instead of thinking it through, they followed a checklist, "relying too much on first impressions, the victims of their own tunnel vision" (Hirschhorn, 1984, p. 89). What they needed was conceptual skills, the kind talented auto mechanics use to rule out causes of unwanted vibrations by building a Gestalt of the whole problem. In 2010 a horrendous oil spill in the Gulf of Mexico proved that point yet again.

"External supervision may correct errors," said Trist, "but only internal supervision can prevent their occurrence." When change is rapid and continuous, even an automated plant is in a constant state of redesign. It cannot be left to function automatically day in and day out. It puts people who work there on a continual "expedition of learning and innovation from which there is no return" (1981, p. 89).

The "Turbulent" Environment

I cannot leave this discussion of open systems in the workplace without visiting the most dramatic implication of all. No workplace can exist in isolation from rapid, unpredictable, and discontinuous changes on the world scene. "The rate of change was picking up so much," Trist told me, "that neither we nor our clients knew what was happening to us" (January 9, 1987, interview).

From this observation came Emery and Trist's most widely cited paper. "The Causal Texture of Organizational Environments" (1964) described how outside events interacted to produce conditions organizations can neither control nor ignore. Increasing unpredictability in technology and markets, Trist told Emery when they were together in Norway, it felt to him like an airplane flight he had taken through extremely rough air. He was upset by the turbulence. So was born the concept of the turbulent field—relentless, unpredictable swings in the economic life of communities, governments, and organizations (Emery and Trist, 1964). This remains the central fact of life for organizations worldwide today, requiring unprecedented forms of planning. This environment, what my friend Peter Vaill (1996) called "permanent white water," requires companies to course correct all the time or face serious disruptions.

This insight confirmed for me that Lewin's unfreezing, moving, and refreezing was no longer a viable model of the change process. In Chapter Eighteen I propose a new practice theory for managing turbulence. In Chapters Twenty through Twenty-Two I describe three modes of action, two of which build upon pioneering work by Emery and Trist.

Communities, States, Nations

It does not take much imagination to see that turbulent environments push us to think about society as the context for effective work design. Employment security, for example, once largely local, had by 2010 become a global concern. Emery and Trist early on extended their thinking to whole industries, communities, societies, and global networks. The noted Jamestown (New York) Area Labor Management Committee, for example, was an extension of sociotechnical thinking to an entire region (Trist, 1985a).

From 1972 on, this effort to increase employment through community cooperation resulted in more than forty workplace innovations, attracted a new Cummins Engine plant, and influenced the renewal of downtown Jamestown. This same spirit infused the twenty-year-old Craigmillar Festival Society, an annual community music and drama event, which brought hope to an economic-disaster area near Edinburgh, Scotland (Trist, 1985). Such projects were commonplace as I revised this book, adding Future Search examples from various cultures (Weisbord and Janoff, 2010).

On several continents, then, we were in a quantum leap into a workplace equivalent of what Star Trekkies know as "hyperspace" and worlds where no person has gone before. It was a workplace shifting from physical manipulation to machine-controlled processes, from doing the work to making sure machines do it right, from predictable sequences to "anything can happen." It was a global society awakening to the interdependence of every living thing.

Three lessons came roaring through for me as I compared this systems redesign history to my own experience. First, we have real choices to make, not trivial ones, about who controls what and who ought to. The future doesn't just happen; we carve it out of what we do today. Second, none of us is expert enough to supply somebody else's answer. If we delude ourselves that we do, we can only make change problems worse. Finally, we have to learn effective participation. We cannot do that with buzzwords, hoopla, and PowerPoints unless we follow by involving people to influence policy, procedure, structure, and division of work.

To sum up, informed self-control, not close supervision, is the only way to operate new technologies without making mistakes so bad we might not live to say "I'm sorry." Knowledge and skill can't be pumped into people the way traditional schools have done it. They can be mastered only by collaborative work on the job. That requires the learner's direct involvement. The future of democratic values—dignity and worth of each person, free choice and free expression, social responsibility coupled to personal opportunity—depends on what we do today. Lewin understood that, and the sociotechnical thinkers, led by Trist and Emery, provided us with the implementation tools. By 2011, the knowledge revolution offered unprecedented opportunity for those of us committed to the integration of social, technical, and economic values.

Remembering Eric Trist and Fred Emery

In 1987, Eric Trist went into semi-retirement in Gainesville, Florida, with Beulah, for twenty-seven years his wife, friend, companion, secretary, and administrative assistant in numerous projects. He died June 4, 1993, in Carmel, California, at age 83. He had lost a leg to diabetes a year earlier and had a stroke two weeks before his death. Eric was my friend, colleague, mentor, gentlest collaborator, and toughest critic. For fifteen years I had enjoyed his calm presence, dry wit, boundless compassion, and intellectual rigor. Eric had a quality shared with his mentor Kurt Lewin. That was the ability to find a kernel of truth in every statement, a seed of constructive possibility in every experiment, no matter how outlandish. I had seen Eric many times take a novel idea, turn it this way and that, and hand it back to its originator richer, fuller, and more insightful. That's what he did when he urged me toward "a conceptual emboldening" that resulted in the learning curve that became the framework for this book.

Eric, modest in the extreme, had a hard time accepting that his concepts had influenced so many people. He was uncomfortable if praise for his work did not include his collaborator Fred Emery. I marveled at the way these two polar opposites had produced so much together. Their relationship surely validated the cliché about the creative use of differences.

I visited Eric often over the years—in Swarthmore when he taught at the University of Pennsylvania, later when he retired to Florida, then at Denman Island in British Columbia, his happy summer retreat. When we met I would tell him of my latest experiments with work redesigns involving the "whole system in the room" and a Future Search model based on confronting chaos rather than rigorous analysis. Eric would listen intently, reflect a while, and unfailingly hand me back the same gift—the courage of my convictions. I always came from a talk with him believing that whether something was "practical" was secondary to whether I believed it was the right thing to do.

Eric often would describe the ups and downs of the trilogy he was editing on the work of the Tavistock Institute (Trist and Murray, 1990–1997). Progress always varied with his iffy health. I saw him for the last time a few months before his death in the Carmel, California, apartment where he had moved so that he could watch the Pacific Ocean from his window. In an intimate moment, he told me that for years he had stifled intense feelings of vulnerability certain to well up in anybody whose passion was changing the world. He was sure that "stiff upper lip syndrome" had contributed to his medical crises, including heart surgery.

At the end he grew more introspective, studying Eastern philosophies in counterpoint to Western science and wondering whether there was still time to change himself. On good days, he read, wrote, edited, and answered his mail. The unflappable Beulah Trist—his wife, business manager, secretary, cook, chauffeur, and best friend—energetically organized their lives to make work and good times with friends doable. On bad days, he fretted and slept.

A fact of his biography haunts me. Earlier I wrote that he had descended from a long line of British sea captains. He alone chose Cambridge. The course he charted irrevocably changed the way we encounter the world. Having turned his back on the sea, still he needed to be near it and walked the beach whenever he could. Eric's spirit was large, generous, and timeless as his beloved ocean. He had a great head for ideas, as I have amply shown. It was his great heart I missed most when he was gone.

A Collaboration Resumed

Fred Emery worked tirelessly after 1969 in Australia to institutionalize new-paradigm thinking. In the mode of "barefoot social scientists," he and his wife Merrelyn Emery stimulated hundreds of projects and Search Conferences with people in every sector. Emery and Trist, after a hiatus of some years, resumed their collaboration in the 1990s. Fred assisted Eric with his Tavistock trilogy, picking up the editing of the sociotechnical volume after Eric's death. Fred died at age seventy-one at his home in Canberra, Australia, on April 10, 1997, four years after Eric. I met Fred through Eric, and while we never became close, I found him a stimulating person to know. Fred had a tremendous capacity for synthesizing and seeing the big picture. He was generous with his time and his papers when I was writing this book. Fred was a better theorist than consultant. He never became much of a group facilitator, nor, I suspect, did he wish to.

Fred had little patience for meetings. I recall him sitting in back, outside the circle, listening, letting people muck around, then coming in with a definitive statement that rendered further conversation unnecessary. Merrelyn Emery was the practitioner, designing and leading hundreds of groups during the development of the Search Conference and Participative Redesign methods. It was Fred who suggested that a dialogue among practitioners was the way to test whether there was the basis for the book that became *Discovering Common Ground* (Weisbord and others, 1992). And both Emerys' insights in that book helped many others crystallize their thinking and improve their practices.

Eric Trist, self-effacing and open to anything, had enormous curiosity. Fred Emery, a blustery character, had a hard time with ideas that did not fit his frameworks. I was conscious in writing *Productive Workplaces* of my debt to Fred for his awesome intellect, to Eric for his unfailing support, and to both for the fruits of their remarkable collaboration.

■ ■ ■

"A CONGRUENCE BETWEEN THEIR VALUES AND MINE..."

BOSTON, MA—In 1983, while a senior Digital Equipment Corporation executive, I took a master's degree in organization development, intending to learn how to apply social psychology to my work at Digital. I read *Productive Workplaces* as I was considering a radical career change from computer engineering management to organization development consulting. I would have to leave a lot behind, hoping that this new field would provide me more socially meaningful work. *Productive Workplaces* pushed me over the edge. I was deeply inspired reading about Douglas McGregor and Fred Emery. I felt the congruence between their values and mine, and I found a new confidence that I was heading in the right direction.

A few years later, I was invited to join the corporate consulting group, where I helped teams be more effective and coached managers in roles like the one I had held. By 1990 our company was in a tailspin. Coaching and team building would not fix a strategic crisis. On a whim, I went off to Workplace Australia to explore the Search Conference, what Bunker and Alban (1997) later called a "large group intervention" [LGI]. There I met its creators, Fred and Merrelyn Emery, and also Marv Weisbord,. It was a joint meeting of business, labor, and government celebrating Fred's work. Inspired by that event, I thought perhaps that whole-system meetings in Digital might help save the company. We held several Search Conferences, but not at a level that might have turned the company around. Meanwhile, Marv and Sandra Janoff were developing what I had wished to do, a search design more appealing for North American culture. I decided to support that work and joined the Future Search Network.

I left Digital in 1993 to start my own consulting firm. That year I helped Katharine Esty with a Future Search in Cambridge, Massachusetts. After that she and I made many trips to South Asia and Africa to work on iodine deficiency disease, maternal mortality, child labor, early childhood development, food security, and population planning. In Bangladesh we trained many NGO staff in Future Search. A recent program on NPR revealed statistics showing that public health in Bangladesh had improved much more than in India, despite the latter's superior economy. I'd like to think that our work in fostering cooperation among Bangladesh's NGOs may have had broader impact than we imagined.

I expanded my repertoire of LGIs, learning from Dick and Emily Axelrod, Kathy Dannemiller and Robert Jacobs, Harrison Owen, Alan Klein, and others. Elizabeth Olson and I put together a three-day LGI seminar that gave consultants an overview of "seminal models." By 2001 nearly all my large group events were custom designed to client needs. Since these events would only happen once, they had to work the first time. And, to my surprise, they did!

I had learned something about the sequence of design elements, listening to the system ahead of the event, framing a relevant purpose, and many other things. I partnered with Nancy Aronson for a seminar series that we call "Advancing the Common Good." Our goals are to teach leaders how to improve every meeting from three hours and up and how to design and lead their own effective large-group interventions.

My client work has created a life of meaning surpassing my dreams back in 1987. I've been blessed with some great clients: the Boston University School of Dental Medicine, which adopted large-group interventions as its way of dealing with systemic change; 3M; City University of New York; Starbucks; and many others.

—Gil Steil, Gil Steil Associates

PART THREE

Learning from Experience

"I think you are wrong to want a heart. It makes most people unhappy," said the Wizard.
"That must be a matter of opinion," replied the Tin Woodman.
"I will bear all the unhappiness without a murmur if you will give me a heart."

—*The Wonderful Wizard of Oz,* Baum, 1900, 1958, p. 114

I retold in Part One the stories of the pioneers who shaped my vision of productive workplaces. I showed how three diverse traditions—scientific management, organization development, and sociotechnical systems design—evolved to integrate social values eroded by the Industrial Revolution. All three targeted authoritarian supervision, irrational work, and unproductive conflict.

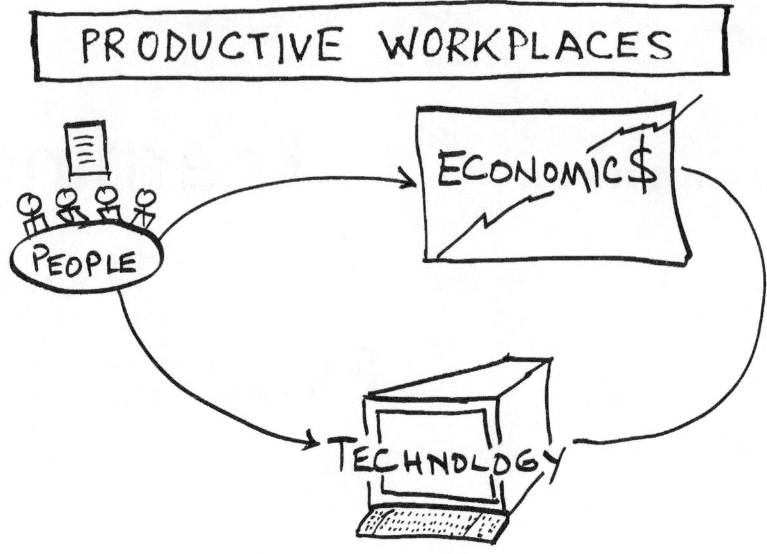

All made possible constructive activities not previously imagined. Each could be misapplied as well. If I learned anything all these years it is that when you set sail to improve workplaces you will always come up short focusing only on technology, only on money, only on human resources. The sensible way to make a commitment to "our people" is to have our people work together in rethinking their own work—as captured in the "Productive Workplaces" drawing.

Participation not only builds commitment. It ensures everybody learns essential things they did not know. You have no better choice than learning how to include as many stakeholders as you can.

In Part Three, I propose a practice for fostering whole systems learning. Chapter Twelve describes how managers and consultants evolved away from Taylor's technical methods toward Lewin's, including people and situation both. In Chapter Thirteen I illustrate this with my own action-research cases and analyze second-generation applications of Lewin's work.

In Chapter Fourteen I critique my early cases and advocate an evolution beyond Lewin's model to one more suited to an increasingly diverse, fast-changing world. In Chapter Fifteen I speculate on two "whole system" cases that changed my approach toward consultation. In 1987 I likened my applications to the early DC-3 airliners—bigger, safer, more comfortable, and faster than open-cockpit Jennies, but not big enough, comfortable enough, or fast enough to suit our fast-changing expectations. Now we are flying jumbo jets and imagining space ships.

I added Chapters Sixteen and Seventeen in 2004. Both involved training workshops, one in a medical center, the other in a steel mill. For decades many in my business assumed that people could not improve workplaces without training in—pick your favorites—assertiveness, communication, computer literacy, conflict management, cultural sensitivity, finance, group dynamics, decision making, leadership, negotiation skills, problem solving, statistical process control, whatever.

We theorized that when every person received the same inputs, they would transform their organizations. "Flavor of the month" programs came and went like songbirds with the seasons. People improved themselves more than their workplaces. What training did not give them was influence over policy, procedure, system, and structure. Eventually, I concluded that the quickest way to empower people was to "get the whole system in the room" to do a consequential task on a relatively level playing field. I came to this conclusion via two remarkable training experiences. Both cases violated a critical training norm. Instead of homogeneous peer groups, we involved people from many levels and functions at once.

Chapter Sixteen describes how doctors, nurse practitioners, and pharmacists learned primary care program management together. Chapter Seventeen tells about making systems "thinking" experiential in a steel mill so that anybody with heart could apply it.

chapter
TWELVE

Putting Action Research to Work

Now they wanted . . . manual control of the rocket! They weren't kidding! . . . How could they be serious!—the engineers would say. Any chance of a man being able to guide a rocket from inside a ballistic vehicle, a projectile, was so remote as to be laughable. This proposal was so radical the engineers knew they would be able to block it. It was no laughing matter to the seven pilots, however.

—Tom Wolfe, *The Right Stuff*, 1980, p. 161

In one memorable scene in Tom Wolfe's astronaut fable, the Apollo pilots force engineers to modify the first space capsule, adding a window, an escape hatch, and manual controls. They renamed it a spacecraft. When an engineer cites high costs, one astronaut says, "No bucks, no Buck Rogers!" Engineers and astronauts enact a high-tech version of omniscient parent and dependent child—Theory X comes to outer space. It is an exact replay of the process Taylor elevated to a high art. (Similar disconnects and narrow cost focus led to the 1986 space shuttle Challenger disaster and in 2010 to the monumental Gulf of Mexico BP oil spill.) Also known as the medical or doctor-patient model, it's typical of transactions built on the belief that only technical experts know a system.

The Wright Brothers designed, built, and flew their own airplane. Theirs was a systems thinking triumph, wedding experimentation, intuition, cooperation, and persistence. They would not risk their lives until they had worked through all the details. The first astronauts had little to say about the design of the first space vehicle. Far from collaborators, they were considered research subjects. Chimpanzees took the same tests as pilots, and a chimp imported from West Africa became the first "American" in space. The astronauts refused the chimp's contract. Unless they could control the spacecraft, they wouldn't fly.

Here was the traditional experts-know-best scenario, enacted with sophisticated pilots, most trained as engineers themselves.

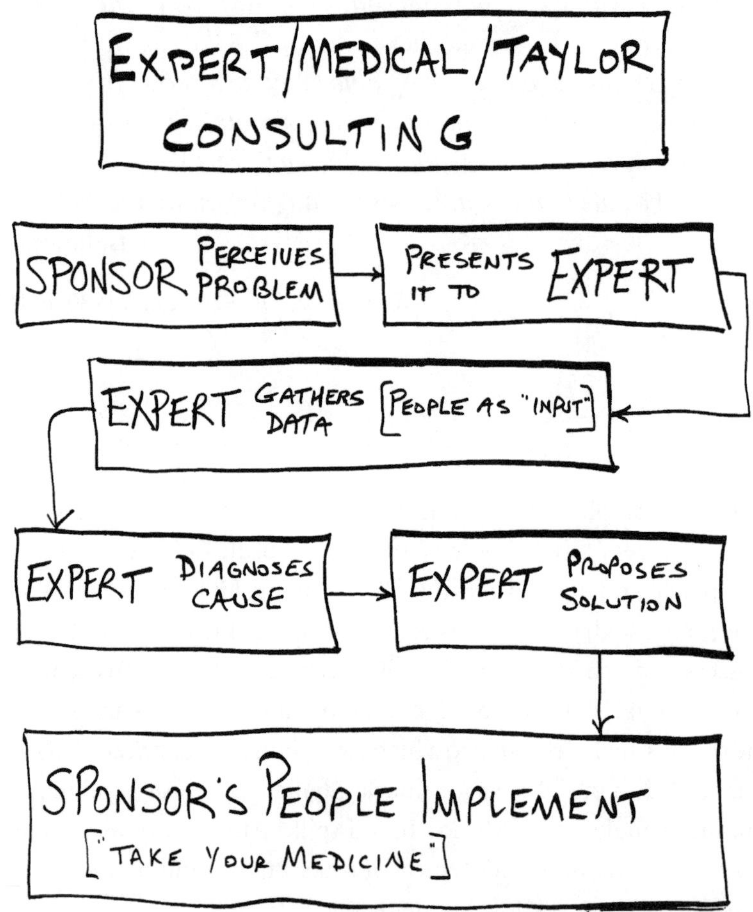

Going Beyond Taylor

Taylor's model assumed that only his experts could get the right data to solve the problem, a left-brain triumph with the right brain in suspension. "Expert problem solving" assumes that every result is traceable to a cause that only experts can pinpoint. Both model and method omit an astonishing variable: whether other actors will play their assigned roles.

The expert model is more likely to succeed the simpler the problem, the more cause and effect correspond, and the less others' motivation matters. Emergencies are classic examples. If clear-air turbulence puts your plane in a dive, rely on the pilot to pull out of it. If peritonitis sets in, trust the surgeon to remove your appendix. I find even these examples insufficient. The way a pilot handles emergencies influences whether people fly that airline again. A doctor's relationship skills may be critical to a surgical patient's recovery. How people perceive the pilot and surgeon—not just what they accomplish—becomes, in science jargon, a "key variable." Over time the process makes as much difference as technical skill. Norman Cousins (1984), the magazine editor who cured himself of an incurable disease with laughter, has cited many examples of physical changes not explainable by the medical model—variables beyond problem solving. The main aha of open-systems thinking is that everything counts.

Taylor knew early on that effective systems required cooperative people. The more work the expert did alone, the less cooperation could be expected. This is hardly surprising in a society in which people believe opportunity, free expression, and self-governance are birthrights. The Industrial Revolution pushed people toward passive dependence on the assembly line, the engineer, and the supervisor. Democratic aspirations pulled them toward more influence over their work.

Yet the tendency of experts to discount knowledge that did not fit their models grew in direct proportion to the 20th Century explosion of technical expertise. The clouds still hang over many workplaces. Lewin saw that segmenting knowledge into discrete packages subtly undermined science and democracy as much as breaking work into little pieces. People interact not only with one another but with their environments—the reason for their work. It is both antidemocratic and unscientific to imagine astronauts would risk their lives in vehicles they could not control.

■ ■ ■

"THIS BECAME A FUNDAMENTAL LESSON FOR ME..."

LEUVEN, BELGIUM—When I read *Productive Workplaces* in November 1987, two things struck me. First, Marvin painted a markedly different picture of Frederick Taylor than the one I had from my psychology studies. I wondered to what extent Taylor had been simply dismissed as an "engineer" by the new "human relations" proponents, who discouraged me from reading his basic work. This became a fundamental lesson for me: always try to understand the complex realities facing an author that must have influenced his or her thinking and theorizing, rather than accept the biases of others.

The second surprise was the simple way in which Marvin expressed his ideas and insights to the reader. The language and flip-chart drawings made it easy for a reader to grasp his messages. He produced "actionable knowledge" before Chris Argyris (1996) coined the concept. I wondered, "Doesn't he make it too simple, leaving out the key role he played in his own work experiences?" I believe he underplayed the importance of his role in containing tensions and uncertainties, his ways of creating a "holding environment," structurally removing and/or encapsulating destructive conflicts to enable groups to do constructive work.

When I was a visiting professor at George Washington University in 1988, I assigned *Productive Workplaces* and Peter Checkland's (1981) work on soft system methodology as basic readings for my OD course. I was prepared to help students see how Checkland's rigorous SSM was complementary to *Productive Workplaces* in dealing with complex organizational design issues. I think that they made more use in their lives of Marvin's principles. PW is still on the reading assignments list of our International Professional Development Programme for consultants and managers, while we teach the basics of SSM in half a day.

One of Marvin's famous one-liners, "Get the whole system in the room," captures an essential principle of studying and developing organizations. That principle had been tested by many social scientists, predominantly in Europe, since the late sixties, for example, Gunnar Hjelholt's (1972) mini societies and my work in IBM World Trade and Unilever's Scandinavisation project (Vansina, 1974). This principle contrasted strongly with the then widespread assumption that organizations could be conceived as large, monolithic groups. "Bringing the whole SYSTEM into the room" is far from easy. It requires careful, structural preparation and facilitation of the work processes so that the diversity and power differentials of the subsystems in the room do not become so socially suppressed that people make a defensive statement like, "We are all in the same boat!" If such statements dominate a meeting, the result may be a happy, even euphoric feeling of achievement, but the outcomes won't stand the confrontation with the realities afterward.

A recent project illustrates the complex psychodynamics of "bringing the whole system in the room." It required clarifying and strengthening five role identities (product sales managers, area managers, product sales merchandisers, a chief butcher, and store managers) in an international distribution organization of foods and other goods. At the beginning, people asserted that, "We are all selling goods!" They denied the specifics, power differentials, and proper accountabilities among them. To claim their role identities, they needed to differentiate and recognize each other's roles within that structure (Vansina and Vansina-Cobbaert, 2008). This illustrates the tremendous power of working with social contexts in temporary systems, an expression, in the spirit of *Productive Workplaces*, of the relevance of a psychodynamic approach within OD.

—Leopold Vansina, Ph.D. professor emeritus, University of Leuven and l'Université Catholique de Louvain-la-Neuve, Belgium, and Fellow of Professional Development International, BV, The Netherlands

---

Adding Action to Research

Lewin in the 1940s sought to improve Taylor's system through action research. He had imagined in the early 1920s that better use of farm implements was more likely to follow from psychologists/farmer teams in the field than from laboratory experiments with farmers as subjects (see Chapter Five). Lewin intended his enhanced problem-solving model to preserve democratic values, build commitment to act, and motivate learning. Indeed, some renamed a variation on the process "action learning" to highlight its vast potential (Revans, 1982).

Few concepts have been so simple or powerful. Yet Lewin's road map, unlike Rand McNally's, does not have scales in miles or kilometers. Indeed, our perceptions of the terrain keep changing as we involve more people and learn more in new situations. The finance manager sees costs going up and blames it on poor motivation. The workers know they could produce more, but for oppressive supervision. The supervisors blame flawed technology. They are all right. It is the systematic relationship among their views that action research addresses.

A New Look at Expert Problem Solving

Building on Lewin, social scientists by the 1960s evolved a significant modification to expert problem solving. With a repertoire drawn from group and interpersonal dynamics, they devised methods to alter situations that Taylor considered immutable. Resistance, instead of a force to be overcome, was seen as a source of energy. The emerging model (see "Lewinian Consulting") took account of feelings, attitudes, perceptions. It required that all who are key to implementation wrestle with the data and arrive at mutually acceptable action plans. This meant a significant shift in the relationship between expert and sponsor. Now experts sought to bring those experiencing the problem into the diagnosis and solution, to treat their reservations and insights as "data," and to consider their relationships with one another a key to implementation.

There are no practical reasons why this model should be owned by behavioral scientists, any more than new work methods by industrial engineers. The reasons are mainly historical. Taylor early on disdained "industrial social workers" blazing trails parallel to his own. Lewin recognized

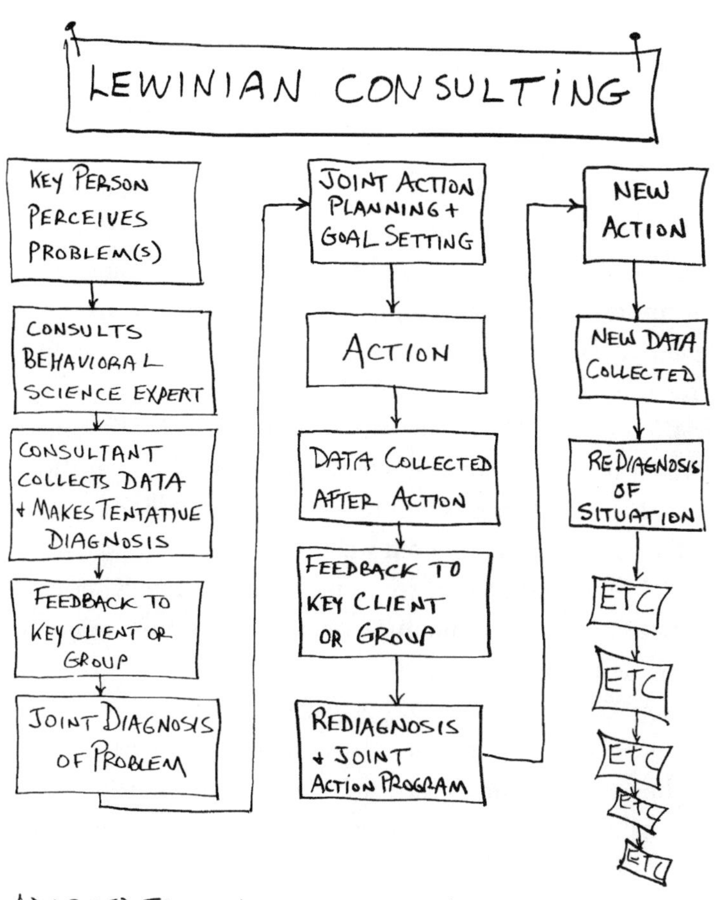

ADAPTED FROM WENDELL FRENCH (1969, P. 26)

the commonalities. He influenced educators and social scientists to follow his path. Follow it they did, quite separately from engineers until Trist's coal-mine studies. We have been a long time bringing the technical and social frameworks together. All the action research projects I described in Part Two—Lippitt's famous authority-democracy leadership experiments, Lewin's and Mead's World War II food studies, the work of Bion and Trist in officer selection, Coch and French's change experiments at Harwood, T-groups, sociotechnical work design, community action projects—were milestones on the road to this generic practice theory. Today, the biggest progress is being made in "large group interventions" where workers, managers, engineers, physical scientists, and accountants cooperate to do valued tasks (Chapter Twenty-Five).

What makes action research unique is the concept that those with a stake in the problem help define and solve it. It becomes a joint venture of clients and consultants, so that everybody learns from multiple realities. The uses of this insight have proved literally infinite: team development, task forces, training course design, technology transfer, rethinking corporate strategies, reorganizing offices and factories, planning cities and towns, devising futures for states and nations. Had they known how, the first space-vehicle designers might have spared themselves much travail by treating the astronauts as partners.

The Middle of the Movie. The expert always arrives in the middle of the movie and leaves before the end. Those unschooled in Lewin's ideas come to believe that only their reality counts. If others' data is needed, they will collect it, analyze it, and point out what to do. Lewin showed how limited this belief is. Without people, economics and technology mean nothing. Without a technical and economic context, fixing people seems pointless, a movie without a plot.

So action research became the opposite of scientific research. Instead of standing outside the experiment, watching what happens and writing up your findings, you become a learner in a situation you helped devise. You develop a stake. You assume responsibility. A hypothesis (unproved theory) is not a neutral statement of possibility; it is a statement for or against a preferred discovery.

Many social scientists and management scientists still place themselves outside the experiment to discover how "people" behave. The main thing you will learn from this activity—other than that it makes a safer thesis than a narrative—is that nobody really gets outside. "Our findings," to quote management professor Peter Vaill, "follow our lookings" (1979, p. 4). Lewin saw collaborative learning as never-ending, based on trial, error, and feedback. He was especially scathing about managers who delegate one-shot change projects. He likened that to a ship's captain ordering a course correction, then going to dinner while the ship sails in circles. What is missing is the feedback loop, steering the vessel in relation to wind and water rather than what goes on below decks.

This understanding opened the door to a generic form of consultation quite different from Taylorism. A new set of consulting skills evolved for helping individuals, groups, and whole systems make constructive changes.

These skills included making solid working agreements, testing commitment, and involving clients in their own diagnosis and action. These skills could enhance expertise in marketing, finance, personnel, production, or research. They could be acquired and used by anybody if—a big if—they had the will to learn and the ego strength to fail while doing it. NTL Institute has run laboratories in this form of consultation for years (Chapter Six). Peter Block (2011), in his "Staff Consulting Skills" workshops, has taught thousands of people with technical skill and no formal authority practical ways to transfer their knowledge to line managers.

Survey Feedback. Lewin's way of seeing things stimulated many other social innovations. The most elaborate action research spinoff was survey data feedback, invented at the University of Michigan's Institute for Social Research (ISR), where Lewin's Research Center for Group Dynamics moved after his death. ISR's Floyd Mann pioneered survey data feedback to investigate supervision, promotion, and job satisfaction among eight thousand Detroit Edison employees. Mann fed back his findings in an "interlocking chain of conferences." Departments that discussed their data made more significant changes than those that heard nothing or received feedback only. Face-to-face discussion, not the survey technique, was the key to constructive change. This discovery became the benchmark for effective surveys (Mann, 1957).

Likert's Refinements

While Mann worked on change processes, ISR's Rensis Likert (1961) correlated numerous leadership and motivation studies to results. He identified four prototype organizations, defined by the degree to which they were open, participative, and satisfying to work in, calling them Systems 1, 2, 3, and 4. (See chart on the following page.) Likert showed that as systems moved toward 4 on his scales, they had lower costs and higher output than those tending toward 1, a finding I have repeated in several workplaces. The key variable was the boss's behavior.

Combining Likert's survey with Mann's feedback procedures produced a method for inducing and measuring change in large systems, a grand-design action-research strategy (Bowers and Franklin, 1977). Until Likert, few managers thought of organizations as systems of measurable

LIKERT'S SYSTEMS

	1	2	3	4
MOTIVATION	SECURITY MONEY	STATUS	GROWTH RECOGNITION	IDENTITY ACHIEVEMENT INFLUENCE
ATTITUDES	HOSTILE	MIXED (-)	MIXED (+)	FAVORABLE
COMMUNICATION	DOWN ONLY ↓	MOSTLY DOWN ↓	DOWN AND UP ↓↑	UP, DOWN ↓ SIDEWAYS ↑ ↔
TEAMWORK	NONE	LITTLE	SOME	MUCH
GOALS SET	TOP DOWN	TOP DOWN	TOP, WITH DISCUSSION	GROUP PARTICIPATION
OUTPUT	MEDIOCRE	FAIR TO GOOD	GOOD	EXCELLENT

ADAPTED FROM *NEW PATTERNS OF MANAGEMENT*, 1961.

processes. They were more inclined to see the workplace as an aggregate of jobs. Likert changed their viewpoint by quantifying "soft" processes such as control, influence, decision making, and goal setting. He fed this data back to natural work groups who compared what they had with what they wanted. Problem-solving skill training helped them move. Periodic surveys provided progress measurements. Keying on leadership, Likert made McGregor's Theory Y assumptions into a comprehensive organization development and information system.

When I started consulting in 1969, I visited Likert in Michigan and wrote several articles about his work. I understood his ideas intuitively from relating them to the business I had managed. In the 1970s I did several surveys using Likert's ideas and methods. I report on two of these in the next chapter. Surveys can be built on a specific problem like turnover (Chapter Thirteen), treated as a thermometer in a systemic "health checkup," or aimed at company-wide tangles like high costs.

My former colleague Eileen Curtin used her own variation on survey feedback more than twenty times to improve office productivity in divisions of General Foods and other companies. She had two major goals: better jobs and lower costs. She would form a participative study team to survey common office practices: phone calls, typing, photocopying, dictating. Every person from president to janitor took the survey. The study group fed back its findings one department at a time, seeking consensus on changes to be made.

Curtin was neither measuring change nor quantifying behavior. She was mobilizing energy for problem solving by having everybody validate needed improvements. Her purpose was building a mandate for change at all levels, in Lewinian lingo "influencing the gatekeepers" to become involved. Next steps usually involved cross-functional task forces or departmental work-redesign teams. These groups consistently improved jobs and cut costs 15 to 40 percent.

Task Forces

Ad hoc task forces early on became essential to functionally organized companies, especially in high-tech industries, because functional structures don't cope well with fast change. "Participation" was often the reason given for task forces, on the vague theory that including people was a good thing. Many of us were unhappy with this simple-minded translation of Lewin's work. Providing "input" did not qualify as involvement. We wanted business-centered participation and legitimate roles for each participant. We insisted that people bring information or skill, in addition to their warm bodies.

Mary Parker Follett, a person light-years ahead of her contemporaries, had recognized this phenomenon years ago. "It is not the face-to-face suggestion that we want," she wrote, "so much as the joint study of the problem, and such joint study can be made best by the employee and his immediate superior or employee and special expert on that question" (Metcalf and Urwick, 1940, p. 60). Using ad hoc task forces enabled people to bypass hierarchy while they figured out changes in policies, procedures, and systems. With persistence—Lewin again—this could be done in such a way that people would absorb the general principles for using task forces on their own. In Chapter Thirteen I recount cases showing the growing dilemma of enacting these methods while holding fast to values of productivity, participation, and learning.

■ ■ ■

"I NEEDED TO SHIFT FROM TOP-DOWN TO COLLABORATION..."

SEATTLE, WA—For many years as director of operations and chief operating officer of a national museum, I led a large, passionate staff serving 350,000 visitors and delivering educational programs to 100,000 students each year. I was struck back then by W. Edwards Deming's demonstration that faulty quality was not the worker's doing. He would ask two volunteers to take a handful of mixed red and white beads from a jar. The volunteer with the most red beads was "informed" that his work was substandard. Deming would then explain that this is how manufacturers often handled quality control. Defective products reflected management's failure to provide a suitable production process.

I saw that the way we treated museum employees affected the quality of their work. Rather than leaving employees out of improving our services, we needed to include them in our design processes. They knew the customers, and they shared an interest in our success. For the museum to benefit from a fully engaged staff, I needed to shift from a top-down approach to leading collaboration, so I set up cross-functional teams to help shape our ideas and prioritize the initiatives to pursue.

I resolved to strengthen my own skills to incorporate employee engagement. I was fortunate to find a master's degree program at Antioch University Seattle that drew on the sciences of human behavior with a strong organization development (OD) component. In my organizational theory class I read *Productive Workplaces Revisited* and found new support and inspiration for a healthy model of leadership and management.

A year after graduating, I left my executive position to become a full-time consultant. While much of my consulting involves technical and management knowledge from my prior careers, I have integrated OD into what I do. The centerpiece of my practice is facilitating groups in creating their own strategic plans.

In preparing to help groups work together, for example, I interview each participant, using techniques I learned from *Productive Workplaces Revisited* to mirror back to the clients what I'm seeing in their organization, seeking to model an open curiosity that group members can employ when working with each other and with staff. In the aftermath of the 9/11 attacks and the Great Recession, many clients come to me with a great deal of internal tension, falling back on top-down, command-and-control-style management. Sadly, this style deprives leadership of an organization's capacity to respond at the time it is most needed. I seek then to get the "whole system in the room." Often I stretch a client's boundaries. However, every time we do it, the results are better and more durable.

In one nonprofit, for example, new management had gotten the facility into good shape, but the organization was frustrated in its fundraising. Board leadership seemed unapproachable. Open dialog was not happening. Using "Lewin's Law" (page 259), I was able to unfreeze the board through one-on-one interviews and in small groups by talking openly about the current situation. Using the "Four Rooms of Change" model (page 326), I was able to articulate that board leadership was in the *Contentment* room while the rest of the board was in *Confusion* and seeking to move into *Renewal.* As a result, the board chair not only decided to step aside but also stayed to guide the transition and remain an active board member. This breakthrough allowed a smooth transition that kept the group together and poised to take on the fundraising they needed to do.

—Richard Beckerman, president,
Richard Beckerman Consulting

chapter THIRTEEN

Rethinking Diagnosis and Action

According to Lewin, bringing about lasting change means initially unlocking or unfreezing the present social system. This might require some kind of confrontation or a process of reeducation. Next, behavioral movement must occur in the direction of desired change, such as a reorganization. Finally, deliberate steps must be taken to ensure that the new state of behavior remains relatively permanent. These three steps are simple to start but not simple to implement.

—W. Warner Burke, *Organization Development: Principles and Practices*, 1982, p. 48

During the 1970s I explored every method I could find to solve organizational problems with Lewinian action research. I did surveys, interviews, participant observation, and so many groups they blur together. I saw myself as a "change agent" whose objective was to help systems unfreeze, move, and refreeze. I never doubted that diagnosing the gap between what people did and what they said was essential for melting the natural resistance of systems to change.

Lewin had described—magnificent paradox—the "creation of permanent change" (1951, p. 224). I fell in love with diagnosis, with its rich overtones of prediction and control. I also discovered systems thinking. My group dynamics training led me to define problems in social-psychological terms, related to personal styles, interpersonal relationships, and group norms (unwritten rules). As an ex-manager, I knew these could not be divorced from economics and technology. "Social researchers," wrote William F. Whyte, "tended to concentrate almost exclusively on human relations. We gave lip service to the importance of technology but tended to treat it as a constant instead of as a variable, which could be changed along with changes in human relations" (1984, p. 168).

In my six-box model (Weisbord, 1978b) I sought to remedy this by introducing purposes, structure, rewards, and helpful mechanisms connected to relationships and leadership. I still used medical terminology, a paradigm in transition. Working in medical schools, though, I realized that the best doctors used their own model cautiously. "There are three things I can do for a patient," my friend Dave Wagner, a surgeon and a founder of emergency medicine, told me one day. "I can cut them, I can drug them, or I can counsel them. Increasingly I find myself counseling them."

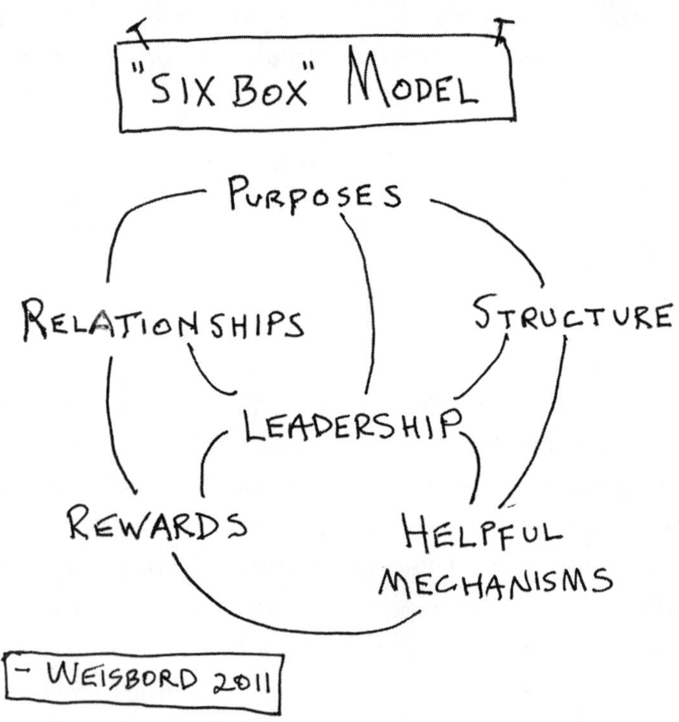

No sooner had I written a book on diagnosis but I grew uneasy with the medical concept—and said so in the book (Weisbord, 1978b, p. 67). I still believe the six boxes have value for people trying to figure out what they need to work on.

To reduce my ambivalence, I began using the terms "snapshots" and "movies" in place of diagnosis and action. The snapshot was a picture of the action frozen in time long enough to identify conditions to be changed. A good movie, I believed, required that a large cast join in the snapshooting, own the dilemmas, and take corrective actions together. Two of the cases that follow employ survey methods that can be used with any diagnostic theory to fit many organizational problems. They assumed that systems required consultant-induced unfreezing before they could move.

These cases exemplify the consulting practice Peter Block, Tony Petrella, and I sought to develop when we teamed up in the 1970s. We wanted a consultancy built on business goals that encouraged people to manage the interplay between task and process.

Our business focus led us to high-risk, high-payoff situations. These cases were largely problem-focused and consultant-centered. However, there was an evolution taking place, visible with 20/20 hindsight. Our methods and models propelled us toward new forms for snapshots and movies and greater unity of the two concepts. In the 1970s my colleagues and I became increasingly aware of how external forces—the marketplace, suppliers, regulators—influenced solutions as much as interpersonal and group skills did. Our telephoto lenses gave way to wide angles. In parallel we grew increasingly uneasy about doing so much diagnostic work for clients. We wanted them more firmly in charge of the camera and the script. The first case illustrates classic Lewinian action research, problem-focused, showing the best that participative experts could do back then.

CASE 1. FOOD SERVICES TURNOVER: ACTION RESEARCH AND HUMAN RESOURCE ACCOUNTING (1970–1971)

> Heck, we have data from India, Pakistan, Sweden, too. Beer salesmen in Sweden. The more the supervisors use System 4, the more beer the salesmen sell. But if you don't think it

applies to you, collect the data. Find out what the differences are between your own high- and low-producing departments.

—Rensis Likert, in Weisbord, *Conference Board Record*, 1970, p. 16

The president of Food Services, operators of cafeterias in factories, colleges, and hospitals, wanted to bring social science thinking into his fast-growing firm. With his blessing, I convened a seminar of volunteer executives, dieticians, and financial and personnel staff to consider new theories, methods, and experiences in other firms. Rensis Likert's "human resource accounting" immediately attracted the group. Likert (1967) had said that treating hiring, training, and people development as investments rather than costs could change the way a company is managed. Our seminar flagged food service unit turnover as an expensive problem.

The Costs of Turnover. A typical cafeteria had from ten to sixty employees: manager, cashier, chef, cooks, food preparers, servers, dishwashers. People worked long hours for low wages. It cost an average of $300 to recruit, orient, train, and set up files for each new-hire. The previous year this company of 35,000 issued paychecks to more than 72,000 people—more than 100 percent turnover. Unit turnover was costing more than $10 million a year, an amount equal to total profits! The company had accepted high turnover as an unalterable cost. Yet a curious thing was going on here. Turnover varied from 6 to 800 percent across units. Scanning figures from more than one hundred cafeterias, we defined "high" turnover as 120 percent a year or more, and "low" as less than 60 percent. We soon noticed that all categories—utility, supervisory, and food preparation—turned over two and a half times as often in the high-turnover units as in the low. Unit differences had more to do with work systems than with job categories.

Mark Frohman, then a graduate student at Michigan, and I devised a comparative study of high- and low-turnover units. We interviewed managers and collected their turnover theories, for example, type of union contract, geographic location, percentage of women, employees' ages, number of shifts. We added other theories based on work at Rensis Likert's Institute for Social Research, such as manager support for new-hires, tools and equipment, and on-the-job training. We tested a thirty-nine-item survey, then selected ten units for the formal study, four with low turnover, two medium, and four high.

Both high- and low-turnover units showed similar patterns in employee ages, length of service, job categories, types of union and service contracts, number of shifts, and labor and food budget deviations. None of these accounted for turnover. The survey data strongly confirmed differences in manager behavior. Low-turnover units responded more favorably than high to thirty-one of thirty-nine questions. Most striking was that employees in

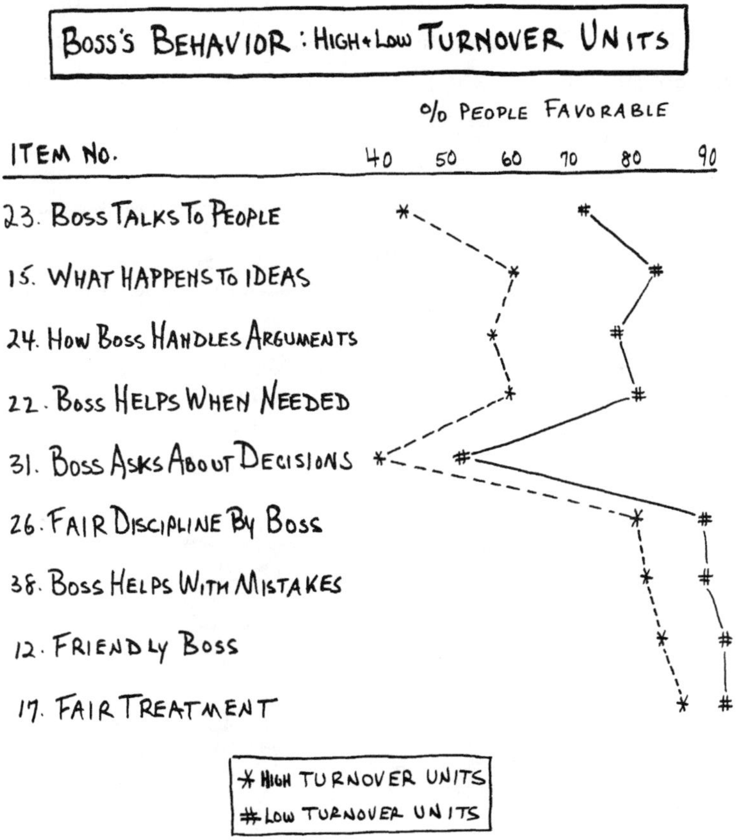

BOSS'S BEHAVIOR: HIGH + LOW TURNOVER UNITS

% PEOPLE FAVORABLE

ITEM NO. 40 50 60 70 80 90

23. BOSS TALKS TO PEOPLE
15. WHAT HAPPENS TO IDEAS
24. HOW BOSS HANDLES ARGUMENTS
22. BOSS HELPS WHEN NEEDED
31. BOSS ASKS ABOUT DECISIONS
26. FAIR DISCIPLINE BY BOSS
38. BOSS HELPS WITH MISTAKES
12. FRIENDLY BOSS
17. FAIR TREATMENT

* HIGH TURNOVER UNITS
# LOW TURNOVER UNITS

low-turnover units believed they had better orientation and training, more helpful and friendly unit managers, and more chances to advance than those in high-turnover units. They also showed greater satisfaction with their jobs and pay (although all pay scales were the same). "Boss's Behavior" on the previous page shows the response pattern on one cluster of nine related items.

To help managers interpret the graphs, we drew a map of the turnover problem, based on Likert's theory of management behavior (see "Manager/Employee Relations" chart). Turnover resulted from employee attitudes shaped by management actions in four areas unique to this company.

Reducing Turnover. We then planned an experimental program to reduce turnover in one region. We offered unit managers training built on survey and turnover data from their own units, which they could compare with the company-wide study. In four workshops they reviewed their own surveys, practiced supervisory and problem-solving skills, and planned turnover-prevention activities. Instead of hearing how-to lectures, managers listed things they

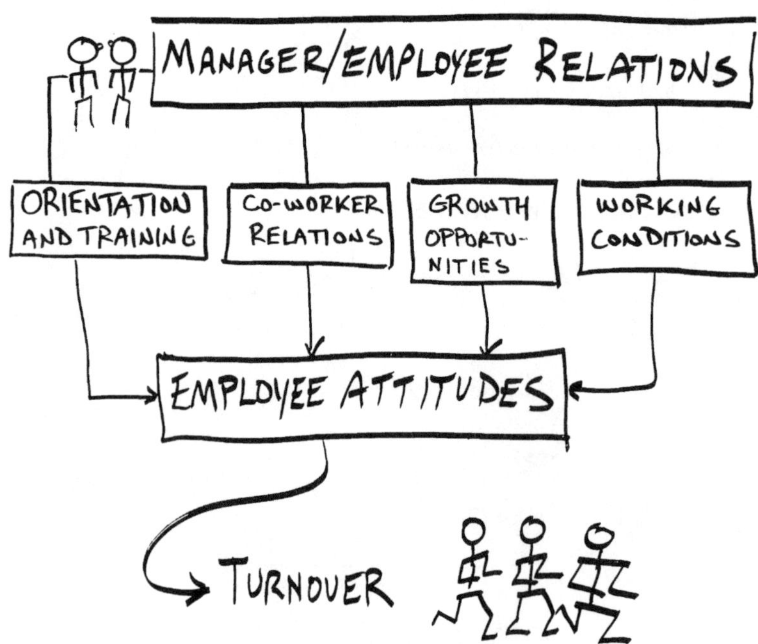

thought new employees wanted to know and things they needed them to know. Then they role played orientation meetings and critiqued their ability to get across important points. They also met with senior managers to discuss problems that could not be solved at unit level.

We later compared turnover in units whose managers did and did not take the training. Of twenty-seven participating units, twenty-four reduced turnover. One twenty-nine-person unit that had thirty-seven turnovers the year before had none the year after. The experimental region cut its turnover rate 50 percent in a year when the company-wide figure climbed to 143 percent—a dramatic confirmation of participative action research for solving intractable problems.

New policies and procedures were established; training was extended to other regions by internal company staff. District managers, one level above units, also asked for training. This led to week-long district manager workshops, the start of a management development curriculum. Within three years the use of experience-based training methods went from nonexistent to an integral part of company management—the president's objective in sponsoring the original seminar.

Limits of Likert Theory. Mann and Likert developed their organizational survey methods with business firms. Likert's research showed that System 4 organizations were likely to outperform System 1 organizations. Likert-type surveys illuminate systems where goals are concrete, formal authority is easily recognized, people must work together to obtain results, and output can be measured. Remove any of these conditions and you see that the systematic effects of any management style begin to blur like an out-of-focus photograph. Although I could repeat his findings in business firms, I found human service agencies and colleges more problematical. Physicians and scientists, for example, expected to maintain control of their own work, no matter who was in charge. They had little understanding of task interdependence, organizational goals, and output measures.

The Likert lens could not "see" what was going on in nonlinear systems because it was designed to look for patterns anchored in high interdependence, repetitive work, and measured output. Likert recognized this when I showed him a medical school survey that used his instruments. Maintenance, housekeeping, and food service graphs varied the way they should, influenced by supervisor behavior. Academic departments showed no consistent patterns within or between. Likert smiled and said, "What you have here is System Zero." How do you induce change in such systems? Not with surveys or by focusing on the boss's behavior. In Chapter Sixteen, I show, based on a project in the same medical school, that "System Zero" needs new structures to influence cooperative action.

Turnover Update at Food Services

Food Services metamorphosed several times in the mid-1970s. Founded as Automatic Retailers of America (ARA) in 1959, the company went public in the late 1960s and became a hostile takeover candidate. The management organized a buyout, acquiring 70 percent of the company. In 1994, still growing, it changed its name to ARAMARK. By 2000 it had numerous divisions in food and many other services, went public in 2001, and then private again in 2007.

Although my old contacts were gone, in January 2003 I went over the earlier study with the human resource vice president for the Business Services Division, David Kahn. "It's remarkable how little things have changed," he said. "You were certainly ahead of the curve with turnover thirty years ago. Manager quality is surely the key to cutting turnover," he continued. "People don't quit companies, they quit managers." He did a rundown of the extensive manager curriculum that had evolved at ARAMARK. In offsite workshops new managers learned the importance of imparting clear goals and expectations, offering feedback, and providing chances for employee development.

Manager trainees also were assigned to selected units where experienced managers, trained as coaches, helped them learn the ropes. Kahn also pointed out the importance of a stable hourly force, used to being supervised by a string of trainees and willing to assist in manager training too. It was company policy to provide more full-time jobs with secure pay and benefits, a key to developing a mature workforce. Turnover, Kahn said, was now averaging about 65 percent and considerably less among managers. "If you treat people poorly they're not going to stay," he added. "If you make it a great place to work, people respond, and do a much better job of serving customers."

■ ■ ■

"PEOPLE ARE DEMORALIZED...IT'S NOT THE PAY, IT'S THE WORK..."

CHICAGO, IL—I encountered *Productive Workplaces* in my Ph.D. program in organization development. I was an industrial/organizational psychologist working as a coordinator in the selection and testing department of a large transportation company. With PW, I gained insight into where I could look for motivators. The book helped me understand the importance of dignity and meaning in myself and in my work. It supported my purpose for being in OD and reinforced my urge to improve my workplace.

The economic recession changed my company. After a hiring freeze, highly paid employees with advanced knowledge, skills, and abilities were doing menial work. In the human resources department, for example, recruiters, analysts, and coordinators helped other departments by stuffing envelopes, creating spreadsheets, updating databases, shredding paper, and answering phones. They had no input into decisions affecting their work. People were demoralized. Management blamed the economy and low pay for low morale. The real reason was the work itself.

Reading PW, I gained confidence to take up new projects. The company, for example, lost valuable knowledge as people with more than twenty years of experience retired or left. I volunteered to find a way of preserving what would be lost and have involved analysts, coordinators, and HR interns who want to do something meaningful to help the company retain knowledge and build a culture of collaboration. We are identifying eligible retirees, planning interviews and surveys to capture their experience, and devising methods to transfer this learning across all departments and job functions.

—Neelima Paranjpey, Ph.D. candidate, Benedictine University

The next case describes a problem-focused survey of a different order from Food Services. First, the angle of vision was wider, taking in relationships among company departments. The snapshot was taken with a homemade survey tool derived from a research tradition based on studying how organizations and their departments adapt to their environments.

Second, I learned here that it was not essential that consultants collect and feed back data. In this case the clients helped develop the survey, collect data, and interpret results. The feedback was handled by managers with the biggest stake in making improvements.

CASE 2. CHEM CORP R&D: MANAGERS DO THEIR OWN FEEDBACK (1978–1979)

From this vantage point we can see why conflict must be accepted as a continuing result of living in a complex civilization. Resolution is not then put up as some final Utopian answer, but simply as a sensible solution to today's issue—with awareness that basic and legitimate differences will generate new conflicts to be resolved tomorrow. From this baseline managers can move more directly toward designing procedures and devices that are adequate for processing the flow of conflicted issues that will surely arise.

—Paul R. Lawrence and Jay W. Lorsch, *Organization and Environment,* 1967, p. 224

Every department in Chem Corp—engineering, manufacturing, sales, and finance—criticized R&D. The R&D vice president, an outspoken veteran, was viewed by his peers with affectionate mistrust. His department played a dual role. It was responsible for developing new products and for troubleshooting process glitches. The vice president argued that his department spent its budget on crises in small plants scattered around the country. He did not have the resources to make a priority of both long- and short-range goals. All his peers saw was a new glass-and-steel building from which only a trickle of new products emerged.

Meeting with the R&D team, I learned that no one liked the situation. Everybody had a favorite "bad guy" in other departments. Together we devised an action-research plan. We would design a "customer" survey of other departments to pin down dissatisfactions and air the resource-allocation dilemma throughout the company. It would be given only if the vice president's peers agreed to participate.

A Company Priority. Top managers quickly sanctioned the project and made cooperation with R&D a priority. The R&D managers brainstormed everything-they-always-wanted-to-know-about-their-relationships-with-other-departments-but-were-afraid-to-ask. I drafted a survey testing each item: response time, quality, service availability, new product development, cooperation. Space was allowed for open-ended responses.

To get at the process side, I added conflict management questions from Lawrence and Lorsch (1967), whose contingency theory I had found useful with scientists in medical schools (Weisbord, Lawrence, and Charns, 1978). This theory says that when organizations set up departments with the right goals, time horizons, and boundaries for their environments, they can expect conflict with departments requiring other structures. Managing conflict constructively, not getting rid of it, becomes a criterion for success in high-performing companies. The engineers and scientists liked the more practical and honest assumption that conflict was a two-way street. (See "Sample Question.")

The R&D managers and I spent a day analyzing more than one hundred survey forms and planning feedback meetings. One interesting finding was the tendency of other functions to see

Sample Question

22. Have you in the last 12 months experienced strong disagreement or conflict with anyone in R&D?

_____ No   _____ Mild Disagreement   ____ Yes

If "yes" please compare the way conflict was handled by R&D and by yourself using the definitions below. Check two modes most often used by self and two by R&D.

Self	R&D		
____	____	Forcing:	People use "power plays."
____	____	Smoothing:	People discuss differences as if no substantive issues exist.
____	____	Avoiding:	People avoid raising sticky issues.
____	____	Bargaining:	People split differences trying to maximize their own interests.
____	____	Confronting:	Despite tension, people openly discuss differences, seeking mutually acceptable solutions.

R&D forcing, smoothing, and avoiding more often, and themselves bargaining and confronting more—just the opposite of R&D's view. Another was that the more different a department's orientations from R&D's, the more likely the two would be in conflict—predicted by Lawrence and Lorsch's research. The most significant result, however, was not in the data. It was a new spirit among research managers, who shucked the "poor us" posture and set out to confront the resources question.

Discussion Meetings. Each R&D manager conducted feedback meetings with his or her "customers," reviewing the data and planning joint action. From these meetings came closer cooperation, more frequent information exchanges, and budget reallocations. When I asked people in other departments how things were

CHANGING PERCEPTIONS OF R+D

"CUSTOMER" UNIT	% CHANGE 1978-79
SUBSIDIARY A	+ 0.9
CORPORATE PLANNING	+ 5.6
ENGINEERING	+ 13.5
STAFF OPERATIONS	+ 14.8
FINANCE	+ 16.2
PLANT OPERATIONS	+ 21.7
OVERALL AVERAGE	+ 10.9

going; their responses ranged from "It's about time" to "I still don't trust them but at least we're talking."

A resurvey the next year showed dramatic improvements. One way results were dramatized was to average responses across seven items: timeliness, technical quality, business mission, sensitivity to department needs, understanding/support, competence, and performance. See "Changing Perceptions of R&D" and

COMPARATIVE R+D PERFORMANCE

	APRIL 1978	JUNE 1979	% CHANGE
TIMELINESS	3.59	2.65	+26.2%
TECHNICAL QUALITY	2.77	2.38	+14.1
UNDERSTANDING AND SUPPORT	3.20	2.37	+25.9

1 = MOST, 5 = LEAST FAVORABLE

"Comparative R&D Performance"—two of several charts used in feedback discussions.

Again the R&D managers fanned out to address problems highlighted by the survey. The R&D vice president remained on the job and the function became more respected and important. From 1978 to 1986 R&D produced more than 150 new product ideas.

It is hard to say how "frozen" Chem Corp was before the survey. The ready support of top managers was certainly a function of the need for new products. However, the survey was intended to change intergroup dynamics. I see its value now as demonstrating that clients could facilitate their own changes. They did not need a consultant facilitating joint discussions to make sure the correct diagnosis was reached and action steps written down.

Chem Corp Twenty Years Later

In the spring of 2000 I phoned an old friend at Chem Corp. He had been a key player in the R&D work more than twenty years earlier and remained in senior management. What, I asked, had happened with R&D?

There were, he told me, a spate of new products in the eight years following the project. During that time the feisty R&D head retired. The survey was forgotten. Chem Corp R&D still occupied the same building, although corporate headquarters had moved.

Despite the new ideas from the 1980s, despite the greater acceptance of R&D by other units, the lab was producing few new products. To improve customer relations, the company had given the business managers a dotted line responsibility for technical staff. Engineering, for example, a particularly sticky wicket, was now housed under plant operations.

The company again had trouble scaling up new products from pilot plant to production. The cultural divide between the people of science and the people of action widened again. "The business managers," said my friend, "want a project that needs a year and $15 million, to be done for $8 million in six months." As a result, they had frustrating delays, missed deadlines, and longer lead times to market. In short, our survey feedback project of twenty years earlier had great short-term impact. Like Solcorp

(Case 4, to follow), no form of consultation could make up for inherent dilemmas of managing a technological swirl in a volatile marketplace.

When I spoke to the former president in 2003, he agreed that departmental relations with R&D backslid in the 1990s. Still, from 1970 to 2000 the cumulative increase in shareholder return on equity was seven and a half times that of the Standard and Poor's 500 corporation benchmark. "We moved from a paternalistic, high control company to high involvement, starting with the work you did back in the 1970s," he said. "We felt the long-term impact of that work throughout the company for years after." (This privately held firm had the same president for decades.)

Inventing "Local Theory"

Next, I will revisit two cases built on another action-research spinoff, the invention of "local theory" from the pooled perceptions of those closest to the problem. This is still consultant-centered work. However, the effort to enlarge the snapshot beyond relationships and motivation—to show connections among relationships, structure, and purpose in each client's own terms—reflects a further evolution of practice. In this instance we were moving toward making two forces—open systems thinking and the empowerment of clients to act for themselves—increasingly practical.

One case involves productivity in a factory where management had made unfounded assumptions about employee capability, the second a race to save a new solar energy firm from strategic ruin. In each, top managers had concluded that the problem called for changing people's behavior. In practice we made outside forces more central in the snapshots. The consultants still did a lot of the work, but we were enlarging the context to connect behavior with history, markets and technology.

CASE 3. PACKAGING PLANT: OPERATORS MEET EXPERT ANALYSIS (1979)

> They're good people. They're just not used to cranking out large quantities. I want them more involved in the business.
>
> —Vice president for operations, Packaging Plant

For years Packaging Plant's lackluster products made a comfortable living for its family owners. When an international giant bought it, new management began a Madison Avenue blitz to wipe out competition. Sales went up like a rocket. The plant could not meet demand. The operations vice president attributed this setback to the fact that workers had never been asked to produce so much so fast—a kind of work ethic crisis.

We assembled twenty-eight people who knew something about how products were packaged—lead operators, schedulers, a production planner, mechanics, quality control inspectors, managers, supervisors. Two consultants (William Smith and I) offered to interview people individually about the situation and conduct a meeting to talk over what we learned.

People were skeptical, wary, unsure what management was really after, and they talked openly about what they thought was going on. Two weeks later Bill and I papered the conference room with newsprint charts about the problems, the company's history, and its dramatic changes in technology, government regulation, the marketplace, and relations with the parent firm. We displayed a map of four conditions that must be met for a packaging operation to function:

1. Quality control must release good product from manufacturing.
2. Bottles, labels, boxes, brochures, and cartons must arrive from inventory.
3. A mechanic must spend four to eight hours setting up the line for a new run.
4. Operators must start up and test the line.

(See "Coordination Means . . . ")

Production planning, a Taylor invention, controlled schedules using a master called the green sheet. It actually was blue, and often was wrong. It showed labels in inventory that were on the unloading dock, released product that was still in manufacturing,

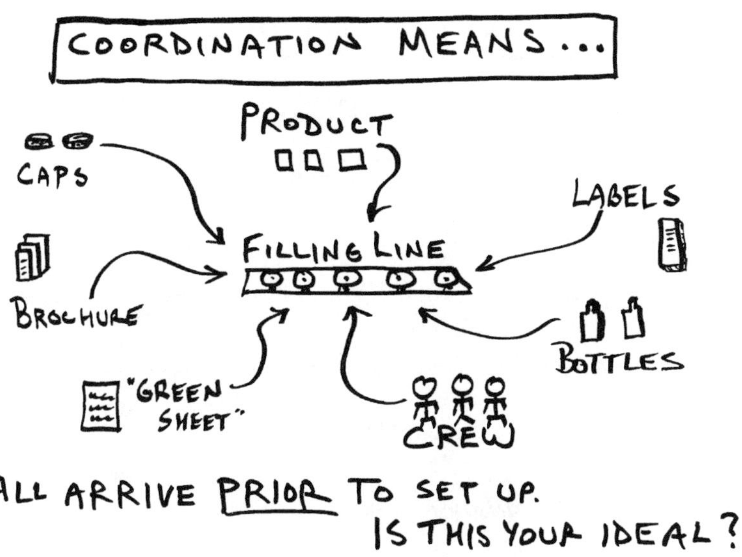

bottles available but not the right size. When mechanics showed up to do a line change, they often found a component missing. Market swings reverberated through the system to show up as missing items at setup time. The problem was coordination, not worker competence. See "Market Conditions."

The workers, middle managers, and staff people had a richer, more complex systems view than the boss did—a phenomenon I had experienced as a manager in the 1960s, and one confirmed by Elden's "local theory" experiments in Norway (1983b). It was no longer functional to go right into problem solving. We needed what Geoffrey Vickers (1965) had called an "appreciation" of the whole system before the right problem could be solved.

Spurred by the broader interpretation of their own data, the group acknowledged that hourly workers had no control over packaging delays. This confirmed the intuition of a systems analyst assigned to improve the green-sheet system. Until then he could not get a hearing for his ideas. A multifunction task force was organized. They mapped the system in detail, identifying exactly where things went wrong. Within a few weeks they ironed out many problems that had plagued the factory ever since sales

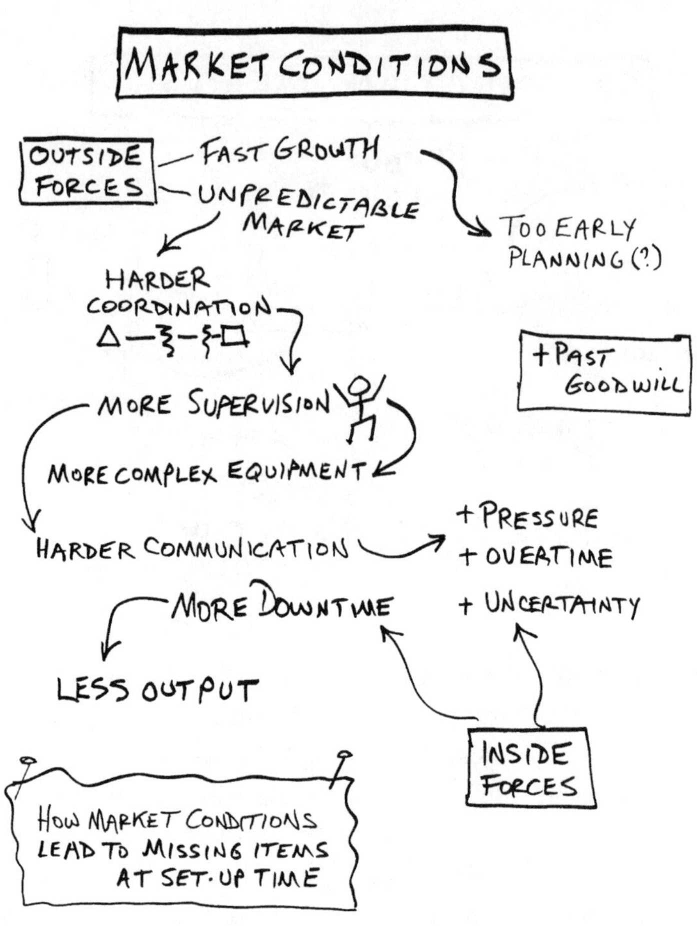

increased. Production went up dramatically. The green sheet, however, stayed blue.

Packaging Plant Revisited

About ten years later I received a call from a Packaging Plant staff person. The company was enjoying boom years, sales going up, with new products in the pipeline. The pressure was on for production, quality, and cost-cutting. There had been many plant managers since I was last there. Now an energetic newcomer had taken over. I sent the new manager the work design chapter from this book. We set up a lunch. He enthusiastically embraced the idea of an employee-based plant redesign. He thought people ought to own their jobs, take pride in their work, and feel responsible for results.

Jill Janov and I undertook interviews to test the feasibility. When asked what they thought of getting everyone involved, many managers said, in effect, "Not much." As one recalled years later, "We had no model for trusting one another. The risk was pretty big. We were conditioned to operate independently, making ourselves look good and being rewarded for it. The workforce was used to an endless parade of managers coming in, declaring productivity, safety, or whatever to be the most important thing, achieving some improvements, and moving on." Suffice to say we spent some months in meetings and "readiness" conversations. We still were doing a form of time-intensive diagnosis to gain commitment. (I doubt people would sit still for this ramp-up today.)

As the concept spread among the 260-person workforce, enthusiasts emerged. One by one, several second-tier managers agreed to support a redesign effort. For some it reflected a wish to please the boss. Others liked the idea of workforce involvement. The plant manager's boss, the director of manufacturing, agreed to go along on one condition: in two years or less the plant had to show significant gains. If he thought they were not moving that way, he would pull the plug.

Eventually, we followed the guidelines in Chapter Eighteen, devising an early version of what Dick Axelrod (2000) would call The Conference Model®. Four volunteer teams representing every function came together to redesign four distinct processes. Each team included operators, supervisors, engineers, quality inspectors, and managers. The teams decided they wanted everything in plain sight. So they had a soundproof room built in the middle of a cavernous, noisy factory. Into this space some sixty employees, one-fourth of the workforce, came each week to document the existing system and design a better one.

The teams engaged in a series of two- to three-day workshops facilitated by Janov and Davidson Jones. The first workshop, a variation on Future Search described in Chapter Twenty-Two, created an umbrella of values, mission, and goals. The second had people analyzing the technical system, the third the social system, the fourth focused on systems redesign, the fifth on implementation. Between workshops the design teams briefed the rest of the plant on what they were learning and tested new ideas.

Not everyone wanted change. Many employees, hourly and staff, not just managers, were happier with the devil they knew than the one they didn't. "I remember one meeting in the auditorium," a former supervisor told me years later, "where an employee asked the plant manager, 'When is this change going to start?' And he said, 'It already has!' The person didn't know it was happening. We needed strong leadership because so many people didn't want to do it."

Employee-Designed Work Teams

The work came together in dramatic presentations—looking back from the future—of how the various redesigned areas—compounding, filling, processing, packaging, mechanical support services—were "now" operating. People attended from all functions. Many staff from the main corporation, who had offices at site, sat in. They were awed and baffled at what the employees were able to accomplish. The company had never seen anything like this.

The teams redid supervisory functions into a team leadership model. They streamlined paperwork, set up troubleshooting task forces to root out longstanding problems. They shortened and sped up the product pipeline, rationalized inventory control, making changes to systems and procedures that would surely have bemused Frederick Taylor. Each quarter the plant managers sat down with the manufacturing hierarchy to review the numbers. They were positive and improving.

The transition was hardest on former supervisors. A decade later one recalled how the redesign effort "was scary, different than anything we ever did before." As a team leader, she lost many supervisory responsibilities that now went to the hourly workers. Despite extreme skepticism about the increasing role of hourly people, the manufacturing vice president kept his word and continued to sanction the project. The plant manager was overjoyed. In mid-1989, employees began implementing their plans, setting up a radical new way of managing the plant. Weekly open meetings were held to talk over novel and unprecedented problems. The numbers kept getting better.

Aye, there's the rub, to steal a line from the leadership secrets of William Shakespeare. A manager who got results like these in a corporation of any size could not expect, and would not want, to remain in the same job too long. Career-path planning dictated that you move every few years or stagnate. Inevitably, as people began to learn how to manage this new culture for the long pull, the plant manager received a promotion he could not refuse. He had no say in choosing his successor, who was brought in from another business to run the plant.

Remembering Changes Past

When I called the former plant manager twelve years later, I found him in a pre-retirement holding pattern at corporate headquarters. He anticipated the day, not far off, when he could take up a new career of service to his church and community. "The project was not popular with the new management," he recalled. "It was seen as very quirky by the manufacturing establishment. I was an outsider. I only survived because we made the numbers. They put in an engineer to follow me who had grown up in manufacturing. His attitude was, 'We have to put it back to the way it was.'

"After I left," the former plant manager went on, "my new office was still in the building. People would come up to me in the hall to say, 'They're changing things.' Rumors held that there was too much power in the hands of the people, and the new manager was not buying into it." He felt pangs of remorse as people told him how their enthusiasm and commitment were draining away. He felt guilt, too, for raising expectations so high only to have them dashed by his successor. As he saw it, coordination and control were being shifted back to managers and supervisors. Many people were demotivated. Key staff and managers left the company for other jobs.

A former team leader remembered the exercise somewhat differently. "Whether you like it or not depends on what happens to your team job," she said. "You can always find people who were enthusiastic and others who simply had to leave." She herself had moved on to a series of staff jobs. By 2002 she was among a very few leaders who had survived the initial redesign.

Was It Worth the Effort?

When I asked her if she would do it again, she did not hesitate. "Absolutely!" she said. "We went through a huge cultural change, something none of us ever had gone through before." She recalled that the new manager within a few years conducted his own reorganization, in which the employees were also involved. "We could not have done it without the first one," she said. And she added, "I think we should do this sort of thing every two years. The technology and customer needs change so fast that none of these systems lasts very long."

I asked the production manager who had raised the question of trust whether he thought it was worth the effort. "How can you say a system that delivers such positive results is not worth the effort?" he replied. "Isn't management's primary responsibility to optimize shareholder value and work toward the overall health and profitability of a company? Doing it with a fully engaged workforce is what we all should be striving for."

"The most satisfying part for me still," said the former plant manager, "is talking with the people who lived through that first redesign and seeing the impact it had on their lives." He mentioned Donna, an engineer now with a consulting firm, and Mike, a product line production manager now running a non-profit children's agency. "What struck me too," he added, "was how people who were not trained engineers could make such significant changes in the factory. One guy, an hourly line worker, said the most moving thing to me. 'In the old days,' he told me, 'I could check my brain at the door. Now I go home and I worry about the business. I can't help thinking about it. It's part of my life now.'

"The ones who suffered most in this situation," the former plant manager continued, "were the rank-and-file workers who struggled to make the turn, had all this excitement and enthusiasm and commitment, and then were told to go back to their machines and stop thinking although the impact of their work was obvious. The numbers were there. We validated the business model in a very short time frame."

I asked him if he would do it again. "Oh, certainly!" he replied. "But I would want more control. I'd need agreement at the highest levels that succession planning would be included, that this was a long-term cultural change, not just an experiment. I would have to be free to hire people who would be open to doing things a new way instead of doing whatever they wanted to make their own mark. I'd need assurances that whoever followed me would carry on in the same spirit.

"When you put so much of yourself in, it's revitalizing and exciting to get so much accomplishment. When I look back on my career, that project is what I am most proud of. And I have such high regard for the leadership team that came so far with me in that project. Many of them found new paths for themselves."

He felt no rancor. "The new guy who came in and turned things around had to make his numbers too. He must have done it or he would have been gone. I guess there is more than one way to do this work."

Learning from "the Environment"

Packaging Plant, like many corporate divisions, had little control of systems that determine the longevity of projects. Its "environment" was controlled in part by remote staff executives overseeing a global empire. A typical career path—move every two years or stagnate—was just the tip of a policy iceberg holding innovative ideas hostage. Had the plant manager stayed, he soon would have come up against centralized cost accounting, compensation and personnel policies, quality initiatives, reporting systems—that did not reflect a high-performing system's real value.

In a big company it is difficult to make "systemic" changes when you cannot control key parts of the system. Since nothing stands still, systems redesign is a never-ending task. Those who aspire to this work would do well to get over the idea that there are powerful change technologies, even "large-group interventions," to bypass all this. It's easy to say "flatter organization" and "get the supervisors out" than to figure out how to help redundant people find new jobs or how to put in measurements that account for the economic value of motivated workers.

That does not make systems improvement less important. We do better, though, when we shelve notions that we can create a new, unified, systemically integrated, holistic, organic, good-to-the-last-drop, for-now-and-forever, workplace culture in a sea of contradictory agendas. No one should expect to improve a corporate culture and have it stay that way. We cannot "build in" policies, procedures, and norms that will outlive all those who come after. Each new crop of managers will want to do things their own way. The best any of us can do is to give every project our best right now. Realistically speaking, we ought to act as if there will be no next time. For most managers in large corporations, that is a fact of life.

CASE 4. SOLCORP: EXPERTISE CAN'T FIX THE OLD PARADIGM (1981)

> I think our goals are unrealistic—I mean having a production line when there's not enough product knowledge in this system to have anything other than an R&D facility.
>
> —Engineer, Solcorp

We come at last to the end of the road for experts on one hand and problem solving, even the participative kind, on the other. Solcorp was founded in the early 1970s to develop an innovative process for making electricity from sunlight. Its creator sold out to a large company eager to commercialize the process. In no time the division had 250 engineers and scientists, a building full of high-tech equipment, and a factory making solar energy cells. The trouble was, they cost too much.

After a few years—way too few, it turned out—the parent company increased pressure on its new venture to cut costs and start making money. The division missed production targets for four years running. To stem the cash drain, management laid off one-fourth of the workforce. Skilled technical people were bailing out as fast as they could type up their résumés. Tensions among marketing, manufacturing, and development ran high. The parent company recommended consulting help.

The president, a scientist, had no management training. He had nagging feelings the company was off track, and he wondered whether they could meet the current objective of a viable product this year and worldwide sales within four years more. He was convinced that new procedures to set goals and hold people accountable would solve his problems.

Cotton Cleveland and I agreed to use his concern as a hypothesis to be tested in a diagnosis of the whole system. Like many managers, he was backed into a participative process by events he could not control. He called in twenty-five staff members from every function who knew the problems and whose commitment was needed for solutions. A joint diagnosis was planned. We consultants took more than one hundred pages of interview notes. Many comments confirmed the president's observation about goals:

"I don't really know what the goals are."

"There are no goals. None."

"Our goals have been wrong. With 20/20 hindsight it's easy to say that."

Still, people had a strong sense of mission and were excited about the work. It appealed to their social values—finding a pollution-free, benevolent energy source. It appealed to their professional aspirations—pioneering a frontier technology.

"I'm engrossed in the high technology. The end result is visible, and it gives me a warm-all-over feeling."

"The public desperately wants an alternative to oil. The sun is too attractive to be ignored. It has to be pursued. We are pioneers, no doubt about it."

"This company is strong in its technical capability. People simply believe in what the company is trying to accomplish. It's something potentially beneficial."

Despite fuzzy goals, the company had a clear mission—to make and sell cheap solar modules based on their new technology. The oft-noted lack of clarity was attributed to the fact that neither production nor sales goals had been met. People believed, deep down, that the goals were wrong. Their comments revealed a deeper strategic dilemma: the plight of a firm seeking to market a product not yet fully developed.

"We lack process knowledge. The basic work hasn't been done. We go by empiricism rather than knowledge—there's a lot of witchcraft and black magic here."

"There's a frustrating shift in quality and nobody knows why. We change direction to make the problem seem to go away."

"We can't produce and then repeat a stable product."

"We should never have gotten into manufacturing as early as we did."

The president had been single-mindedly tuned in to the high-potential technology. His unfounded optimism brought economic pressures from a corporation happy to believe that profits were just around the corner. The social consequences had become too grave to ignore. Nobody had hope—a classic example of the way technical, economic, and social problems interact. Top managers took to public blaming, a symptom of anxiety and fear.

"I've seen people ripped to shreds in group meetings."

"I don't want to be humiliated in front of my peers."

"Upper management always takes comments as personal attacks."

The twenty-five people reviewed these and one hundred other comments in a day-long meeting with the president. They readily owned up to five conclusions based on their own heretofore never shared observations:

1. The product was not ready for market without more basic research.
2. Nobody could say how long this would take.
3. The sales force was promising potential customers more than the factory could deliver.
4. The factory was in a constant state of crisis, trying in real time to iron out the bugs of a technology not fully developed.
5. Each function went its separate way, with little interchange, coordination, or joint problem solving.

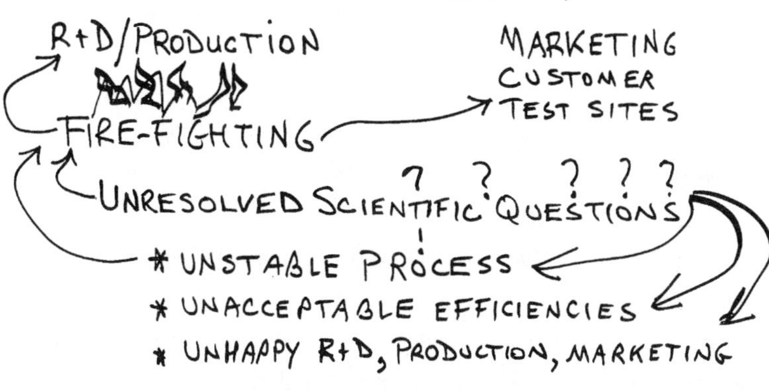

In short, it was a research lab trying to act like a business. People continually fought fires. The president desperately wanted to believe that the solution was just one experiment away. He knew research findings could not be scheduled, that some breakthroughs take years, others forever. Manufacturing goals—which could be scheduled—proved unrealistic because of quality breakdowns. To succeed they had to make the same product the same way

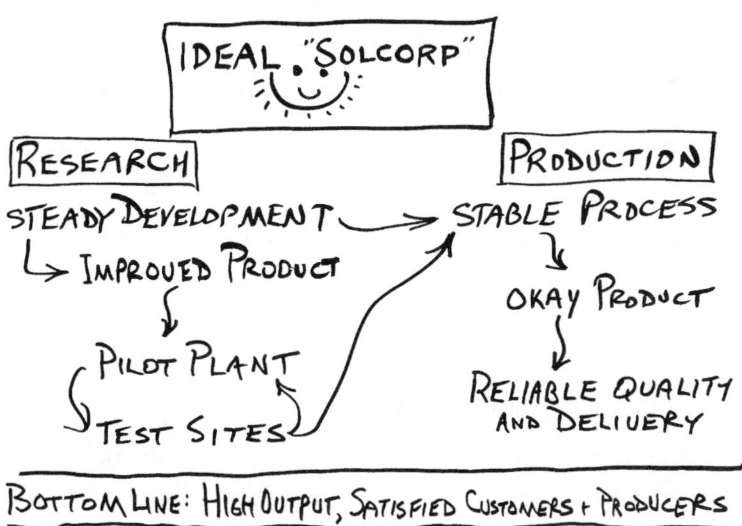

each time. See "Cat Chasing Its Tail," a local theory for this situation, and "Ideal Solcorp" (both on the previous page) for the gap between reality and aspiration.

It was probably too late to salvage the dream. Involving employees more fully might minimize the damage. Two alternatives emerged from the joint discussions. Solcorp could stabilize a minimally acceptable product, maximize sales, and decouple production from R&D. This would mean a narrow market in the short run, hardly enough to stem the losses. Or it could eliminate marketing entirely, reduce manufacturing to a pilot plant, and free up the researchers to become again an R&D facility.

In follow-up meetings, the top-management team decided on the second course of action. The consultants, not cognizant then of participative options for downsizing, terminated their work. Within a year, the parent had agreed to further cutbacks; half the workforce was laid off, and the facility focused on R&D.

From the standpoint of this book's theme, several interview comments also reveal the depth of the need for employees to be involved in the problem solving and decision making from the start:

"This meeting is the last chance. It can't go on. Management has to change or people will leave."

"If we change direction, everybody should share in that and the sooner the better. But I need commitment behind me."

"My people and myself want to help and don't know how."

"For representing such a large number of people, I don't feel part of the team. That makes it extremely difficult to plan."

"We have great difficulty working in concert and it's clear we can't work independently and be successful."

Searching for Solcorp

Solcorp, real name Solar Energy Systems (SES), fell off the radar screen in the 1980s, not long after the events just described. I learned of its demise a decade later while seeking to contact someone who had been there. I called a company with a vaguely similar name in the same locale. Wrong company. One veteran executive recalled SES and even remembered the president's name. He had no idea where to find him. He could not recall the year they closed up shop.

In the 1980s SES was a Shell Oil subsidiary, so I checked the company website. Shell again had an active solar entity, in Europe. The online history made no mention of SES. I called Shell and exchanged emails with staff in Texas, California, and the Netherlands. No one could tell me what had become of SES. An industry historian thought it had folded in the 1970s.

On the web I found that the cost of solar cells had fallen by 50 percent since 1990. "Photovoltaics," said an executive vice president of Shell Solar, "is one of the fastest-growing of all the renewable energy technologies. We have the people, the reach, and the resources to build a sustainable, commercially successful solar energy business around the world."

When I visited the website a few months later I found that the company was closing two European factories and laying off 170 people. "These have been difficult decisions for us and job losses are deeply regrettable" said the same VP. "The PV market faces a glut in supply and . . . we believe the way to maintain a competitive edge is to focus on our leading position in technology development and our sales and marketing operations" (de Renzy-Martin, 2002). I was encouraged to note that the company planned to help those laid off to find new jobs. The technical problems of the early 1980s had been solved. The industry remained volatile and uncertain. In 2006 SolarWorld, a German company, acquired Shell Solar's assets, becoming, for the moment, the largest solar panel manufacturer in the United States. Anyone who sought to do "change" projects in such companies could expect a bumpy ride.

One measure of change: In 2010 the Weisbord family installed fourteen solar panels on a south-facing roof, something inconceivable when I first wrote this case. We were making 30 percent of household electricity from the sun.

The story illustrates, under the worst conditions, the hunger for productive workplaces. It also shows how technical values tend to drive out social values and the power of collaborative action research for untangling the mess. Without the involvement of his managers, the president could not gain perspective on his sinking feeling that he had been wrong to hold on so long. Without focusing on the whole system, he could not confront the parent with its unrealistic expectations. This sort of dilemma continues to frustrate 21st Century managers. The movie was merging with the snapshot. That called for a wholly new way of building on Lewin's road map.

■ ■ ■

"AT FIRST GLANCE, IT SEEMS RIDICULOUS..."

CHICAGO, IL—For Emily and me, the legacy of *Productive Workplaces* is the idea of getting the whole system in the room. The chapter on Future Search was transformative for me. We were planning a workshop with the American Fishing Tackle Manufacturers Association on protecting Great Lakes water quality and fisheries and had invited fishing club members, commercial fishers, environmentalists, and state officials. Future Search's elegant simplicity was what this group needed. I ended up doing two more Future Searches with AFTM, on fresh water and salt water fisheries.

In 1991 The Axelrod Group began integrating Future Search principles and sociotechnical design into what would become the Conference Model®, a large group process for workplace redesign. At RR Donnelley and Sons, North America's largest printing company, we were able to compare our method with traditional processes. Organizations using our conference model, with the "whole system in the room," experienced much faster implementation.

We now have conducted hundreds of processes with organizations large and small using Future Search, other large group methods, and our own model. In one unlikely application, for example, prisoners were involved in the redesign of a jail. They pointed out, among other things, that moving door hinges from the inside to the outside of the cells would make prisoner suicide more difficult.

Had we not seen *Productive Workplaces* in 1987, we would not have the Conference Model, and Boeing would not have increased engineering employees' satisfaction by 40 percent,

Hewlett-Packard's Microelectronics Division would not have increased productivity by 18 percent for five consecutive years, Calgary Health Authority would not have reduced wait times 10 to 40 percent, and the Chicago Arts Partnership in Education would not have the funding to provide its important services.

—Dick Axelrod, The Axelrod Group, author of *Terms of Engagement: New Ways of Leading and Changing Organizations* (2010).

---

chapter
FOURTEEN

Managing and Consulting in Permanent White Water

If you want to understand what a science is, you should look in the first instance not at its theories or its findings, and certainly not at what its apologists say about it; you should look at what the practitioners of it do.

—Clifford Geertz, *The Interpretation of Cultures*, 1973, p. 5

Peter Drucker (1976) pointed out that the trouble with Taylorism was that the engineers who followed Taylor stopped where he did. Lewin's descendants face the same dilemma. You can get caught in the labyrinth of social technologies, lose sight of core values, break off chunks of psychological reality, and prescribe activities for workplaces that no longer exist. The world we live in calls for new forms of diagnosis and action. Peter Vaill (1996) aptly named this environment "permanent white water." Vaill makes the point that, while anything is possible, "what cannot be planned for is the continual occurrence of further surprising, novel, ill-structured, and obtrusive events" (Bunker and Santana, 2010, p. 57). In this chapter I will critique the cases presented in Chapter Thirteen to show the direction required for a 21st Century practice theory of managing and consulting.

To appreciate why I want to refocus the playing field, I would like you to join me on a trip through the thickets of organizational change theory. For decades OD case studies have reflected two improvement processes coexisting uneasily. One was a theory of diagnosis based on the expert's data-collecting skills. I liken diagnosis to snap-shooting, grabbing a picture of "reality" at a moment in time. Another was Lewin's brilliant theory of participative action. I call that moviemaking, creating conditions for effective collaboration. Most practitioners know that the two theories are really one. How you take the snapshot determines the quality of the movie.

There are two critical decisions affecting the snapshot and the movie:

1. Who takes the picture?
2. Where point the camera?

The only Lewinian requirements were that people and situation be looked at together, and that consultants and clients work as a team. Any problem, large or small, could make a movie, so long as its dynamic aspects were considered, meaning people's feelings, perceptions, and behavior, which change from moment to moment. Yet all of us have one foot in the old paradigm—Taylor's cause-effect reasoning. Taylor fragmented work into manageable pieces. Action research, despite our whole-systems rhetoric, was often problem-focused. That's no surprise when you consider the concept's origin.

Social science early on imitated medical science. "Diagnosis" is medical jargon for specifying the gap between sickness and health. As biology exploded in the 19th Century, the human body was divided into manageable components. Specialist physicians became the industrial engineers of the human physique. Their claim to expertise was the ability to factor in every variable and thus heal the sick. It is no surprise that early psychologists thought the same way about mental processes. Indeed, until the biologist Ludwig von Bertalanffy (1952) proposed a general systems theory, people educated in Western societies could hardly think any other way.

Process Thinking

Lewin highlighted processes unseen in the 19th Century because nobody had a conceptual lens that could see them. His force fields made possible "process" snapshots—feelings, motives, intentions, and other intangibles related to results. Lewin portrayed diagnostic gaps in more dynamic terms: as an interaction of relevant social forces—personal, group, company-wide, societal. Who are the gatekeepers, he asked, whose behavior must change to assure constructive action? What forces prevent or encourage their involvement? In that way, he showed more precisely under what conditions action-taking led to change. Still the old medical vocabulary endured. From Lewin I inherited two practice theories making possible my transition from manager to consultant. One was the task-process relationship, a construct telling me where to point the camera. The other was changing a system by unfreezing, moving, and refreezing it. For this to work, the people in the picture had to be involved in taking it.

Task-Process Snap-Shooting. The task-process connection describes a chicken-egg interplay between ends and means, methods and goals, motivation and output. A task is concrete, observable, and purposeful. You can convert it into criteria, measurements, and targets. Devise a plan for reducing turnover 10 percent in Region A, for example. Find out and fix what blocks output on the packaging lines.

Process describes the "how." It reflects perceptions, attitudes, feelings, reasoning. "Why aren't we making progress?" or "Do people feel involved and committed to this?" Not when, where, and how many. Rather, why, how, and whether. Process thinking stimulates questions about attitudes and motivation. Who will be interviewed? Who will do it? You, an expert, or the people themselves? Alone or in groups? If you split the task from the process, you come up with a plan you can't implement.

A Dual Image Paradox. Task-process thinking can be likened to the famous visual paradox of the Old Woman/Young Woman, reproduced on the next page. Do you see a young beauty facing away or a wizened crone in profile?

You can't see both at once. By some mental gyration you can shift between them. Does one picture cause the other? Cause-effect thinking that underlies both Taylorism and the medical model may lead you to imagine that defining a goal causes its achievement. Industrial managers developed an exquisite left-brain approach: linear, rational, A causes B, three steps, nine phases, be precise, don't waste my time, gimme the bottom line. Diagnosis is a task requiring structure and precision. Whether your

Reprinted from *Gestalt Therapy: Excitement and Growth in the Human Personality* by Frederick Perls, M.D., Ph.D., Ralph E. Hefferline, Ph.D., and Paul Goodman, Ph.D. Copyright © 1951 by Frederick Perls, M.D., Ph.D., Ralph E. Hefferline, Ph.D., and Paul Goodman, Ph.D. Used by Permission of The Julian Press, Inc.

categories are "hard" or "soft," listing and prioritizing them puts your left brain into high gear.

Action reflects process. Once you have a destination in sight, you fly largely on automatic pilot, fueled by little explosions of energy in the right brain—of creativity, energy, synthesis—especially when choosing among uncertainties (Mintzberg, 1976). Lewin ingeniously expanded left-brain thinking. He shifted the diagnoser's viewpoint to focus attention on processes invisible only because nobody was looking for them.

From his work came a simple practice theory I learned when I started consulting: process "issues" always block work on tasks. Through trained observation you can find ingenious linkages. If the work isn't getting done, for example, look for what is not being talked about. The concept, like the picture of the woman, is an artifact of how our brains work. Your train of thought can be derailed by either picture—too much or too little task orientation. And you can fasten on any issue or combination, depending on your upbringing, education, genes, even what you ate for breakfast.

You will find a task-process interplay any place you look. Neither task nor process adequately describes reality. They exist only in relationship. Lewin does not tell you how broad or narrow your gaze should be, only that you should look at people and situations together. If Food Services has too high turnover, what makes folks leave? What is the link connecting cost, motivation, output, and manager behavior? If your framework is narrowly economic, you might (like Taylor) engineer the jobs for speed and pay more. From a social systems perspective, you might conclude (with Likert) that manager behavior and conditions of work must change. And you might then proceed to force changes without involving anybody.

Task-Process and Systems Focus. Many consultants in the 1970s were learning to see the task-process linkage not only with interpersonal relations but also in an organization's relationship with its environment. My six-box diagnostic model (Weisbord, 1978b) reflected this effort to move toward a more complete view of reality than group dynamics alone would permit (Chapter Thirteen, p. 222).

Two realities make task-process applications problematical. One, social engineers can abstract process issues out of their economic and technical contexts for problem solving the same way industrial engineers break down machine operations. That's because all economic and technical problems have a "people" component—the unwritten rules (norms) evolved to cope with work. However, diagnosing norms does not make them treatable. Suppose the process issues derive from the structure of the work itself? The sort of OD I was practicing in the 1970s did not permit that question. Moreover, my clients, still not shaken enough by world events, would not have found the question actionable.

Second, even with a systems model it is possible (even probable) that you will become problem-focused too soon. Managers hate to sit looking at something from all angles; they like to get on with it. That's what I did for many years. In a left-brained industrial world, with computers tracking output, Wall Street watching quarterly results, and the Dow Jones stock index changing daily, you can hardly avoid it. It is tempting to zero in on a process issue in one box and start fixing it. You say, "Let's get a new reward system in here," and, presto, a compensation expert is working out the details, independent of purposes, relationships, or anything else. You say, "I want effective communications around here," and soon everybody is in workshops (communicating how much they hate being there).

A manager's aspiration should be to go back and forth between task and process, structure and behavior, the way a pilot scans the instruments—from gas gauge to altimeter, to air speed indicator, to artificial horizon—continually keeping all of them in sync. As soon as one dimension checks out okay, you shift your gaze to another. If you see a serious deviation, say you've let yourself drift 1,000 feet too low, it would be disastrous to keep focused on the compass. Correct your altitude or risk a run-in with another plane going elsewhere at the same height.

You Can't Fly on the Compass Alone. Unfortunately, left-brain diagnostic thinking leads us to pay attention to the compass and to consider the altimeter a luxury or a frill. The assumption is that the diagnoser stands outside, impartial, objective, and aloof from what is observed. If you add to this our propensity to defer to authority—parents, bosses, experts—you have a setup for disappointment. If ever a whole civilization was built on left-brain behavior, it is the world of work in industrial societies. None of us is immune.

Group dynamics' great contribution to management—whether from the Bion or Lewin traditions—was its relentless gaze at the process picture inseparable from the accomplishment of the task, the diagnoser inseparable from the diagnosis, a leader's skill inseparable from follower contributions. One big aha for me in unstructured learning groups was how I reinforced my anxiety and frustration. My efforts to do things perfectly, and to get everybody doing likewise, I now trace to my unfounded assumptions about what I and others could and should do.

The big aha for a task force making no progress is the need to resolve process issues. Chem Corp's R&D department could not gain credibility through team building at the top. People at many levels had to commit to removing the blockages. Until these were cleared out, things could only become worse.

There is no by-the-book process issues list. One clue that things are off track is in your own reaction to what's happening. If you hear the same information recycled without being acted upon, that's a process issue. If you want to contribute something and hold yourself back, that's a process issue. If people run away or fight, abandoning the task, that's a process issue. All can be seen as the "how's" that block the "what's."

Unfreezing, Moving, Refreezing

My second important practice theory was what I called "Lewin's Law." Lewin saw human systems as almost but not quite static and resistant to change. A consultant's goal was to accelerate the rate and direction of change in response to a social problem or conflict, and to stabilize constructive actions. What was to be unfrozen were the unconscious behaviors that worked against productivity. In the four cases in the last chapter, my diagnostic snapshots were intended to make people want to act, to melt the ice of indifference, ignorance, or uncertainty and unfreeze the system. Once melted, it would follow more natural channels, flowing downhill, so to speak, until cooled enough to refreeze into more functional patterns.

At Chem Corp, Food Service, and Packaging Plant, I think the need to unfreeze was a defensible hypothesis in the 1970s. While all three firms experienced "turbulent environments" (Emery and Trist, 1963), most employees did not know it. In Packaging Plant, for example, nobody but

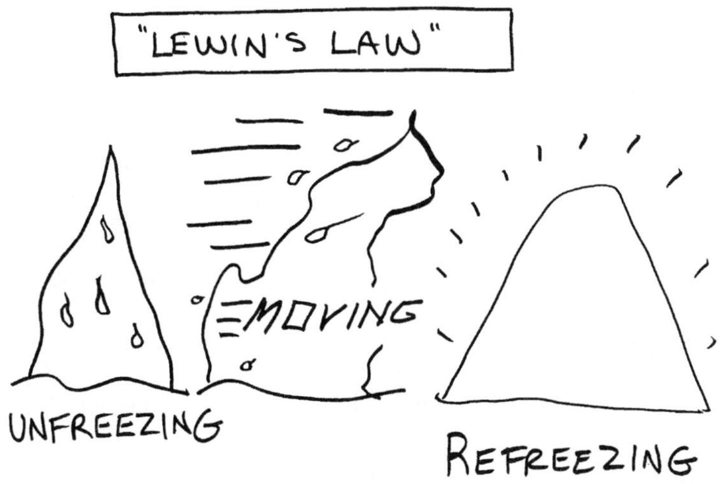

top management saw anything amiss with the filling lines until the consultants assembled a cast of twenty-eight people and held up a mirror to the dilemma. At Chem Corp, although the top team and R&D managers wanted to do something, other departments were indifferent until the survey created awareness of the need to act. Food Services assumed turnover as an immutable business cost, not a clue to systemic dysfunction. The carrot of cost reduction attracted top managers to study what had been, until the consultant's seminar, a non-problem. Hence the comparative diagnostic survey enticed people to take a second look and galvanized action. Although a traditional unfreezing diagnosis was attempted at Solcorp, I believe it was largely for the consultants' benefit. If I were doing it again I would not diagnose the system's failures; I would seek to mobilize energy for change. In Solcorp's case I probably still would have been too late.

Change Theory

Now, let us visit the linkage between the task-process cycle and the process of unfreezing, moving, and refreezing. This linkage made possible the organization development (OD) profession. Unresolved process issues accumulate in organizations like junk in an attic. People freeze in dysfunctional patterns; nobody listens, appreciates, celebrates, communicates. Output and quality suffer. Reacting to crises drives out future thinking. This self-perpetuating ice storm over corporate headquarters was what Lewin sought to unfreeze with action research.

If the stored-up stuff could be put out into the open, if people could express their resistances and skepticism, energy would flow. People would become aware of their own contributions to their problems. The blockages would be removed and new behavior would emerge—a possibility that might be accelerated through skill training. Unfrozen, people would redo strategy, policy, procedure, relationships, and norms more to their liking. Implementing new action plans would move the system, and reinforcing mechanisms—periodic review meetings, for example—would refreeze the system into more functional patterns.

Could you measure the results? The best answer was to check people's attitudes and actions before and after and compare their answers to service levels, product quality, quantity, cost, profit. That's what Likert did with his systems surveys. At Food Services and Chem Corp we measured outcomes that indicated new behaviors had taken root with excellent results. At Packaging Plant we changed the production system, and the incompetent workers fallacy disappeared.

How long would the refreezing last? A long time, we hoped. But not a moment longer than the perception that unfreezing was needed again. That became the rub. How does a system become self-regulating? What does it take to spot and free up process blockages as you go along, instead of building up to a crisis before doing anything? The key was believed to be learning—not just learning how to solve the problem in cause-effect terms (if I do A, then I get B) but also learning how to flip back and forth between task and process, and to realize that both "pictures" are there all the time.

Learning to shift your gaze between task and process could become a way of life rather than a one-shot. Results were feedback loops, a built-in monitor for self-regulation. In the cases in Chapter Thirteen we intended that managers not only solve their problems, but that they evolve a new way of doing business. Then people would approach future dilemmas with more thoughtful diagnoses. They would take responsibility rather than play helpless or blame others. They would stop jumping to conclusions and become more aware that involving others would lead to faster, better, and more committed action. They would, in effect, learn how to learn, to generalize new behavior into better future responses. Those were the OD assumptions of change. They beautifully capture the spirit inherent in Emery and Trist's new paradigm behavior in contrast to a more mechanistic, manipulative Taylorism.

All OD cases fit this framework of diagnosis and action. At the heart of the diagnostic act was a confrontation: the clients had to accept the incongruity between what they wanted and what they had—the normative demon to be exorcised before healing could begin. Although Lewin's model does not assume sickness, it is easy to infer for those of us socialized to the medical model with diagnosis its most sacred act. Lewin believed action research should be a joint venture of experts and those with the problem. While action was the client's bailiwick, unfreezing the system was the consultant's.

In the 1950s and 1960s people began working out a new form of third-party behavior—consulting skills—to facilitate these assumptions. It was based on Lewin's insights that people are more likely to act on solutions they have helped develop. It included a minor fiction: that questions, methods of inquiry, data presentation, analysis, and action steps would be jointly planned. I say "fiction" because the methods inevitably belonged to the consultants, and so did the theories of task and process, unfreezing, and the rest. The feedback meeting was the pivot point of social change. There the data were "owned," resistance melted, and movement initiated. So long as OD consultants considered unfreezing their special province, they could not avoid the role of expert, models and rhetoric to the contrary.

Four Cases Revisited

My four cases from the 1970s represent stages in my own development and that of OD practice. Better movies required progress toward greater stakeholder involvement at every step. The path toward better snapshots led from analyzing discrete problems toward understanding whole systems—the subtle interplay of economics, technology, and people. In Chapter Eighteen I suggest guidelines for merging snapshots and movies that make simpler, more radical change projects feasible. To appreciate them we must acknowledge the shortfalls of older methods: focusing groups on too narrow a problem or having too few people in on the diagnosis. Worst case, we do both—the agony of the expert problem solver.

From Problem Toward System Focus. Problem focus means worrying over one piece of the puzzle unconnected to the others—economics, or technology, or people. System focus means treating the whole as one piece of a larger puzzle, for example, one that includes world markets and employees hungry for dignity, meaning, and community.

If you look at the four cases along the snapshot continuum from problem focus to systems focus, you see this picture:

Problem Focus	**Transitional**	**Systems Focus**
Food Services (turnover)	Chem Corp (interdepartmental relations) (innovation)	Packaging Plant Solcorp (economics, technology, people)

At Food Services we worked on manager behavior, not food service unit structure. At Chem Corp, we sought to improve relations between R&D

and everybody else—a classic OD intervention, but with a do-it-yourself "new paradigm" survey twist. An unexpected outcome was the flow of new products. At Packaging Plant we started with a problem focus—motivate people to put more product out—and found the solution in describing the way the whole system worked from suppliers to factory to market. At Solcorp, swamped by change, our action-research orientation moved us quickly from teamwork in setting goals toward the heart of the issue: the connections among strategy, technology, markets, structure, and behavior. In short, we used (appropriately) a wide-angle lens, even when the president wanted a telephoto.

There is no necessary connection between the wideness of the lens used for snap-shooting and the degree of stakeholder involvement. To make good our participative aspiration, people have to be deeply involved from the start in methods, concept development, data collection, and diagnosis. To make good our whole open-system aspiration, we need to put the system and all its problems at the center of the action. If we would fully experience the snapshot and movie as one process, nothing less will do.

My cases reflect a mix of old and new paradigms. When all stakeholders were involved and the clients generated hypotheses and led feedback meetings, the movie tended toward the new (Chem Corp). When consultants made problem maps for the client (Packaging Plant, Solcorp), the movie looked more like the old, even though the systems maps were state of the art.

A quality movie requires systemic participation in the snapshot. People need to describe their own gaps, make their own maps, find their own variances, instead of having consultants do it for them. The more technically competent consultants are, the greater the challenge to transfer their knowledge.

From Expert Toward Stakeholder Involvement. If we now put the cases on a movie continuum—from expert involvement to stakeholder involvement in the whole process—we see this:

High Expert Involvement	**Mixed Involvement**	**High Stakeholder Involvement**
Food Services Solcorp	Packaging Plant	Chem Corp

In my four cases, my colleagues and I still did most of the front-end diagnosis. In our zeal to be effective, we became another kind of expert, striving to understand the client system, to draw maps of how it works, to explain it to those who work there, seeking to transfer "ownership" by negotiating questions to be asked, timetables, and objectives. In short, we did whatever it took to unfreeze them. But we did it.

The four cases reveal varying degrees of whole-system focus and high stakeholder involvement. The best systems analysis was at Solcorp, where the clients had the least involvement in the diagnosis. The best client involvement was in Chem Corp. The cases reveal assumptions and aspirations for both snapshot and movie beyond the scope of my techniques. Nonetheless, I easily persuaded myself that unfreezing by third parties, movement by principals and third parties together, and refreezing by the principals constituted a strategy for cultural change.

Science could be mobilized to beat back authoritarianism and bureaucracy. If the norms of data collection, communication, relationships, and problem solving were changed, all else would follow. What made this different from Taylorism were its participative techniques—learning to do things with, not to or for, others. Whatever its shortcomings, this brand of action research, like scientific management in 1900, was a great advance over what people did before.

Rethinking Lewin

I now find my old practice theory unsatisfying from two perspectives. First, global markets, technologies, and worker expectations change so fast that a frozen workplace is a temporary phenomenon. Today change goes more like a bullet train than a melting iceberg. The rate has accelerated since Kurt Lewin died in 1947. Conventional diagnoses may serve useful functions, but unfreezing systems is not one of them. We change our behavior when we are ready to do it, not because an expert tells us we should. Nobody is skilled enough to push the river. The best a consultant can do is create opportunities for people to do what they are ready to do. If we apply a linear bag of tricks, only the content differs from Taylor's. The process comes out uncomfortably the same.

Second, despite my use of systems models, I cannot know enough about any system to isolate, analyze, and synthesize its many moving parts. My systems perspective is the most useful thing I have. However, the perspective, or way of thinking, matters more than the factors, dimensions, or boxes in my model. Systems models are best thought of as tools for coalescing people to do something together, helping them to undertake a systems-improvement task. Collectively they know more than any consultant about what it will take for them to move.

If you accept that proposition, you will see why I worry more about responding to needs for dignity, meaning, and community than about supplying "right" answers. There is considerable anxiety and confusion everywhere. I think it is wrong to assume people's dilemmas mean sickness, as if only the diagnostician were whole and in control. Nothing holds still long enough to be changed anyway. So consultant-centered diagnostic activities intended to unfreeze systems, even when welcomed by clients deferring to authority, even when holistic in concept, may inadvertently deter people from taking charge of their lives.

To honor Lewin requires reconfirming his values and insights. It also requires that we devise methods closer to our aspirations for wholeness, involvement, and self-control. I'm conscious of profound paradoxes. I have at my fingertips diagnostic techniques for every issue in the cosmos. On my bookshelves I find more models for fixing things than there are stars in the galaxy. Yet, I am strangely undernourished by this intellectual cornucopia. My objective, I keep reminding myself as I pant to keep up with change in a new era, is not to diagnose and heal sickness, but to help people find dignity, meaning, and community in work. *Those* are the conditions that sustain productivity.

The consultants' dilemma is that we always arrive in the middle of the movie and leave before the end. The script has many subplots and informal directors. The consultant negotiates a role—sometimes major, sometimes minor, but always limited by the willingness of others to play along. My view of the consultant's role has turned upside down from what I once thought. I imagine it now as helping people discover and act upon a more whole view of what they are doing than any one discipline or person can provide.

I find that proposition fraught with uncertainty. To the extent I can help people integrate their values and tasks, I make an important contribution. Yet that means being at some level an expert and accepting people's projections on authority, even when I don't act the authoritarian. None of us knows, exactly, how to be both an expert and just one of the gang—when we value collaboration and mutual learning more than being right. I know that people can learn how to learn. But that any of us can teach others explicitly how to do that is in my opinion an old paradigm theory full of iffy-ness.

Toward Assessing Possibilities. We come at last to the heart of it: it is not always practical or desirable to negotiate a consulting role that, at its simplest, is helping people do what they are capable of doing, even when they don't know that they know it. The consultant's task in the movie is to see confusion and anxiety through to energy for constructive action, and to learn along with everybody else. That has an odd ring to somebody like me, who grew up at the tail end of the Industrial Revolution. I now believe that assessing the conditions (and they are narrow) under which such an unusual partnership is feasible should be the first task of consultation. Not how to help, but whether to make the offer.

Diagnosing gaps is not what I mean. Anxiety is not a sickness; it is a sign of bottled up energy for learning. Managers need simple ways to assess the potential for action, focus attention, and help people learn together about the whole contraption. That is quite different from consultants collecting and analyzing data. I am not against expertise, only the assumption that the expert knows everything required to improve a situation. This is especially true in complex work like reorganizing, a task governed largely by the right brain, and not amenable except in discrete details to problem solving. Staff-centered activity is not necessarily conducive to productive workplaces, whether named "participative management" or "dynamic synergistic holistic transformation." If people don't join in planning their own work, it's old Fred Taylor all over again, with social-psychological window dressing instead of time and motion study.

Whose Movie Is It? It is important to grasp this point if a productive workplace is your goal. An effective snapshot, seen as a dual image—task and process—portrays the whole system in relation to a valued purpose. People can do that accurately only when they all, to the extent possible, take the snapshot, appear in it, and look it over together. When the whole system is in perpetual motion, every relationship changing, no one person can take a coherent picture. As soon as people start making a collective self-portrait, it is not a snapshot. Suddenly it's a form of cinema vérité, as messy as life itself.

Only those most involved can make that movie. The best role a consultant can hope for is stage manager. Managing the dialogue required does not require elaborate unfreezing exercises. Most systems are destabilized long before a consultant comes in.

To influence committed action today requires a practice theory that (1) respects the past, (2) enhances productive workplaces, and (3) is responsive to the tide of change. Such a theory requires imagining under what conditions people will cooperate to improve whole systems, and under what conditions a consultant can help. In the next chapter I report two more cases pointing toward new ways of consulting and managing that many people are now evolving.

■ ■ ■

"ADDING A CREATIVE APPROACH TO LEFT-BRAIN PLANNING..."

PORTLAND, OR—I first read *Productive Workplaces* in 1990. It was given to me by a manager at Intel in appreciation for what I had done with his engineering group. It reminded him of the work I did as a "connector of people." I appreciated the theoretical and historical context and the framework in PW for putting theory into action.

I had been noticing in my work in my large corporation that we knew how to do problem solving but had no expertise in effecting lasting change. The quote, "We change when we can think out loud together with others whose actions affect us," plus the consulting advice in Chapter Thirteen [now Chapter Fifteen], were pivotal in my decision to pursue a degree in the Organization Systems Renewal program at Antioch University in Seattle. I wanted to know how to get folks together to think out loud and consequently make changes that would be beneficial.

Pursuing this end, I engaged a group at Intel in Future Search as a way of beginning the company's rigorous strategic planning process. Participants added a whole systems and creative approach to their usual left-brain planning. Not only did we come up with a couple of brand new ideas, but by having the members from other parts of the organization who were connected to us, we increased our total organizational output.

I have since designed and facilitated several Future Searches. My most significant challenge was in 2004, co-designing and co-facilitating with Ray Redburn, another Future Search Network member. This was a unique FS for a large, once-successful spiritual congregation that had dissolved rather dramatically. The community needed a unifying effort that would generate energy to propel itself into a new identity. Over the next five months about 150 congregants signed up. They faced many challenges, for example, a spiritual community in turmoil, disillusionment and anger, the resignation of the senior minister, little experience with operational structure, processes, and decisions, and severe financial constraints. Staff reductions meant stress and overload on remaining staff and volunteers. There were communication breakdowns and a flurry of activities which led to confusion. The congregation's viability and survival were at stake. To involve everyone who wanted to participate, we conducted two three-day conferences, followed by a day-long Action Planning and Implementation event attended by people from both prior meetings. We then put on a Vision Fair for congregants to explore action themes and sign up to participate on teams.

In 2007 I followed up with a smaller conference for the same spiritual community, incorporating a major learning from the earlier meetings. To maintain momentum we developed a team of action "champions" who met regularly to ensure progress on our identified actions. The result has been a spiritual community united since 2004, continually building on the foundation of renewal that emerged from chaos and confusion at the start. I knew from the beginning that the FS technology would unite the community and help people move forward and that I was the person who could provide that opportunity. PW, my graduate studies, and my experience with FS gave me that confidence.

—Jeannine Yancey, Jeannine Yancey Consulting

chapter
FIFTEEN

Involving Everyone to Improve the Whole

We are witnessing the most rapid, complex and thoroughgoing corporate restructuring in modern history.

—Alvin Toffler, *The Adaptive Corporation*, 1984, p. 4

At last I revisit two cases somewhat different from the previous four. Although I did not know it then, they put me on the path toward "getting the whole system in the room." Since the turn of the century, many practitioners have developed high involvement practices that equal people's aspirations for dignity, meaning, and community. Case 5 below opened my eyes to the value of stakeholder engagement in saving a system. Case 6 confirmed for me that involving the "gatekeepers" is the only form of reorganizing that works. Each was a move beyond problem solving toward wholeness.

CASE 5. MEDICAL SCHOOL: STAKEHOLDERS PLAN THE FUTURE (1969–1971)

The president and dean of Medical School, faced with dramatic changes in medical education in the late 1960s, charged a faculty/administration task force to make a "plan for planning." Members included the vice president for planning, physicians, a hospital administrator, heads of nursing, microbiology, radiology, and social work. An associate medical dean, having heard that I had helped a large foundation, asked me to meet with the president, who described his many dilemmas. A few years earlier medical deans performed surgery before breakfast, taught a class in mid-morning, saw patients in the afternoon, and ran a faculty meeting over dinner. To be CEO now meant more fundraising, less everything else. Research dollars were growing scarcer, escalating conflicts among specialties. The college and teaching hospital were at odds over their respective missions. Cost-containment pressures and a shortage of primary-care professionals triggered a clash between advocates of broad-based care and newer specialties.

Meeting with the task force, I saw that faculty and administrators could hardly discuss the weather without arguing. As an ex-journalist I knew how to interview people. As an ex-manager I knew something about business. This did not sound like a business. So I proposed interviewing department heads and key people on behalf of the task force, seeking clues to effective planning in this conflicted situation.

People Talked About the Process. Interviews revealed faculty mistrust and skepticism toward the planning effort and the dean. People mentioned internecine conflict more than medical education. There were deep rifts between faculty and managers, and between Medical School and its teaching hospital at the far end of the same building. Medical professionals, I learned, attributed conflict mostly to personalities. They had no concept of how task pressures could frustrate everybody.

Department heads flagged three major areas: a mission crisis; wanting a clearer organizational structure; and needing to influence programs and budgets. I reported to the task force the widespread skepticism, perceived needs, and obvious conflicts. What to do now? Medical schools, like the printing business, could not spend more money than they took in. The schools too had customers—students and patients—and hundreds of employees. That much I knew. But the managers (called "administrators") did not enjoy the respect accorded their business counterparts. High status was reserved for professors, researchers, and clinicians, with one exception. The dean was considered a super-being, whose broad shoulders carried all medical education problems. If doctors were God, medical deans were the whole Trinity.

When deans fell short, as inevitably they did, the earth shook. Associate deans, charged with integrating programs, had the least standing to do it. The president/dean, who had the standing, had no training and could not get support. I followed this in a myopic sort of way, like I did Spanish in Mexico, knowing some words but missing much for not having lived in the culture. Managing medical education was not like managing a business.

There comes a time, in Mexico or medicine, when you need to speak up. I proposed an experiment to the task force. We could build on Likert's studies at the Institute for Social Research of participative processes that had never been tried in medical schools. It was a gamble, certainly, but one worth taking given the high stakes. We would treat the planning process as an action research project to change the school by involving everyone. The research flavor appealed especially to the basic scientists, who understood learning by trying something new.

Using Link Pins. So we adapted Rensis Likert's (1961) link-pin concept. There would be three interlocking planning councils. Each would include doctors, nurses, basic scientists, students, trustees, and administrators. Each would have two members in common and two who served on a coordinating body with the president and vice presidents. Why two links? People missed

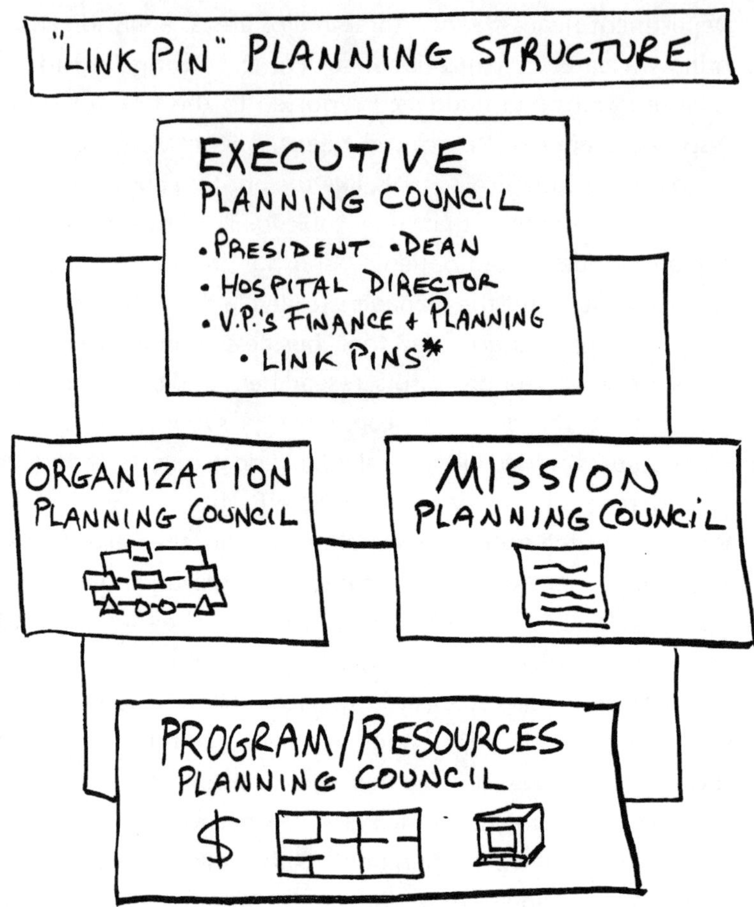

meetings too often, or ran out in the middle, said task force members. This process would address the three major areas of need (the task) and the demoralizing skepticism of those who had no influence (the process). (See "Link Pin Planning Structure.")

I drafted this plan, and task force members took it to their constituencies. After several stormy meetings, a consensus formed that high participation beat the status quo. We recruited forty volunteers to attend a two-day planning council start-up session. They reviewed research on coordination in hospitals (Georgopoulos and Mann, 1962), decided how link pins would operate, and chose chairpersons for each council. A friend of mine whose day job was corporate management training taught them cooperative problem solving. We rewrote a famous conflict management exercise, "The Prisoner's Dilemma," in terms of allocating space among medical departments. It was so realistic nobody considered it training.

Over several months I met with each council weekly as they studied their institution, proposing changes in mission, structure, priority setting, and budgeting. The councils scheduled meetings with medical and nursing staffs, attending physicians, trustees, and students—to review early drafts before finalizing proposals. The process gave influence to angry people previously left out. The meetings, tense and mistrustful at first, turned to problem solving as council members, armed with new information, talked with their peers. Commitment grew for change.

Changes. The Mission Planning Council went on to revisit the famous three-legged stool of academic medicine—research, teaching, and patient care—and made a radical proposal I will get to shortly that altered the school's future. The Organization Planning Council worked out a new concept of relationships between administration and faculty, medical school and hospital. The Program and Resources Council involved faculty and students in studying the financing of medical education.

Still, Medical School was never a bed of roses. The concept of having representative stakeholders work on structure and budgets was easy to grasp. Doing it, though, required great commitment from people on overload with patient care and teaching. Many people, despite high anxiety and frustration, worked hard for months to establish a new way of operating. Some faculty left. The president/dean moved on and the two jobs were separated. A candidate accepted the president's job, met with the planning task forces, and then backed out. One respected physician active in the planning councils was named interim president and dean. Those who stayed struggled to reorganize their medical school.

Medical School Revisited (2003)

Thirty years went by in an eye-blink. The need for confidentiality was gone, along with most of the players. What had been Women's Medical College in 1969 became Medical College of Pennsylvania (MCP) in 1970. And MCP survived until it was done in by egregious mismanagement nearly three decades later. Allegheny Health Systems, a Pittsburgh-based for-profit health care company, purchased the school and hospital in the late 1980s. It was merged by Allegheny in 1994 with Hahnemann Medical College into a corporate medical megalith, the MCP Hahnemann School of Medicine.

Allegheny went bankrupt in 1998. Several executives were indicted for fraud. Among other things, they used restricted grants for private purposes, including foreign junkets, costing some departments their research budgets (Stark, 1999). At this point the California-based Tenet Healthcare Corporation acquired Allegheny's facilities. In 2002 the school's assets were transferred to a new nonprofit entity, the Drexel University College of Medicine. What had been the smallest private medical school in the United States metamorphosed into the largest and became viable again.

Recalling the Planning Councils. What I could not write in 1987 is central to understanding what the planning councils actually did. Perhaps the most significant change was that the only all-women's medical school in the United States decided to admit six men (10 percent) into the class of 1970. The decision resulted from heated debates in the Mission Planning Council. For graduates and board members this breaking of the gender barrier was an act of betrayal to a mission dating from 1850. In 1969, only 6 percent of U.S. medical students were women, and 50 percent of all U.S. trained woman physicians were graduates of Women's Medical College! (Equal opportunity cut both ways. By the 2000s the national male-female medical student ratio was roughly 50–50.)

Dave Wagner, the surgeon who had sparked the planning project in 1969, was now the chair of emergency medicine. In the intervening years he became a founder and past president of the American Board of Emergency Medicine. With his help, I convened a meeting with planning council members from thirty years earlier. These included faculty members Phyllis Marciano, a pediatrician and 1960 WMC graduate, and June Klinghoffer, an internist who graduated in 1945.

Bernard Sigel, now retired, a respected surgical researcher who became dean and president at the height of the crisis, attended. So did Donald Cooper, chair of surgery in 1969, later vice provost, also retired. We met in the emergency medicine conference room.

The project remained vivid for all of them. The issues in 1969, said Dr. Marciano, were inextricably linked: whether to admit men to an all-women's school and where to find money. Good students were transferring to co-ed schools after two years, and, as a women-only school, WMC was denied access to government funding in the early days of the gender revolution.

The talk turned to outcomes. "There was no tangible outcome from the planning councils that I can recall," said Dr. Cooper. "I have thought a lot about it. I later came to believe it didn't work for two reasons. One, you need good will and we lacked it then. And, two, you need time to achieve consensus and we were out of time. Two-thirds of our budget came from outside sources, government, and state. The financial VP and hospital head kept a tight rein even though the dean/president was the nominal head. The issue was how to manage without authority." He was referring to a structural artifact from the days when a medical dean had a part-time job, the hospital and college were managed as one entity, and a full-time financial officer made budget decisions affecting educational priorities.

Why, then, did people stay with it? "We talked like we had never talked before," said Dr. Klinghoffer, "across all lines. We were all in it together."

Added Dr. Marciano. "We ventilated, we expressed our views, and it was helpful in that regard. What came out of it," she went on, "was a much better understanding of each other's problems."

"Given what you know now, would you do it again?" I asked at last.

"Absolutely," said Dr. Sigel. Several heads nodded in agreement.

"Why?" I asked. "The planning process kept us from flying apart at a critical time," said the former president. "Had we not been involved, I don't know whether we would have survived."

"Under the same circumstances," added Dr. Cooper, "I surely would do it again."

Finally, Dr. Wagner reiterated a point he had made for years: "In my opinion, faculty involvement in planning and budgeting to this day is traceable to the work we did in 1970. That was a key turning point for all of us."

Implications for Practice. What lessons did I derive from this case three decades later? One, we can never know going into a project what will come out of it. "Deliverables" represent wishful thinking. Two, creating dialogue across all boundaries is a healthy response in open societies, no matter what happens after. Three, what we call "managing change" may be more an exercise in endurance than management. And that, in my opinion, is not necessarily a bad thing.

Two of three planning councils had significant impact. The admission of men to an all-women's school resulted from the work of the Mission Planning Council. And faculty involvement in planning and budgeting over the next thirty years was traceable to the Program and Resources Council from the tumultuous meetings in 1970. Nothing was implemented from the Organization Planning Council, which had worked so hard rethinking the school/hospital relationship. What people remembered decades later were the passion and the dialogue.

Their work, however, extended far beyond one school. Building on the Council's report, Paul Lawrence and I teamed up to do differentiation/integration research with nine academic centers and twenty-five hospitals, under the auspices of the National Institutes of Health and the Association of American Medical Colleges (Weisbord, Lawrence, and Charns, 1978). These studies influenced medical school management and change projects in many places (Weisbord, 1974). In Chapter Sixteen I tell more of that story.

Learning (the Wrong Lesson) from Experience. Some years and many medical schools later—now an "expert"—I wrote a controversial article, "Why Organization Development Hasn't Worked (So Far) in Medical Centers" (Weisbord, 1976). I did not report the preceding Medical School case. Only later did I become aware that it represented one of the few cases on record at that time where physicians had collaborated with other stakeholders to improve an institution. I know now that Medical School was an excellent early example of the practice theory I now see widely applied. The case also illustrates an indisputable fact: no procedures can trump upheavals in society. Sometimes mutual support is the best people can do.

CASE 6. PRINTING INC.: GETTING THE REPORT OUT OF THE DRAWER (1981)

I began studying the report-in-the-drawer phenomenon a decade after Medical School. I was working on organizational structures and change processes in both medicine and industry. One day the general manager of Printing Inc., a small division of a global company, phoned me. His boss at world headquarters told him he needed team building and his staff had recommended me.

Their market, the GM said, had been flat for a long time. Some products were dying, a few others growing, all made and sold by decades-old processes. The rising star, an electronic label maker, was buried in development. In his old functional organization everybody specialized, nobody cooperated.

My potential client was an ex-bomber pilot, meticulous and careful, a planner, not a risk-taker like the fighter jockeys who had flown cover for him. When I asked him what *he* wanted, never mind his boss, he reached down into a bottom desk drawer and, using both hands, pulled out a document with more pages than *Gone with the Wind.* He opened it to two organization charts, which I have simplified on the next page as "Now and Proposed." Two years earlier, unable to grow, he had called on a firm noted for its organization studies. The consultants spent months talking to employees, doing library research, holding meetings. This was the result. They had recommended a decentralized product line organization that would be more flexible in the marketplace.

Why had he not implemented it? He hemmed and hawed for five minutes. It would change every manager's job. The GM considered himself a sensitive "one-on-one" manager. He had talked the report over with each person privately. No sale. All had different opinions about what to do, but on one thing they agreed: none wanted management jobs changed. My god, old Charlie had run manufacturing for twenty-three years.

That afternoon the general manager convened his subordinates. We began talking about the report like a black-sheep relative who had skipped the country. I asked whether they would be

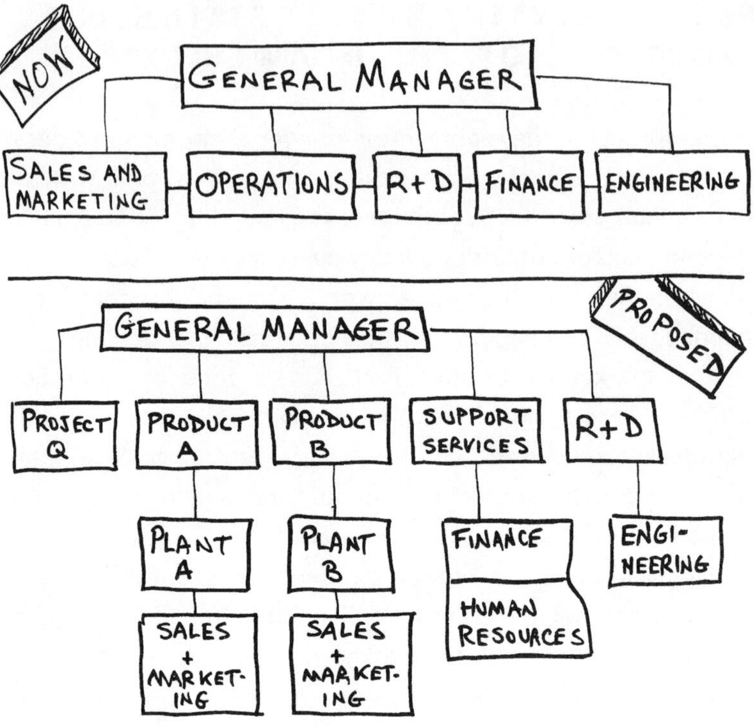

interested in comparing what was in the report (furtive glances, would it explode?) with structural ideas they had raised in our meeting. We decided on a two-day retreat to do it.

There are, broadly speaking, three ways to organize a business: by function, by product lines, or by some combination, called matrix. Variations on each form depend on local realities, technology, markets, and the rate of change. An organization study tends to recommend the structure you don't have. That is based on the theory—faultless, when you think about it—that if what you have isn't working, you need something else. All structures reach their limits after a while.

Companies reorganize because any structure's weaknesses eventually sap its strengths (Weisbord, 1978b). I knew that from years of medical school research and from consulting in many companies reorganizing from this to that. The need to reorganize, I had learned, does not mean that things are screwed up. It's a sign of growth, evolution, the earth turning on its axis the way it should.

Functions tend to build in-depth expertise, along with high walls and "silos." They make it hard to bring in new products. Product-line organizations maintain flexibility; the cost may be in losing touch with state-of-the-art marketing, engineering, manufacturing, and human resource practices. Big central staffs reassure top managers they have control, an illusion bought with high overheads. Small central staffs mean more local control and less overhead but more uncertainty at the top. Nothing comes free.

At Printing Inc. we discussed the options for an hour. Then the managers divided into three groups. One championed the old report; the others devised alternatives. Each listed the pros and cons of their proposal. We agreed that the first task was to come up with a structure they believed they could operate successfully. Suppose you were the sole owner? How would you organize? Once that was agreed upon, the job would not be finished until we had found appropriate slots for each manager.

The meeting was equal parts excitement and anxiety over the impact on jobs. Within twenty-four hours the managers had added some wrinkles to the expert consulting report and closed on a new structure. After two and a half years of aggravation, the report was implemented in a few months with jobs for each staff member. Old Charlie, after two years of worrying, took over a plant in another city.

A New Structure, or Just a Report? I have reflected for years on two questions raised by that experience:

1. Why do reports—even excellent ones—end up in bottom desk drawers?
2. Under what conditions can they be implemented?

I have two answers to question number 1. The first is that some managers want reports, not implementation. It has taken me a while to accept that, a triumphant integration (for me) of right-brain intuition with relentless rationality. Expertise has many uses besides solving the problem. Why would you want a report you do not intend to implement? One reason might be political—to satisfy a boss that you're on the case, yessir, or to placate a boss by using a highly recommended resource, let's say the parent company's favored consultant. (That, after all, is how I came in.)

A second reason might be unconscious—to act by turning the problem over to an expert. Most of us have ambivalence about tough dilemmas. Wilfred R. Bion, the psychoanalyst whose work I told about in Chapter Ten, could explain that one. The wish to struggle through and to run away from the labyrinth is played out as dependency on the consultant. If the consultant acts the expert authority and accepts the task of coming up with the perfect solution, the client is off the hook. The analysis and recommendations may seem too idealistic or too complicated. Not doing anything becomes a prudent decision. The more comprehensive the expert's work, the harder it is for anyone else to get a piece of the action—the perfect "successful failure." Two University of Pennsylvania social systems consultants have described this pattern as unconscious forces that can trap unwary consultants. The better the consulting job, the more helpless the consultant becomes (Gilmore and Krantz, 1985).

As for the second question—how to get reports out—some people, like Printing Inc.'s general manager, really want solutions. They shelve the report because they don't see how to implement it or because it violates a deeply held value. Those reports—and only those—are easy to get out of drawers. However, getting them out requires a process assessment—whether to try, how to do it, and who would be involved. Printing Inc.'s general manager purchased a state-of-the-art diagnosis of the marketplace, the technology, and the limits of his structure. It assumed that, given the "right" technical and economic solutions, reasonable people would do the right thing. That assumption had been smashed to smithereens by the machinists' union in the Watertown Arsenal strike against scientific management in 1911 (see Chapter Four).

Rethinking Diagnosis. It is easier to see now that implementing technically correct solutions calls for another form of diagnosis.

At Printing Inc., economics and technology got their due, but the people most affected, the managers, got an identity crisis. Structure is not an organization chart. It's a division of labor—who does what. Here was the general manager's paradox: he could not see how to invite participation when the outcome threatened jobs.

"Ah," say you hard-nosed realists, "the solution is obvious. Forget participation. Tell people to take the new job or go see a headhunter." The general manager knew he had the power to do that. But here is the kicker: He would not because it violated his values. He would not force people to act against what they saw as their own best interests. More, he believed forcing them would hurt the business.

In music stores you can buy CDs of standard tunes entitled "Music Minus One," a full band except for piano or horn. Supply the missing line and the room swings. Without it, it doesn't sound right. The consulting report was a music-minus-one exercise, all the right technology and economics changes with the people part missing. The action needed is so simple that people often will not believe it works. Have those with the biggest stake in the change sit down together with the experts and figure out what to do. Their emotional stake in the outcome is not a reason for avoidance. It is exactly the reason they should be included. At Printing Inc. that course of action supported the manager's values. He had been a prisoner of old assumptions, feeling that he alone had to meet everybody's needs, just the way the dean did at Medical School.

After reorganizing at the top, Dominick Volini and I helped Printing Inc. do a series of work redesigns. People joined planning teams from all levels in customer service, art and graphics, and planning and scheduling. Each group devised its own multi-skilled, self-directed model. With each implementation, lead times from order placement to delivery were reduced, along with errors and costs. Even the press room reorganized. By the early 1980s, the employees, from a sense of ownership bred of designing their own work, turned an ink-spattered slap-dash area into an industrial space neat enough to be a cafeteria.

Printing Inc. Revisited (2002)

In 2002 I called the plant and was told that it soon would be no more. A few days later I drove the seventeen miles that would take me back twenty years, from the freeway to a residential street to a one-story stone-faced building on a large tract across from a row of 1950s duplex houses.

This February day there were patches of snow in the street. A sign on the corner announced, "Available 117,000 square feet, 11.8 acres." The last time I was there the woman who greeted me from a glass booth to the left of the door would have been a team member rotating from other work.

The controller in a sports shirt and casual shoes greeted me, a squarish man with a brush cut and a nice manner. He told me that his main job was closing down the plant. The customer service and printing operations were moving south. Only the machinery business would remain as tenant or in a new facility.

We entered a light, bright, open office, once the customer service and art and graphics areas. The old partitions were gone. I noted big modern desks to the left and right, half of them vacant. The place was eerily quiet. No bustle. No hum. I recognized Don, a former plant manager, the same smiling, garrulous guy in a sweatshirt, except twenty years older, still slender and with most of his hair. He talked to me with one foot up on the desk. Having outlasted seven general managers in as many years, he now ran order processing and customer service. Of forty-four people in his area, only eleven remained. A pall of sadness hung over the room, for this had been a good place to work. Now the survivors would lose their jobs. I met a woman who had participated in the work redesign years earlier. She had become a team of one at a computer terminal, headset around her ears, doing the whole job much like the folks at my old company in the new century.

"We once had ninety middle managers," said Don. Now operations had four supervisors and needed only two. "They are called team leaders," he added, "but they do little leading. They provide support and problem solving if needed. They have their own accounts and their own jobs. We found that the multi-skilling worked so well that teams became unnecessary. People know what to do, have all the tools to do it, and work on their own." Most had their own customers, and they could back up each other because all had computer access to every account.

The work that began two decades earlier had continued, despite several reorganizations, clear up to the year 2000. "Actually," Don went on, reflecting on the past, "you don't need teams when everyone has his own customers and knows what to do. The focus now is on how good your system is. And hopefully you develop the system with the people who do the work. That's what we have done ever since you left."

In the factory the machines remained as the design teams had rearranged them years before, in clusters related to certain markets. However, the workers were back in functional teams based on the size and type of press. "We tried organizing around the customer with three different machines," said Don, "but that turned out to be flawed thinking." Now, the organization was okay but the old layout worked against them.

"Efficiency is high," the controller said, "the quality good, and the customers like us. We just can't afford two plants. Our overseas business is growing, but domestic sales are dropping 10 percent a year." This day on a mid-week, mid-morning shift only three of ten machines were running.

The manufacturing was going to North Carolina, although some functions had been brought back from Mexico for a customer who required American-made tags and labels. Employees had nine months' notice plus counseling and job-search services. Many would receive up to a year's severance.

Some months later, Don, now retired, sent me an email. "I wish there was a way to capture the real story. The endless parade of 'Professional Managers,' " he wrote, "and the decisions ranging from questionable to really bad, the individuals who refused to listen because they 'knew' that theirs was the only way and the focus that moved off of what was good for the customer and onto making the 'numbers' look good." In short, Printing, Inc., like many small acquisitions of global giants, had become, despite the best intentions of its workforce and middle managers, a dysfunctional stepchild.

Implications for Practice. This story repeats experiences for more than a century. In a market-driven business, no matter how good the work system, no matter how involved and happy the people, a workplace lasts only so long as its economics add up. At Printing Inc. key decisions came to be made by itinerant managers with no stake in the hard-won designs of those doing the work. In such cases there is nothing you can "build in" to assure continuity. This lesson is especially poignant in publicly traded corporations. Employee and customer satisfaction may be highlights of the mission statement. But in the new millennium, distant market and stock price strategies determined the work lives of countless people around the world.

The Case for Process-Focused Assessment

In my first four cases, the consultants acted as unfreezing and diagnostic experts. Neither Printing Inc. nor Medical School needed unfreezing. The consultant was called in because the systems were caught in the bumpy turbulence Emery and Trist described in 1963. Medical School had a planning task force struggling to figure out what it should plan. Printing Inc. had a good consultant proposal they could not act upon. It took only a half-dozen interviews and a two-hour meeting to help the managers own up. They knew they needed to reorganize, but were stuck procedurally. By involving them in planning, it became possible to make a movie that was not implicit in the proposed reorganization scheme.

At both Medical School and Printing Inc. you notice that further content diagnoses were done by the clients. In the first case that happened because I hardly knew what to do about medical education. At Printing Inc., however, I was an ex-printer who knew costs and markets, production and sales, capital and labor from having managed for a decade and consulted for another. I could have told my clients what to do.

There are two flaws in this approach for a whirlwind world driven by knowledge work, rising expectations, and a crisis of values. One, I could be wrong for the same reasons that any extrapolators of past data for future purposes are wrong. I could be wrong for the same reason the engineers were wrong when they told Jimmie Lee Jones, the Jet Press operator in Chapter Two, that he did not know how to improve their contraption. I could be wrong for the same reason the aerospace engineers in Chapter Twelve were wrong when they excluded the astronauts from the capsule design. Experts can never have all the relevant data.

Two, most people would not take my advice unless it squared with what they wanted to do. They might pretend. That's a good way to hedge a relationship with authority figures. They would not follow through if they thought it against their best interests.

Strategy zigzags, mergers, reorganizations, downsizing, decentralizing, centralizing, retraining, redesigning work—that's all complicated, high-level stuff. If managers don't know what to do, and consultants don't give them answers, how can they possibly do the right thing? That answer is that there are answers, just not the sort most people expect.

The snapshots needed now are of a qualitatively different kind from those designed to find "the one best way" or to unfreeze a system. Accept that problems are everywhere, like flowers in the woods. But not everybody is ready to be helped. There is a season for this work. What is worth "diagnosing" are the conditions for success—finding the leadership and focus likely to turn people's anxiety into the constructive energy and mutual support needed to transform a system.

You can't separate structure from behavior any more than you can people from their economics and technology. Engineers, psychologists, and physicians can't do it. Neither can you or I. However, that is not the only point behind my wish for a new practice theory. I also believe that the task-process linkage makes an excellent whole-system concept, not a discrete technique. For that reason I think that solving the big problems of corporate life—costs, markets, quality, customer satisfaction, money-making, fulfilling work—lie in systems improvement, not in problem solving.

Systems can be improved only to the extent that everyone who works in them understands how they work. That takes deep engagement. Helping people rethink the whole is the best way a consultant can reinforce dignity, meaning, and community. That requires a qualitatively different activity from soliciting input.

In the first edition I cited British Airways' efforts in the 1980s to anticipate increased competition by "putting people first"—customers and employees both. They repeatedly brought thirty to forty thousand employees to London for day-long events geared to learning more about one another's jobs, airline economics, customer preferences, teamwork, competitors' advertising and service (even eating other carriers' in-flight meals). It was an ongoing systems improvement strategy British hoped would make it the "best airline in the world" (British Airways "Customer First Newsletter," spring 1986, issue No. 5). That no longer seems like a radical idea. With the proliferation of "large-group interventions" since

1990, dozens of similar examples now exist (Bunker and Alban, 1997; Holman, Devane, and Cady, 2007).

You can buy all sorts of useful advice. I will give you some for nothing. If you want a plan implemented, a company reorganized, work redesigned, or many problems solved all at once, get as many key stakeholders as possible in one room and ask them to work on the task together. Reaffirm dignity. Help people find meaning in their lives. Create a productive community in the workplace.

This prescription is not the "one best way," to borrow from Taylor. It is quite simply the only way, if—always a big if—what Lewin called "life value" matters as much to you as technology or money.

■ ■ ■

"A SHIFT IN THE QUALITY AND DEPTH OF MY WORK..."

ALBANY, NY—I read *Productive Workplaces* in graduate school while working towards a master's in OD. PW had a profound influence on my work and life. Through PW, I discovered Future Search—a concrete model, method, and approach that helped me fine-tune my consulting and design skills toward principles of "organizing and managing for dignity, meaning, and community".

From there it was only a short step to learn to apply the principles and values to a wide spectrum of development work—planning, training, coaching, and large group interventions. I aligned my consulting work with my personal beliefs and values and found, most importantly, that I could deliver consistent, successful outcomes for clients.

Strategic planning became for me much more than data collection, assessments, and decision making. Change initiatives became much more than changing structure, systems, space, reporting lines, people, and jobs. Interventions became more than conflict resolution processes and negotiated agreements. I saw a fundamental shift in the depth and quality of my work as clients took responsibility for their current realities, owned their futures, and discovered their greatest potential for collective learning and action.

For sixteen years I've been fortunate to have had opportunities to apply my learning from PW and Future Search toward helping clients restructure global financial organizations, improve communications in the United Kingdom Mission to the United Nations, implement policy, process, and technology changes in the British Home Office/UK visa-issuing posts across North America, establish a new Northeast U.S. Region in the National Parks and Conservation Association, negotiate ownership, financial, governance, and succession concerns in family businesses, and help partners find common ground despite divisive issues in law firms.

In 2010 I was engaged to help a not-for-profit health insurance company pursue cutting-edge approaches to improve access, quality, and cost of care in New York State. "Health-Value Strategy" was a major departure from the ways things had historically worked, demanding partnerships across the system, greater coordination of services, greater use of technology, and a new payment model that allowed providers to practice medicine as they've been trained to practice. They were advocating evidence-based medicine as decision criteria, moving from a financially driven emphasis on volume to providing the highest possible quality of care.

I was able to help my client use collaborative planning processes to launch a new medical affairs division, effect a strategic alliance with a large medical group, and restructure its network and contracting division to emphasize building partnerships rather than simply negotiating.

In every aspect of this work I drew on the lessons from *Productive Workplaces.* Steering committees and planning teams worked collaboratively to help design change initiatives and whole-system conferences where everyone had a voice in creating a new direction, making system and process improvements, and in shaping collective actions to realize a better future. The people closest to the work designed their own training. The entire division partnered across departments to design new work flows and processes.

By year's end, there were twenty-four patient centered Medical Home pilots up and running, involving hundreds of providers and 100,000 members. The jury will still be out for the next few years as to the degree of success these efforts will have on changing the status quo. There is no question, though, that the company has taken bold action to change its business model, practices, and infrastructure in pursuit of a vision for better health care for all.

—Shem Cohen, Change Events, Inc.

chapter
SIXTEEN

Revising Theories of What Works

Historically, health professionals have tended to learn management skills in their own groups, physicians with physicians, nurses with nurses, and so on, thus replicating the model in which professional training was provided. However, effective management practices require integrative behavior and nowhere is this more obvious than in the relatively new and rapidly expanding area of primary care.

—Rachel Z. Booth, associate dean, University of Maryland School of Nursing, December 4, 1979

Diagnosis means specifying gaps between the way things are and the way they should be. The first law of diagnosis is this: "Seek and ye shall find." Whatever you worry about lurks in the closet, waiting to pop out and bite you the moment you name it. A favorite organizational bugaboo is "resistance." When I started consulting, the systems reputed to be most resistant to change were staffed by expert professionals—medical schools, hospitals, laboratories, law firms, and universities. Had I known that, in my first ever OD project at Medical School, I surely would not have asked physicians to collaborate.

As a result of that project, however, I enjoyed a decade of consulting and research in medical schools and teaching hospitals, collaborating with Paul Lawrence and Martin Charns to apply Lawrence/Lorsch (1967) organization theories to medical education. I learned a great deal about resistance in those years. Facilitating a one-hundred-person retreat of stakeholders in a state medical school in 1972, for example, I saw a respected neurosurgeon go to the door and announce before storming out, "It is a waste of my time to discuss these matters with nurses and medical students!"

I described this work in several articles, notably one on why OD had not worked (so far) in medical centers (Weisbord, 1976). While updating this book in 2004, I decided to revisit that work too to see what I could learn. My last academic medical project was with the University of Maryland's primary care program between 1978 and 1980. In helping to develop an interdisciplinary training seminar, I was able to apply everything I had learned about medical systems. How I came to revise some of my cherished ideas about what "works" is the subject of this chapter. Like any mystery story, there are a few twists that I will save for the end.

The DIAGNOSIS: Great Differentiation, Little Integration

OD grew up a hybrid of many experiments dating back decades. Some of its origins were odd indeed. I date the leadership style industry to the 1939 studies of preadolescent boys' clubs by Ron Lippitt, Ralph White, and Kurt Lewin. I trace the pioneer research on participative management to Lewin and Margaret Mead seeking to change the food habits of Iowa housewives in World War II (Chapter Five). That same war saw the birth of self-managing teams in a method used by Wilfred Bion and Eric Trist to select British Army field officers (Chapter Ten). T-groups and later team building originated from Lewin's workshops with the Connecticut Interracial Commission to train community workers (Chapter Six).

Boys clubs, housewives, Army officers, social workers—not a businessperson among them!

Output- Versus Input-Focused Organizations

Despite its non-commercial origins, OD, promising improved performance through cooperation, got its most enthusiastic reception in business and industry. Working in business firms and academic medical centers in the 1970s, I discerned that medical systems lacked the systemic factors that made businesses amenable to OD. Business leaders managed *output-focused* organizations, emphasizing quantity and quality of goods and services. Customers voted with their wallets.

Output-focused systems typically had

1. Clear-cut formal authority;
2. Concrete goals;
3. High interdependence; and
4. Agreed-on performance measures.

Academic medical centers were *input-focused,* evaluated by the staff's professional credentials and state-of-the-art practices. Such systems tended toward

1. Diffuse authority;
2. Abstract and often conflicting goals;
3. Low interdependence; and
4. Few or no agreed-upon performance measures.

Professionals had personal standards for quality care, based in part on individual patient needs. So variable were (and are) these standards that it was (and is) hard for third parties to impose standard diagnoses and treatments to control costs. Indeed, until hospitals began competing aggressively in the late 1980s, there was little organized effort to satisfy patients. Today, in an age of free market medicine, I see TV testimonials from patients, ads for doctors and hospitals, and an emphasis on outcomes. None of this was evident in the 1970s. (See "Comparing Systems.")

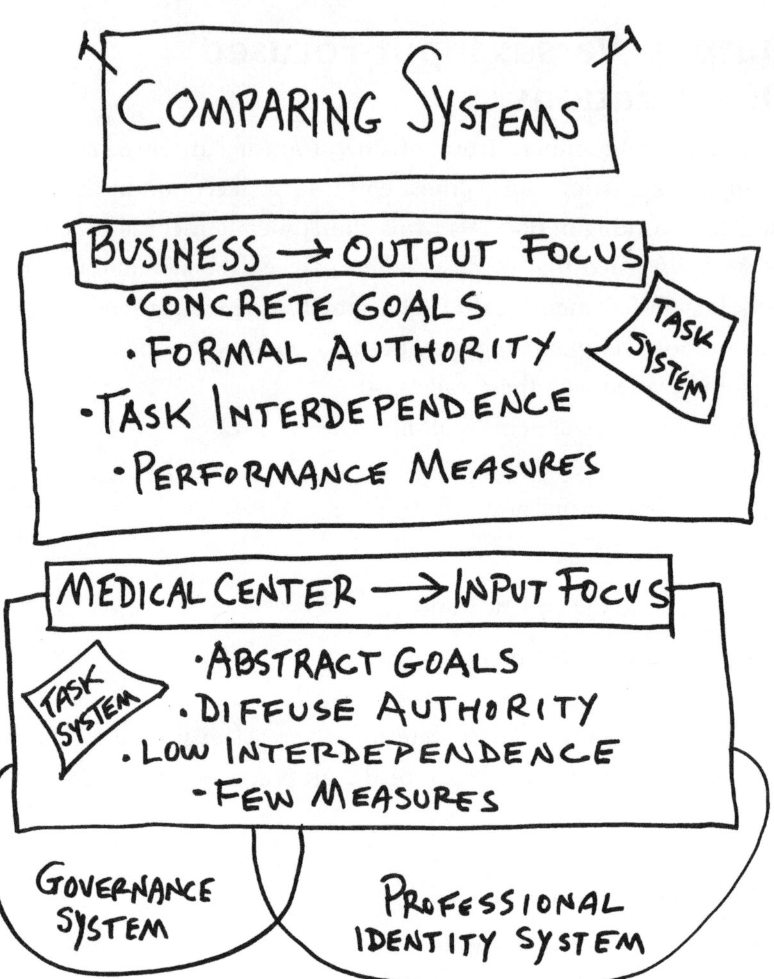

COMPARING SYSTEMS
BUSINESS → OUTPUT FOCUS
•CONCRETE GOALS
•FORMAL AUTHORITY
•TASK INTERDEPENDENCE
•PERFORMANCE MEASURES
TASK SYSTEM
MEDICAL CENTER → INPUT FOCUS
•ABSTRACT GOALS
•DIFFUSE AUTHORITY
•LOW INTERDEPENDENCE
•FEW MEASURES
TASK SYSTEM
GOVERNANCE SYSTEM
PROFESSIONAL IDENTITY SYSTEM

There was another key difference, peculiar to medical schools. In industry, people tended to wear one hat at a time: production, sales, R&D, engineering, etc. Industry honored general managers who could integrate specialized functions (Weisbord, 1978). In medical schools, faculty members wore as many as four hats at once: administration, patient care, teaching, and research. Each had two, three, or four *individual* bottom lines. (See "One Hat Versus Many.")

Administrators could hardly keep track of who wore which hats when. Faculty could do research, patient care, or education, alone or all at once, depending on the month, the day, or the hour. They could switch in an eye

blink, a phenomenon I came to call "the hat dance." Individuals had no trouble sorting out their work. They might use one program's budget to subsidize another's. Those in charge, however, could hardly keep track of, let alone prioritize, so much differentiated activity. This was made more mind-numbing by two dozen board-certified specialties (medicine, pediatrics, obstetrics, surgery, and so forth) and countless subspecialties (more than two hundred today). No wonder medical faculty shunned administrators. Their attempts to integrate threatened everybody's freedom.

During our years of action research in academic medical centers, my colleagues and I interviewed scores of faculty (Weisbord, Lawrence, and

Charns, 1978). We often heard stereotypical personal traits named as problems, particularly for associate and assistant deans. This one was too young, only recently out of residency. ("Prejudice toward youth?" I wrote in my notebook.) That one was a woman, and women had a hard time gaining acceptance from male faculty. ("Women too?") Another was black, at a time of few black faculty members. "No prejudice," an interviewee assured me, "but . . . you know." (What I knew was that I could find racism anywhere. "Prejudice toward nonwhites, too?" I mused.)

Then there was the veteran faculty member, semi-retired, who was "over the hill." ("I think they don't like seniors, either," I wrote.) But the interviewee who confounded me was the one who said of a distinguished, prize-winning clinician, "He used to be a pretty good doc, but ever since he got on the dean's staff, he seems out of touch." ("They don't even like each other!" I observed.)

One day at my desk I took out my notebook and contemplated this grim litany of isms. Except for a storm of negative projections, what could these diverse medical professionals have in common? And then lightning struck. They were all administrators. Each sought to impose order, predictability, and modest controls where personal preference and free choice defined the work. Standard procedures were unwanted bureaucratic intrusions for professionals who thrived on specialization.

People in diffuse structures with few organizational constraints tended to personalize everything. Anyone integrating on behalf of the whole was seen as interfering with good research, teaching, and patient care. No wonder that, except for nurses trained in coordinating care, I found so few takers in professional systems during those years for methods based on self-awareness, teamwork, and shared goals.

In business firms, rewards and prestige went to generalists who could manage on behalf of the whole. In medicine, rewards went to awe-inspiring specialists. Consulting to business firms and medical schools, I lived in contradictory worlds. I became aware that most management technologies were adopted first by industry. All were designed to affect what I called the "task system," the core process of delivering products or services. Task systems thrived on clear authority, goals, interdependence, and measures. Business was relentlessly bottom line: higher profits, lower costs, increased shareholder value. Self-awareness, personal growth, and collaboration—core OD values—were touted as paths to more productive workplaces, not just better human beings.

Three Systems, Not One. Medical centers in the 1970s, by contrast, represented a force field of three interlocking systems. There was a task system, to be sure, producing education, research, and patient care. Administrators, drowning in paperwork, ran the task system, with its diffuse goals, dispersed authority, unrecognized interdependence, and few measures. Indeed, as Just Stoelwinder, an Australian physician and medical administrator, pointed out, physicians controlled up to 90 percent of hospital costs in the 1970s. Doctors decided who was hospitalized, what treatment and medicines patients received, and how long they stayed in. Administrators were left with supporting these decisions as efficiently as possible (Weisbord and Stoelwinder, 1979).

Medical professionals danced to more subtle melodies than bureaucracy's relentless drumbeat. The two most powerful of these I dubbed the "identity system" and the "governance system." Professional identity in medicine was based on academic training and certified by outside agencies and licensing boards. Credentials were the name of that tune. If you asked the general physician with the little black bag who visited your grandparents' house in the 1930s what he did for a living, he would say, "I'm a doctor." If you asked your personal physician forty years later, she replied, "I'm an internist" or "I'm a family practitioner." They were board certified, their identities validated, updated, and policed by diverse civil and professional agencies—the governance system—where the rules for professional conduct and competence are made.

No wonder many medical professionals, socialized by training and licensure to autonomy, resisted collaborative methods. Why would surgeons care whether psychiatrists showed up for work? Many doctors considered administration a necessary evil, inimical to good patient care, research, and teaching.

The PRESCRIPTION: Training as Action Research

It was from this perspective that I began working with William S. Spicer, Jr., a feisty physician heading up the Office of Coordination of Primary Care

Programs (OCPCP) at the University of Maryland in Baltimore in the late 1970s. Spicer's goal was a joint training program in medical management for primary care doctors, nurse practitioners, and clinical pharmacists. He hoped to train a generation capable of integrating multiple disciplines on behalf of patients. The vehicle would be an annual three-day workshop for interns and residents in medicine, nursing, and pharmacy.

Spicer had attended the Management Advancement Program of the Association of American Medical Colleges at MIT. He had recruited a physician and hospital administrator with a master's degree in management and a noted nurse-educator to help plan the program. He invited me to join them by virtue of my medical systems experience.

The plan was to develop content similar to what the physicians had learned at MIT, then pilot the course with primary care faculty. We would start with a five-day workshop for faculty in the three disciplines. They would be expected to support and staff three-day training events with graduate students. Modules included large systems change theory, management practices, group dynamics, interpersonal skills, and personal leadership.

I would coordinate the design meetings and manage the faculty workshop. Something troubled me about the plan. My years working in medical schools had taught me that administrators valued the managerial bag of tricks more than medical professionals did. The OD theory and practice taught in business schools derived largely from industry. I was reluctant to prescribe this medicine for doctors, nurses, and pharmacists without a clinical trial.

For years I had heard colleagues tell me that doctors insisted that you be an expert too, a projection I resisted, although with much anxiety and self-doubt. How could I force collaboration on people and unilaterally insist on more democratic practices? I considered my medical school consulting a form of Lewinian action research. None could say for sure what would work in upside-down organizational settings. Pushing content that some professionals considered antithetical to good medical practice might increase negative resistance in this system. We needed to enter into joint inquiry with the professionals.

I liked Lewin's model of shared agreement between clients and consultants on goals, procedures, and outcomes. That medical systems required expert solutions troubled me. In fact, our research had shown that much medical school integration took place inside individuals—who did some mix of patient care, education, and research—rather than by administrators. Even Spicer's title reflected this. He was the "coordinator" of primary care programs. He couldn't order anybody to do anything.

Building on Individual Autonomy

With these thoughts rattling in my head, I proposed another format for the faculty workshop. Instead of treating the OD repertoire as essential, why not invite the faculty to evaluate proposed training modules with us? We would present personal style instruments, interpersonal, group, and meeting skills, role analysis, problem solving, and large systems change strategies. The faculty/participants' task would be to (1) try each activity as potential content for graduate training and (2) decide what could be dropped, modified, or offered to students.

Nobody was expected to change his or her behavior, work systems, or organizational norms. Participants needn't like everything. We needn't defend anything. The deal was accepted. Despite much anxiety, we conducted this experiment with twenty faculty members in January 1978. We refined the program's content to everyone's satisfaction, emphasizing aspects of the training repertoire faculty considered most useful for medical professionals in building program manager skills.

No Right Answers

A key feature of the Maryland program centered on cases written by faculty members. Trainees would use the cases to "diagnose" organizational problems and work out new solutions. One typical case had a person coming into the primary care clinic with severe dizziness. She says she is taking "pressure pills" four times a day. Except for unusually low blood pressure, the nurse practitioner finds nothing wrong. A medical resident confirms her findings. "Just get her to take her pills right," says the resident. "You've got to educate these people to use this sort of medicine." The nurse points out that the patient took her medicine for months and was fine until now. The nurse also notices that the records show a different dosage from the patient's bottle. "The pharmacy messed up again!" she says. "I'm calling them."

"Don't bother," says the resident. "They don't listen. Give her a new prescription." The nurse practitioner writes and the resident signs a new Rx. A few days later the woman is back in the emergency room after a fainting spell. This time she brings two bottles of the same medicine, one generic, one brand name. She is taking both, thinking she has two medicines. A resident on duty calls the pharmacist, who finds two prescriptions written two weeks apart.

"You should have caught this!" says the resident to the pharmacist. "Don't you talk to your clients?" To which the pharmacist replies, "This is what happens when doctors just countersign Rx's and don't really evaluate the case!" Whereupon the screening resident calls the clinic resident and both agree it was the nurse's fault for not taking the first bottle away from the patient. The nurse practitioner says, "This is what happens when you have physicians sitting around in offices reading journals instead of helping us out!"

Finding an Organizational Solution

To work on the case, we formed groups differentiated by specialty: nurse practitioners, clinical pharmacists, and physicians. We asked each group to "diagnose" the situation. How did the patient get into trouble? Each group presented a diagnosis emphasizing its blameless behavior. Now we reorganized into cross-disciplinary groups and introduced them to the technique of "responsibility charting" (Beckhard and Harris, 1977). Across the top of a newsprint sheet, groups listed the roles involved in the case: resident, nurse, pharmacist, patient. Down the left side they listed the key decisions made at each step, from the woman's first visit until the discovery of her double dose. For each decision, they assigned one of four letters to each role:

"R" (Responsibility)—Initiates action to ensure procedures/decisions are carried out.

"A" (Approval Required)—Reviews, approves, or vetoes each action.

"S" (Support)—Provides what may be needed to carry out the action.

"I" (Inform)—Receives prior notice (but does not decide).

Each integrated group then made a responsibility chart ensuring that this troubling case would not occur again. No two solutions were exactly alike. What happened next remains etched in my memory. One young physician jumped up from his chair, clapped a hand to his head, and said, "Omigod, there's no right answer to this!" He had found the outer limit of expertise. Putting the system at the center of the action, he realized that the right answer could only be collaborative—the one everybody agreed upon.

We repeated the workshop with similar cases for several years. It had considerable faculty support and a positive impact on primary care.

Learning from Experience

Two noteworthy things happened in Maryland to challenge what I had considered OD gospel. First, we expected the primary care faculty to put systems theory and matrix management high on the list for graduate training. This was high-level systems thinking. We expected personal, group, and interpersonal skills training to rate relatively low. This was the "soft" stuff that people needing control often found threatening. In fact, the faculty rated both hard and soft content as relevant. To our surprise, they suggested sacrificing some large system concepts in favor of personal, interpersonal, and group methods of interaction. Personal skills, they said, would be instantly useable on the job!

Huh? This was the very content I had heard many medical professionals dismiss as "touchy-feely." Given first-hand experience, no pressure, and no expectations, the faculty wrote its own prescriptions. Despite the temptation to play the medical game and prescribe desirable techniques, our training staff got more openness to new ideas by treating the techniques as hypotheses for action research. Had we not done that, the faculty would surely have confirmed our built-in prejudice about their built-in resistance.

Whence Cometh New Behavior?

My second "aha" had to do with "transfer of training," the conditions under which people apply at work what they learn in seminars. Earlier research had shown that newly learned skills and attitudes faded quickly once a workshop ended. To overcome this, trainers would devote up to 20 percent of workshops to "back home" applications. People would write and even rehearse action plans. Despite this, they often had a hard time affecting their systems. This was especially so when people came alone and went back to find that existing organizational norms, policies, practices, and/or leaders did not support new behavior.

There were no "back home" exercises in our faculty experiment. All we asked was help in refining the curriculum. We did not anticipate that the faculty—researchers, clinicians, and teachers—would begin applying what they had learned anyway! In follow-up interviews, many reported using responsibility charting, conflict management techniques, and meeting skills on the job. OD wisdom had it that "just training" was an inferior way of inducing organizational change. Here we saw the stirrings of significant changes in the way primary care professionals worked with each other. Our faculty was not constrained by the corporate sanctions reported by businesspeople. This was not "organizational change" in the strict sense. Yet many people were acting in new ways.

How could this be happening? I concluded that the same features that led Cohen and March (1974) to call universities "organized anarchies" also made possible effective action by individual faculty. In systems with diffuse authority, abstract goals, low interdependence, and few performance measures, all were queens and kings of their own domains.

"If the fans won't come," baseball's legendary phrase-maker Yogi Berra is reputed to have said, "nobody can stop them!" In academic medicine, if faculty wished to act constructively, then nobody could stop them! Professional autonomy could work for, as well as against, better organizational practices. After Maryland, I stopped stereotyping experts and dropped "resistance to change" from my vocabulary.

■ ■ ■

"FUTURE SEARCH LAID THE FOUNDATIONS FOR A NEW RESEARCH ORGANIZATION..."

ADELAIDE, AUSTRALIA—In the early 1990s I was a consultant in occupational health and safety, making links between healthy and safe workplaces and management practice. To find out why so many managers seemed unable see a link between quality and health and safety, I took an MBA at the University of Adelaide, South Australia. I didn't find the whole answer; so I undertook a Ph.D., following a manufacturing enterprise through three years of massive change in which workers had significant influence in management decision making. Seeking successful examples of participation and collaboration, I came across *Productive Workplaces*, Marvin Weisbord's story of worker participation in his family business. To read the unfolding argument in favor of letting "those with a stake in the problem help define and solve it" was riveting. It affirmed and informed my research and my practice as a consultant to industry,

After twenty years of consultancy, I am now a full-time, university-based researcher in organizational change, organizational culture and occupational health and safety. My special interest is how participative processes, built on a foundation of dignity and respect, contribute to workplace safety, health, and productivity. A workshop I facilitated recently brought together fifty senior academics, business leaders, union officials, and government officials to develop a strategy for research on work, work systems, and workers. They included researchers, the researched, and research funders of a group of high-achieving people, many of whom held conflicting views. Some were vigorously competing for funds. They found common ground, agreeing to work together strategically to make a difference and to commit time and other resources. Together they laid the foundations for a new research organization, built on the cooperation of many contributing organizations.

—Verna Blewett, associate professor, Occupational Health and Safety, the University of South Australia

---

chapter **SEVENTEEN**

Making Systems Thinking Experiential

". . . the process of becoming increasingly competent amounts to an increasing understanding of a subject in what can be called systems terms. What [successful learners] become good at is not fragmented for them, not isolated from its environment, not isolated in time or in space. They know the relevant elements and their interrelations intimately. These learners have a feeling for the meaning of the subject beyond its technical details and its formal structure. They have operative knowledge about this system, which is to say they know how to get this complex something to work in the way they intend . . ."

—Peter Vaill, *Learning as a Way of Being,* 1996, p. 111

For decades I have lived with a keen awareness of the secret niche that Frederick Taylor, "father of scientific management," fills in the human psyche. You need not look far to find "electronic sweatshops" using employees' computers rather than stop watches to dehumanize work (Garson, 1989). Yet, paradoxically, many old economy giants by the 20th Century's end had shucked the yoke of Taylorism. One notable example was Bethlehem Steel Corporation, the place where Taylor's system flowered more than a century ago.

I cannot overstate the priceless lesson in systems thinking that I received at Bethlehem in the early 1980s. What I valued most about that experience I could not put into words until years later. Now I can say it in a sentence: Ordinary people can use systems "thinking" in workplaces only to the extent they can *experience* the whole for themselves.

Getting Ready for Labor-Management Cooperation

Frederick Taylor exited Bethlehem Steel in 1901, forced out by managers whose power he usurped in service of higher productivity. I met Bethlehem's Ben Scribner, an idealistic, doggedly effective operations researcher, in 1978. In mid-career Ben had taken up consulting and earned a doctorate in psychology. He told me he was determined to help Bethlehem throw off the yoke of Taylorism and would one day invite my consulting firm to help. I considered that a foolish pipe dream. His company's executives had not long before punched time clocks. So I was surprised to receive a phone call one spring day in 1981. "The time is now," said Ben.

Taylor's ingenious solutions that cut costs and raised wages had regressed to mindless time-and-motion studies eighty years later. The company had eleven steel plants, fourteen levels of management, 3,400 wage incentive plans, and four hundred industrial engineers timing jobs and setting rates. Bethlehem's workforce averaged 130 percent of base pay. Yet, the company was losing $80 million a month, the cost of poor quality pegged at $1 billion a year, almost exactly the losses.

Labor-management antagonism, a chronic problem in Taylor's day, had reached mythic proportions. A consulting firm studying the situation had flagged labor-management cooperation as critical to survival. After decades of workforce strife, management did not know where to start. Block Petrella Weisbord's charge was devising a "readiness" program for managers. We visited the plants, met top managers, and proposed a plan for teaming with line managers in each plant who would be dedicated to a concerted effort to change management assumptions and practices.

Although top executives supported this idea, we, like Taylor in 1898, found skepticism everywhere. Mid-level managers believed the hierarchy impregnable. United Steelworkers of America leadership rebuffed our bid to include union members. This hot potato, they said, was management's alone. We determined to help the company gain credibility with its workforce. Working with designated line managers, we started programs shaped by local needs in plants across the country.

Sparrows Point Plate Mill, 1981

Thus began my education in translating open systems from a theoretical construct into action plans involving all the players. Sparrows Point, Maryland, was a sprawling complex of blast furnaces and finishing mills, company housing, schools, and stores. It was one of half a dozen major plants where Tony Petrella and I came, hoping to enable "readiness." We soon learned that the giant Plate Mill would shut down for maintenance early in 1982. Workers would be furloughed for two weeks with pay while technical crews tore down, refurbished, and reassembled the mill.

That meant that some eighty non-union managers and staff (five levels!) could be available for readiness training. Here was a chance to work with a whole system and its leaders. John Dupre, a new BPW associate, and I met with the mill managers and the internal consulting and training staffs. Several had just returned from Japan. They described their shock at seeing the integration of new technologies with employee participation into work systems that defined "world class." We discussed what it would mean to involve everybody in improving the Plate Mill. Could people imagine a world-class Sparrows Point?

What I recall most about that seminal meeting was the anxiety. It was palpable, bouncing off the conference room walls, a vortex of fear, fueled by the possibility that we might, just might . . . do . . . something . . . new! The norm was for training up to twenty people for a few days at a time. The human resource staff was understandably nervous at having eighty managers from five levels working in one room for two weeks. What would we do with all that time? How would hands-on managers used to grime, grit, and piling up steel plate in the yard put up with a long talk fest? Even if the talk was tied to making plate steel?

Scribner spoke in favor. The consultants talked risks and benefits. The grizzled old mill superintendent at last threw up his hands. If top management wanted it, that's what we would do. The issue was settled. In the words of Kris Kristofferson (1970), "Freedom's just another word for nothing left to lose." In the Plate Mill in the dark days before Christmas 1981, people had nothing to lose. The shutdown would take place a few weeks later. For the first time the staff, instead of taking a vacation, would study the whole system together. We consultants had an unprecedented opportunity: carte blanche to use our training repertoire—individual, group, and organization—with all the key actors. Nobody could say, as we had often heard, "The wrong people are in the room!" or "What's all this stuff have to do with making product?" We had the right people and ample time to connect learning with doing.

A Two-Week Systems Workshop

The two-week workshop plan was as follows. All eighty Plate Mill managers—superintendent and assistants, foremen and their assistants, and service staff—would study the whole together. "The system" was defined as relationships within and among five centers of action:

1. Individual ways of thinking and acting;
2. Interpersonal relations with co-workers;
3. Teamwork;
4. Mill-wide organizational problems; and
5. Customers and suppliers, the mill's "environment."

People would work alone and in four groups: pairs; natural work teams; cross-functional problem-solving teams; and customer and supplier study teams. (See "Whole System Learning.") My knowledge of systems theory was then largely conceptual. I had done "open systems planning" exercises, usually with natural work groups or task forces. I could diagram environmental demands and constraints on a chart pad until the paper ran out. I had never tried to facilitate learning on every level with so much of a system in the room. In short, I could imagine doing what I am about to describe. I had no idea what would happen. It has taken me many versions of that experience to appreciate what power the right people can exert on their systems when they have access to each other all at once.

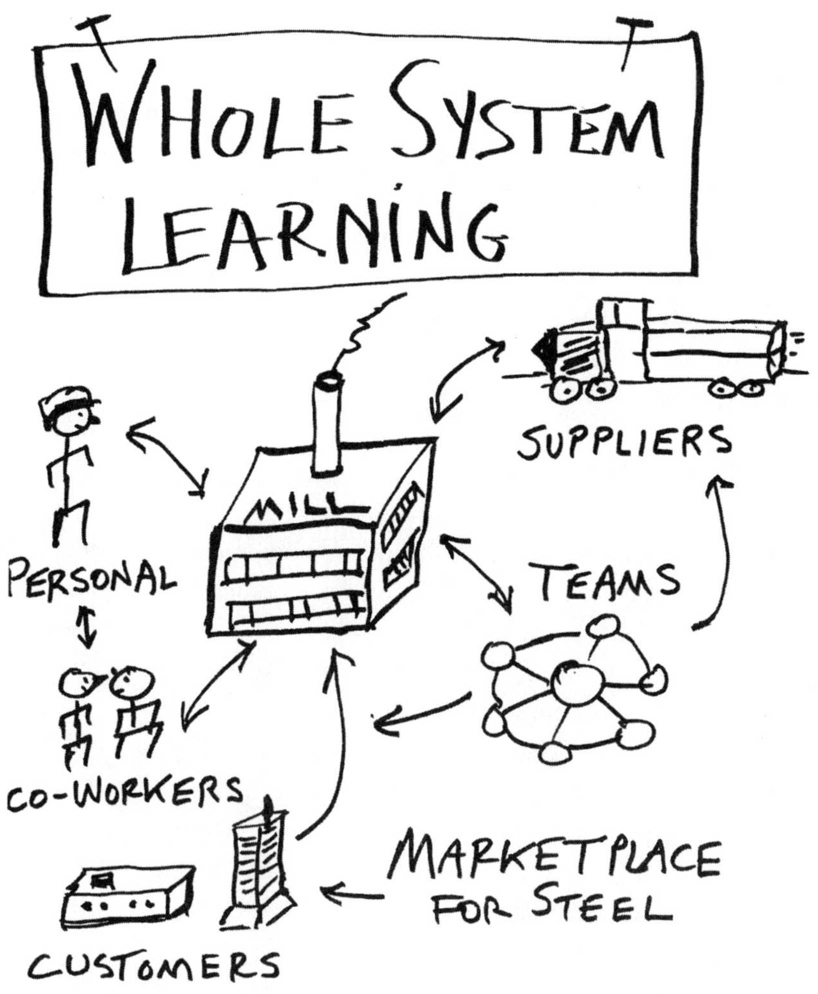

Experiencing the Whole System

In advance of the two-week seminar, managers and staff met to describe the problems hampering their work. During the first week we taught group problem solving and formed cross-functional teams to devise solutions. Team members also filled out "personal style" surveys and found out how their ways of thinking and doing affected their working together. On other days, people met with their supervisors. They talked about the changing role of supervision, from goals imposed by management, for example, to shared goals set jointly.

Teams studied their "process issues," for example, communications, control, trust, decision making, motivation, and the use of each other's capabilities. At each step people were asked to make notes alone, to share them with others in their groups, and then to report out and discuss what they were learning. A typical question might be, "What do personal styles have to do with the mill problems we worked on this morning?"

At the start of week two, sales and marketing staff, who may as well have been Martians, came with overheads and spreadsheets. Everyone filed into the auditorium and saw the big picture on a large screen—the marketplace for steel plate and what was known about customer uses. In late morning, groups of five or six got into their cars and went to visit customers within driving distance of the plant.

The next day they reported to each other what they had learned. The room crackled with excitement. One veteran foreman told a story that raised the hairs on my neck. "This customer bought a crane," he said. "Spent $25,000 on it, just to turn our plates over. They said we were shipping 'em 'upside down.' Hell, we don't care. We told 'em we'd ship 'em right side up from now on. They didn't need that crane!" That day we heard many similar stories, of changes easily made to the work system as a direct result of meeting customers and seeing how the product was used.

Later that week the groups visited their raw steel suppliers, Sparrows Point's blast furnace and steel-making department, a quarter of a mile away. Again, reports and revelations. "I've worked here thirty years," one man said, "and I've never seen those guys make steel. We do a lot of complaining about what they send us. Well, I can tell you they have the same problems we do, and they are busting their butts the same way we do. We have to work with them if we're going to keep our quality up."

Systems Thinking as Systems Doing

At Sparrows Point I first became aware of what ought to be a core principle of workplace education. Drawing "environmental scans" on flip charts is no substitute for interacting with those who *are* your environment. "Systems thinking" becomes useable in workplaces to the extent people experience the whole for themselves. During those two weeks I gave up a fantasy that had haunted my consultant identity for years, that if only I could master systems concepts, tossing off words like "equifinality" and "negative entropy," I would, at last, become a transformer of workplaces. Such ideas could not be acted on unless people identified systems improving with everyday experience. They had to gain control of their own work. At Sparrows Point, without any big words, we expanded systems thinking into everyday experience, linking minds, hearts, and hands with making steel plate.

Cloning the Experience. In the months that followed, the internal consulting staff got the "whole system in the room" repeatedly as each mill shut down for maintenance or closed temporarily for lack of work. Eventually, they involved two thousand people in studying the whole and improving their work. Soon, customer-supplier teams sprouted up throughout the plant. One group, for example, took on the problem of moving raw steel from primary to finishing mills while still warm, eliminating a costly reheating process. These teams became standard procedure for all cross-functional problems. Eventually, union leaders in each mill, wanting to be part of the action, officially unable to back the effort, began attending readiness sessions anyway.

The internal staff sought training in sociotechnical work design and began involving workers in redesigning their systems. Management and union signed a local memo of agreement assuring cooperation on new technology. For the first time, a joint labor-management team installed a new continuous caster that became one of the best performers anywhere. At Sparrows Point "readiness" metamorphosed into effective action as managers and steelworkers implemented new forms of cooperation.

BPW also developed a team training program to enable the use of Joseph Juran's statistical process control methods. We taught it to thirty Bethlehem managers, who implemented it with teams in all the plants. One was Davidson Jones, an engineer who grew up in the company town and later joined my company and had a successful consulting career. Another was Barbara Bertling, whose personal story appears on page 313. Sparrows Point also sought help from Eli Goldratt, the Israeli engineer who had written a novel called *The Goal* that elucidated a "Theory of Constraints" for systems improvement (Goldratt and Cox, 1985). They changed everything after that—new markets, new products, the works. By the end of the 1980s, Sparrows Point became what seemed an impossible dream a decade earlier. They were a world-class operation.

Sparrows Point Fifteen Years Later

In 2000 I called up the late John ("Rocky") Rockstroh, lead internal consultant for the Sparrows Point work. Retired now, facing cuts in health and retirement benefits because of steel industry instability, still he was glad to reminisce. "From '81 to '83 the culture changed," said Rocky. "We realized the way to manage the business was to get everyone involved. We put a stake in the heart of Taylorism. We changed the role of the industrial engineer." By the year 2000 the IE's, instead of just timing jobs and setting rates, also had become process and methods improvement experts, doing post-mortems on outages and other problems.

"The place was never the same after the Plate Mill project," said Rocky. "It became natural to ask, 'Who else do we need in the room to solve this problem?' " He recalled how one manager, after seeing what the finishing mills had done, insisted on system-wide readiness training for the "hot" side, even though the furnaces could never be shut down. "I was fresh from a consulting skills workshop," Rocky recalled, "so I used words I had never said in my life. I told him that for me to help him there were certain things I wanted him to do too." He would have to get together managers from all the operations to help solve the problem of training everyone while keeping the furnaces hot. Eventually, they came up with a plan to get one-fourth of the managers together in each of four workshops that would include a cross-section of people from operations, electrical, and mechanical departments. What had he gained personally from this, I asked Rocky. "Always look downstream and upstream to learn the whole system," he said.

Today, the Sparrows Point training program, state-of-the-art in 1982, seems overloaded to me. We threw in everything we knew. The critical learning was what the steelmakers went out and got for themselves. Now there are many large-group processes for involving everybody and many elegant experiential learning methods (Holman, Devane, and Cady, 2007). Some processes (Future Search is one) do not require new skills or self-awareness training at all before people improve their systems. Nonetheless, the principle remains durable. Getting the whole system in the room and giving all a chance to learn from one another is surely a no-fail productivity enhancement strategy, no matter what procedures you use.

Systems Improving 101: If You Can't Get the "Whole System," Use the "Three-by-Three Rule"

From Sparrows Point I derived my Three-by-Three Rule, a practical way to start people improving the whole. This is not quite a recipe. You will have to choose your own ingredients, preparation time, and serving size.

Pick your bureaucracy. The key thing is that you have a legitimate reason for calling a meeting. Be clear about what your responsibility is and who else you need. Whether you are staff or line, high or low, doesn't matter, only that you have the standing to invite others.

Pick an issue that affects people at more than one level. Make it something in which people have a big stake, where the solution would be a blessing, not a threat, to almost everyone. (I say "almost" because I never found an issue so benign that it didn't threaten somebody. Be good to yourself and accept reality. You will never please all the people all the time.)

Make it an issue where you have to act. It helps if you are not sure what you ought to do. Even if you know what you would do, this meeting is the fastest road to surfacing potential roadblocks and to getting help. You are inviting people to advise you on what to do. You are not giving up your responsibility to decide.

Here is the key step. Do not compromise. Get a minimum of three levels in the room from the unit where action is required (vice president, director, supervisors, or directors, supervisors, workers) and a minimum of three interested functions (manufacturing, sales, research; finance, human resources, engineering), depending on the issue.

Have everyone hear from everyone else about his or her stake in the issue before proposing anything. In groups of thirty or fewer you can keep everyone together; ask each person to make a statement in a minute or less. In larger groups, have each group talk together for fifteen minutes about its stake and report to the whole. This is called "differentiating," which is the key to integrating anything.

Organize cross-functional groups—if necessary—to plan action steps.

Have everything happen in public. Don't end the meeting until all commit publicly to what they will do next.

Bethlehem Steel in the 21st Century

I also did an Internet review of the new millennium steel industry in the United States. While workers became ever more productive, globalization had altered the face of steel production. Modern mills in Europe, Asia, and South America were making good steel at lower cost and shipping it around the world. Consolidations were taking place everywhere. Experts debated endlessly whether governments ought to subsidize critical industries like steel making.

In the 1980s and 1990s Bethlehem Steel closed or merged one facility after another, going from eleven plants to four. Having lost $1.5 billion in 1982, the company started making money again. But not for long. In 1995, the erectors of the Golden Gate Bridge and the Empire State Building ceased making structural steel altogether.

In December 1997 the corporation announced the closing of the coke works in Bethlehem, Pennsylvania, ending 140 years of steel making there. The last vestige of the plant where Frederick Taylor had created the world's most efficient machine shop and invented high-speed steel was no more. Henceforth, the Sparrows Point blast furnace would import its coke from Asia. About the same time, Bethlehem bought Lukens Steel, a company with two plate mills. The Sparrows Point plate mill, world class at last, was shut down again, not for maintenance but for good.

In September 2001 the corporation hired a noted turnaround specialist, Robert Miller, Jr., as chairman and CEO. He had his work cut out for him, with six retirees for every active employee, a $5 billion liability. A month later *The New York Times* reported that Bethlehem Steel had filed for Chapter 11 bankruptcy protection. They would go on with a reduced workforce and radically changed product lines. New talks began with the United Steelworkers aimed at an unprecedented realignment of workplace restrictions built into earlier contracts that would mark the complete demise of Taylorism. "We need a comprehensive restructuring," said Miller, "so that our employees can be part of a globally competitive steel industry in the future" (Miller, 2002).

In 2003, I received a note from Connie Fuller, who had worked with Ben Scribner years before at Bethlehem and was now a human resource manager in another company. "I think a case could be made," wrote Fuller, "that the change initiatives enabled the company as a whole, and Sparrows Point in particular, to remain viable for much longer than it would have otherwise. I know that the work done at Bethlehem Steel changed the culture forever." (See Fuller's personal story on page 36.)

A few days later I read that the company had cut off health and insurance benefits to retirees and arranged to sell its assets to International Steel Group of Cleveland, a firm noted for innovative work systems. The major remaining facilities at Burns Harbor, Michigan, and Sparrows Point, Maryland, would be renamed ISG/Bethlehem. On April 30, 2003, roughly one hundred years after Frederick Taylor invented scientific management and twenty years after I had learned to increase productivity by getting the whole system in the room, the Bethlehem Steel Corporation was no more (Caruso, 2003).

■ ■ ■

"WE CHANGED BETHLEHEM STEEL FOREVER..."

BALTIMORE, MD—I not only read *Productive Workplaces*, I lived it at Bethlehem Steel in the 1980s when I started working with Marv Weisbord, Tony Petrella, and John Dupre of Block Petrella Weisbord. Their task was helping managers learn to cooperate with labor, hoping to save the company. I had never heard of sociotechnical work redesign or process management. I had graduated from a local high school and started as a statistical clerk in Bethlehem's blast furnace department (the first female ever to work on the "hot side"). My parents believed college was a "waste of time" for one who was just going to get married and stay home raising kids. Not surprisingly, Bethlehem's management viewed women the same way—as clerks or secretaries until they left to start a family.

In 1980 I was sent as a maintenance foreman to the rod and wire mill. I had no idea where it was located, nor had I a clue as to what I should do. I was being sent to do a "management job" as part of an affirmative action agreement in which Bethlehem had to promote blacks or females. I was told to sit in my new office for a couple of months, fulfilling the company's obligation, then inform management that I was unable to do the job. This plan was against everything I valued. Instead, I worked double shifts with the mechanics I "supervised" to learn everything I could about the mill's equipment and processes. After six months, I was sent to take the "foreman's test" with the expectation that I would fail and go back to my clerical position. I scored 97 out of 100.

Now management did not know what to do with me. Then, along came Marv Weisbord and sociotechnical work redesign. I was sent from the rod mill to become an internal consultant. (Again, I had no idea what this meant.) My new boss was John "Rocky" Rockstroh, heading up an internal consulting team that consisted of one person from each department, representing the entire steelmaking and finishing operations of the huge Sparrows Point plant. This concept of the "whole system working together" was absolutely unheard of.

We did unbelievable things and changed Bethlehem Steel forever. We learned and practiced sociotechnical work redesign and whole systems management in every department at Sparrows Point. In each mill we worked with one hundred managers and foremen in a room together with their support services, suppliers, and customers. We helped people analyze and improve hundreds of processes. More than two thousand people were involved in examining, problem solving, and changing the way they worked. No one would ever be the same again. I was one of them. What a gift we had been given!

I left Bethlehem Steel in 1986 to become the manager of organizational development at American Trading and Production Corporation, owned by the Blaustein family of Baltimore, Maryland, founders of AMOCO. Dr. Blaustein, based on my Bethlehem experience, selected me over candidates with master's degrees and Ph.D.s. (While in this job I earned my degree at College of Notre Dame in Maryland and did a year of graduate work at Johns Hopkins in organizational communications and development.)

At American Trading I worked with manufacturing plants, hotels, oil and gas, and transportation companies to analyze their systems and redesign their work. In 1992 I left American Trading to form my own consulting firm, practicing sociotechnical work redesign and process management with clients in manufacturing, mining, banking, real estate, radio, and government agencies. I also started a non-profit animal rescue organization in 2000. Drawing on my Bethlehem Steel experiences, I work to change the lives of the people I touch the same way my life was changed by my mentors and friends.

—Barbara Kunaniec Bertling, president,
The Bertling Alliance, Inc.

PART FOUR Integrating the Past into the Present

I'm not much of a magician . . . but if you will come to me tomorrow morning, I will stuff your head with brains. I cannot tell you how to use them, however; you must find that out for yourself.

—The Wizard of Oz to the Scarecrow, Baum, 1900, 1958, p. 114

In Part Three I reviewed projects to develop better workplaces, suggesting that in "permanent white water" we needed methods equal to our values. Part Four begins in Chapter Eighteen with a new road map for managers and consultants toward involving everybody in improving whole systems. Chapter Nineteen presents a case employing this map in the rescue of an economically troubled company. The case illustrates my effort to integrate two forms of action originating in the 1950s—organization development (OD) and sociotechnical systems (STS) design—both stimulated by Kurt Lewin's fertile mind. Sharing Lewin's practice-theory road map and values, each method enabled work on different pieces of the same puzzle.

When I started consulting in 1969, I expected to do what I had done as a manager—help people install autonomous work teams. However, I came in through the NTL door, went to T-groups, and learned team building. I soon found myself in country clubs and boardrooms with chief executives and top managements. Imbued with Beckhard's concept (1969) of a large-systems change as a top-down strategy for reorienting management culture, I had faith that, layer by layer, every corporate onion could be peeled.

After some years I realized that my top-down projects stalled before they got to those on the bottom. I might survey front-line workers but rarely consulted with them. I might train supervisors, but I only met supervisees during a quick walkthrough. What I hoped to do belonged to sociotechnical systems (STS), a tradition practiced in different circles from the ones I was going around in during the 1970s.

Where ODers sought new behavior and relationships at the middle and top, STSers designed work systems to reduce the need for management and supervision. STS design metamorphosed in the 1970s into a worldwide movement labeled "quality of working life" (QWL). It became especially attractive as a framework for uniting management and organized labor to improve products and services, making work more secure. OD moved toward "organizational transformation" (OT): discontinuous, rapid culture change helped by novel questions about myths, heroes, rituals, unwritten rules, values, and so on. Practitioners of each movement inevitably adopted methods, techniques, and perspectives from the other.

Emerging New Millennium Practices

Chapters Twenty through Twenty-Three illustrate a synthesis of methods in what I call "21st-Century management and consultation." These are my how-to chapters, procedures based on open-systems methods, the dignity of each person, and the responsibility of all for the common good. These surely are not the only methods that fit my beliefs. They are the ones I know. They come from Lewin and laboratory learning, from McGregor and Lippitt, Emery and Trist, and many others—all infused with my biases, managerial and consulting experiences.

To succeed in democratic societies, to harmonize personal and general interests, people need to work together on economics and technology. In finding more humane and sensible solutions together, we may also learn to accept one another the way we are. If I could ask one thing of a crystal ball in every new situation it would not be "What's wrong and what will fix it?" It would be "What's possible here and who cares?"

"I DESIGNED AN ARCHITECTURE FOR CREATING THE NEW WORLD..."

RIXEYVILLE, VA—Wired as a change agent, I had intuitively led change projects for years without formal authority or academic training. In my first job, for example, I changed the pre-press layout function in the printing plant of a local newspaper. Later I led autonomous work team development, action research, and technology projects for eleven years at the U.S. Geological Survey—all before I learned there existed a field called "organization development" (OD).

In 1998 while pursuing an undergraduate degree in OD at Union Institute and University, I read *Productive Workplaces* (PW). Little did I know that it would lead me to my life's work—a grassroots, global movement to unite people everywhere to create a new world together. My journey began in a systems theory class. I was to write a summary of what I found most compelling in PW. I'd read about the evolution and trailblazers of OD. I found the theories and approaches interesting, but the expert model from the early days of "Taylorism" and the closed, hierarchical systems of focus for OD felt constraining to me. My world lit up as the assigned chapters brought me my first academic affirmation for what I already knew to be true—that people, communities, organizations, nature, and the world we live in are dynamic, organic, living systems. I knew then that if I wanted to be an "expert," it would be in unleashing the creativity and talents of people in a system toward their own highest aspirations.

With this foundation, I stepped into a fruitful career developing change models for adult learning, strategic planning, and leadership development. PW became my dog-eared resource. In the early 2000s I undertook a project that brought me to Marv's doorstep, designing and managing for the U.S. Department of Health and Human Services, a process to create a fundamentally new way to address poverty in the 21st Century. We convened eighty key stakeholders from public and private sectors over four working sessions, including Marv Weisbord and Sandra Janoff, who brought the experience and resources of Future Search Network. (When Marv walked in, I asked him to sign my copy of PW, like a groupie after a rock star.) The three of us later built on the HHS report to develop a national action strategy, which we called *Prosperous Communities, Prosperous Nation (PCPN).* During our four-year collaboration, I found myself *living* PW. We trained several local teams organized by the American Baptist Churches, USA, to support its Children in Poverty initiative and helped people organize Future Searches to that end. During that time, I grew by leaps and bounds, experiencing the value of mechanisms that use community as the unit of large-scale change. And I discovered a deeper song within me that longed to be sung.

I went on to weave my systems change experiences into an architecture for a way forward, engaging humanity-as-whole-system to take us beyond a world in crisis. I designed a world-building workshop where people can experience that we have the reason, the vision, the power, and the technologies to create a brighter future, starting immediately. I have dedicated my life in service to this goal. I have joined with many individuals and networks around the world holding the same goal. I'm deeply indebted to PW and the cascade of events it initiated in me for the privilege of this work.

—Nancy Polend, founder, Creating the New World, Inc.

chapter EIGHTEEN

21st Century Managing and Consulting

The results of this generalized speedup of the corporate metabolism are multiple: shorter product life cycles, more leasing and renting, more frequent buying and selling, more ephemeral consumption patterns, more fads, more training time for workers (who must continually adjust to new procedures), more frequent changes in contracts, more negotiations and legal work, more pricing changes, more job turnover, more dependence on data, more ad hoc organization. . . . Under these escalating pressures it is easy to see why so many businessmen, bankers, and corporate executives wonder what exactly they are doing and why . . . they see the world they knew tearing apart under the impact of an accelerating wave of change.

—Alvin Toffier, *The Third Wave,* 1980, p. 230

Anyone who had or lost a job in the 2000s knows that a sea tide of change has surged through the work world for decades. Futurist Alvin Toffler called it "the third wave" to differentiate it from bygone agricultural and industrial revolutions. In the new century, we are changing ever more rapidly from physical to knowledge work, mechanical to process technologies, manufacturing to service economies, and central to local control.

Here I lay out an integrated practice theory for preserving dignity, meaning, and community in a stormy sea of change. A practice theory, in Peter Vaill's (1979) words, is one which resembles a formal theory but is in no sense identical. It is based on experience, not systematic research. It constitutes a mental map of what's important and what to do about it. I have no doubt that research studies can be devised to substantiate what I will say. However, I base my theory on mental maps drawn up while rethinking the cases in Part Three in light of the history in Part Two.

In this edition I have the good fortune to include forty supporting stories from contemporary managers and consultants who were influenced by this history. I wrote these guidelines while consulting full-time in the 1980s. I have not changed my mind about any of them, despite the technological explosions since. Rather, I present them with greater certainty, for they have been replicated by colleagues around the world.

I evolved my practice-theory from studying my own experiences with the issues highlighted by "A Century of Learning." In 1900 Taylor had experts solve problems for people—scientific management. In 1950 Lewin's descendants started everybody solving their own problems—participative management. About 1965 experts discovered systems thinking and began improving whole systems for other people. The challenge, I wrote in 1987, was getting everybody improving whole systems. By 2012, a great many people had figured out how to do that; hence the new stories throughout this book.

I suggest practices going beyond problem solving and participation to give people direct influence over the economics and technology of their work. Keeping this objective in mind, you can think your way beyond panaceas that don't work. The guidelines that follow reflect my vision of what managers and consultants can do to make a new paradigm live. Some people apply them intentionally, others without knowing it. I have sought to describe effective responses to the great dilemmas we face and to wide aspirations for dignity, meaning, and community.

I write both as an ex-manager and consultant. "Ninety percent of living," comedian Woody Allen once said, "is just showing up." Hidden in the joke is a grain of wisdom. Getting the right people together is probably

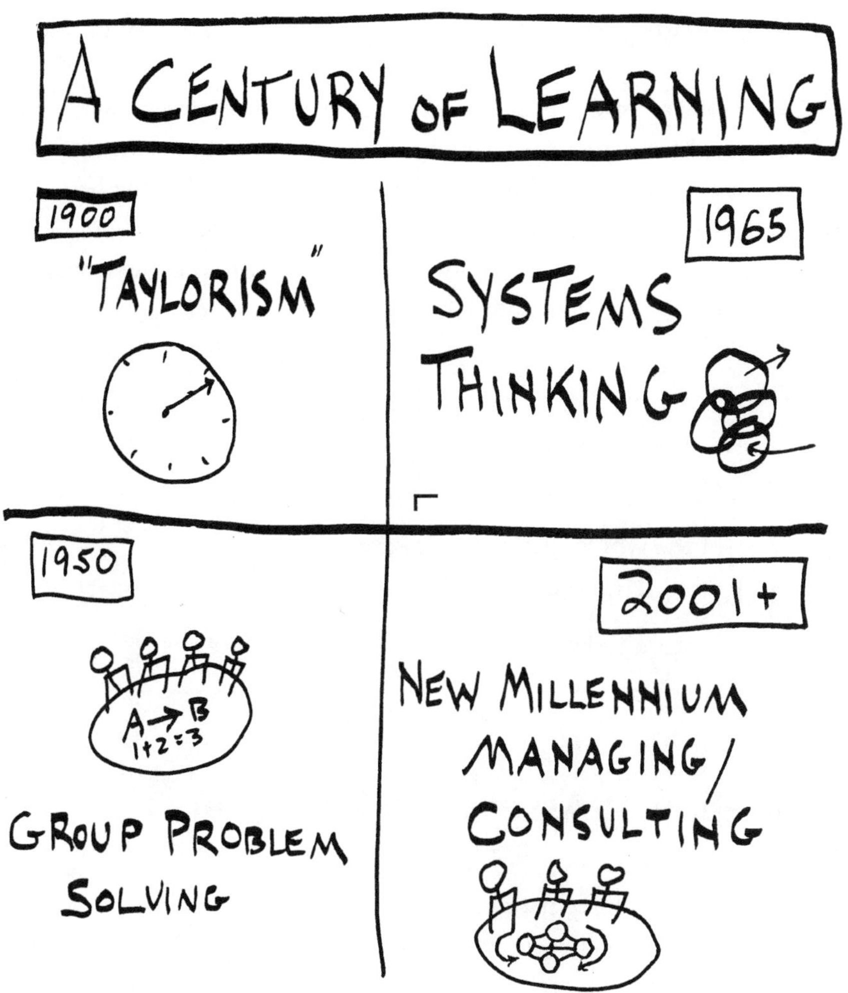

90 percent of 21st Century managing. What remains is helping them commit to valued purposes and tasks.

No person, not even an expert, unfreezes another. We move in our own way at our own pace, regardless of techniques used. We change as we have face-to-face contact with others and receive new information. We change when we listen and respond in new ways, hearing ourselves say things we never said before. We change when we can think out loud with those whose actions affect us. Applying techniques piecemeal to problems, big or little, provides an illusion of progress. Looking together at how the whole system works is the shortest route to solving handfuls of problems at once.

I have moved away from flagging discrepancies between words and deeds toward testing people's willingness to take on important tasks together. The assessment I recommend is to find out whether the season is right for action. Reviewing my projects from many decades, I notice recurring patterns related to leadership, energizing situations, and energized people, that I have distilled into four guidelines.

Four Practical Guidelines

1. Assess the potential for action.
2. Get the whole system in the room.
3. Focus on the future.
4. Structure tasks that people can do for themselves.

Guideline 1: Assess the Potential for Action

This guideline has three parts, as shown by the flip chart "Snapshot: Potential for Action." I moved away some years ago from diagnosing gaps between the way things are and the way they ought to be; that's the client's job. Instead, I find myself asking under what conditions I could make a contribution. That leads me away from problems toward an assessment of three local conditions: leadership, business opportunities, and sources of energy.

Committed Leadership. Do the people authorized to hire me have itches they want to scratch badly enough to put their own rear ends on the line? Consultants make better contributions when a person in authority says, "I think this is so important I'm willing to take a risk too." I'm wary of requests to fix somebody else or to supply "expert" answers. I admire leaders who stand up and say to co-workers, "We're in this together."

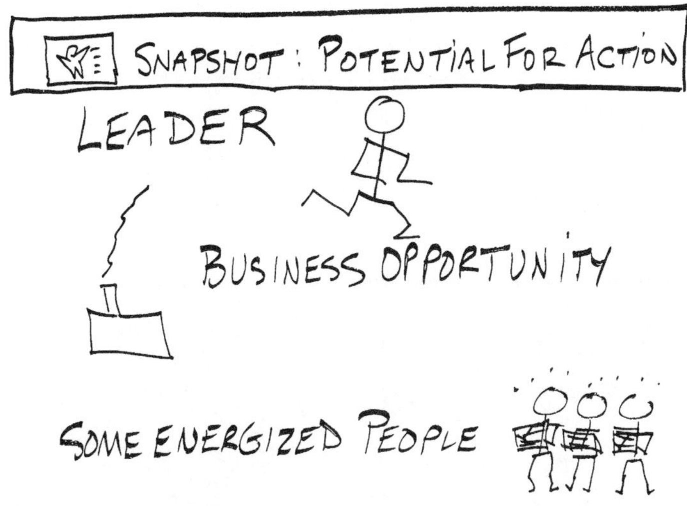

Good Business Opportunities. These come in packages labeled "economics" and "technology." They can be the rich source of dignity, meaning, and community—or the death of them. So I listen sympathetically to the "people problems." I focus, though, on opportunities for cooperative action, chances to innovate products or services, and ways of making or delivering them. These occur in mergers, acquisitions, reorganizations, declining markets, overhead crises, nonfunctioning structures, new technologies, and changes whereby people will lose existing jobs. The potential benefit has to be worth the cost. There ought be no economic reasons for not using these guidelines.

Example: The Medical Products Division of Atomic Energy of Canada, Ltd., in 1985 rescued itself from economic disaster and mass layoffs by assuring jobs for a year and employing much of its workforce in market studies, work redesign, and new employment opportunities. The payoff was a viable business managed participatively by its employees. That's a good business opportunity. I tell this story in Chapter Nineteen.

Energized People. This dimension is a little trickier. We all drag our feet some days and burst with energy on others. Claes Janssen, a Swedish social psychologist, devised a simple model for visualizing where the potential energy is. Each person, group, department, company, says Janssen (1982, 2011a, b), lives in a "four-room apartment" that in the 2000s he was calling the "four rooms of change." Note how the rooms correspond to the positive

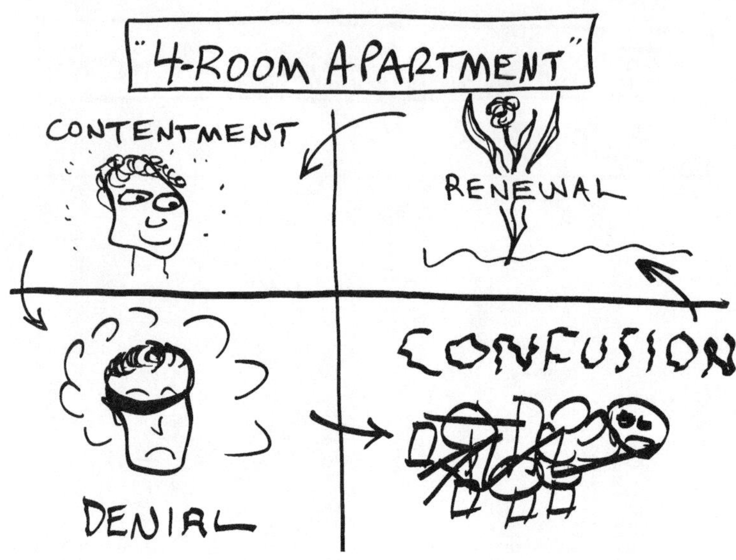

and negative aspects of Theories X and Y (as described in Chapters Two and Nine).

We move from room to room, depending on perceptions triggered by external events. The rooms represent cyclical phases, not unlike the process of death and dying. Indeed, change represents a "little death," a letting go of the past to actualize a desired future. However, it's not an ever-upward spiral where things only get better. It's a circle game. Our feelings and behavior go up and down as outside pressures impinge on our life space. How much energy we have for support and commitment depends on which room we're in.

In Contentment, we like the status quo. We are seen as—and feel—satisfied, calm, and realistic. Any change—a merger, new leader, market crisis, job threat—can move us into Denial. Now we are perceived as unaware, afraid of change, insensitive, although we do not (consciously) feel that way. We stay there until we own up to fear or anxiety, thus moving through the door into Confusion. Here we are seen as—and feel—different, out of touch, scattered, unsure. Mucking about in Confusion, sorting out bits and pieces of our lives, we eventually open the door to Renewal. Now we are perceived as—and feel—sincere, open, willing to risk.

Anxiety (in Gestalt terms, "blocked excitement") is the emotional decor of the Confusion room. Far from a state to be avoided, it signifies readiness to learn (Perls, Hefferline, and Goodman, 1951). Anxiety is the place we store energy while deciding whether to invest it. Every new project, course correction, major change requires optimal anxiety. If there's too much, we are paralyzed; too little, unmotivated. In every Confusion room there are people already taking constructive action. It is they who will carry the movie forward—if they can be brought together to learn how their initiatives integrate with the whole.

People in Contentment or Denial are not frozen. Events will move them soon enough. Little can be done to hasten the day. People have the most energy in Confusion and Renewal. If you were to revisit OD cases from this perspective, you might see that "failure" correlates closely with pressuring people in Contentment or Denial to do things they'd rather not. The seeds of success are sown in Confusion and sprout in Renewal. Those are the rooms where people welcome chart pads, models, and OD methods.

■ ■ ■

"I SOUGHT TO LET GO MY PRESUMPTIONS AND LISTEN TO THE PEOPLE..."

STOCKHOLM, SWEDEN—I bought *Productive Workplaces* after meeting Marvin in a consultancy training program in Sweden. I had read many books and participated in many OD seminars. With *PW*, I put it all together. The text brought profound meaning to the profession I had decided to make my own—helping people in organizations become self-helpers. I have practiced that work since the late 80s, training and coaching other consultants, and giving classes at universities in Sweden and the United States. I took on my most challenging consulting task in the winter of 2009 in Afghanistan, helping a large organization improve its management systems. It had almost 6,000 local employees, 99% of them Afghans. I made two field trips, supporting efforts to manage with "dignity, meaning, and community" in a country torn by war, insurgents, and foreign forces. I sought to let go of my own presumptions and prejudices and listen to the people. My job was to collaborate with management in changing this one organization from within. People had experienced tension, conflicts, and turf-wars, losing energy and inspiration. The more I encouraged people to take charge of their own reality, and the more I turned back their questions and need for expert solutions, the more realistic we all became about what needed to be done

Drawing on what I had learned from PW, in running Future Searches, and in using The Four Rooms of Change, I found it surprisingly easy to work in a culture very different from my own. Using the principle of "everybody improving whole systems," I helped the central management build upon the whole organization's experience of the present and dreams for the future. The people proved to be capable of redesigning, reinforcing, and taking responsibility for a system that hadn't been working well for some time.

The Four Rooms of Change worked well in this environment. Many managers at first diagnosed themselves as being in *Denial* and *Confusion*, and close to the end they put themselves in true *Inspiration/Renewal* and *Contentment.* Using the "Organizational Barometer" (a diagnostic tool), people transformed problems and anxiety into action items within a few hours. They simplified their organizational chart, reduced misunderstandings between line and staff, and, according to many employees, created an efficient organization capable of delivering more aid per invested dollar to Afghanistan's people.

I learned that there exists among the Afghan people tremendous resources and capacity to rebuild and redesign their own futures. Given an opportunity, they took on such difficult issues as relations between men and women, the bribing culture, and the traumatic experience of trying to live normal lives in a country at war for decades.

What the people of Afghanistan needed as much as security was capacity building. It is difficult to imagine a society with greater need for large group interventions based on the principles of *Productive Workplaces*, Future Search and the Four Rooms of Change. Having come closer than ever to rocket attacks and car-bomb blasts, I better understand the dilemmas in supporting people to learn to take responsibility for their future while under attack. Nonetheless, I found it an extraordinary experience and returned hopeful after meeting so many Afghan men and women seeking, under the most difficult conditions imaginable, to create better health care, education, infra-structure and security, all built on basic human needs for dignity meaning and community.

—Bengt Lindstrom, Ander & Lindstrom AB

Lewin showed that the attitudes and feelings of those being diagnosed are critical to the change process and that situations matter as much as personalities. If you want a diagnosis to lead to action, said Lewin, you must include those who will have to act. That changes the diagnostic objective from "being right" to "helping others learn."

The forces working for and against a given change can be charted in a force field analysis. I think Lewin had it right to advocate reducing resistances rather than adding pressures. This may not be a matter of rational problem solving, even in groups. The urge to hold on to familiar patterns, relationships, and structures is as old as human history. Donald Schön called it "dynamic conservatism," defined as "a tendency to fight to remain the same" (1971, p. 32). Robert Tannenbaum and Robert Hanna, developers of a powerful learning laboratory for "holding on and letting go," explained this tendency as the profound losses that change represents for each of us—loss of identity, of certainty, of meaning itself. Under these conditions no unfreezing techniques are likely to help. "Realistic patience and a sense of an appropriate time scale must underlie and guide the change process itself," counsel Tannenbaum and Hanna (1985, p. 114). We can help by giving people a chance to come together, to experience their mutual dilemmas, to make their own choices about when and how to move.

Oddly enough, the T-group, a closed-system application of action research, was initially taken up by Lewin's successors as the way to induce change in the workplace. It could not succeed because, by design, it eliminated past and future, created an isolated cultural island for learning, and removed everyday tasks so that people's here-and-now behavior would come sharply into focus. What the T-group did was heighten our understanding of the task-process relationship. It taught us first-hand that feelings and perceptions, as I showed in Chapter Seven, can block task accomplishment as surely as lack of money, time, or tools.

Any task, at some point, may shake people into Denial when the going gets rough. When that happens, I am inclined to keep talking and wait it out. The movement toward Renewal is always in doubt. We are all subject to anxiety and craziness under stressful change. People need support to stay where they are a while longer under those conditions, not admonitions to hurry up and change faster.

Pockets of Innovation. There is something else you can do, even when all hell is breaking loose. Some people have a knack for constructive action. They need to be found and put together with those who don't know what to do. Often the two groups ignore or mistrust each other. Creative seeds tend to sprout independent of each other. See "What to Do in Each Room."

Consultants only add to the resistance when they merely collect the data and present back what others have already figured out. We have more power than that—we have the standing to bring people together who can make new things happen.

Hooking together many disconnected activities requires only a little linear planning. If we provide the right container, people will fill it with the right elixir. This happens spontaneously as the other guidelines—getting the system in the room, focusing on the future, constructing doable tasks—are applied. Important tasks, mutually defined, building on existing initiatives, greatly enhance both survival and self-control.

The "Should We/Shouldn't We" Dialogue. The activities I like best, because they involve whole systems, are joint planning of business strategy (external focus), work redesign (internal focus), and reorganizations, which embody both strategy and structure. In each mode the people most affected help devise and test various structural models. I don't mean to make this sound easy as pie. I often found myself in long "should we/shouldn't we" dialogues, hours or days of hashing out the pros and cons of whether to include others, whether there's time to do it all, whether short-term results will suffer, what alternatives exist. Both clients and consultants need the dialogue to decide whether to become personally involved.

So I look for a leader, a business opportunity, and a "should we/shouldn't we" discussion. If we decide to go forward, I help people plan how to raise a crowd, structure a task, and provide some methods for getting started. And they could be left-brain methods. As right brains are activated, they take care of what can't be planned in advance.

Now I take up what I call the "Movie Guidelines."

Guideline 2: Get the Whole System in the Room

There are many ways to get a whole system together. A system can be there, for example, in your head—a conceptual rather than logistical feat. For example, try the "All-Purpose Viewfinder" and see how fast you can become a systems thinker.

However, knowing what's going on is not the same as enacting dignity, meaning, and community. That requires living the open system. How many

"MOVIE" GUIDELINES

WHOLE SYSTEM IN THE ROOM

FOCUS ON FUTURE

TASKS PEOPLE DO THEMSELVES

ALL-PURPOSE VIEWFINDER

	INSIDE PICTURE	OUTSIDE PICTURE
ECONOMIC$	COSTS + OR – ?	REVENUE + OR – ?
TECHNOLOGY	DO SYSTEMS WORK AS INTENDED?	ARE PRODUCTS + SERVICES BEING IMPROVED?
PEOPLE	HOW DO PEOPLE FEEL ABOUT WORKING HERE?	HOW DO CUSTOMERS FEEL ABOUT BUYING HERE?

functions, levels, managers, operators, staff, line can be mustered to work on their own organization all at once? Could you bring in customers and suppliers?

I tend to push for more and let others say what's realistic. In 1987, I wrote that I didn't know how to involve a cast of thousands. If the Wright brothers figured out how to fly like birds, however, somebody else would figure out how to get whole companies or communities together. By 2012, many people knew how to convene large interactive groups. And the Internet had become the venue of choice for involving countless people in anything you can think of. (See Chapter Twenty-Five.)

When people meet across levels and lines of status, function, gender, race, and hierarchy, treating problems as systemic rather than discrete, wonderful (and unpredictable) things happen. Long-standing lockups are resolved. Relationships improve, walls come down, problems are solved, norms change. These results can't be planned except in the sense of making them more probable. Such happenings lead to more creative and committed actions, more secure and engaging work.

Some Examples

- In the merger that created Sovran Bank, making it the largest bank in Virginia, the operations departments used an interlocking chain of conferences, starting with top executives from each of the merger partners, cascading to the next two levels, culminating in a mass meeting of hundreds of employees. People planned their own roles and divided up the work—an exercise many believed was impossible.
- Bethlehem Steel's Sparrows Point Plate Mill, the focus of Chapter Seventeen, reorganized during a two-week training marathon attended by eighty people. The key new management behavior: paying people to come in and learn instead of taking a two-week vacation during a maintenance shutdown.
- A fast-growing software development company, McCormack & Dodge, lacked the structure to implement a new strategic plan. Top management convened four conferences for fifty people representing all levels and functions. Design teams organized by product line analyzed the system and created new organization designs, based on their values about

employees and customers. They closed information gaps, improved career paths, and developed more accountability and self-control. This was the unpredictable part: twenty-four hours into the first meeting they began making changes to existing practices. Long before a design was finalized, people were acting in ways neither planned for nor diagnosed in advance. As a design emerged, the fifty talked over implementation issues with one thousand others, extending to all the influence over next steps.

News Note. Perhaps it will come as no surprise to you that Bethlehem Steel shut down the Sparrows Point Plate Mill years before going bankrupt in 2004, while Sovran Bank and McCormack & Dodge disappeared in a tidal wave of mergers. The latter case provides another example of environmental vagaries nobody controls. Dun & Bradstreet acquired M&D in 1983, about two years prior to the events just described. Under Frank Dodge, a founder and CEO, the company grew profitably from $38 million to $180 million in annual sales, reaping the fruits of its employee-managed reorganization. At the end of 1989 D&B, without consulting Dodge, acquired a leading competitor and put the two companies into a software division, headed by the rival CEO, whereupon Dodge left.

After the merger, the company lost money for three years, laid off much of its workforce, went through several "cultural" changes, and was sold to a Canadian firm. When I spoke with Frank Dodge in 2002, he had a new career as executive in residence at Babson College in Boston. "This could be a case study," he said, "of how large holding companies fail when they try to acquire entrepreneurial firms."

■ ■ ■

"I HAD HUGE MISGIVINGS ABOUT TRADITIONAL CONSULTANCY..."

BUCKINGHAM, UK—In the early 1990s I was just starting out as an OD consultant. Trying to find the essence of what being an excellent OD practitioner meant, I read books by Edgar Schein (1987), Warren Bennis (2009) and Dick Beckhard (1977). Then, in a bookshop in my home city of Oxford, I stumbled across *Productive*

Workplaces. There was almost an audible pop in my brain when I came to the chapter on whole systems working. I was utterly compelled by the idea that my role was to assist whole systems find or rediscover their own way forward. I had huge misgivings about "traditional" consultancy models, which sought to *do* change to an organization rather than work *with* the people. I realized I was part of a growing community of people who believed this too.

Productive Workplaces still influences my practice as a leadership coach, change facilitator, and blogger (http://jonharveyassociates.blogspot.com). I have used "whole system in the room" ideas to tackle such issues as reducing gun and knife crime in the UK, developing women leaders in a large public service organization, and assisting psychotherapists renew their voluntary association. Recently, I facilitated a process to help integrate a range of professional agencies about to move into a single building. The client wanted to make sure that the co-location also resulted in significant partnership building and streamlined inter-agency processes—an ideal application for helping a system improve itself.

—Jon Harvey, Jon Harvey Associates Ltd.

Guideline 3: Focus on the Future

This guideline derives from work by Ronald Lippitt (1983), coiner, with Kurt Lewin, of the term group dynamics. In 1949 Lippitt began tape-recording planning meetings. The tapes revealed people's voices growing softer and more stressed as they listed and prioritized problems. You could hear the energy drain away. Lippitt decided that problem solving depressed people. In the 1950s he started using what he called "images of potential," rather than gripes, as springboards for change. In the 1970s he created new workshops merging group dynamics with future thinking, teaching people to visualize preferred futures as if they already had created them.

This simple concept has enormous power. Enacting future scenarios energizes common values. Taking a stand for a desired future provides purposeful guidance for goal setting, planning, and skill building. Successful entrepreneurs, notes Charles Garfield (1986), are uniquely skilled at projecting alternative futures. They get "feed-forward" from their imaginings, a qualitatively different experience from feedback on past behavior. Lawrence Lippitt (1998) describes a large group method for doing this in eloquent detail.

A word of warning. This concept—"visioning" is one name for it—is so attractive that many people want to go out and run a group through it. The technique will not work in the absence of committed leadership, a business opportunity, and some energized people. It won't work with people in Contentment or Denial either. Nor will it work without a good description of the way things are *now.*

Guideline 4: Structure Tasks That People Can Do for Themselves

Assuming leadership, opportunity, and energy, what structures enable people to learn and plan for themselves? A conference series designed by clients and consultants together is one strategy. I'm suggesting interactive task-focused meetings to reorganize work or refocus effort. I believe all people have unique contributions to make. What they require are clear goals, structured tasks, and adequate time frames. For a consultant to manage such events requires, first of all, sanction from credible parties. Then, any plausible bag of tricks will do. It is here, at the very last, we get to techniques. You need a few of what Hackman and Oldham (1980) call "task performance strategies." One example (of hundreds) is responsibility charting (p. 383). Others include simple worksheets to help people analyze and redesign their own work. In Part Four I give many examples of specific methods.

Merrelyn Emery, a leading advocate of this perspective, points out that the purpose of consulting technique is to create a learning climate, not solutions. This is a subtle and important distinction. It is essential that we do nothing that would reinforce the idea—both undemocratic and unscientific—"that people cannot make sense of their own experience." Creating a learning climate, said Emery, results in "an almost immediate increase in energy, common sense, and goodwill" (1983, p. 4).

Notes on Getting Whole Systems in a Room

In 1987, six years before Future Search Network began, I put in this book nine tips for managing "whole system" meetings. I recommended clear tasks, sticking to time, self-managing small groups, and handouts that facilitate the work. I also noted keeping myself out of the action so that people could do their own work. No lectures. No diagnosis of group behavior. I had by then learned to ask the group when I didn't know what to do (somebody always knows). I took my first of many swipes at windowless rooms that deplete the human spirit, making productive anything difficult.

A quarter-century later it all reads as old hat. Sandra Janoff and I have since written (and twice revised) *Future Search: Getting the Whole System in the Room for Vision, Commitment, and Action* (1995, 2000, 2010), and *Don't Just Do Something, Stand There! Ten Principles for Leading Meetings That Matter* (2007). Add to these the writings of Barbara Bunker and Billie Alban; Dick and Emily Axelrod; Juanita Brown; Harrison Owen; David Cooperrider; Kathleen Dannemiller; Robert "Jake" Jacobs; Lawrence Lippitt; James Ludema et al., Peggy Holman et al. and you have more excellent big meeting advice than you can apply in a lifetime. You'll find all these authors in the bibliography.

New Way of Consulting

Working in these ways, I found myself doing things that did not come naturally at the start. I had to shift my focus—a real mental wrench—away from content diagnoses and problem lists, even of process issues. I stopped fantasizing some time ago that I could become expert enough to tell people what they should do. Anybody who offers to sell you an exemption from the clarifying experience of muddling through to Renewal is a charlatan. When the whole system gets into one room, when people have a valued task to accomplish, when they focus on future potential rather than past mistakes, I believe the right diagnoses and action steps occur in real time. Designing somebody else's work cannot be an expert task.

Nor do I imagine that I can take away by any magical mystery trick, technique, system, jargon, book, speaker, or smart phone app, the travail, confusion, chaos, and anxiety that are as natural to our species as breathing. These conditions fertilize growth, excitement, creativity, joy, energy, and commitment. As a consultant I was often credited with the power to grant people exemptions from Denial and Confusion. Alas, like the Wizard of Oz, who knew he was a fraud, I can't do it. I don't believe you can either.

I hate to hear anxious people labeled "change resisters," as if the natural cycle of human experience is an evil legion to be defeated by superior methodological firepower on the force fields of organizational strife. Resistance is as natural as eating. I am learning to accept my own resistance too, especially to client expectations I cannot meet. The people I work with are moving, too, in some or all of these ways:

Away from	**Toward**
"Solve the problem."	"Create the future."
"Give it to an expert."	"Help each other learn."
"Get a task force."	"Involve everybody."
"Find the technique."	"Find a valued purpose."
"Do it all now."	"Do what's doable—in season."

In sum, I believe that elaborate consultant- (or manager-) centered diagnoses are unnecessary to reorganize workplaces flooded by sea tides of change. That may surprise some fans of my widely used six-box model (Weisbord, 1978b). Yet that model, as many have discovered, has many uses besides diagnosing problems. It can advance organizational learning. You can use it to encourage thinking about how the whole contraption fits together. That is its strength. Now, I'd steer away from zeroing in on problems within boxes. Rather, I'd seek connections between boxes, among whole sets of problems to the values, beliefs, and assumptions that support them. That describes any model's "expert" function—to make better open-systems analysts of each of us.

However, a model's "everybody" function need not be diagnostic at all. Its best "everybody" function is as a planning tool. What sort of system do you want three, five, ten years from now? In terms of Purposes, Structure, Relationships, Rewards, Helpful Mechanisms, and Leadership? Does your work design or reorganization plan account for each category in a way that's consistent with your values? How does Purpose influence Structure? What kinds of Relationships do you seek between units? How should you manage disagreements?

A model may reduce anxiety and frustration, but it can't take them away. I have learned to greet them as familiar traveling companions in every white water voyage. I try to rejoin them each time with good humor and to forgive myself when I can't. I recall Rudyard Kipling's poem about keeping your head "when all about you are losing theirs and blaming it on you" (Sisan and Sisan, 1973, p. 69). Dignity, meaning, and community in the workplace are for me the anchor points for economic success in democratic societies. We need to preserve, enhance, and enact these values for reasons at once pragmatic, moral, humanistic, economic, technical, and social—take your pick.

That for me is the song and dance of restructuring workplaces. I am interested in preserving economic stability beyond quarterly dividends because I believe that democratic societies depend on creating employment. More, I advocate these guidelines to help people discover new ways to manage economic and technical innovation, to stimulate new economic activity, and to find for themselves dignity, meaning, and community in work.

■ ■ ■

"THE VISION WAS STILL ALIVE AFTER TWENTY YEARS..."

COLUMBUS, OH—In August 1989 I was trying to make sense of experiences that left me both energized and disoriented. I had been working with colleagues in an automotive supplier's factory. A quality problem had surfaced and the company could not identify the cause. The team leader suggested inviting that area's entire workforce to a large ballroom for team building and conversation about the problem.

As someone rooted in small group OD dynamics, this struck me as a horrible idea. I agreed to join so that I could watch and learn, anticipating that I would be called on to help clean up the mess. To my amazement, when front-line workers talked together, they discovered several ways in which team members had solved problems that management wouldn't address. By the time the next shift started, workers had fixed the latest problem without any new financial or human resources.

Later that year two colleagues asked that I help facilitate a "summit" to lay the foundation for reorganizing the youth corrections system in an Eastern state. They proposed that diverse internal and external stakeholders spend two days creating a shared vision for the new structure. Because of this state's historic past—one of America's original thirteen colonies—our lead consultant proposed to start by reflecting on the history of youth corrections in the context of world events. I still resisted the idea that large, diverse groups could work productively in such limited time, but given my earlier experience, I remained open to the possibility. I saw the group make a palpable shift while reflecting on their history when they realized they were all in it together.

Shortly after, a colleague told me about *Productive Workplaces.* Attracted to the idea of dignity, meaning, and community in the workplace, I read it cover to cover. I was struck by three things. It reconnected me to the roots of my training and work, suggesting that I reconsider some of what I had learned. I found also that the lessons Marv had learned trying to move theory into practice resonated with my own. My epiphany came in the third section where Marv describes the evolution of whole-systems thinking and practice. Suddenly my earlier experiences began to make sense.

I attended the 1991 Cape Cod Future Search training, and that year I ran my first FS, working with two colleagues, the Ohio governor-elect, and the Ohio Head Start Association to create a vision for serving the state's children and families. Participants identified core values and minimum critical specifications for a statewide service system. They committed to increased collaboration among systems at all levels and to including families in case and system planning. In 1993 the legislature set up state and local "Family and Children First Councils" and the Governor created a "family cabinet" to assure that relevant appointees collaborate. After four governors and three political party changes, the cabinet and councils were still active twenty years later.

That Future Search led to two more on improving the quality of early childhood care and education. As a result, the local Board of Developmental Disabilities, the largest Head Start agency, the Columbus City Schools, the YMCA, and other organizations partnered to set up a broadly inclusive child care and early childhood center. The Ohio child care partnership has now been operating for a decade. In the 2010 planning retreat they invited parents and families to help create an environment in which family members move beyond their active involvement in their own children's development to join in program development for the entire partnership.

I have continued working with multi-organization, multi-sector partnerships to build inclusive communities based on "getting the whole system in the room"—in health care, human services, early childhood, and intercultural understanding.

—Chris Kloth, ChangeWorks of the Heartland

chapter
NINETEEN

Changing Everything at Once

Transition begins with an ending. Human beings cannot move into new roles with a clear sense of purpose and energy unless they let go of the way things were and the self-image that fit the situation.

—William Bridges, "How to Manage Organizational Transition," 1985, p. 28

The case that follows describes a permanent white water rafting trip down an uncharted river. Numerous industries are caught up in having to rethink both costs and markets in a period of relentless discontinuity. Reimagining a business requires a profound letting go of past assumptions, habits, familiar niches. This case documents one company's experiences in pushing beyond severe economic and technological limits by removing the limits on employee involvement. It embodies the guidelines discussed in Chapter Eighteen.

A Division in Trouble: Technology Meets Economic Limits

Atomic Energy of Canada Limited (AECL) was a Crown (government) corporation dedicated to peaceful uses of nuclear energy. It operated world-class research facilities and businesses competing in global markets. One business, the Radiochemical Company (RCC), had for years profitably made radioisotopes and equipment for treating cancer and irradiating many products.

RCC's Medical Division—subject of this case—manufactured and sold cancer treatment and treatment planning equipment. In the 1950s it built the first commercial cancer treatment device using the radioactive element cobalt 60, and became the world's leading supplier of cobalt machines. In the 1960s the linear accelerator began replacing cobalt. To remain a radiotherapy leader, Medical in the 1970s invested in an advanced accelerator—the Therac 25 (T-25). An innovative breakthrough promised a new high-energy machine smaller and less expensive than the competition's. Ironing out the complexities proved difficult. At $1 million a copy, the new machine had a limited market. AECL faced serious doubts about the T-25's commercial prospects.

In 1982 Bill Hatton, a chemical engineer and stern taskmaster, took over RCC after upping productivity in a heavy-water plant. A story is told about Hatton that reveals his stubbornness. Ken Round, the last of many project engineers managing the accelerator, had once been technical manager in Hatton's plant. During a drought the lake was dangerously depleted. Round told Hatton they would shut down in a week for lack of process cooling capability. "That's totally unacceptable," said Hatton. "You must make it rain. I know it's technically feasible." Round hired Indian rainmakers and aerial cloud seeders. What happened? "It rained," said the teller of the tale. "In that part of the country it always rains if you wait long enough."

This time, however, Round could not make rain. The T-25 was a technological marvel and an economic nightmare. Even if its bugs were ironed out, the market was too small to recoup the investment. Hatton and his team soon proposed two drastic steps to AECL: one, withdraw from accelerators; two, slash costs. Neither move would be easy, particularly as more T-25 development work was needed to support units already in the pipeline. Still, if costs could be cut, the product might break even and be a success. Late in 1983 Hatton reluctantly sought approval to downsize by 20 percent—220 people through voluntary retirement and layoffs—RCC's largest reduction ever. Cuts were made across all product lines. People in profitable segments were demoralized and worried. With no new T-25 orders in prospect, more layoffs were inevitable.

Hatton asked his human resources staff for remedies. Their report pulled no punches. Most people were job-security oriented, knew little about customers, and had never met top management. Planning was secretive; functions were rationalized that shouldn't be done at all. They noted an "inflexible structure . . . resistance to intergroup cooperation . . . assigning blame for problems to other groups . . . duplication of responsibility . . . buck passing . . . exclusion of almost all employees from decisions . . . low morale." The report noted that companies had turned bad situations around by reducing layers, increasing teamwork, and devising more flexible systems. They recommended outside consulting help.

In July 1984 Maurice Dubras, a mechanical engineer, internal consultant, and a twenty-year AECL veteran, introduced me to Hatton. "I've got a three-million-dollar problem and no way to solve it," he told me. "The only way management knows is to lay everybody off. We have one hundred surplus people right now. I'm not sure what to do. What we went through before is not right. I want to redirect that effort."

Dubras, I, and Dominick Volini, a member of our firm who had lived in Canada, met with RCC's management team. AECL's motivation was not only cost-cutting. It was also to avoid further layoffs—a source of guilt, anger, and despair among senior managers. We agreed to assess the feasibility of a participative rescue effort. Managers would discuss our findings throughout the company. Only then would we decide whether to go forward together.

In July 1984 Dubras and Volini were joined by Eileen Curtin and Jack Ollett of our firm. All had facilitated reorganizations in offices and factories. Curtin and Volini had recently helped a small Philadelphia manufacturer cut costs $1 million a year without layoffs. Dubras hoped the approach could be applied in RCC.

The team interviewed fifty-eight people across levels and functions, using the technique of following the flow of office paperwork and raw materials to finished goods in the factory. The local union presidents—Ed Devaul of the Energy and Chemical Workers (ECWU) and Frank Amyot of the Public Service Alliance of Canada (PSAC)—were open, helpful, and worried. So was Reg Waterfall, the local head of the Commercial Products Professional Employees Association (CPPEA), an engineers' group active in the company.

Managers and supervisors were discouraged. All knew that the lack of T-25 sales was a cloud of doom for the workforce. Many wanted to help and had little confidence in management's leadership.

Three dilemmas threatened the company. One, the T-25 tied up major resources and had to be let go. Two, tangled systems, inefficiencies, and work rules kept everybody busy. Three, while stopping work on the T-25 and redesigning work would mean more layoffs, these steps could not save the company. Solutions required more sales in a stagnant market.

Time had run out on incremental change. More layoffs were imminent, making a cooperative salvage effort improbable by overworked and demoralized survivors. A few managers remained stubbornly committed to accelerators. Others argued to expand manufacturing, still others for marketing agreements with Japanese or European firms.

In our feasibility summary we wrote, "In terms of our model for required starting conditions—committed leadership, a significant business problem, and a high degree of awareness and energy to solve the problem—RCC qualifies on all three counts." But initiatives were needed on two fronts at once: costs and markets. I could hear in the situation uncomfortable overtones of Frederick Taylor's magnificent failure at Simonds Ball Bearing (Chapter Three). By focusing on production, he had cut costs, raised wages, reduced working hours—only to see the firm fail in a volatile market. Unless we addressed markets and strategy along with production, we faced a similar prospect.

Hatton was attracted by the example of Lincoln Electric Co., an innovative "guaranteed employment" company that had weathered a recession by giving redundant workers a crash course in selling. Could that notion work in a government-owned company? Canadian law required sixteen weeks' notice of impending layoffs. Suppose RCC put 150 redundant people to work exploring options instead? Suppose labor and management cooperated to search for new markets, better technology, more efficient methods, and alternative jobs? The responses of RCC's top team ranged from skeptical to incredulous. Opening the company to influence from so many directions would release forces management could not control.

Hatton had tentative support too. Ken Round desperately wanted to iron out the T-25's bugs, support existing customers, and cut the product loose. The former manufacturing head, Frank Warland, an expatriate British engineer and AECL veteran known for his exuberance, had grown discouraged at his inability to influence change. Bob Wolff, head of human resources, had good relations with union leaders and liked the idea of increased involvement. Yet he saw pitfalls in traditional practices and animosities on the shop floor.

Hatton's group discussed a radical proposition—guarantee employment for a period longer than normal if people would participate in the rescue attempt. This might include work redesign, phasing out the T-25, an internal job search agency, entrepreneurial training, sale of the existing business, new services using existing technology, product line extensions, and/or joint ventures. The list was a chicken-egg tangle of interlocking dilemmas. How can you redesign manufacturing for an unknown market? Or build new products when your internal systems need overhauling? Managing so many objectives at once required an enormous leap into the unknown.

In the film *Starman*, an alien sent to study the planet Earth is pressed to explain his culture's motives for wanting to know more about human beings. "You are one of the most interesting species in the universe," he replies. "You are at your best when things are worst." That's as good an explanation as any for the events that followed.

Building a Company-Wide Mandate

AECL's corporate management, meanwhile, had decided on a bold move. "We had made classic mistakes—merging winners and losers into one company," said President James Donnelly, a pragmatic Scotsman with high standards. "It didn't work." To give RCC's viable products a fighting chance, he proposed to reorganize yet again.

He would set up a new division, AECL Medical Products, for the losing accelerator lines, cobalt therapy, simulators, treatment planning, and manufacturing. RCC, a viable radioisotopes business, would stand alone and become a major customer for Medical. AECL would withdraw from accelerators, while supporting existing customers. The new division would lay off 150 of 480 people and an uncertain future. Those in a downsized RCC would have relatively secure jobs.

Many aspects troubled Donnelly. "It was more than just going out of the accelerator business," he said later. "It meant going out of the cobalt therapy business, and that was a much harder problem." Customer anxiety about the company's future could jeopardize successful products. Donnelly also wanted to tell employees that this was the last layoff—the same message as a year earlier.

At this juncture Hatton brought Donnelly the proposal that he and his team had worked out with the consultants. He wanted a fighting chance to turn around the existing RCC. Donnelly offered him an unattractive option—heading up Medical, the weaker division split off from RCC, and managing its further downsizing and withdrawal from accelerators.

Harry Hughes, AECL's corporate human resources vice president, urgently believed the company needed participation. Hughes and Donnelly asked the consultants what could be done to help Hatton after downsizing. Now we had a dilemma. For moral and practical reasons we could not support unilateral layoffs. I called my friend Eric Trist. "Tell them exactly how you see it," he advised. "This could be a damaging situation, socially and politically, and five hundred people could lose their jobs."

Next day we met with Donnelly and Hughes. We said we couldn't help if they undertook a unilateral layoff. The survivors would not participate in saving a business that had laid off so many of their friends and relatives. It would be a mistake to tell people layoffs were over unless costs were cut and sales increased. The only way we could imagine saving the business was to put the redundant people to work searching for innovative solutions.

Donnelly pondered the pros and cons. "If we guarantee jobs and search for ways to save the business," he reflected at last, "we can tell people the truth! We are dropping accelerators, protecting our customers, and looking for options to carry on. We could satisfy ourselves that we had explored every choice."

All at once the meeting turned to problem solving. The cost to guarantee five hundred jobs for a year when only 350 people were needed would be $5 million in wages and salaries. But dropping accelerators and laying off 150 people would cost $3 million in any case. Even if Medical floundered, involving people in searching for new businesses might set a learning precedent for the company. With a hiatus in peaceful uses of nuclear power, layoffs were a prospect throughout AECL. Demonstrations were badly needed that the trend could be reversed.

The ball bounced back to Hatton. Would he take the Medical assignment if it included a layoff moratorium? By now Hatton was invested in the idea of all-out participation as the only solution to uncertainty. He abhorred the "hatchet man" label he had acquired and concluded he had no choice but to go for it.

Hatton's team was ambivalent. The proposition made more sense to them before the decision to split off the profitable business. Had they been tapped for self-liquidation? Round characterized it as "an appallingly difficult problem, caught in conflicting objectives between employees, customers, and shareholders." Wolff, the human resources manager, worried about splitting two union locals. How could they bargain jointly with one company surviving, the other in jeopardy?

Top team members and consultants met for days on end, bouncing back and forth between how to do it and whether anybody really wanted to. Many questions were unanswerable. Who would run the existing business and who would search for new options? How would candidates be selected? Could the process be kept voluntary? If some people were tagged "redundant," would that not amount to a layoff with twelve months' notice? Suppose the unions balked?

It was now late December. The impending split had to be kept secret until a January 15 announcement. In the interim, Medical Products Division employees would be told of the proposal to put a one-year moratorium on layoffs in return for their cooperation to save the company. Two unions and the professional employees society would have to agree to co-sponsor any plan before it could be set in motion.

A Tangled Web. In tense meetings between Christmas and New Year's, Hatton and his team worked out the complex details—announcements, reassuring customers, offers to the unions, employee briefings, starting up the search for new products and markets. Several times they reached dead ends. Did they really want to go through with this? All options looked unattractive.

Warland somehow found in the ambiguous challenge extraordinary reserves of energy. Each night he recharged his batteries by writing out notes and plans on his personal computer, coming in the next day with printed "to do" lists, ideas, questions, schedules. His enthusiasm fed the rest of us. Inevitably, we decided there were no ideal alternatives and no expert solutions. The skeptical financial manager opted for transfer. His place was taken by Rod Arnot, a self-identified "bean counter" who proved to be a great deal more. With enormous anxiety and misgivings, the group decided to plunge ahead.

A formal proposal went to the AECL board: defer layoffs for a year while the division involved people to explore new uses for existing assets, create jobs for all within AECL or outside, fulfill customer obligations, supply basic products to RCC, and enhance AECL's reputation as a responsible employer.

If the unions agreed, up to 150 people would be engaged in pursuing options and redesigning work systems. Others would maintain the existing business. A third track, still ambiguous, would explore outplacement. Medical Products in transition would have two major departments, Operations under Warland to carry on the existing business, and Search, guided by Round. The latter would include new markets and products, work redesign, and outplacement. A transition team, representing all employees, would manage the effort. Somebody noted that, even if employees agreed, they really didn't have a year. The law required sixteen weeks' notice for layoffs. That reduced the practical window to eight months. It seemed a near impossibility.

The wish to preserve employment united everyone. It struck me as the corporate analogy to a barn raising, a ritual of community survival that enabled each farmer to remain viable in the face of adversity. Of all managerial acts, none is more hateful than burning the barn. The practice of involuntary layoffs grows from deep-seated, unexamined assumptions—that people are spare parts, that no one can influence impersonal economic forces, that management is unilaterally responsible for what to do in good times or bad.

In a layoff everybody loses. The victims lose self-esteem. The survivors suffer guilt and demoralization. The community endures economic and social hardship. The unemployed and their families may be severely depressed.

Usually a last resort, layoffs compromise a firm's ability to rebound. The assumption that layoff is a necessary management tool is what makes layoffs necessary. That assumption can be altered, McGregor would have said, only by testing it in each situation. That layoffs hurt business has been amply documented (Pfeffer, 2010).

Achieving a Mandate. There began an emotional roller coaster of euphoric highs and depressing lows, an all-out effort to salvage a business most had written off. Between Christmas and mid-January a "buy-in" of all parties—AECL board, union leaders, middle managers, professionals, unorganized staff—was sought in tense meetings. Top managers, consultants, and officers of the Energy and Chemical Workers Union (ECWU) and the Public Service Alliance of Canada (PSAC) met to discuss the proposal.

Henri Gauthier, ECWU's articulate national representative, posed tough questions. "Why are we always junior partners in good times and senior partners in bad?" was the first. Management replied that AECL would open its records to union officials over the weekend. Participation would be a way of life at AECL Medical if the company were saved. Gauthier also challenged what he called the consultants' "blueprint." He recalled another company in which the union had been handed a plan and told it could not be changed.

This proposal, he learned, was open-ended. A transition team representing all parties would form two steering groups to organize search and work redesign (see "The Blueprint"). All further decisions would be theirs. A joint U.S.-Canadian consulting team would assist. To test each other, the parties had to plunge ahead. Gauthier, in fact, had had more experience with labor-management cooperation in Canada than any of the parties. His union had partnered with Shell in the startup of the Sarnia, Ontario, chemical plant, a notable innovative work site. He knew the potential if the parties learned to trust each other. He also understood the pitfalls. Union officials insisted that there be no changes in job descriptions or the collective agreement without mutual decision and that either party could terminate if it wished to.

Union leaders balked at including nonunion office workers. "They're unorganized. How can anybody represent them?" said one official. In this uncharted water, past rules, norms, and labor-management practices offered little guidance. After some old-fashioned bargaining, it was agreed

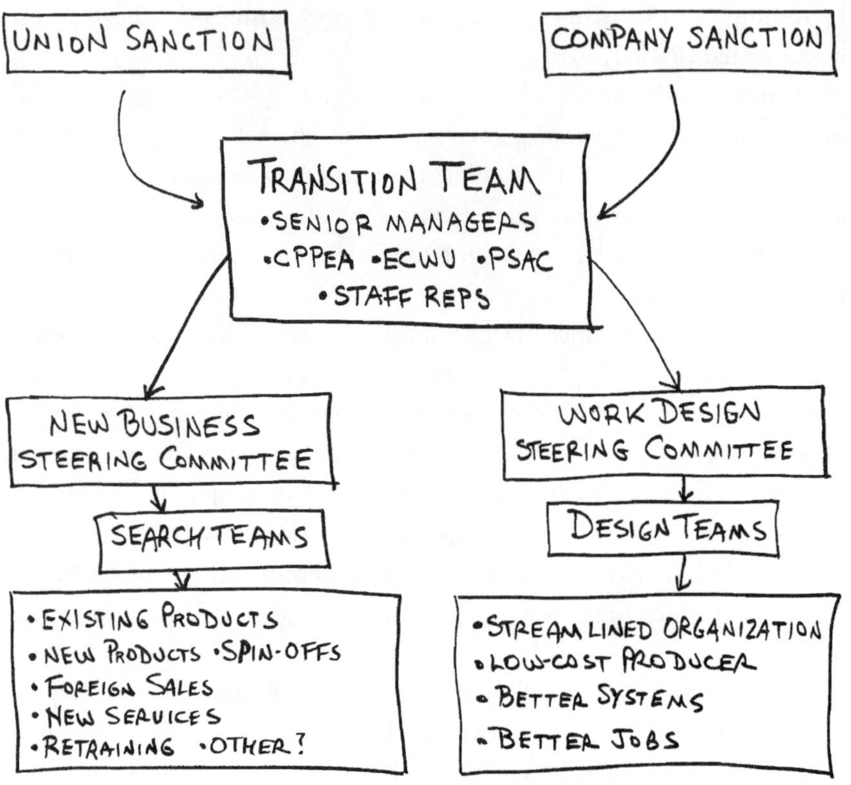

that the transition team would include five top managers, one representative each from employees' association, middle management, and unorganized workers, and two from each union—the local president plus a national official—thus keeping significant union influence. The deal would be contingent on union votes after a public announcement.

Next day Hatton told his "old" RCC management of the plan. "We would like to see unions, managers, and all employees involved on teams," he said. "This will work if we practice openness, honesty, and participation." The next day Donnelly announced the new AECL Medical to an employee mass meeting. "While existing business conditions and work load would traditionally dictate a layoff," he said, "we will undertake an innovative participative management program for twelve months to involve and tap the creative energies of all employees. We feel it has a reasonable but by no means guaranteed chance of success."

Now began a frantic three days of communicating and asking for a buy-in among Medical Division employees. Managers, supervisors, and union officials were given special briefings, asked to assume leadership, communicate to their people, bring back questions. "What will happen," asked a union shop steward in one meeting, "if we go along and pull it off?" Hatton: "I think we'll look a little smaller, walk a little taller, and make a little profit. I'm just giving you my personal feelings, because in this I'm one of 486 people."

Supervisors and middle managers now had to manage a risky transition wholly outside their experience. Warland offered them a list of anticipated questions and answers: how people were sorted into divisions, under what conditions a layoff might occur, whether the company would sell assets to employees, what to tell customers. Volini reviewed tips for dealing with likely reactions to the change. (See "Guidelines for Helping People in a Major Change" on page 355.) All managers agreed to circulate and collect additional questions that afternoon.

Next day all sixty-five managers pooled the collected questions and concerns and worked out answers to be distributed in French and English. They identified twenty high-priority themes for a company mass meeting that afternoon. Confusion was evident. "It's worse than two years ago," said Hatton to his managers. "I take full responsibility for that. What we're discussing here is whether we will buy into a new way of trying to turn it around."

Voice from floor: "Will it be democratic or management veto or what on this transition team?"

Hatton: "It will be all things—tough, soft, mixed up. Until I get on the team, I don't know."

Facing Facts. At the mass meeting Hatton outlined the facts. The new company had few orders, was losing $1 million a month. To survive it had to turn around by 1986–1987. Although there was too little work, employment would be guaranteed for a year if employees joined in finding new markets and redesigning work. The goals were two:

employ everybody and become profitable. The transition team could meet only when all parties had agreed and picked representatives. People talked it over at their tables with union leaders, managers, and supervisors. That evening both unions voted separately to participate. Professional employees and supervisors voted yes the next day and unorganized workers a few days later. All recognized that the choices were few and unattractive.

Mobilizing a Productive Workplace

On January 23, 1985, less than a month after AECL's embarking on this risky journey, the new division had a transition team of top and middle managers, union leaders, and unorganized office workers—a diverse group that had never worked together. They were starting cold turkey with a tight deadline. Hatton said that he expected all major company decisions to be ratified in this forum. He would serve only as another group member. It was a startling (and unsettling) statement from an executive viewed as an autocrat. Uncharted water again. The consultants agreed to run the first few meetings until transition team members figured out an acceptable leadership mode.

The transition team began by naming a Business Opportunities Steering Committee (BOSC) and a Work Design Steering Committee (WDSC). Urgency and anxiety led to improvisations and goofs. The transition team decided not to have its members "link pin" with steering committees. Instead, mindful of employee suspicions that management might spy on activities in this more open climate, they offered each group maximum latitude. Management had backed way off to avoid being seen as manipulative. Ken Round, as search manager, would be link enough. Round's charter was ambiguous. Did the teams work for him? Or was he an ex officio member?

Management also assumed that its distant U.S. sales force could not participate. A few days later in Dallas, sales managers confronted Hatton: this was stepchild treatment from the home office. They made a conference call to the transition team, suggesting a U.S. member be added. Union reps interpreted this as a management power play. "How can we exclude our U.S. operation?" asked Hatton. "They represent most of our sales." A few days later the unions accepted a compromise: Only four of the five top managers would attend transition team meetings, to create a slot for a U.S. manager.

Guidelines for Helping People in a Major Change

Mostly, it's common sense. Here are practices usually found helpful:

1. Give as much information as possible. Repeat as often as needed. You may not be heard or understood the first time.
2. Tell the truth. It's okay to say, "I don't know but I'll find out and get back to you."
3. Don't argue. If you feel misunderstood, ask people to repeat what they thought you said. It can save a lot of explaining.
4. Accept all feelings—good and bad—as real honest expressions of the other person. Don't tell people how they "should" feel. It's okay to be down. Your feelings change eventually, even if you don't do anything.
5. Guard against self-fulfilling prophecies, such as, "That won't work." We don't know yet what will work and what won't. We intend to explore every opportunity.
6. Let people see you write down things that need follow-up. It's reassuring.
7. Follow up all questions, rumors, or concerns. Don't let anything go by. Get the facts!
8. In short:
    - Give information.
    - Listen, accept feelings.
    - Make notes.
    - Follow up.

The transition team began writing a charter (see "Transition Team Charter"). With anxiety, touchiness, uncertainty, and vague mistrust, the joint rescue operation was launched.

Transition Team Charter

The transition team is a joint, representative, decision-making body. Our aim is to ensure employment for all employees of AECL Medical by making it a viable, participatively managed business with a strong customer focus. This will be accomplished by promoting the voluntary participation of all employees, who will provide ideas for business opportunities and redesign of the work performed. We will assume an ongoing leadership role by managing the change process, by motivating and encouraging the free flow of ideas, and by ensuring that all necessary information is communicated promptly to all employees. With employee cooperation, we will make every effort to provide employment beyond the one-year guaranty within Medical, elsewhere in AECL, or outside the company.

Focusing on the Future. The Business Opportunities Steering group (BOSC) organized a two-and-a-half-day Future Search of one hundred people from all levels and functions. Together they looked at the past, present, and future of AECL Medical. The conference featured a "skills fair." Every function touted its capabilities in booths improvised on the spot. BOSC also had collected more than five hundred business ideas—novel, practical, farfetched—from those who stayed home to run the business. These were sorted by four tough criteria. To merit further exploration, an idea had to (1) create jobs, (2) use existing skills, (3) require little or no capital, and (4) likely provide profits in one to two years.

A dozen task forces emerged. Nearly all involved expanding, refining, upgrading, or cutting costs on existing products. Union shop members supported subcontracting, for example, selling excess plant capacity. High priority went to a low-cost cobalt therapy machine, a product line extension that could open new markets.

Management had feared that people would opt only for "blue sky" pursuits. In actuality, most clung to a belief in existing products "if only" this or that happened. BOSC, alarmed now that there would be no innovation, insisted on a second-round poll. It yielded endorsement of ideas such as a novel home decoration called an electron tree and X-ray machines to survey hidden structural damage in buildings and bridges. As traditional projects were completed or proved unfeasible, new teams would investigate innovative ideas.

At last, twelve volunteer search teams met in a blur of anxiety, enthusiasm, and bewilderment. They organized team leader and member roles, reviewed purposes, picked meeting dates. What were they allowed to do? Whatever they believed was necessary. Who could they talk with? Anybody they thought could help. How much time could they spend? Negotiate with supervisors. Suppose supervisors balked? BOSC or the transition team would deal with it—another unprecedented problem to be worked out. Claudia Chowaniec of our firm and Larry Schruder of AECL joined Dubras and Volini in consulting to the search teams.

Each team would meet monthly with BOSC and the transition team to report progress and decide next steps. The clock was ticking. Seven months remained before a layoff decision had to be made. The "whole system in the room" monthly review was the only integrating mechanism, based on the premise that goal-focused people exchanging information and organizing their own tasks was the shortest route to survival.

Search Crisis. Within a few days of startup, management made a high-risk decision: to place under BOSC two sensitive merger discussions already underway. This meant opening up secret negotiations to hourly employees, an extraordinary display of trust. The initiatives, mutually exclusive, would make work for different functions. Opening the issue to influence, said management, was the only sure path to implementation if either venture panned out. Confidentiality agreements were signed—and respected. To stop the perception that this pet project would be railroaded over all opposition, Hatton and Warland refused to take any further actions until BOSC decided who could join them on the team and give them a mandate to proceed.

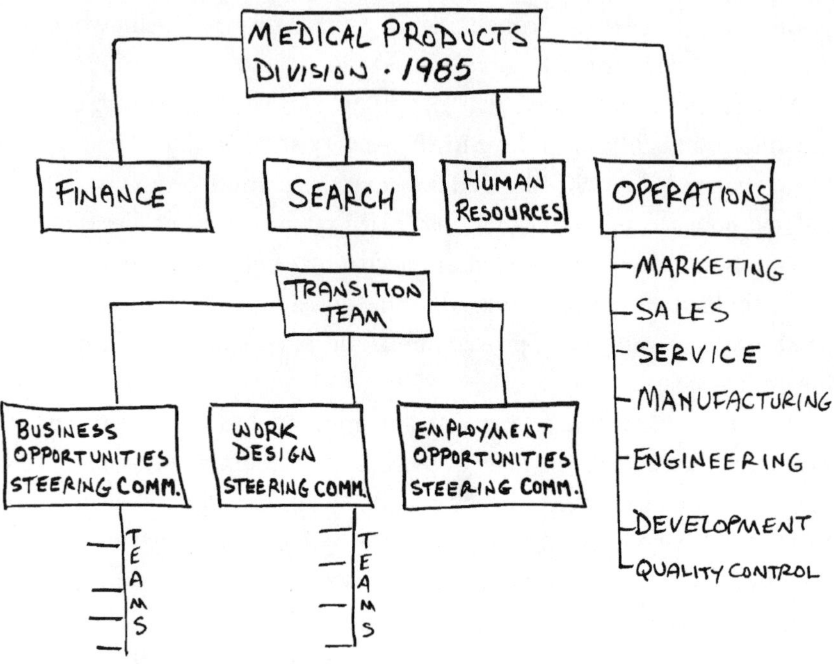

Hatton took an extraordinary stand: the transition team would become the company's management committee. He deliberately held back in meetings, insisting that the team confront all business dilemmas together. This discomfited both his top managers and union leaders. The managers were frustrated that he was not more forcefully directing; the union leaders wondered whether they could share management decision making and still bargain for their members' best interests. With heads of finance, search, human resources, and operations involved on the transition team, it became difficult to separate day-to-day operations from future-oriented search. More, the transition team became a forum for airing every ongoing problem. The "Medical Products Division" chart shows the operating structure.

Were management's and labor's interests incompatible, aligned, or some of both? Were their relations grounded in natural law—adversarial to the end—or different in each situation? It was an issue baffling to those most committed to its constructive resolution. One thing was obvious. Both management and union leadership had to change. They would move together or not at all.

Contrary to conventional wisdom, Hatton had created a leadership vacuum. His action reflected complex motives—anxiety, faith in this process, uncertainty about what to do, acknowledgment that this management, exercising its prerogatives, had often made mistakes. He readily accepted that the buck stopped with him. Who would share the risk and join in thinking through the tough decisions? Would people fight, run away, or confront their mutual problems? The answer was not long in coming. Union members of BOSC insisted that hourly people be added to management's merger negotiating teams. High-level managers argued that BOSC itself included members of these teams already. Two union officers walked out of BOSC, saying that this was one more example of how management put down hourly workers.

The issue dredged up long-buried resentments. The consultants, determined not to let people fight or run away, joined the fray. After tense discussions, relative harmony was restored. The issues would recycle many times as anxiety mounted about which potential businesses would be pursued. Some managers, upset at top management's patient acceptance of union members' volatile behavior, felt bruised and abandoned and began updating their résumés.

Starting Work Redesign. Meanwhile the Work Design Steering Committee (WDSC) set up tables in the company cafeteria and solicited employees' ideas. Nearly five hundred suggestions came in. The committee identified three priorities: order processing; building new product prototypes; and improving the Materials Resources Planning system. Volunteer task forces received an orientation to basic work-design principles, set goals, flowcharted the existing systems, and scheduled meetings. They would rationalize systems and work flows for products, technologies, and markets that in fact might not survive the search process.

Review Meetings: Getting the Whole System in the Room. The first review meeting, in a church hall that could hold everyone, opened a Pandora's box of tangled systems, accumulated inefficiencies, and strategic dilemmas. Never before had the whole system's intelligence assembled in one room: manufacturing, marketing, finance, engineering, management, factory and office workers. Work-design teams reported bad due dates and inflated factory lead times. Orders passed through production planning four times. Prototype parts needing sixteen hours of machine time took forty-eight days in process. Simple parts orders passed five times between three buildings and took fourteen working days to ship. New procedures could save $200,000 to $300,000 a year and vastly improve customer service.

Search teams reported customer interviews, analyses of service failures, costs, market data. Joint-venture initiatives in Japan and the United States were being explored. Teams had found attractive markets and extraordinary dilemmas in tapping them. Customers preferred the competition's cancer treatment simulators, for example, despite the excellence of Medical's. "We have to clean up our act, improve service support to customers, reduce irritations," said the team. Subcontracts surfaced a puzzling dilemma: the factory had excess capacity, yet existing products were consistently late.

People were stressed by the scarcity of resources to carry on daily work and explore options. There were sore backs, stomach aches, weariness from long hours, and high anxiety. Despite supposed redundancies at all levels, few managers could work full time on teams. Fear grew that participation was too little, too late. After the meeting, a marketing executive confided that he believed the division would close its doors by year-end. As if to punctuate his remarks, two experienced engineers took new jobs elsewhere.

There was worse to come. Pressure on union-management relations grew. By April work-redesign teams realized that many order processing jobs held by PSAC members could be eliminated. Without warning, the national union withdrew its members, citing joint management of layoffs as a dangerous precedent in government service. PSAC members had been among the most dedicated participants. Their union's unilateral pullout left them vulnerable to early layoff should management choose. Yet many continued on search teams as individuals, and management did not exercise its option.

Middle management was in disarray. Many of its problem-solving prerogatives had been assumed by search teams. A "management initiatives group" was convened to encourage this group—the one most threatened by change—to take charge of their futures. Only thirty-five of sixty-eight responded. Many could not face the dilemma that when hourly workers had direct access to management through participative teams, supervision must undertake a wholly new role. Union members heightened the tension by using the more open climate to publicly criticize unpopular bosses.

Arnot showed the group the latest business plan. They could lose $18 million in 1986, including the cost of letting go 250 people, and $3 million more in 1987, "tantamount to closing our doors." All products but replacement sources were losing money. They had no orders for the next three months. What next? A half-dozen volunteers agreed to organize work-redesign orientations for middle managers not on teams. Pessimism ran high. One subgroup offered to start exploring alternative employment and termination compensation.

By June the need to revamp marketing, sales and services, production, and control systems was apparent. Externally, the assessment was gloomier still. Although good ideas abounded, few could be taken far enough in one year to employ everybody. After each review meeting Arnot updated his spreadsheets, feeding in new data and assumptions, looking for a mix of product lines, services, and costs that netted a survivable business.

The Phoenix. A few bright spots emerged. The feasibility of a simple, inexpensive, high-quality cobalt therapy unit (nicknamed Elsie–LC—for "low cost") was quickly established by a search team. It would be ideal for Third-World and rural hospitals, likely to take 33 percent of the market by 1989. Given the many factory glitches, it would take a year to produce. After weeks of demoralizing debate, Warland seized the initiative. He got together union machinists and a cadre of engineers. "Let's cut the red tape and get on the market," he said. "Can you build a prototype without detailed drawings?" A union inspector asked what the quality specs were. "If you're proud of the finished product, Jack," said Warland, "that's good enough for me." The team produced a prototype in eight weeks. They named it Phoenix, symbolizing a reviving company. Two team members flew to Miami to display the machine at an October trade show—a big lift at a critical moment.

Another team identified a chance to market a U.S. firm's low-cost simulator overseas. It made no jobs, but was "one of the few things likely to produce revenue this year," strengthening chances for survival. Meanwhile, the subcontracting search team had sold a new contract. This good news was quickly tempered by the discovery that a subcontract job shop required systems different from a manufacturing plant. They must be selective in accepting jobs lest they foul up regular production.

Now BOSC sought to initiate a second round of search teams focusing on innovative ideas. Only seven people signed up. "If we have 250 people on a potential layoff list," asked one steering team member, "why aren't they available?" The answer seemed to be that it took all the experienced people to patch the system's inefficiencies. BOSC sought financial help to assess old programs, get marketing input on potential sales of new products, and train members in compiling and analyzing business plans.

On the work-design front, people revamped production control and engineering despite some supervisory foot-dragging. Three more teams started—in packaging, cobalt adjuster rods, service contracts. Potential efficiencies were identified at every turn. Yet the gap widened between the quality of problem solving and people's gloomy feelings about the future. "There are many obstacles to better manufacturing," said one steering group member. "Morale is low. It's certain now we won't have 480 jobs come January." On paper, one-third of the jobs in selected areas had been cut out in the first three projects. How would they choose the right people and assure work for those whose jobs disappeared? Strong leadership was needed. Where would it come from in this ambiguous participative climate?

Can This Business Survive?

Would any strategic scenario save Medical? Perceptions of the situation began to change. The division was not avoiding a layoff of 150 people. It was discovering whether the business could survive at all. By now financial manager Arnot was putting every team's analysis of costs and markets into spreadsheets weekly and discussing the resulting scenarios in every forum he could reach. Employees at all levels learned the economics and technology of the business—an unprecedented sharing of information, knowledge, and responsibility.

Despite the anxiety, great surges of energy also had been released. Nobody knew how to run this unprecedented system. Yet run it they did. Control had shifted from top management, where it was illusory anyway. Self-control at many levels emerged. It could not be seen, touched, or put into job descriptions, and not everyone had it. But some people, in this situation, had chosen that path. Something vital was happening.

In the June progress review, the mood was quiet, somber, rational—and sharply focused. Both anxiety and excitement had gone. Time had come for concerted action. "Our shop is underutilized," said Hatton. "Our sales force can do four times the volume with little increase in cost. But is the business there? We're in crisis now." A few days later, Arnot's spreadsheets revealed dim outlines of viable business strategies—with and without manufacturing, with and without marketing competitors' products, with and without divesting certain product lines. The alternatives were built around either high-tech fabrication or the medical marketplace.

Hatton convened fifteen top managers to consider options. What would motivate them to want to build a future company? What sort of plan would get their support? The consensus: one that included a new management style, more influence from everybody, more ownership at all levels. And it had to have growth potential. They could build a survivable core business from the pieces surfaced by the search. They noted treatment planning, servicing competitors' products, selling other companies' lines, and subcontracting as viable if they improved office and factory systems. "We must maintain a customer focus in the future," said Hatton. "Management must be much closer to the customers."

The future rested on two observations. One, cobalt therapy, the cash cow, was good for the foreseeable future, even without the T-25. It could provide revenue to underwrite new initiatives—a real breather—if costs were cut and service improved. Two, Medical had to make a fair profit on sales to its sibling company, RCC, the customer whose orders provided a major source of stability.

Perhaps they could survive with two hundred jobs. A layoff was still a prospect. Agonizingly, the transition team activated the Employment Opportunities Steering Committee (EOSC), under Bob Wolff's leadership, to consider career counseling, résumé writing, entrepreneurial training, early retirement, and voluntary resignations. EOSC boldly proposed that union, nonunion, and management people together create voluntary severance packages to meet as many needs as possible.

Meanwhile, pressure built at the top. At a private lunch, Hatton told Arnot, Round, Warland, and Wolff—the "direct reports" who had come this far with him—"I think my role is largely over. I realize people have had a hard time with my leadership. I'm ready to move on." The others had mixed feelings. Said Wolff, "I think Frank [Warland] is the man for the job. He has support in the plant and can pull all the factions together." The changeover could coincide with reorganization. That could be done when they had a process for reducing the workforce and selecting a new management team.

By the end of June a consensus had emerged on a short-term strategic plan based on retaining manufacturing and keeping other options open. A few weeks later EOSC presented an employee-designed plan for early retirement and voluntary resignation. They set up job-search and retirement-planning seminars. Wolff saw enormous advantages over traditional labor-management practices. If people found it beneficial to relocate without following seniority guidelines, there would be no layoffs and no recall list. Yet self-selection meant that some skilled managers, engineers, and machinists surely would go. Certain experienced people were offered inducements to stay through the reorganization. Round, for example, agreed to supervise the completion of the THERAC-25 engineering so that customer support services would exist for the discontinued product.

New Beginnings. In midsummer the transition team undertook a formal review. Big disappointments were lack of new products and difficulties in gaining middle-management support. Despite the lengthy decision process, diffuse leadership, and union-management dilemmas, none wished to scrap future participation. What parts did not work? Team members said they felt out of control most of the time, missed direct links to steering groups, lamented the loss of minority ideas, and (despite, or maybe because of, Hatton's laissez-faire approach) wished management had pushed harder.

What did work? Only one grievance was filed throughout this period. There was much better rapport between senior management and others, freedom to speak out at all levels, and a great increase in employee understanding of the business. The value of having people who do the work redesign it was undisputed. However, the difficulty of achieving results when the outcome was loss of jobs was undeniable. Eliminating pyramids, identifying employee skills, more dependable feedback, and better decisions were applauded. And they noted one thing more: the division had met its first-quarter financial objectives for the first time in living memory!

The future? The consensus was that a representative team could not perform ongoing management. Instead, they proposed an employee advisory group, elected by each department rather than the constituencies previously identified. People at all levels should be consulted on policies and procedures. Employees in all departments would be directly involved in the design and planning of their own work.

By the end of August the future leadership was resolved. Hatton accepted a post with CANDU Operations, AECL's reactor business in Toronto. With little fanfare, his transfer and Warland's appointment as vice president of AECL Medical were announced in September to coincide with the retirement and voluntary termination list. It had been little more than a year since the managers first discussed salvaging the company. It was almost a certainty that the new organization would employ perhaps 260 people, many more than anyone dreamed possible eight weeks earlier. Most others, secured by generous severance, had found jobs elsewhere. No layoffs would be needed now or—as the survivors vowed—ever again. They would manage the business to assure employment security.

Management and labor, organized and not, had forged a community of interest out of the need to survive. In December Warland issued a notice in French and English headed "Participation." A few sentences are worth quoting:

> "AECL Medical has made a firm commitment to Participative Management as the future style of the Division. We began with the formation of the Employee Council. . . . I am now pleased to announce a second step. The formal process of Work Design will be instituted throughout the Division. . . . I have appointed Bob Wolff to direct the Work Design Program and his first task will be to assemble a team of knowledgeable employees to formulate a master plan."

A Backward Glance. Rereading my notes during the project, I saw constant references to slow decisions, uncertainty, ambiguity, conflicting goals, short tempers, profound disagreements, misunderstandings. I found managers lamenting the lack of clear focus and concrete end points. I also found words like energy, creativity, and innovation. More than a year later, I saw a division, unprofitable for years, that had in twenty weeks:

1. Evolved a new mission
2. Developed a new strategic plan
3. Reorganized its workforce
4. Involved everybody who wished to be
5. Created a new level of labor-management cooperation
6. Turned around its sales and costs
7. Implemented a participative, no-layoff downsizing
8. Established a firm future base

Defying theory, AECL Medical had turned itself around. It had retained employment for more than half its workforce and avoided further layoffs. By the end of 1985 its sales already were running ahead of projections. By early 1986 the shop was working overtime. By early 1987 the company had shown a profit for six months in a row. A renewed sales force had turned in so many orders the factory could not keep up. It became necessary to hire back people who had left. By April 1987, 309 people were employed.

In April 1986 Medical surveyed those who opted out to determine, in Warland's words, "what your views are of what we did right and those things that could have been done differently." Most respondents agreed that participation was the right path. Many felt it came too late under too much time pressure. They were disappointed that more innovative marketing and work-redesign ideas had not been implemented before taking the decision to cut back. Several felt the termination options were implemented too hastily, that they had no way to judge whether they should go or stay. Some who left expressed regret now that the company was doing better. More than half said their economic situation was unchanged. Supervisors, those people in the middle pulled apart in every change effort, remained generally negative. Nearly everybody said they had learned "a great deal about how organizations operate and are managed." Two-thirds said they would participate again if given the chance.

■ ■ ■

"YOU CAN RAPIDLY MOBILIZE WHOLE ORGANIZATIONS AND COMMUNITIES..."

MONTREAL, QUE—I found in *Productive Workplaces* a clearer understanding of where I was coming from, where I was, and where I could go as a management consultant. It reinforced my values. I remember my puzzlement at discovering that F. W. Taylor was not the "bad guy" he was depicted to me at the School of Social Sciences. I found out how much consultants, managers, and employees were indebted to him. This reading gave me a new insight into labor-management cooperation, driving me to learn more about work redesign. Eventually, it provided me with a powerful tool to do projects in an egalitarian, participative, and effective way in workplaces as diverse as hospitals, a major seaport, and a large brewery.

I also discovered "getting the whole system in the room." In the fall of 1993 I attended a Future Search workshop and from then on, until I left consulting in 2008, "getting the whole system in the room" became a key driver in my work. I experienced repeatedly that, under the right conditions, you can rapidly mobilize whole organizations and communities by getting all key stakeholders to focus on their common ground. I found this strategy much more effective for strategic planning than the traditional top-down approach by senior management and experts that I had used before.

Now, in a new stage of my life, one of my great satisfactions as a consultant and as a father, is that my son facilitates Future Searches. A quarter-century later the loop is closed and at the same time reopened.

—Jean-Pierre Beaulieu, J.P.Beaulieu, Conseil en gestion inc.*

*Beaulieu became a fine art photographer. His work can be viewed at www.pbase.com/jpbeaulieu5

Medical Products Fifteen Years Later

In the fall of 1999 I called Frank Warland, the retired former CEO, to learn how he viewed the AECL adventure now. "No one expected Medical Products to survive," he said. "That the company still exists is a tribute to the work we did together and a lot of resolve during some difficult times after that." The employees who had lived through the traumas of 1985 pulled together at critical moments in the years that followed. From early days, Warland recalled, they had faced the distressing deaths, due mainly to faulty software, of several cancer patients treated with the discontinued T-25 accelerator. The company undertook intensive remedial work. By 1988 they had fixed the software and upgraded the hardware too.

Thereafter AECL Medical made money into the early 1990s. Still, it had too little capital, too few products, and giant competitors. Its plant was too large a facility for the volume. The company cut costs by building offices inside the factory and moved from three buildings into one.

In the late 1980s the Canadian government divested the two companies that had been split asunder years earlier. Medical Products became Theratronics International, and The Radiochemical Co. was renamed Nordion International. Nordion was sold to a global giant, MDS Health Group, and in 1991 became MDS Nordion. Theratronics' employees, given a chance to buy their company, met with a financial consultant and decided their best chance was a sale to a going business. A Canadian-French partnership put in a suitable bid. Just as the deal was closing, the U.S. Food and Drug Administration, under pressure from legislators to crack down on imports, determined that Theratronics had fallen short in its Good Manufacturing Practices. It could not export to the United States until it had redone its policies and procedures. On its own now, sans government subsides, Theratronics put on hold a major new treatment machine and lost 40 percent of its product lines.

The firm went to four-and-a-half-day work weeks, cutting income for management and workers alike. "If we hadn't gone through 1985," said Warland, "the place would have shut down long ago; we wouldn't have had the spirit to enable us to carry on during those tough times. I don't think there's any doubt that our union relationships were important. Both Hank Gautier (of the ECWU) and I spoke of the need to share the benefits and share the pain. And people responded with commitment again." A few years later Warland ran into a former employee who had lived through the organizational traumas and now had lung cancer. "I wouldn't be here," said the veteran, "if we hadn't pulled together back in '85. I now know what it means to be under one of our machines!"

After two years of struggle to upgrade quality, Theratronics became in 1993 one of the first Canadian medical device companies to qualify for ISO-9000 certification, a key condition for resuming U.S. exports. Now, however, the Canadian government would not approve its prospective merger partner. So the company began serious talks with David Evans, a senior MDS Nordion executive, who had been with the Radiochemical Company during the turmoil of the 1980s.

In December 1995, while talks were in progress, Frank Warland, CEO for ten years, retired. His successor, a popular marketing and sales executive, died of a heart attack some months later. Again the company was thrown into white water. Rather than recruit another president, the board set up a senior executive team headed by the chief financial officer. The government exerted pressure to get the company in shape to sell. Turmoil at the top reverberated through the workforce, affecting morale.

Everyone scrambled again. "Our middle and senior management," recalled an executive, "were by then a battle-hardened group. We had been through trials that few companies face, and we had an intense sense of accomplishment and pride in that." One tangible success was a computer-based treatment planning system that increased safety and effectiveness of cancer therapies.

Together Again!

Then, in the summer of 1998, this story, which began with an agonizing decision to separate two businesses, took a new twist. MDS Nordion acquired Theratronics. The two businesses that had been split off from each other thirteen years earlier were reunited! Unlike the original company, however, MDS Nordion had a long-term strategy. It had bought up several small companies, giving it a global presence with a wide range of related products. With access to capital, Theratronics introduced a new version of the old T-25, the Theratronics Elite, with a state-of-the-art computer interface.

Under MDS Nordion, a culture of employee participation and high involvement was enhanced and extended. In 2000, I spent a couple of hours with David Evans, who was then in charge of Theratronics. Evans had built a new management team. "We don't believe in autocratic styles," he said reflectively. "We believe in teamwork." Moreover, the company now had the resources to invest in training, team development, and regular workforce meetings. The company had survived once again to emerge stronger under a more secure corporate umbrella. "Still," one executive who had come through the bad times told me, "there is something about crisis and uncertainty that gives you an intensity of focus. There's a kind of high in that too."

In one of our conversations, I asked Frank Warland if, knowing what he knew now, he would go through the traumas of 1985 again. "Yeah," he said, after a moment's reflection. "I'd do it again."

I asked why. He said, "Because I was motivated to succeed and believed that we needed all the help we could get from employees to make a major cultural change. That was the only thing that would save us." He recalled how so many people pulled together to improve manufacturing processes, and what that meant to him as an engineer. "There were many who opposed the original search process at senior levels in AECL," he recalled. "Comments such as 'letting the inmates run the asylum' and 'having the animals running the zoo' were very hard for me personally.

"On reflection, I was more concerned about the lack of respect for the knowledge and abilities of the employees. Even those who opposed us, such as the Public Service Employees Union, were important. While they couldn't support layoffs, many employees quietly helped us survive. When the labor disputes are over," he added reflectively, "you still have to work together. So we better learn to respect each other's views. Someday, I want my grandchildren to drive by that plant in Kanata and say, 'My grandpa used to work there!' "

Implications for Practitioners

What can we learn from this revisit? One, we have further evidence for a key point made in the first edition of *Productive Workplaces*: no amount of employee involvement and training can make up for lack of capital and market clout. I'm certain that principle will endure until human beings find a way to create an economic paradise on earth. Nor can yesterday's innovations withstand new managers' needs to make their mark. As Ed Liddy, a Sears executive who helped shut down what was arguably the most famous mail-order catalog in history, said, "It's amazing how quickly you can dismantle a business that took a hundred years to build" (Cohen, 2003).

Two, with determined leadership, people are capable of incredible survival feats. The ancient Chinese, Greeks, Romans, Egyptians, and Polynesians knew that long before anybody conceptualized "development." The Theratronics case represents one modern example.

Finally, I reiterate something I did not have the words for, or the conviction, until the new millennium. To get people together in the workplace, to involve people in the control of their own lives, work, and destinies, to "keep meeting like this," is existentially right, no matter what the outcome. I can think of no higher form of leadership. Acting in accord with economic values that also honor dignity, meaning, and community in the workplace is a widespread aspiration. That vision was the common ground for Frank Warland and many others I revisited years later. Engineers, doctors, marketers, staff and line alike—all would do it again if they had the chance.

■ ■ ■

"THE COURAGE TO TRY SOMETHING DIFFERENT..."

CAMBRIDGE, MA—In 1989 I was director of an expert systems group in a major telecom company. We were using new technology to improve internal operations. During a strike we deployed our first expert system to diagnose problems with the local telephone system. After the dust had settled, the system was deployed in forty-two maintenance centers across our service area, from Maine to Manhattan. Some maintenance centers adopted the new technology aggressively and had good results. Others sought to bypass or shut it off. We wondered why. Thus, I began my learning curve in sociotechnical systems.

Productive Workplaces became my tutorial and constant reference. I became interested in developing technology that was used and useful, and that meant learning more about what makes work systems effective. As I came up the learning curve, I was asked by a senior executive to build an expert system to streamline the data line provisioning process. Data services were taking more than thirty days to install. Nimbler competitors had taken away almost half of our business in a major metropolitan market.

By this time, I had been swimming in the broader view of technology introduced to me by *Productive Workplaces*, and I responded differently than I once would have: instead of beginning the process of systems design and specification, we went out to understand the work. A veteran of telco operations was paired with a knowledge engineer. They found that the work was fragmented. There were nine systems in use and a service order was touched forty-two times during a typical install; an order went through nineteen transformations from paper to electronic form or back. We concluded that another system was not likely to solve the problem.

Following the admonition to get the "whole system in the room," we proposed a design team of nine first-line workers, from order writers to central office engineers, to design a new process. This was at the height of the re-engineering boom, and experts were counseling companies to "start with a clean sheet of paper" and to redesign the work from scratch. Most of the corporation used this techno-centric approach. One vice president decided to take a chance on something radically different, and he sponsored the project.

The T1 Provisioning Design Team spent the first few weeks in conflict. These people affected one another's work and had never met face-to-face. Then someone suggested that they do departmental tours and each explain to the others what they did, what caused them problems, and what would make life easier. When they returned, they had become a team.

The design process took several months. In the end it required no new technology. Instead, they co-located two work functions that needed to communicate in real time and added a new integrating role, which assured that all installation work was coordinated across functions. Neither change would be apparent on a traditional workflow map. The Turf Coordinator role would be considered "non-value-added." The time to install a line, however, dropped from more than thirty to less than three days, market share reversed its decline, and the cost of installing a line was cut in half.

Productive Workplaces provided me with the framework and the courage to try something different. I have gone back to the book for inspiration and insight over the years (and given copies to many others). It remains a great puzzlement to me why these principles, which work, are not more frequently adopted. Even the T1 Provisioning process was eventually dismantled by new management. The problems recurred, and I understand that the company was again searching for a systems fix.

—Jim Euchner, visiting scientist, MIT
Sloan School of Management

chapter
TWENTY

Teamwork in a Fast-Changing World

Conventional organizational theory has focused almost exclusively on the individual . . . and has tended to ignore the problems of groups or teams. . . . Certainly, a strong strain of individualism is alive in all of us nurtured in the spirit of democracy. However, the complexity of the environment and the goal structure of the enterprise create a situation in which it is no longer possible to comprehend or conduct the operation of the enterprise without some form of teamwork and team building.

—Douglas McGregor, *The Professional Manager*, 1967, p. 181

Teamwork has been a contradiction in American society clear back to Alexis de Tocqueville, the astute French observer. "Each man is forever thrown back on himself alone," he wrote of Americans in the 1830s, "and there is danger that he may be shut up in the solitude of his own heart." He called this tendency—lest you wonder where we got that word—"individualism" (de Tocqueville, in Bellah and others, 1985, p. 37). It is our great strength, the bedrock of the entrepreneurial spirit and innovation. Overused, it becomes our strongest weakness.

Productive workplaces need individual effort *and* teamwork. People call work groups teams even if they rarely meet. "Team" rivals "empowerment" as a business cliché. "I have to see my team about that," says a company president. "Individually, of course," she adds. "I don't want to open a can of worms."

Sometimes people develop teamwork spontaneously, like schoolyard kids playing basketball. My self-managing teams in the 1960s taught themselves to cooperate by serving customers rather than a boss. Sometimes teams need help. In 21st-Century managing I think this help takes two forms: (1) unlearning self-limiting assumptions about individualism, authority, and responsibility that defeat cooperation and, paradoxically, individual success and (2) looking outward toward the wider social and business networks that shape mutual effort. Improving relationships by focusing together on environmental requirements is what I mean by transforming teamwork. There is no more important task for 21st-Century managers.

Teams and Team Building

Teamwork can be fostered using a simple meeting format a few times a year. Team building, the most predictably helpful tool in the OD kit, takes many forms. It evolved in the early 1960s to counter the transfer-of-training dilemma—how to use workshop learning in real life. A T-group was (and, for a few, still is) an education in self-awareness. The exchange of perceptions of self and others can unite groups if people learn to accept themselves, to trust one another, and to resolve their differences. (See Chapter Seven if you missed it).

Two insights emerged from external executive T-groups in the 1960s: (1) participants had powerful aha's that they could not translate into organizational policies and procedures and (2) when they sought to remedy this defect with "in-house" T-groups, they found people dredging up emotional issues too sensitive to be properly dealt with in that setting.

Developing self-awareness remains a useful but not sufficient activity for changing companies. A T-group learns by observing its own behavior as a temporary closed system. Teams develop from observing their behavior in relation to their organization's environment, economics, and technology. Group norms and interpersonal feelings are pieces of a large jigsaw puzzle.

Team building came to mean everything from interpersonal encounter with co-workers (a format I do not recommend), to joint work on tasks of mutual importance (a format I strongly support). The earliest modes used an exchange of interpersonal feedback as the key building block. In my practice I was more committed to helping each team member take a public stand on critical issues the team faced. The most powerful team building occurs in the mutual revisiting of an organization's central tasks, the design of its jobs, policies, and systems, in light of external pressures on costs and markets.

Many Methods. Many routes are available—from self-guided workbooks and DVDs to facilitators and consultants. Team building remains durable, flexible, and broadly useful for starting new teams and task forces, reorganizing, managing conflicts between departments, setting goals, planning strategy, integrating cultures—any activity people cannot do alone. In team meetings, well-motivated groups routinely learn how to manage with less frustration and higher output. They usually report more openness, more mutual respect, trust, and cooperation over time. Even well-intentioned groups flounder for a while the first time they have this sort of meeting. After that, maintenance requires perhaps one or two meetings a year, during which team processes are on the agenda. This becomes more important when a team gets new members.

Conditions for Success. Team building succeeds under four conditions:

1. *Interdependence.* The team is working on important problems requiring cooperation.
2. *Leadership.* The boss wants so strongly to improve group performance that he or she will take risks.
3. *Joint decisions.* All members agree to participate.
4. *Equal opportunity.* Each person can influence the agenda.

In a typical scenario, the boss calls a meeting, states some personal goals, and asks for discussion. When a consultant is involved, the parties need a get-acquainted meeting. Often the consultant interviews team members to discover their concerns and wishes. Questions might include each person's objectives, tasks, problems, the extent of help needed from others, and their views on costs, markets, innovation, etc.

I'm not talking about interviews in which the consultant (doctor) learns enough to prescribe a cure. An experienced team-builder knows that interviews have purposes more important than a consultant's education. One, they help team members figure out what they really want to say. Two, they reduce the fantasy about the consultant's motives and working methods. The consultant will learn about the organization in any case. What the consultant wants most to know is how much each team member will take responsibility for the meeting's success.

Deciding to Proceed. The consultant presents a summary of interview themes to the team, inviting discussion of the pros and cons of continuing. If the team decides to proceed, it schedules a two- or three-day offsite. Usually the team chooses important tasks: mission and goals, strategy formation, reorganizing, dealing with technologies, costs, markets, quality, or customer problems. What is novel is that team members also specify what it is about their own processes they wish to improve. This makes it possible for them to periodically step back and observe what they are doing that helps or hinders progress. This discussion can be helped by process-analysis forms like that in "Rating Teamwork," a grandchild of early group dynamics.

You can spend days in the library tracking down the issues that decades of research have shown contribute to good teamwork. Or you can ask team members and get roughly the same list in ten minutes. Nearly always people put up "trust"—a validation of Jack Gibb's contention (1978) that without it nothing worthwhile is likely to happen.

Making such a list is useful as a learning tool when used once or twice to help people recognize key processes. Done by rote, it becomes a meaningless ritual. A more powerful way to help teams experience themselves is with videotape. Indeed, these days a smart phone will do. Reviewing ten minutes of meeting video and asking people to recall what they were thinking or feeling is probably the simplest way to facilitate team learning (the same way sports teams, tennis players, and skiers learn by watching themselves).

RATING TEAMWORK

1. PURPOSES

AMBIGUOUS 1 2 3 4 5 CLEAR

2. IN/OUT

I'M IN 1 2 3 4 5 I'M OUT

3. ELBOW ROOM

I'M CROWDED 1 2 3 4 5 I'M EASY

4. DISCUSSION

GUARDED 1 2 3 4 5 FREE

5. USE OF SKILLS

POOR 1 2 3 4 5 FULL

6. CONFLICT

AVOIDED 1 2 3 4 5 WORKED ON

7. SUPPORT

SELF ONLY 1 2 3 4 5 EACH TO ALL

I have three success criteria:

1. The team resolves important dilemmas, often ones on which little progress was made before.
2. People emerge more confident of their ability to influence the future.
3. Members learn the extent to which output is linked to their own candor, responsibility for themselves, and willingness to cooperate.

Practical Theory

I want to describe a team-building theory in business terms, paraphrasing an extraordinary consultant, the late Mike Blansfield, who pioneered the method years ago with TRW and other companies. He called his

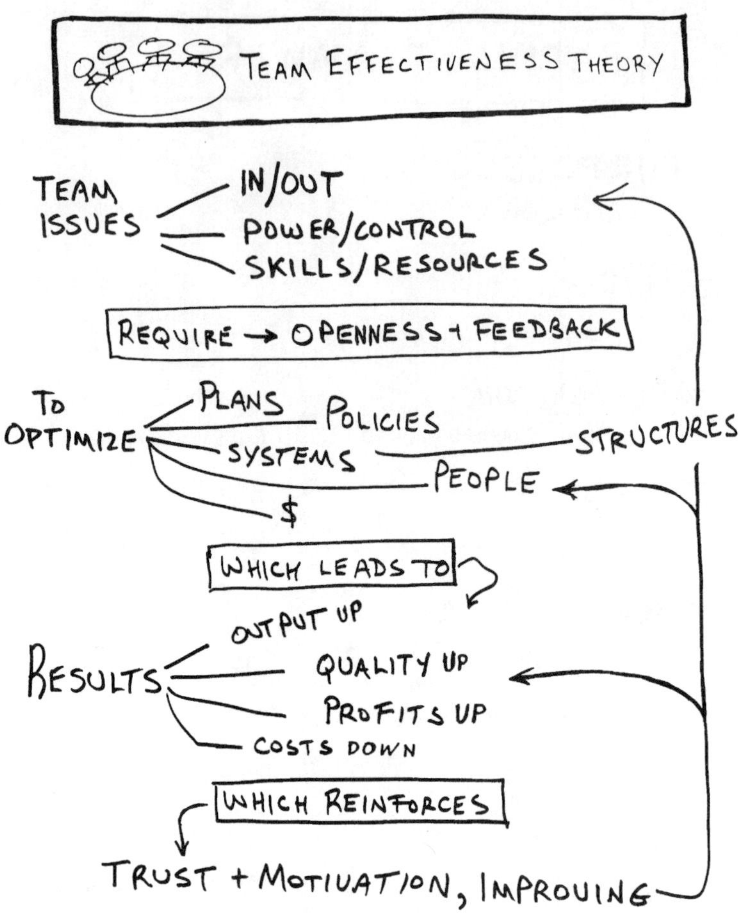

concept "Team Effectiveness Theory," outlined on the chart above. Blansfield's method was based largely on interpersonal feedback. Yet he had a practical grasp of business issues. When I heard him present this theory in 1970, I understood my decade as an executive in an entirely new light. I have since used it to help many others do the same. The key to team building in this century, I believe, is a dual focus on task and process under conditions of rapid change, not a narrowly interpersonal focus.

Blansfield's model highlights processes always present that work teams rarely connect to results. The chart makes the linkages by bringing together a vocabulary for output with a vocabulary for teamwork. Most managers define positive results as higher productivity, better quality, more profits, and lower costs (bottom of the chart).

When something goes wrong, people may feel out of control and incompetent. They search for mistakes in techniques, policies, systems, plans (the middle list), or they seek to finger a villain. In extreme cases, bosses fire people. Few consider the impact of their behavior on the key processes affected by the situation. These are the three factors on the top list.

From Taylor to Lewin to McGregor to Emery and Trist, observers have identified management's behavior as the starting place for improving systems, cooperation, output, work satisfaction, culture, whatever. Blansfield's model highlights the differences between managing a problem one on one and managing a group in which people depend on one another. Hearing it the first time, my mind flashed back to the computerized order processing system I managed in the business described in Chapter Two. A systems consultant told us what we needed. A programmer instructed the computer. I never considered that this new technology would change every job, including mine, reduce our control of customer policy, and force us to rethink non-routine problems. I had never seen a computer. Hardly anybody had. Two decades before PCs, we underwent an aggravating initiation.

It never occurred to me to have the affected people plan the implementation. I told people to carry out their assigned tasks, never imagining the extent to which they might thwart one another. Installing the system was the expert's job. Running it was ours. I vividly recall the disruption, missed deadlines, angry customers, tearful order processing clerks, bewildered systems analyst, and general turmoil that cost two resignations and a few lost customers. I fell prey to a common tendency of task-driven managers. When things went wrong, I pressured people to work overtime. I chided the office force for not cooperating. I reiterated my goals for rapid implementation. I fiddled with the system. In short, I belabored the daylights out of the effectiveness factors. Managing one on one like a whirling dervish, I drove everyone nuts, including myself. I had no vocabulary for feelings and motivation.

Adding Teamwork to Effectiveness

I considered myself a nice guy. Yet, managing a new technology, I acted as if each person were a cog in the machine. I triggered social dynamics about which I knew nothing until I heard Blansfield's team theory. Each person in a work group, he said, struggles with three questions each time he or she faces something new:

1. Am I in or out?
2. Do I have any power and control?
3. Can I use, develop, and be appreciated for my skills and resources?

In or Out. Most of us want to belong, to have tasks that matter, and to be valued by others. The more "in" we feel, the better we cooperate. The more we feel "out," the more we withdraw, daydream, or fight. When I sought single-handedly to patch up the computer system, I drove others out.

Power and Control. Power and control need little explaining after Taylor, McGregor, and the astronauts. Faced with changes we can't influence, we feel impotent, lose self-esteem, work hard, and do worse unless we regain control. That happened to me in the 1960s, and I made life worse for everyone else.

Skills and Resources. People in all workplaces have untapped skills, experience, and common sense. We keep these resources hidden by making outdated assumptions about who is allowed to do what. During my computer installation, I thought that people's vast experience with the old system was irrelevant. I pressured folks to turn on a dime and master something none of us had ever done. Lacking a team concept, I saw no way to help people support one another.

I was not only managing a computer installation, I was managing the destruction of a social system built up over many years. Here is the simple truth: there was no way I could manage this interdependent changeover one on one. The process issues could be resolved only when the tasks were seen as team tasks, not the boss's problem.

Candor and Feedback. These two processes, openness and feedback, link team issues with results. People need to talk over what each needs to do and their anxiety about doing it, to own up to uncertainty and differences of opinion. I've been in dozens of these meetings. Somebody always brings up trust, the bedrock of commitment. A team-building meeting is one way people develop trust.

Feelings about membership, control, and skills influence motivation, which determines the quality of work. It's all one system. Pull on any thread and you untangle the whole net. That's the function of a dual-focus meeting.

Structure. Usually a team-building meeting starts with a discussion of goals and agenda: why, how, what, who. Sometimes there are prearranged "stop-action" points to review their process observations or review a videotape. Sometimes a consultant calls time out if people are fighting or avoiding the task. Usually a short process discussion is enough to get people tracking again.

If people report frustration with interpersonal conflicts or difficulty in communicating, some focus on personal style (maybe a self-report paper-and-pencil survey) may trigger half a day's discussion. In such exercises people learn to value their differences, accept their strengths, and express themselves more clearly.

Sometimes teams engage in role negotiation, a procedure devised by consultant Roger Harrison (1972). Each team member writes down what he or she wants each of the others to do less or more of, and what to keep doing the same. These requests are posted and negotiated. For example, "I'll give you at least a week's notice of schedule changes, if you'll refer customer complaints directly to me." There's no deal unless both parties agree.

Another useful format, responsibility charting, is indicated if the team's self-diagnosis is that important tasks are falling between the cracks. An "R" chart (see example below) lists who makes which decisions, who must be

R = RESPONSIBLE A = APPROVE
C = CONSULT I = INFORM

DECISIONS	ACTORS				
	GENERAL MANAGER	PROJECT MANAGER	FINANCE DIRECTOR	MARKETING MANAGER	HUMAN RESOURCES
CHANGE BUDGET					
ASSIGN PEOPLE					
CHANGE SCHEDULE					
CALL REVIEWS					

informed, who must support, and who has the power to veto (Galbraith, 1977). All these activities increase communication, provide feedback, take account of each person's needs, more equitably distribute influence, and promote orderly procedures for managing interdependence.

Leadership and Consensus. Nearly every team gets around to relations between the boss and team members. The boss laments, "They act like children, bucking everything to me." The team members echo, "He treats us like children and does too much himself." The usual aha is how each acts to reinforce the other in this age-old parent/child drama. Inevitably this triggers talk about the meaning of individual versus group decisions, when each is appropriate, the practical limits of formal power, and whether open decision making means "doing whatever the group wants."

I find consensus decision making the least understood and most useful dimension of teamwork. Consensus means support derived when each person feels heard and understood. Unanimous decision is desirable. With or without it, a boss has the responsibility to decide. This task is made easier if each team member feels free to speak openly. Indeed, the simplest team-building technique is the "go-around," where all participants have a chance to say what they would do. Bosses can facilitate this task by openly sharing their own dilemmas and having the willingness to hear people out. To maintain team cohesiveness, all should be satisfied that they had a chance to influence the decision and declare their willingness to support it. When a team member can't do that, the team still has a problem to solve.

The Future of Team Building

A team-building meeting can become a procedural nightmare of consultant-orchestrated exercises. It also can be run simply, directly, and to the point. My former partner Tony Petrella (1974), for example, evolved many procedures to put responsibility in members' hands. In one variation he interviewed each person in front of the others, asking questions all had agreed to in advance. Everybody took notes. People reviewed their notes in subgroups and diagnosed their team's needs and priorities. They discussed their diagnoses, built an agenda, and spent the remaining time working out new relationships and improving policies and procedures.

In another variation, Petrella and Mike DiLorenzo interviewed managers and wrote down everything they heard—the traditional approach. In a follow-up meeting, before unveiling their notes, they simply asked people to repeat for one another what they already said, a request carried out with enthusiasm.

These simple procedures reduced passivity and put people more firmly in charge of their lives. The consultant's role was to help people talk constructively about their work, to learn, and to act. I share Petrella's conviction that most folks can discuss, learn, and act as readily with a little structure as with a lot. If you consider the "right" answer the best one that is implementable, this less-is-more approach will be welcome where commitment matters for success.

Large systems need teamwork. Team building is useful at some point. Most team members come away feeling more "in," more influential, more competent, more supported, and more committed. They may have solved some problems, devised a new strategy, moved toward a new structure, consolidated a future vision. They are still stuck with the dilemma of implementing action among those who were not there. That's where the next three chapters on work design and Future Search come in, offering complementary activities for involving people up, down, and sideways.

■ ■ ■

"WAYFINDING FREES US TO DO MORE..."

NASHVILLE, TN—Reading the closing thoughts in *Productive Workplaces* (1987), I recalled when the year 2000 felt like the distant future. Suddenly I'm one decade into the new millennium and I don't see any "long stretches of stability" coming soon.

We now require the skills of ancient navigators canoeing the vast Pacific, trusting their inner knowledge to find tiny islands. Their ancient form of navigation today is called "wayfinding." PW, with its historical sweep and whole-system context, became a vessel that made voyagers out of many readers, including me. I gained greater insight into resolving the conflict between autonomy and the need to belong.

For nearly two decades, I worked with Doug Williams to expand the benefits of diversity in the workplace beyond culture, race, and gender to a much larger palette of differences. To avoid workplace tensions, we may make a passive assumption that we are "all the same." Doug and I invite people to explore their assumptions and experience, actively engaging their differences in the spirit of learning. The question we ask is: How do we create a workplace wherein diverse people feel their talents and gifts are welcome and they can collaborate on improving the whole?

There is a costly, unsustainable "energy drain and pain" inside many workplaces. We are severely limited by "darker impulses" for control at all costs. The irony is that we have an enormous capacity within us.

I support individuals at a crossroads who know they have something more to be and do with their lives, helping them to find their inner resources. Wayfinding a sustainable future frees us to do more while tuning into the inner world of possibilities. External structures change rapidly. Perhaps the center of our being is one place we still may find "long stretches of stability."

—Nancy McMorrow, president, seeds: sustainable, engaging and empowering designs for success

---

chapter
TWENTY ONE

Designing Work for Learning and Self-Control

People in our plant are responsible for millions of dollars in equipment. . . . If we can make decisions at work, surely we can make decisions about work. . . . If we are talking about job redesign to make our jobs more interesting, we have to be concerned about company effectiveness. That's not just a management concern. It's part of our increased responsibility for ourselves. Our livelihood is too important to leave to managers.

—Judy McKibbon, chief union steward, Shell Sarnia, *QWL Focus*, 1984, p. 15

The quickest way to increase dignity, meaning, and community in a workplace is to involve people in redesigning their work. That is also the short route to lower costs, higher quality, and more satisfied customers. I learned that in my own business in the 1960s. Having repeated that experience in factories and offices, large and small, union and nonunion, in banking, chemical, pharmaceutical, printing, steel, software and other businesses, I remain dedicated to this mode of workplace improvement.

Designing New Structures

The simplest way to start is to have workers, technical experts, and managers sit down together and describe how the whole system works. If they listen to each other and hang in long enough, they can create satisfying and effective workplaces beyond Taylor's most extravagant dreams.

Work-Design Protocols. The methodology is relatively simple. Stakeholders form a steering group that formulates the values and philosophy that led them to a design effort. In union shops this will always be a joint labor/management venture. This group makes people aware of the meaning of the effort. It chooses one or more design teams to analyze work systems, recommend options, and set up progress reviews. (See "Work Design Structure.")

Design teams differ from traditional task forces. First, line workers and engineers, top executives, and staff supervisors serve together. Second, they look at the whole business, seeking Emery's "joint optimization" of technical and social systems. This form of social learning changes management and worker perceptions of problems and solutions.

The perceptual shift can't be overemphasized. All parties see aspects of their business they have never seen before. To do it, they must get past strange feelings born of invisible walls between jobs and levels. Nobody quite knows how to work together in this odd mixture of status, role, level, gender, knowledge, skill, and authority sitting around the same table.

Orientation seminars help. Simulation exercises, case studies, and visiting other companies are good team-building tasks for work-design teams. Group and interpersonal process work can help. A few hours with a simple personal-style instrument (for example, the Work-Style Preference Inventory [McFletcher, 1983, 2011]) may accelerate mutual acceptance. Some teams set norms by listing desired behavior for members and leaders. Teams are best focused at this stage on tasks—learning about their own system and how to redesign it. If they get into fights, avoid the task, or insist a consultant "give us the plan," they may need to stop action and talk about how they are doing.

The Generic Menu. Here is a generic menu of work designer tasks. I derived it from managing or consulting in organizations seeking to translate into action the principles articulated by Emery and Trist.

- A person who has formal authority usually:
  1. Identifies the window of opportunity, the compelling business need, and invites outside or internal help.
  2. Encourages others to visit innovative sites, attend workshops, read up on what's happening.
  3. Convenes a steering group.
- The steering group usually:
  1. Revisits the organization's purposes and the objectives of the design effort.
  2. Articulates values and philosophies a new design should embody.

3. Selects design team members or criteria for self-selection.
4. Reviews design team progress regularly.
5. Validates new designs and implementation plans.
6. Manages the implementation.

- A design team usually:

1. Examines outside forces to which the organization must respond: customers, regulators, suppliers, government, and so on.
2. Specifies the most desirable responses.
3. Does two analyses of how the system works now:
    a. Technical: linear layout, what "steady state" means, where and why errors or upsets ("variances") occur.
    b. Social: what constitutes "good jobs," what skills are required to operate the system in steady state, handle upsets, and do administrative work, who has which skills, and who needs training.
4. Educates itself about innovative solutions (visits to other sites, reading, seminars).
5. Drafts one or more new scenarios.
6. Presents emerging scenarios to the steering group and (in redesigns) to other departments for feedback on feasibility.
7. Prepares a design plan and implementation proposal.
8. Discusses the plan and proposal with all affected parties before its approval by the steering committee.

A detailed guide for getting started is William O. Lytle's (1997). Implementation follows a learning curve. Consider a graphic illustration of the ups and downs of a redesigned customer service department, which once needed nineteen days to process new orders; see "Customer Service Weekly Progress." A design team estimated the job could be done in three days. The chart shows how a multi-skilled team achieved a dramatic new high.

Design Contingencies. The best-known innovative workplaces have been startups ("greenfields") like the Gaines Foods pet food plant in Topeka, Kansas (Walton, 1982), and the Shell Sarnia oil refinery in Ontario,

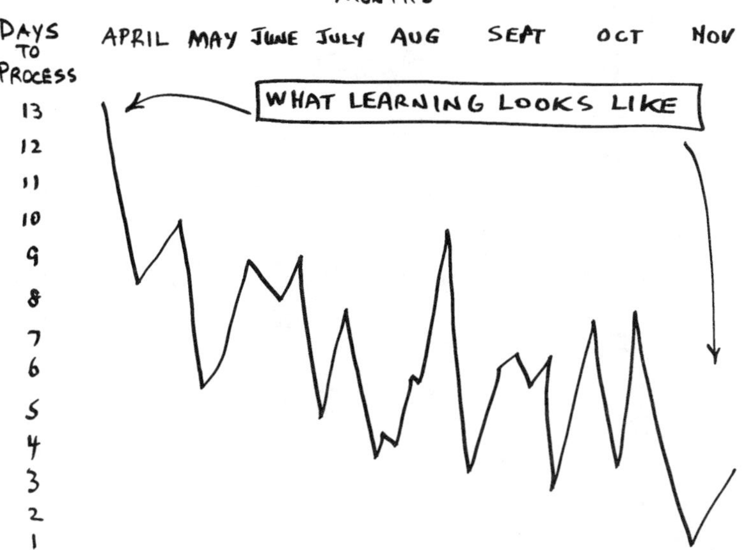

Canada (Davis and Sullivan, 1980). However, a great many organizations have undertaken the reorganizing of ongoing operations since I first wrote this book.

Although originating in mines and factories, work-design principles remain applicable to offices, research laboratories, government agencies, and service businesses. New computer technologies have given people the potential to control their work beyond anything previously imagined. Work-design techniques now have been put directly into the hands of those who do the work. They have been used with equal success (and failure) in union and nonunion settings, with young and old, and with men and women from diverse racial, ethnic, and cultural backgrounds. Multiethnic workplaces present special problems of language and culture. Yet the principles hold for those able to see work design as an action-research process rather than implementing a predetermined structure.

"Work Design Contingencies" shows factors designers usually consider. A unionized office doing accounts receivable and billing calls for different procedures from a nonunion research facility or a batch processing factory.

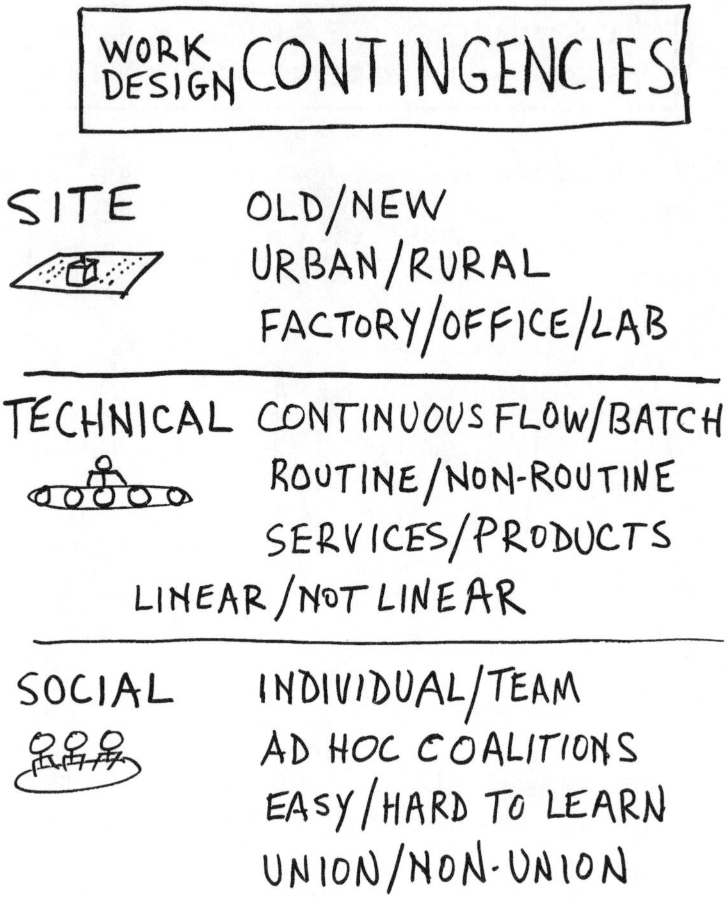

WORK DESIGN CONTINGENCIES

SITE	OLD/NEW URBAN/RURAL FACTORY/OFFICE/LAB
TECHNICAL	CONTINUOUS FLOW/BATCH ROUTINE/NON-ROUTINE SERVICES/PRODUCTS LINEAR/NOT LINEAR
SOCIAL	INDIVIDUAL/TEAM AD HOC COALITIONS EASY/HARD TO LEARN UNION/NON-UNION

Applications vary with geography, local community, workforce composition, even between sites with the same products or services. The "right answer" is best worked out by local teams.

Three Analytic Tasks. Design teams usually make a map of "environmental demands"—what the customers, regulators, suppliers, and the community want from the organization and how it responds now. They also do a technical analysis, flow charting how the system works now and where errors occur. The group analysis of key variances always excites and stimulates people. Finally, a social analysis reveals how satisfying each job is now, indicating how to build a system wherein every job is a good one.

Consultants have invented endless variations on Emery's (1980) classic procedures. The traditional first step was scanning the environment. My preference is to start with technology and flow charts, because the product or service itself is often the one thing the diverse people around the table have in common. They need each analysis to fully understand the others, a chicken-egg paradox that leads to iteration—going around the same mulberry bush several times. Inevitably people discover deeper meanings in their work, and modify it accordingly.

If you start a design team, expect a few frustrating "why are we here?" meetings. Some managers see this as a defect in the process that more efficient techniques could cure. In fact, everything learned about group development since Lewin supports the view that floundering around is an essential precondition to learning and high output.

Laying Out a New Work System. After a design team figures out how things work now, they try out alternatives. They propose systems that (1) eliminate errors and (2) have no crummy jobs. They redraw boundaries among functions, departments, and tasks, making jobs larger, giving people more responsibility. They redefine supervisory and staff roles.

The new system must account for every necessary function: hiring, firing, training, controlling, planning, scheduling, compensating, repairing, filing, reporting, and so on. In unionized places, task force members try to distinguish between problem-solving issues and collective bargaining issues. They soon find the issues cannot be separated. To maintain union-management cooperation in such an effort requires considerable behind-the-scenes negotiating and political skill. Visible outcomes tend to be embodied in new contracts guaranteeing secure jobs, for example, in return for task flexibility.

Designers inevitably alter supervisory roles, and nearly always the title changes to "coordinator" or "team leader." Leaders manage resources, training, and relations with other departments. Teams coordinate and control their own work, something few know how to do until they learn on the job.

However, redesign does not stop there. People draw up hiring and training plans. Choices for new jobs, retraining, or transition help are offered to workers who are not needed, interim methods (and incentives) devised for the transfer of people's skill and knowledge.

None of this is quick or easy. However, people have continuously reduced the cycle. When I first wrote in 1987, design teams took from three months to a year to come up with plans. By the 1990s, the accelerating rate of change called for quicker ways to do the job. It also made obvious that work redesign was not a one-time fix. People needed to continually update policies and procedures. This is analogous to the continual software updates every computer user accepts as a cost of higher productivity. You'd better do it, even if you'd rather not. Many ideas have emerged for accelerating work systems design (Lytle, 2002). See also the IKEA example in Chapter Twenty-Three in which people compressed six months of old-style work into under three days to redesign a global supply chain (also see Weisbord and Janoff, 2010).

In new designs people worry about whether "it" will work. As "High Performing Startups" shows, when a team takes its time and does things

HIGH PERFORMING STARTUPS

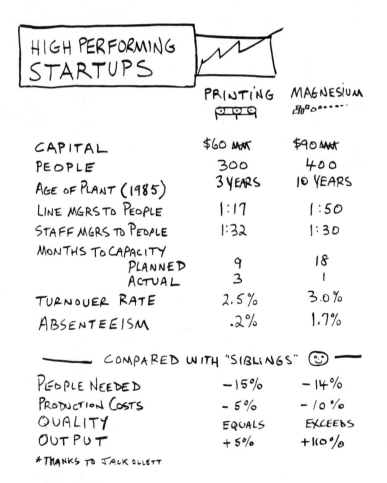

	PRINTING	MAGNESIUM
CAPITAL	$60 MM	$90 MM
PEOPLE	300	400
AGE OF PLANT (1985)	3 YEARS	10 YEARS
LINE MGRS TO PEOPLE	1:17	1:50
STAFF MGRS TO PEOPLE	1:32	1:30
MONTHS TO CAPACITY		
PLANNED	9	18
ACTUAL	3	1
TURNOVER RATE	2.5%	3.0%
ABSENTEEISM	.2%	1.7%
COMPARED WITH "SIBLINGS"		
PEOPLE NEEDED	−15%	−14%
PRODUCTION COSTS	−5%	−10%
QUALITY	EQUALS	EXCEEDS
OUTPUT	+5%	+110%

*THANKS TO JACK OLLETT

right, startups can be accelerated dramatically. Note two ratios in particular: staff experts to workers and managers to workers. These indicate how broadly responsibilities have moved directly to operators.

Special Problems of Redesigns. Redesigns involve more ambiguity and anxiety than startups. The biggest legitimate worry among designers and steerers alike is "What happens to me?" A design done right alters every job. Functions are combined, eliminated, farmed out. Supervisory functions are taken over by those once supervised. Members of self-managing teams usually acquire more skill, knowledge, and responsibility than their former supervisors had. That is what makes teams so flexible, cost-effective, and challenging. It also reinforces the threat to middle managers and supervisors.

This reality requires additional principles:

1. It is wrong and impractical to ask people to design themselves out of work. A way must be found to assure employment for people as their jobs change. There are creative options—new technology and market teams, special projects, ad hoc training groups—that add value not accessible before. As new technologies displace more people, you cannot apply sociotechnical redesign without imagining new forms of economic activity, a reality I explored at length in Chapter Nineteen.

   Displacement is a two-way street. Some people who could and would still be employed discover that they don't want to work this way.

2. Choices should be offered. In many redesign situations jobs are rebid, leadership roles opened up to all who think they meet the criteria. Those who are not selected to their first choice retain former pay and benefits until equitable arrangements can be made.
3. Displaced people should influence their own futures, sharing responsibility for what comes next. It ought not be management's sole job.

These principles alter the authority-dependency games between labor and management. One practical observer has suggested that management and labor reverse their traditional roles: management would take responsibility for job security, labor for productivity (Hickey, 1986).

Supervisory and Staff Roles. Rethink leadership roles only after all other aspects have been figured out. Unless this practice is observed, people may defeat their own design by reinventing traditional supervision. One sign of learning is when an ambivalent supervisor on the design team says, "Well, I do that now. But with what we're talking about, you don't need a special person." A "Responsibility Chart" developed by a General Motors' Packard Electric division design team shows what might happen to staff and supervisor roles. I have found this chart useful for helping people visualize the changeover problem. New teams start with only a critical minimum few tasks because they (1) do not have all the skills and knowledge, and (2) cannot know what coordinating problems they will have with other departments. So the tasks are phased in, teams taking on new responsibilities gradually. Former staff and experts help with training and implementation.

Special Problems of Professional and Managerial Work. In a routine technical analysis, the system is flow-charted and errors pinpointed. In a routine social analysis, tasks are merged and blended to create "whole" jobs. You can see that knowledge work happens differently from repetitive production work. The flow chart spills in all directions. Many knowledge workers have multi-skilled jobs, with decision latitude. What they lack is a map of the informal processes, apparently random, required for optimal results.

One sociotechnical design scheme to account for this maps nonlinear tasks in terms of discussions people must have on the road to a solution, invention, discovery, decision, or plan (Pava, 1983). Pava calls these "deliberations," a word that covers everything from new-product development to sales and service policy. The places where deliberations happen Pava calls "forums." These might involve anything from doodling on the backs of envelopes over coffee to long offsite meetings.

A map comparing required with actual deliberations reveals the teamwork individual contributors, already multi-skilled, need from each other. To enhance the social side, Pava specifies the shifting cast of characters who come in and out of the deliberations as they progress. These he calls

Packard Electric's Responsibility Chart

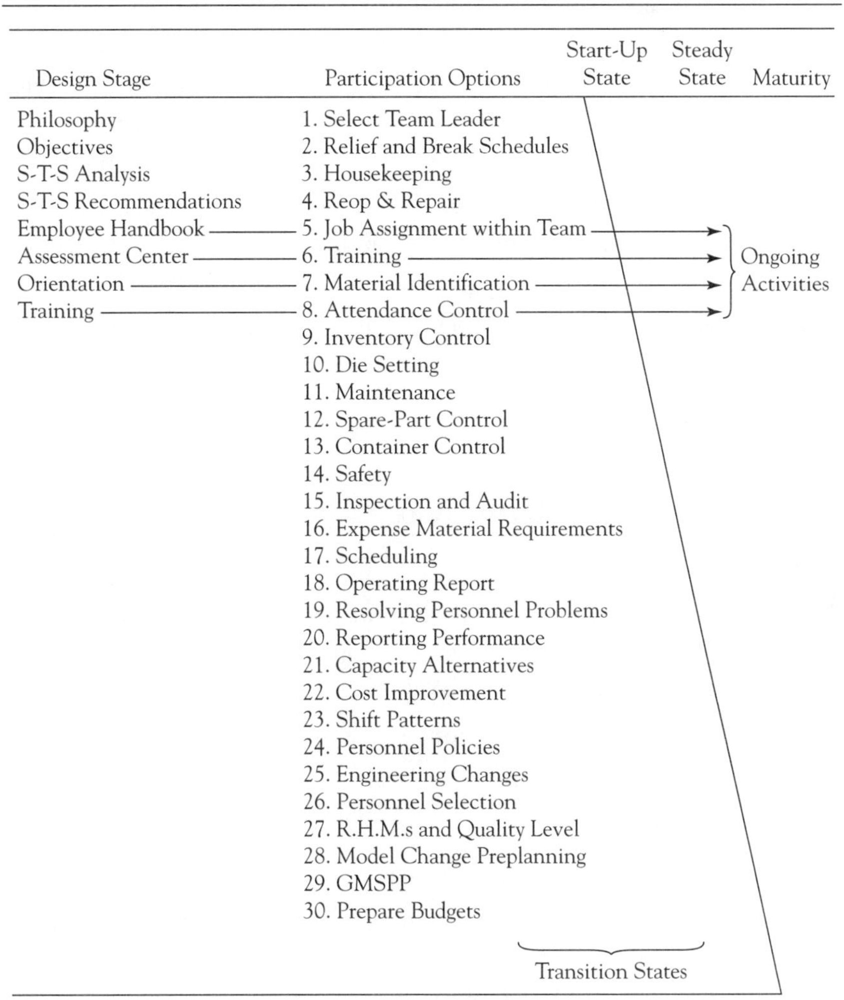

Design Stage	Participation Options	Start-Up State	Steady State	Maturity
Philosophy	1. Select Team Leader			
Objectives	2. Relief and Break Schedules			
S-T-S Analysis	3. Housekeeping			
S-T-S Recommendations	4. Reop & Repair			
Employee Handbook	5. Job Assignment within Team →			Ongoing Activities
Assessment Center	6. Training →			Ongoing Activities
Orientation	7. Material Identification →			Ongoing Activities
Training	8. Attendance Control →			Ongoing Activities
	9. Inventory Control			
	10. Die Setting			
	11. Maintenance			
	12. Spare-Part Control			
	13. Container Control			
	14. Safety			
	15. Inspection and Audit			
	16. Expense Material Requirements			
	17. Scheduling			
	18. Operating Report			
	19. Resolving Personnel Problems			
	20. Reporting Performance			
	21. Capacity Alternatives			
	22. Cost Improvement			
	23. Shift Patterns			
	24. Personnel Policies			
	25. Engineering Changes			
	26. Personnel Selection			
	27. R.H.M.s and Quality Level			
	28. Model Change Preplanning			
	29. GMSPP			
	30. Prepare Budgets			
		Transition States		

From Zager and Rosow, 1982, p. 133. Used by permission.

"coalitions," formal or informal allies thrown together by mutual need on individual and shared tasks.

A non-routine design team's technical analysis, then, consists of mapping necessary versus actual deliberations and coalitions, then designing a realignment of forums to produce more satisfying outcomes. Sociotechnical principles remain intact.

John Dupre and I modified Pava's procedures and applied them in 1986 to the reorganization of McCormack & Dodge, a 1,200-person software development firm I cited in Chapter Eighteen. An M&D innovation was having each staff vice president take on a product or customer service responsibility in addition to support functions like human resources, finance, or information systems. The top team also devised a forum for each function in which business units and field offices joined to make corporate policy. They rejected the alternatives—building large corporate staffs or having a full-scale matrix organization—as too expensive and contrary to people's aspirations for broader career paths. The "Work Design Contingencies" chart on page 392 shows some issues to consider when planning what methods to use.

Implementing New Work Designs

> Events to Ponder Department: Thomas Edison, the inventor, spent ten years on the nickel-iron-alkaline battery. After eight thousand experiments, an assistant suggested giving up, seeing as there were no results. "Results?" said Edison. "We have lots of results. We know eight thousand things that don't work!"
>
> —Popular story

When a design team draws up a new plan, you can bet your last nickel that the designers have concluded that many old practices will not work. You can be equally sure that they do not know which of the new ones will. People who have been doing one task for years don't suddenly become multi-skilled. Supervisors used to handling daily problems don't suddenly become "boundary managers."

Organizations need transition structures. In one case, for example, newly created multi-skilled teams were complemented for nine months by a temporary technical team of former supervisors and staff experts. It had two tasks: (1) transfer its skills and knowledge, and (2) develop new roles for its members.

My advice when in doubt is to try it out. One steering committee was skeptical of a design team's plan to put orders into the shop in three days instead of two weeks. They gave five design-group volunteers their own room and began feeding them orders. In a week the team got the cycle down to three days, learning new wrinkles they put into the emerging plan.

Minimum Critical Specs. Another basic is "minimum critical specification," a breakthrough concept devised by David (P. G.) Herbst (1974) during the redesign of Norwegian merchant ships. The term means not making decisions for another group that its members can make for themselves. By this principle, a steering group passes along values, philosophy, and limits of space and money. A design team recommends structure, quality, output, safety, and legal requirements, a process for member and leader selection, a training plan, and personnel policies.

Many problems people actually encounter often cannot be foreseen. So details like housekeeping, job rotation, relief schedules, and monitoring safety are best left to those closest to the work. Specialists or supervisors may need to remain in ad hoc support roles, gradually transferring what they know to the work teams. Creative companies offer staff and line people promotions if they serve well in this role. One company invited retirees back part-time to teach its new plant teams special technical skills. Outside expertise will always be needed, especially for new product and technology development. In new-design sites, engineers, scientists, and marketing specialists interact with line operators regularly.

Sociotechnical systems case studies abound. (See, for example, the personal stories accompanying this chapter.) You will discover that each site writes its own textbook—of philosophy, mission, values, assumptions, and specific twists. Sometimes it invents new analytic tools. There are so many ways to skin this cat nobody can imagine them all. The only constant is asking, "What principles do we want to apply?"

Perhaps five hundred factories were designed in North America by new-paradigm principles by 1985 and countless others since. Nearly all have features similar to what my multi-skilled teams worked out in the 1960s (Chapter Two). They integrate work and learning, pay skill-based salaries, organize around natural production segments, include maintenance, safety, and clerical tasks, have workers train one another, rotate jobs to acquire skills, have joint team-manager evaluations for pay raises, and coordinate through a committee or task force. The most successful ones treat their own cultures as unique features requiring constant attention. Many install a process review board to keep their norms and principles intact (Hirschhorn, 1984).

Implementation: Possible Pitfalls. People can mess up new designs too. The reasons, broadly put, are too much structure or too little. In some cases management panics when production curves drop during early stages. Anxious managers may re-create traditional supervision at the slightest hint of variance, undermining learning, making a self-fulfilling prophecy. Managers who fear being labeled authoritarian may abdicate responsibility, leaving people too much on their own. They may imagine a collective magic in participation born of good intentions that absolves them from tough choices. Laissez-faire management, as Lippitt and White showed years ago in Iowa (Chapter Five), creates as many problems as capricious authoritarianism. Too little structure is as bad as too much.

Managers everywhere discover, as Lewin pointed out, that while authoritarianism is everybody's old friend, democratic methods must be learned. Effective managers provide goal focus and instruction. Effective participation requires leaders who exercise authority without becoming authoritarian. They learn to give over responsibility gradually to teams, a trick mastered by doing it.

Relearning to Manage. How do you learn and lead at the same time? How do you walk the tightrope in emergencies between taking over and leaving people to struggle? How do you speak for your own goals and visions without preempting other people's? How do you lead while developing other leaders? How will you reassure people when you don't have answers? How do you maintain the short-run economic integrity of an enterprise while people learn to keep it viable for the long haul? These are new paradigm challenges. Each company writes its own treatise.

Experiments founder on two other kinds of shoals. One is a leadership change. A new leader who cannot leave a self-managing system alone re-creates traditional supervision to reduce his or her anxiety.

A more common situation is the boundary that can't be bridged. This happens to experiments within one department or division of large companies. Other departments continue business as usual. Eventually they swallow and digest the maverick. One large corporation fostered sixty self-managing team experiments in the 1960s, only one of which survived into the 1970s. The others sank without a trace, leading researchers to observe that the umbrella of values and commitment must be particularly strong from top to bottom for these innovations to continue (Trist and Dwyer, 1982).

What about workers who refuse responsibility? A few years ago the United Auto Workers sent a delegation to Volvo in Sweden to study alternatives to the assembly line. These factory hands concluded they would rather have high wages and machine-paced work than assume the Swedish system's responsibilities They could not imagine a system they controlled.

In earlier editions of this book, I cited such new-design auto factories as the joint Toyota-GM venture in California and the General Motors Saturn factory in Tennessee. Alas, neither survived the 21st Century business meltdown. In a new era managements will have to learn all over again how to offer job security and unions how to focus on flexibility and output.

The only safe work-design strategy, in this fast-changing world, is to build up workers' ability to learn how the "black box" works so they can detect errors no one has seen before. This principle, I believe, outlasts all foreseeable economic and technological revolutions. People will always be in a tug-of-war between output and learning, what Larry Hirschhorn (1984) called "developmental tension." People fail if there is too much to learn too quickly. Still, external controls are self-perpetuating; the more you have, the more you need.

Another dilemma is the multi-skill system itself, in which everybody may eventually reach the top rate. Designers are learning to plan job progression so that people don't move too fast, compromising safety, quality, and learning. The emphasis must be on knowledge and skill, not on rapid advancement. Even so, teams could experience malaise when everything becomes routine and everybody has mastered all skills. Introducing new products or equipment and systems is one way to keep work teams fresh. Another solution is continually providing new learning opportunities, inside or outside the system. Some companies pay for job-related college courses for workers. Others encourage community service.

The problem is a relatively new one in the world. The more successful a new design, the quicker the demand for novelty, stimulation, and new challenges. In my 1960s experiment, people began prowling the office like restless cats after the day's order crunch was over, looking for excitement.

I know of an instance where one team stole another's work just to keep busy! Compared to boredom and alienation, those are good problems to have. However, it takes constant attention to devise novel solutions.

Finally, people resist peer salary reviews. It takes a mature, experienced team to make peer review work without input from management or the human resource department. Skill-based evaluation responsibility seems to work best when shared between teams and management.

Changing Consultant Roles. If workers, managers, and supervisors move toward new learning, can consultants do less? It is one thing to advocate new paradigms from the sidelines and skewer those who fall short. It is quite another to get into the ballgame, which means joining in the vulnerability, risk, and egg-on-the-face messiness that attends forays into the unknown. Can consultants keep up their old ways and expect to succeed? An early answer from Norway, where they had been thinking about these matters for a quarter of a century, was "No way." Max Elden (1978), at the Institute for Industrial Social Research in Trondheim, wrote about third-generation work democracy as a synthesis of sociotechnical thinking and participative change.

Elden's first generation (the 1960s in Norway) aimed to prove that industrial self-managing teams were feasible outside British mines. Sociotechnical experts did the diagnosing, designing, and implementing. Experts sought to get the "right" merger of technology and social psychology, bulldozing Lewinian ideas with work analysis techniques.

In the second generation (late 1960s, early 1970s) the goal broadened—to change pay schemes, to alter middle-management and supervisory roles, to apply new concepts to service and educational organizations. The expert became a consultant, contracting for a limited number of days to help organizations redesign their work. In this evolution, the influence of the NTL Institute, group dynamics, and the consulting practice that flowed from them, became more important.

While consultants involved clients more in diagnosing and prescribing, they still directed and often performed the search. They also devised an ever-growing repertoire of models and techniques such as environmental scanning, variance analysis, role analysis, demand systems, and core transformation processes. It became hard for people to "own" their daily lives reinterpreted through so many unfamiliar frameworks.

What coal miners had invented spontaneously now became a grueling process. Groups started and could not finish. Just as Taylor built scientific management from pieces tried out in different places, consultants imagined comprehensive change strategies incorporating all of social science knowledge. Sometimes they left out common sense—like the facts that people remember only a few things at once, short-term problems drive out long-range thinking, and dogged persistence is required to keep up anything.

In the third generation—there were more than fifty examples of employee-managed redesigns in Norway (and a growing number in the United States)—some companies moved further away, paradoxically, from outside experts. I say "paradoxically" because more knowledge exists than ever before. Hundreds, perhaps thousands, of managers have had the sort of first-hand experience I did in the 1960s. Many now understand how to find novel, workable solutions to unprecedented problems by turning them over to players once considered ineligible for the game.

Fred Emery, in particular, devised simple methods for transferring sociotechnical knowledge (Emery, 1982). He invented the participative design conference working with the Royal Australian Air Force in 1971, simplifying the methods to reduce dependency. He introduced the procedure into Norway in 1973. It required that natural work groups, given a few simple inputs, then assist each other in doing redesigns. My firm used variations in the United States in printing, textiles, contact lens manufacturing, and steel mills. We found ways to make useful contributions throughout the design phase and into implementation without doing the work for people. By economic and technical standards, results have been dramatic. See "Printing Inc. Redesign" on the next page for one example achieved without layoffs.

Two Important Lessons. Sociotechnical experts have learned two profound lessons by now.

First, given some minimal guidance, most work groups produce designs 85 to 90 percent congruent with what the best outside pros can do—with vastly more commitment to implement. Nobody can implement commitment for you.

Second, a work design is not an all-at-once activity finalized the way plans for building a house might be. Herbst's "minimum critical specification" is a key new-paradigm design principle. That means, bluntly, don't try to figure out every contingency in advance. The best engineers can't do

"PRINTING INC." REDESIGN

	1983	1984
People	227	195
Shipments	$15.9MM	$18.1MM
Direct Costs	45.2%	43.1%
Variances	$557MM	$337MM
Indirect Costs	23.7%	20.5%
Overtime Week-Ends/Month	4	1
Gross Profit	26.8%	33.6%

Bottom Line: +25% Net

it, as Hirschhorn's (1984) studies of Three Mile Island show, and neither can you or I. Even if we could, doing it would cut down others' chances for learning, self-control, and ownership.

Because the multi-skilled self-managing team is reinvented so often, some folks believe work design means, by definition, work teams. That is an understandable mistake. The defining factors of work design are (1) participation in the analysis and problem solving by all relevant players and (2) changing the supervisory role to managing boundaries instead of the work itself so people practice self-control.

For routine and repetitive work, multi-skilled teams are an excellent solution. It should be obvious that such teams do not fit individual jobs like computer programming. People who do non-routine work tend to invent different kinds of solutions per Cal Pava's (1983) office technology scheme. You also can find excellent guidance in William O. Lytle's (1998) work design textbook and in the team-based organization book by Mohrman, Cohen, and Mohrman (1995).

Virtual Teams in the 21st Century

In a new millennium "virtual teams" required further updating of sociotechnical practice. Just as 20th Century automation freed factory workers from heavy lifting, the 21st Century's wireless networks liberated knowledge workers from offices and meeting rooms. People could work in planes, trains and coffee shops, connecting to others at the speed of 4G. Technology allowed virtual teams to coordinate and control their own work. The "cloud" gave everyone access to the same information. Decisions could be decentralized as never before, a new paradigm fantasy-come-true.

Except for one detail. "Modern technology no longer allows a separation from home and work," wrote Kimball and Mareen Fisher (2011) of the virtual team leader's mixed blessings. "Many people find that their relationships, volunteering and service opportunities, and personal health suffer as a result." The Fishers cited a *60 Minutes* segment, "Working 24/7" (CBS News, 2006) dramatizing "how technologies intrude into every area of a virtual team leader's life." One interviewee worked until midnight, another jogged at dawn each day to a virtual Internet café meeting, a third put a web connection in the shower. If authoritarian work systems oppressed people by depriving them of choices, virtual self-directed work left people with lots of attractive choices collectively oppressive.

This tension between work and home life had been building for some time. I became aware of the benefits of "telecommuting," as it was then called, in a 1988 Future Search for Jossey-Bass Publishers (before Wiley acquired them). The questions then were how to coordinate, motivate, and compensate people who only showed up at the office once a week. Twenty years later, with people carrying computers in their pockets or pocketbooks, the issues were more old-fashioned—how to balance work and family life so that neither suffered.

This was as much a work design question as designing production and distribution systems. The solution, if I take my own advice seriously, ought to be the same. Involve the people who do the work in designing it. Now comes a new twist. How do you organize the designing and involving? In the virtual world nobody can create one-off systems for tens, hundreds, or thousands of others. If ever one size did NOT fit all, this was a problem with no template.

"Don't expect your team or organization to ask you how they can help you," wrote the Fishers. "You'll have to take responsibility for managing your life." In the world of virtual work, each of us had become a design team of one. Thus I sit here juggling new chapters for this volume, releases from the book's contributors, an in-box full of emails, a dog that wants walking, snow that needs shoveling, a visiting daughter-in-law I haven't seen for too long, my jazz group buddies wondering if we're playing this weekend, a wife expecting me for dinner, a virtual editorial meeting to be scheduled, a colleague calling from a distant place for advice, and a book deadline imminent. I'm not even a virtual team member. Google cannot help me. And next week it all will change.

The Fishers compiled many tips from virtual team members on walking the tight rope between work and family—reserve regular family times, keep virtual team members aware of your home commitments, introduce your family to your workplace and associates, call your kids each night when you travel, get regular medical checkups, eat right, exercise, and make time for community service. Good advice and hard to do even for those working 9 to 5 in places that still resemble the 20th Century. The only rehab for those of us addicted to virtual technology is a personal philosophy of work and life. Reading this today, I realized I had faced these same issues as a freelance writer in the 1950s and 1960s and as a consultant for decades after that.

The 21st Century dimension was the pervasive technology and interdependence of virtual teams. Consultants and freelancers work for themselves. They are lone wolves, responsible to a client or an editor, not needing six others in far places. Eric Trist talked about the coal miners who invented multi-skilled teams finding their way—at a higher level of technology—back to how their grandfathers worked when a miner did the whole job. The Fishers' work suggested a useful analogy. People in corporations, requiring teamwork, freed in time and space by technology, were re-discovering what those who work for themselves had always known—the burden is on you. Your organization can make it hard or easy, but nobody can do it for you.

Back to Group Dynamics

In our effort to understand what it takes to do complex work under conditions of continual change, we come at last, in an age of cybernetics, robotics, and process controls, back to group dynamics. How important is group skills training? What kind? When? Does it apply to the Internet?

I am attracted to a classic piece of action research showing that a balanced use of leadership and authority is the key to effective self-managing teams. Videotapes by Beth Atkinson reveal people using information, expertise, connections, communications skills, and charisma to exercise influence in positive and negative ways (Hirschhorn, 1984). People willing to risk disclosure of feelings and ideas and to confront differences created a better power balance and more effective teams.

Atkinson changed the climate of self-managing groups by teaching people to use, not abuse, power, and to recognize abuses by literally raising little red flags in meetings. Not surprisingly, she also found that pep talks and exhortation, such as "win one for the Gipper," had little value in motivating quality or output. "People who use charisma as a base," noted Atkinson, "produce the most stifling group climate" (Hirschhorn, 1984, p. 146). They abuse others, and powerless people (as Lippitt and White showed long ago) cease to act.

I conclude that cross-functional teams from three or more levels can invent innovative systems with minimal direction. To operate them over time, however, they need help to learn. In team settings, people need to build up their power bases, to talk to one another on an equal footing. Most of us cannot do this without greater skills in supporting and confronting others, and in taking and yielding leadership in groups (Weisbord and Maselko, 1981). For practical guidelines in developing personal power in large corporations, I recommend Peter Block's book (1991) on constructive politics.

It is worth noting here that the Emerys, working in a highly unionized country, Australia, believed that gaining the legal right to control and coordinate your work rendered group, interpersonal, and communications techniques unnecessary. In the United States, with enormous diversity and political pressures, I found that attractive hypothesis hard to test. I took it seriously because of my 1960s experience with self-managing teams. If I could go back to the 1960s again, I would certainly figure out how to transfer whatever knowledge and skill in managing the task-process relationship I now have. The dilemma, I think, is not whether but rather when and how to do it so that we do not deprive people of choice and control.

We have come full circle—from early group and leadership experiments to T-groups to coal mines to textile mills to nuclear power plants to a merger of technical and group processes in web-based worksites drawn from all these settings. Such is the convergence of OD and STS, two social learning traditions, one dug out of the British coalfields, the other stumbled upon in a Connecticut race relations conference, the one highlighting structure, the other relationships, one developed by Tavistock Institute, the other by NTL Institute, all influenced by Kurt Lewin, the "practical theorist."

■ ■ ■

"A RADICAL CHANGE THAT RAN COUNTER TO CORPORATE CULTURE..."

CHARLESTON AFB, SC—In 1987, I was a rare "new hire" recruited from the academic world to serve as an internal change agent at BellSouth during its post-divestiture transition into the age of rapid technological change and intense competition. When I read *Productive Workplaces*, I realized how big a challenge I faced. Most BellSouth managers worked from the command-and-control mental model they learned from their bosses. Ma Bell never held building dignity, meaning, and community in the workplace in high regard.

Like Weisbord, I discovered leaders who instinctively involve people in setting important goals, structure the chance to learn, offer feedback and support, provide tools and ideas, and stay out of the way. I found myself doing most of my OD work with these leaders and their groups.

Weisbord also said that the best a consultant can do is create opportunities for people to do what they are ready to do anyway I experienced this when BellSouth placed Fred Hamff and Dave Hollett in charge of the poor-performing, grievance-ridden North

Carolina Revenue Accounting Office. A staff member encouraged them to ask for my assistance. I facilitated a series of training, coaching, process mapping, and team-building interventions. In fifteen months, the Charlotte Revenue Accounting Office results were tops in the Comptrollers organization and grievances had dropped to zero.

In 1992, BellSouth consolidated twelve revenue accounting offices scattered across nine states into a new organization with Fred Hamff in charge. "I want to do what we always talk about at conferences but never do," Fred told me. "I want to create an organization where people invest their hearts as well as their heads and bodies, and I want you to help me do it."

Fred used his authority to recruit the best directors, managers, supervisors, and employees from all the offices. I asked each senior director to invite to a vision and mission planning session the manager in their unit most likely to resist the new culture. All new employees attended an orientation session in which Fred explained the business reasons for a new culture and what "walking the talk" would mean. Participants, even the reluctant ones, committed to the enterprise. I worked with directors, managers, and supervisors to use what they had learned about total quality. In less than two years, an energized organization was processing more bills with greater accuracy than ever before. The BellSouth president told Fred, "I want the entire company to have the spirit you have here." Indeed, the spirit asserted a positive influence across the company until AT&T purchased BellSouth in 2007 and returned it to the old Ma Bell command-and-control culture.

In 1995, after nine years, I returned to teaching. I took with me what I had learned about building productive workplaces. If business leaders could create cultures where diverse people choose to invest their hearts, heads, and bodies, I could do the same with a university learning community. I adopted these assumptions:

- Students like working together in a learning community to achieve shared goals.

- Seeking out differences of opinion and people different from one's self is paramount. Every student has unique knowledge, skills, and experiences to offer.
- Helping students discover what only they can add to the learning community is critical.
- Encouraging synergy is important; that is, learning is not a competitive event.

I see my role as building dignity, meaning, and community into the academic program and within the institution. When problems arise, I step back and ask myself, "What's possible here?" and "Who cares?" Invariably, people with different perspectives contribute to resolving the issue.

—Keith H. Griffin, Ph.D., program coordinator,
Southern Illinois University Workforce Education and
Development degree

chapter
TWENTY TWO

Future Search: The Whole System in the Room

On the way to the moon the Apollo astronauts made tiny "mid-course corrections" that enabled them to land at an exact predetermined spot. The corrections were small, but because the moon was far away they made a big difference. It is like that with us. Some of the changes we make in society, in our lives or in our organizations seem insignificant, but over the years they can have major impact.

—Edward B. Lindaman and Ronald Lippitt,
Choosing the Future You Prefer, 1979, p. 4

"In this chapter I will describe an extremely promising method for getting whole systems in one room and focusing on the future—the 'Future Search.' Like so many workplace innovations, its origins are traceable to creative extensions of Kurt Lewin's insight that you steer a ship by feedback from outside, not by how the rudder, engines, or crew behave."

Thus began in 1987 what was then Chapter Fourteen of this book. Future Search integrated into one short action planning meeting insights from the history, research, consulting cases, and training experiences I have described. I had found this method a practical way to "get everybody improving whole systems." The meeting enabled ordinary people to explore whole systems and commit to action plans in an era when many people considered meetings a waste of time. In the 1980s I used the method in strategic planning, mergers, reorganizations, and the introduction of new technologies.

A great deal happened on the Future Search front after 1987. To my surprise, Future Search went around the world. People improved water quality in Pakistan, introduced credit cards into Eastern Europe, demobilized child soldiers in the Southern Sudan, made business plans in Spain, improved school systems in the United States, cut factory costs in Brazil, shaped health care policy in Canada, developed women leaders in Siberia, got the bankrupt town of Stahnsdorf, Germany, out of debt, and formed coalitions to combat AIDS in South Africa, Senegal, Nigeria, and Ghana. Thousands of people repeated my experiences.

■ ■ ■

"WITHOUT WATER, THERE LITERALLY IS NO LIFE..."

JOHANNESBURG, SOUTH AFRICA—I began my working career in cost accounting, then information systems. Twenty years later I was consulting in information systems architecture development and business planning. During the early 1990s, I developed a personal interest in systemic approaches, for example, those of Russell Ackoff (1994), Peter Senge (2006) and Jay Forrester (1998).

Working with a small consulting company in 1993, I joined a project to look at how the South African property transfer and registration process might be affected by the changes following our first democratic elections, particularly a government led by the African National Congress. We had to confront the thorny issue of land ownership and restitution the country has yet to effectively deal with. Using traditional approaches and scenario planning, we produced many recommendations early in 1994; little action followed. We were struck with the challenge of how to get people with a wide spectrum of views to act together.

Visiting my favorite bookshop after our historic elections in April, I picked up a copy of *Discovering Common Ground* (Weisbord, et al., 1992) and was immediately captivated by a subtitle that promised ways to "bring people together to achieve breakthrough innovation, empowerment, shared vision, and collaborative action." Reading that book changed my working life and has influenced all my work since. It opened up a new world that explicitly recognizes the need in all for dignity, meaning and community in a complex and changing world.

My curiosity was sparked, and in 1995 I read *Productive Workplaces* to more fully understand the history and theory; for more detail on practice, I read *Future Search* (Weisbord and Janoff, 2010), In 1998 I joined Future Search Network. The following year I planned and conducted my first Future Search, visited the USA for further training, and went on to manage fifteen Future Searches in business, education, community development, conservation, and water management.

Of many examples, two stand out. On the lower Zambezi River in Zambia, we used Future Search to create new partnerships among the community, government, and private sectors for wildlife conservation. Participants overcame a significant history of conflict, went on to initiate local conservation programs, and form a community trust to govern and manage the funds and income they generated. And in a historic gold mining area west of Johannesburg, local community groups, fragmented, isolated, and in extreme poverty, found a collective voice, organized themselves to engage local government and are now included in local development planning (as distinct from being planned for).

I also brought the Weisbord-Janoff workshops in "Managing a Future Search" and "Leading Meetings That Matter" to South Africa. The underlying principles of this work have become a core of my practice. What has had most impact on me, I believe, is the challenge for the 2000s first identified so eloquently by Marv Weisbord in PW in 1997—"Getting everybody improving whole systems". Marv's theory-based practice continues to be a living learning laboratory for me. While developing interests in many interrelated theories and approaches, I keep returning to those outlined in *Productive Workplaces.*

I'm currently collaborating with several colleagues on the issue of water—learning to live with climate uncertainty and managing this vital resource more responsibly. This seems to be an area that touches on everything: health, agriculture, food security, poverty reduction, sustainable livelihoods, energy, business, recreation, local, regional, international and global governance. Without water, there literally is no life. We simply have to keep on exploring new ways of working collaboratively on the future. The principles and approaches set out in *Productive Workplaces* are a powerful foundation.

—John Goss, founder partner, Cinnabar

The Agenda. Because it was a learning laboratory, not a definitive answer, many practitioners added refinements. These are documented in a how-to book now in its third edition (Weisbord and Janoff, 2010). A typical Future Search lasts sixteen to eighteen hours spread across three days. It involves sixty to eighty people, working at times in stakeholder groups (those with a similar relationship to the task), mixed groups of diverse stakeholders, and in a meeting of the whole. The focus is "the Future of X," usually five to twenty years out, X being an organization, community, network of shared interests, or an issue needing cooperative action.

There are five segments—the past, present, future, common ground, and action. (See "Future Search Agenda.") At each step, people (1) build a database of their own experiences, (2) look at the whole together, and (3) interpret through dialogue what they are learning. At the end, those who wish make action commitments. A key feature of Future Search is that all do the same tasks together prior to action planning, gaining a view of the whole that none could get alone. The outputs are three: a "common

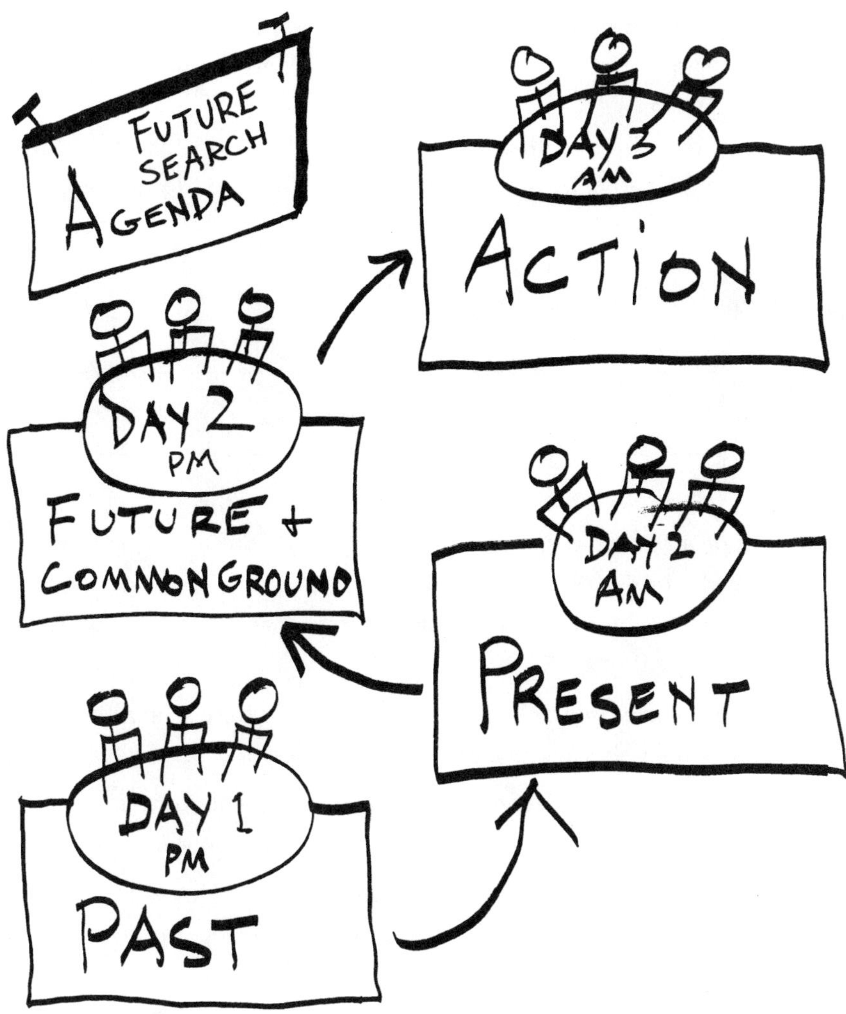

ground" statement that every person supports, action plans not imagined a few days earlier, and high commitment to follow through.

Principles Over Techniques

The meeting employs time lines; mind maps; "prouds and sorries" lists; and future-oriented scenarios. The principles, however, are more important than the techniques (see "Future Search Principles"). Indeed, hundreds of techniques could be found for these principles. The principles assume a leader with an itch to scratch, a "business opportunity," support from people energized by the focal topic, and the guidelines from Chapter Eighteen.

Be aware that you can misapply this method like any other. I have not found techniques to substitute for attractive goals, good leadership, and people who care. The hard work comes in the planning. You have to match the participants to the task. Without "the whole system in the room," it's just another meeting with novel procedures.

Future Search Principles

- Get the "whole system" in the room. The quotes imply that you never get everybody. You can get in the same room people with Authority, Resources, Expertise, Information, and Need. Just calling this meeting can be a radical change, making possible many others.
- Explore the whole before seeking to fix any part. Every person develops a richer picture than each had coming in.
- Put the future and common ground front and center. Treat problems and conflicts as information, not action items.
- Invite self-management and personal responsibility. Each time managers or consultants do something for a group, they deprive others of initiative.

Development of Future Search Principles

Future Search principles emerged for me during years of applying in businesses and medical schools ideas from Kurt Lewin and his followers. After the first edition of *Productive Workplaces* appeared, I was surprised by calls and letters from people who had had run meetings based on my brief account and were astonished at what happened. People everywhere had an insatiable hunger for simple methods promising wholeness and cooperation. In the late 1980s I called these stories to the attention of

Fred Emery and Eric Trist. Braced by their support, I began a systematic inquiry into the use of search processes. This led to the book *Discovering Common Ground* (Weisbord et al., 1992). While compiling that book I uncovered many experiments for involving people in improving whole systems. I found confirmation for the value of principles over techniques. Below I summarize how this inquiry into effective planning influenced Sandra Janoff and me as we began refining the practice with members of Future Search Network in the early 1990s.

Principles from Eric Trist and Fred Emery

Emery and Trist invented what came to be called "the Search Conference" in a 1960 planning meeting in Great Britain. A merger had led to a serious market crisis in the Bristol/Siddeley aircraft engine company, one partner making piston engines, the other jets. Trist was asked to help, and he brought along his young associate Emery. The pair had recently begun work on the managerial dilemmas of "turbulent environments." To the firm's top managers, caught in a technological culture clash, they proposed a weeklong collaborative inquiry.

It would be a new kind of strategic planning meeting designed to set up "conditions for dialogue" that Emery had derived from the research of social psychologist Solomon Asch (Weisbord et al., 1992). When people experienced themselves living in the same world, subject to the same laws of nature, having the same psychic needs, and willing to accept each other's perceptions as shared resources, they would plan together effectively.

During the meeting, piston and jet engine proponents compared notes on the state of the world and their industry before dealing with their differences. Talking about the same world changed the meeting dynamics. When each person's perspective was validated, people stayed with the task without having to defend themselves or attack others. Moreover, comparing multiple perspectives before acting gave each manager a view of the industry that none had before. This wide-angle view enabled crucial strategic choices, including building a new jet engine that, Fred Emery wrote me, was still in use forty years later.

Trist and Emery (1960) also made two key discoveries. First, when people explored the wider world together, they were less likely to fight or flee than in a problem-oriented session. Second, they discovered a contradiction in the consulting role. The pair drew hostility from the group when, having come in as experts, they refused to interpret data and suggest actions. They concluded that effective searching could not mix expert input with self-management. Rather, people would be primed to accept responsibility for their data, interpretations, and actions (see the Barford Report, in Weisbord et al., 1992). The facilitator's job was managing time and tasks and staying out of the way when people were working.

In future years Emery, collaborating with his wife Merrelyn, refined the methodology (Emery, 1982). The Emerys' conference typically lasted two or three days. They began by mapping the networks of people and external pressures linked to the focal task, what they called the "extended social field." They ended with action planning. In between they drew on a flexible menu—history, desirable and undesirable features, constraints on change, values to be carried forward, desirable futures—based on data produced and analyzed by the participants.

Others made adaptations, from downsizing business firms (Hirschhorn and Associates, 1983) to refocusing social service agencies (Clarkson, 1981). Trist did various conferences in this mode, noting in a memo to me the emergence of other search models, for example, Michel Chevalier's search position conferences in Canada for executives who couldn't be away more than a day a month and Russell Ackoff's (1974) idealized design sessions.

Design Dilemmas of Searching

The Search Conference inspired two of the four Future Search principles: exploring the whole before seeking to fix any part and having groups self-manage their work, a principle traceable to the Tavistock coal mine studies described in Chapter Ten. The techniques, however, proved to be more of a challenge than I expected. While preparing *Discovering Common Ground* (Weisbord et al., 1992), I found that the Search Conference was closely held by a cadre of practitioners trained by Fred and Merrelyn Emery, whose insistence on "the Asch conditions" for dialogue I considered a major addition to group dynamics theory.

In Future Search experiments, we had sought to activate dialogue by having each person record life experiences in parallel with global and local events, making people's personal histories part of the system. This quickly enabled the discovery of shared psychological needs, a key "Asch condition" for dialogue. I was surprised to discover that the Emerys ruled out personal information in a task-centered conference.

Other Search Conference features puzzled me. Groups were asked, for example, after listing global trends of concern, to imagine what would happen if they "did nothing" and to contrast the usually gloomy predictions with their future dreams. Janoff and I tried this and gave it up for two reasons. First, we had never known a group to decide to do nothing. Second, nobody could predict the future. Extrapolating the future from a static present contradicted people's experience.

The Emerys also saw theoretical drawbacks to inviting customers, suppliers, family, or community members to, say, a company conference. "Outsiders" would dilute the use of the "second design principle" intended to further democracy by flattening hierarchies, eliminating supervision, and placing control and coordination with those who did the work. From our point of view, redefining and enlarging a system's boundaries by inviting key stakeholders—"the environment"—was a way to put open systems into action, the essence of democracy.

Colleagues around the world had confirmed that "whole system in the room" led to new forms of cooperation within and between organizations and communities. Fred saw this as a dilution of his central goal rather than a parallel discovery. I considered this unfortunate, for the Emerys had made giant strides in workplace improvement practices. Without them Future Search would not exist.

Parallel Universes

Ludwig von Bertalanffy, author of general systems theory, once observed that the same ideas often spring up in parallel in diverse places. Many people in the 1960s and 1970s were seeking ways to bring diverse stakeholders into the room. Meetings cascading down from the top were a recipe for frustration in large bureaucracies in a speeded up world. New information came up in every meeting that was not available at the top. Why go slowly nowhere in numerous meetings when one with all the right people could produce information and action both? Among the early practices I sought to emulate were the intergroup events pioneered by the late Richard Beckhard (1969) and the imaginative "collateral organization" design of Dale Zand that got people at all levels in a hierarchy looking at the same problems (Weisbord, Lamb, and Drexler, 1974; Zand, Miles, and Lytle, 1970).

By the end of the 1970s many of us became convinced that having diverse "stakeholders" working together in real time was the key to rapid systems improvement. The person who opened my eyes to large groups was Ronald Lippitt, Lewin's student and colleague in the evolution of group dynamics. I was fortunate to spend many hours talking with Ron during several summers when we both were at NTL Institute in Bethel, Maine.

From the 1940s on, Lippitt, like Emery and Trist, had sought to extend group dynamics to large organizations, networks, and communities. He too had moved from small-group problem solving to future-oriented conferences with diverse participants. What started him down this road were tape recordings secured (with Douglas McGregor's help) of thirty strategic planning groups in action. Lippitt was appalled as he heard people build long problem lists, set priorities, generate solutions—an outgrowth of his pioneer group dynamics work. He noted that voices grew more depressed as people attributed problems to causes beyond their control, using words like "hopeless" and "frustrating." Action steps tended to be short-term, designed to deal with symptoms and reduce anxiety. The motivation, noted Lippitt (1983), was to escape the pain induced in part by the method. As early as the 1950s Ronald Fox, Lippitt, and Eva Schindler-Rainman (1973) began eliciting "images of potential"—envisioning what could be instead of lamenting what was.

In the 1970s, Lippitt and Schindler-Rainman, a community development consultant, pioneered large-group future-oriented conferences for more than eighty cities, towns, and states, many organized by Eva's longtime client, the Junior Leagues of America. Diverse interest groups—community, business, labor, government, health care, education, social agencies—sometimes hundreds of people at a time—jointly envisioned desirable futures. People were invited from all walks of life, ethnicities, and neighborhoods. The pair devised a menu of activities geared to the past, present, and future: a history, a list of events, trends and developments shaping the future, "prouds and sorries" about present operations, preferred futures, action planning.

Principles from Lippitt and Schindler-Rainman

From Lippitt and Schindler-Rainman derive the principles of getting a whole system in the room and focusing on the future. Lippitt also teamed with the late futurist Edward Lindaman, who had directed planning for the Apollo spacecraft that made the first moon landing. Lindaman believed that the future was created by our present ways of confronting "events, trends, and developments." The "preferred future"—an image of aspiration—could be a powerful guidance mechanism for making far-reaching course corrections. Lindaman and Lippitt (1979) found that when people presented future action plans as if they had already happened, they developed energy, enthusiasm, optimism, and high commitment.

Schindler-Rainman's and Lippitt's large-group work (1980) had little influence in the business world of the 1970s. It remained for Kathie Dannemiller, of Dannemiller-Tyson Associates, to make the conceptual and practical leaps that would enable as many as two thousand people in such companies as Ford and Boeing to do significant systems change together on the Lippitt/Schindler-Rainman foundation (Dannemiller-Tyson, 2000). Inspired by talks with Ron Lippitt, I too found myself lobbying clients to bring more people into the room. I saw it as the most practical path to valid information and committed action.

In the early 1980s, I made my first foray into community dynamics, using an NTL "organizational diagnosis" laboratory in Bethel, Maine. In years past we had sent teams out to visit single organizations. Now, eager to apply the large group knowledge then emerging, we decided to involve the community in action research. Teams would investigate the relationship between NTL's summer program and local sectors—stores, restaurants, churches, schools, medical facilities, hotels, and banks.

Each team would interview, observe, prepare a report, and invite people to a large meeting of the whole. Eva Schindler-Rainman, working that week in Bethel, gave us the benefit of her years in community building. And she joined in the meeting that brought all the parties together. A major issue was the culture gap between lab participants and service people in stores and restaurants, leading to mistrust and mutual irritation. A joint committee of townspeople and NTL staff, facilitated by Eva, continued to build a collaborative community long after the meeting. Only in a face-to-face discussion by many stakeholders could this new spirit be infused into an old relationship. And I had my eyes opened to the feasibility of multiple stakeholders from many sectors planning joint actions when they shared an important goal.

Facilitator Dilemmas of Large Groups. Early in my journey I faced a contradiction between the principle of self-managing groups and the refined, technique-rich Lippitt/Schindler-Rainman meeting model. In 1969, when I took up group dynamics, I learned to facilitate small groups using procedures (agenda setting, brainstorming, prioritizing) and process analysis (time out to look at decision making, control, communications, commitment, and so on).

Lippitt and Schindler-Rainman, using this repertoire, would train, say, twenty lay facilitators for a two-hundred-person conference, one for each group of ten. It was a good investment, for the facilitators were learning skills that would last a lifetime. While I liked the premise, I worried about reinforcing dependency when the intention was the reverse. If a facilitator were assigned to my group, I need not concern myself if things went wrong. Instead, I could sit back and watch what the leader would do.

Reducing Dependency. The facilitator's goal in the early days of group dynamics was teaching people to observe their own behavior and "learn how to learn." That skill, many of us imagined, would enable people to monitor and self-correct whether we were there or not. As some of us started working with Future Search, we became convinced by the Emery/Trist experience that people were capable of self-managing their small groups, even without training, if they had a clear task. Then a team of two could easily manage groups of sixty to seventy and more. This seemed both feasible and cost-effective.

What's Good for the Goose . . .

In 1983 the late Ronald Lippitt helped Block Petrella Weisbord organize a Future Search with clients from AT&T, Bethlehem Steel, McNeil Consumer Products, Smith Kline & French, Soabar Corporation, Warner Cosmetics, and consulting colleagues from the United States and Sweden. Together we looked at the future of the work world, and the meaning for all of us.

Our decision to open a private meeting to clients and friends was triggered by a startling statement in *Megatrends* (Naisbitt, 1982). Producers fear losing control if they invite consumers into strategy and policy discussions. "Too many corporations that should know better are terrified of this whole idea," Naisbitt wrote. "I do not think it an oversimplification to state that producers can only become more successful by learning how better to satisfy consumers" (1982, p. 178).

In our conference we compared notes on major trends reshaping business firms. Clients noted the need for constant retraining, the emergence of a world marketplace, a smaller gap between blue-collar and white-collar work, fewer jobs at the middle and top. The ways in which our company's future scenario must take account of these trends became plainer to us. My confidence in participative work design and reorganizations was greatly strengthened by the managers in this conference.

Yet, as small groups grew to ten or more the need for facilitation increased. If large meetings were organized into subgroups of eight, rather than ten, people's ability to self-manage was enhanced. Why eight? You can find support in academic studies cited by Russell Ackoff (1974). While teaching Future Search in Singapore, Sandra Janoff and I also learned that eight was the luckiest number in Chinese culture and that eight groups of eight, our ideal structure, was lucky beyond imagining. Social science or Chinese numerology? Take your pick.

Although I moved away from training small group facilitators, I considered as priceless the change strategy wisdom I got from Ron Lippitt and Eva Schindler-Rainman. They had discovered the incredible power of having a "whole system" in the room. They had proved the dynamic virtues of focusing on the future rather than the problem list. These tenets too I wrote into *Productive Workplaces.* Later Janoff and I adopted them as core principles of Future Search.

Honoring the Pioneers

The pioneers who inspired me had made unprecedented conceptual breakthroughs. The way that Lippitt and Schindler-Rainman defined a community to include everyone, high and low, rich and poor, all ethnicities and professions, and actually got them there was for me a triumph of moral imagination in action. More, their emphasis on the future was the precursor for visioning and futuring methods that would leap like a flash fire through corporate boardrooms a decade later. The way that Emery and Trist had built Solomon Asch's research into a task-centered meeting to create conditions for dialogue I considered a model lesson in putting theory into practice. So too their discovery of the power of self-managing work groups.

Hence Janoff and I formally adopted "Future Search" as an apt name for the methodology we were practicing. "Future" honored the community futures conferences of Lippitt and Schindler-Rainman. "Search" acknowledged the seminal Search Conferences of Emery and Trist. We saw Future Search as a learning laboratory for theirs and many other ideas, where people could discover new ways of working together.

All the trailblazers from whom I learned were mentored by Kurt Lewin, who pioneered action research, group dynamics, and collaborative consulting. Although I portray Lewin in this book as a long-dead giant in the history of applied social science, there are in fact only two degrees of separation between him and you. I hope that many who read this will be inspired by this tale of origins to extend Lewin's reach further still down the generations.

■ ■ ■

"THE MAJORITY OF STUDENTS ARE ARMY AND AIR FORCE OFFICERS..."

NORMAN, OK—I teach in the University of Oklahoma's Human Relations Department through Advanced Programs, which provides graduate-level courses on military bases in Europe and the U.S. I also work full-time at OU's Center for Public Management as a project manager. providing human resource development (HRD) support to Oklahoma Child Support Services, a state agency.

In a recent human relations course at Fort Sill in Lawton, Oklahoma, I included *Productive Workplaces Revisited* and *Don't Just Do Something, Stand There* (Weisbord and Janoff, 2007) as required texts. Most students are Army and Air Force officers, women and men in their thirties, both in graduate degree programs with international relations (IR) and human relations (HR) majors. The IR majors had never participated in a course based on experiential learning, involving small-group work and "hands-on" activities. They agreed that the assigned books were enlightening, especially *PWR.* Several mentioned that involvement and taking responsibility—key elements of Future Search—were fundamental to successful leadership. One summarized by saying that having the "whole system in the room" represents the first step toward people taking responsibility for their futures. He said that people will do almost anything to see projects succeed because involvement builds personal commitment and ownership for follow-through.

I also showed the Santa Cruz video of the process (see www.futuresearch.net). During a closing activity, several students mentioned how much the video moved them, because it showed how working with groups could really change communities in positive ways. Another student made the point that he remembered people he knew as a kid in his old neighborhood who might not be in prison today if they once had experienced the empowerment process he had witnessed in the video.

—Marilyn Durbin, project manager, Center for Public Management, University of Oklahoma

"...KNOWING I WAS ON THE RIGHT PATH..."

SONOMA COUNTY, CA—I read *Productive Workplaces Revisited* as a prerequisite for the master's in OD program at Sonoma State University. I came to understand the distinction between expert and process consulting and the historical context for both. I realized how models can illustrate concepts and that letting a group find its way to meaning and understanding through democratic means is more productive and rewarding than supplying answers.

I was most intrigued by Future Search, which I considered a nexus of the democratic approach to workplaces. As part of my studies, I did a consulting job with a local nonprofit cultural arts agency, working with the "whole system." We were able to run meetings in which managers heard from secretaries and directors heard from maintenance crew. People at first were confused about their roles and responsibilities, leading to frustration and poor performance. They reframed their problems and regrouped to solve their challenges together, rather than looking for others to blame. The group, for example, addressed the budget, a painful topic for everyone, and all became involved in creating the budget proposal for their board, a tremendous leap for this group.

There were personal breakthroughs too. The event coordinator realized she could evaluate her work after each project, based on criteria that reflected her values and needs. Another manager found she felt isolated and did not like her job. A few months later she had a new role and title, happier doing something integrated with the core mission.

—Talia Eisen, Clarity Professional Organizing

chapter
TWENTY THREE

Cross-Cultural Future Searching

"The principle of surviving in a multi-cultural world is that one does not need to think, feel, and act in the same way in order to agree on practical issues and to cooperate."

—Geert Hofstede, *Cultures and Organizations*, p. 237

Future Search has now been used since 1982 in corporations and communities on five continents. I never found a more cost-effective or time-efficient planning method during decades of experimenting. Nor one more responsive to values of dignity, meaning, and community. In this chapter I summarize a few Future Search applications and speculate on why so many diverse cultures took it up.

In this regard I must mention the role of Sandra Janoff. When we met in 1987, Sandra had a decade of teaching in an experimental school where city and suburban children formed a self-managed learning community. Her experiences paralleled mine in business firms. We had separately concluded that structure was a shaper of behavior that people actually could control. Together we began to fine-tune Future Search principles, practices, and structures that best enabled people to transform their capability for action.

I had been experimenting since the early 1970s with meeting designs aimed at involving the whole person and not just the "left brain." This meant offering ways for everyone to participate regardless of learning styles. Janoff and I set up tasks that would require people to move around, on the theory that if you want to move, start by moving. We gave everyone access to the walls and the chart pads to write or draw pictures from the start. This showed that every person's experience counted and the technology belonged to all.

Adopting a Lippitt technique, we had people act from the future, describing their desired futures as if they had already happened. This, we believed, engaged people physically and emotionally, making action more probable as they got the feeling of success in their bones. Sandra began to integrate into the facilitating work insights from her training in system-centered group dynamics. In particular she showed that so long as each person had at least one other who shared his or her thoughts and/or feelings, a group would stay whole and "on task." It was not necessary to process relationships, only to validate subgroups when issues became sticky (Janoff and Weisbord, 2001).

We refined these ideas with many organizations, notably in 1988 with Resources for Human Development, a nonprofit umbrella agency with 140 human service programs, that became the home of Future Search Network, described by Sandra Janoff in the story below. RHD was growing 25 percent a year with diverse programs for housing, employment, mental health, child care, the arts, and drug and alcohol abuse, among others. The agency sought to implement values of inclusion, diversity, dignity, responsibility, accountability, and cooperation while operating on 15 percent overhead. We later ran two more Future Searches to decentralize what was becoming a mini-bureaucracy with three thousand employees, and to create a strategic direction for accelerating growth. (For insight into this unique non-profit business model, see www.rhd.org.)

■ ■ ■

"WHAT A NEW CONSULTING PARADIGM MIGHT LOOK LIKE..."

PHILADELPHIA, PA—Long before I read *Productive Workplaces*, I worked for ten years in a small, experimental high school, managing in the paradigm Marv came to call "Everybody Improves Whole Systems." The program, started in the mid-1970s, included urban and suburban public school students. We had a flat operating structure, made decisions democratically, and involved parents, students, and adjacent school districts in our planning. Despite great success, the school was closed in 1984 for economic reasons.

I then enrolled in a Ph.D. program at Temple University that emphasized Kurt Lewin's field theory, action research, systems thinking, and group and organization development. There in June 1986, Marv ran a workshop. When he put up "The Learning Curve" chart (page xx) I saw my whole systems experience in a context beyond schools. I was studying clinical psychology and recognized that each combination of "who" and "what" on the Learning Curve represented developmental assumptions that were not mutually exclusive. Each quadrant suggested more capacity in the system, describing behaviors against which you could test your values. In our school we had intuitively enabled people to build a learning community. Marv brought us examples from his own work that showed that this way of managing and consulting was good for the human spirit, good for the bottom line, and good for society.

Some months later, reading about "Taylorism" in PW, I saw how easy it is to become wedded to techniques and, as Marv put it, divorce the values. I also felt a tiny shock when Marv described applications of Lewin's "freezing, unfreezing, refreezing" model as analogous to scientific management. Both sought to "engineer" change and impose permanence on constantly changing systems.

My high school staff had struggled with the tension between the polarities of task and process, certainty and confusion. Extrapolating this to other organizations, I imagined that the bigger the system and the more diverse the players, the greater the tension, but the more opportunity for innovation. I understood the benefits of enabling people to learn from their own experience. I became excited by Marv's chapter on Future Search, and he invited me to join him in several projects. About the same time, he, I, and Allan Kobernick, my husband, started experimenting with video case studies based on themes from PW. (These can be viewed in an online archive housed at the University of Pennsylvania. See www.organizationaldynamics.upenn.edu/onlineresources.)

In 1991, after I received my Ph.D., we did our first experimental Future Search training on Cape Cod. In 1993, we founded Future Search Network, involving hundreds of colleagues. Over the years, we have refined the Future Search process and deepened our understanding of the dynamics. As a result, I have worked with thousands of people on every continent to further "dignity, meaning, and community."

To cite one example, I began consulting in 2008 to the Ilex Regeneration Company, charged with the renewal of Derry-Londonderry, a Northern Ireland city with a troubled past. We held a dramatic Future Search in 2009. People formed joint working groups across sectarian lines and set up a citizen's strategy board. Hundreds of people began working toward a shared vision for equality in economic renewal, education, health care, tourism, and social services (Weisbord and Janoff, 2010).

I helped by structuring large meetings where people could learn from each other and decide on next steps. I have learned that—especially in a four-hundred-year-old city with a divisive past—"transformative change" means one step at a time. Political tension persists in a place with high numbers of underserved and unemployed residents. Still, I experience a growing sense of dignity as people create a new story based on shared purpose, hard work, and hope for the future.

—Sandra Janoff, Ph.D., co-director, Future Search Network

Reaffirming Self-Management

A notable for-profit example was a Future Search in 1990 with the Gaines pet food plant in Topeka, Kansas. Built originally by General Foods, it was then the longest-running team-based factory in the United States. It had won fame for "the Topeka system," a low-overhead, high-productivity process driven from the bottom by the people who did the work. General Foods, as is often the case, could not clone its system, even in a factory making the same product. Eventually, it sold Gaines to Anderson-Clayton, who sold it to Quaker Oats.

The Future Search celebrated Topeka's twentieth anniversary and was intended to set a direction for the Topeka system over the next twenty years. A subtext was the survival of that system in a corporation imposing centralized policies that speeded its erosion. Participants included workers, executives in the Quaker Oats manufacturing hierarchy, raw materials suppliers, and corporate human resources, finance, and information systems staff.

Years later I vividly recalled a passionate dialogue about the subtle shift away from self-management under each new corporate owner. Workers looked increasingly for team leaders to solve their problems. Team leaders increasingly saw the workforce as inept and dependent. In the Future Search, both groups had a shock of recognition: each perpetuated a self-fulfilling prophecy.

The meeting ended with a resolve to restore autonomy and responsibility at all levels. For me the high point came when a senior Quaker Oats executive said in a voice quivering with conviction, "What I realize today is that when we acquired your company, we tried to 'Quakerize' you." A bolt of electricity shot through the room. "For that I apologize. We did not appreciate what you were doing here." He then publicly charged his staff to collaborate with the plant to support the local system.

One thing we learn from the past is that organizations never learn from the past. In 1996, Quaker Oats sold its pet foods division to H.J. Heinz, which moved to "Heinz-ize" it. According to one account, "Management shut down half the plant, eliminated the team system, suspended all the costly ongoing training that made the team system viable, and cut 150 jobs." Six months later Heinz, with declining productivity in Topeka, did an about face. They restored training and team meetings and revalidated pay-for-knowledge and self-management of job rotation. "The system in Topeka has evolved to a much higher level than any of our other plants," said a Heinz vice president. "We look at it as a model of where we'd like to go" (Kleiner, 1996). Each generation, it seems, learns all over again for itself.

Merging Future Search and Work Design

Perhaps my most eye-opening Future Search experience came in 2003 when Janoff and I joined with Tomas Oxelman, an internal consultant with the global furniture company IKEA, to do a feat of systems redesign I had thought impossible. The company had decided to overhaul its "pipeline," the flow of products from the drawing boards in Almhult, Sweden, to its far-flung factories, thence to assembly and distribution points, stores and customers. With eleven major product lines, 186 stores, eighteen hundred suppliers in fifty-five countries, and seventy thousand employees, this would be a daunting task.

Oxelman and other executives had attended Future Search workshops. They persuaded us that extreme action was needed and observed that FS principles supported their corporate values. They would guarantee the right people in the room. Together we adapted the Future Search method to a single product, the "Ektorp" sofa, to re-imagine its journey from design center to customer. This would be the prototype for all product lines. Catarina Bengtsson, the business group manager, had ambitious goals for Ektorp: double sales, improve quality, and cut the price 30 percent without cutting profit, make sofa shopping easier for customers, and cut delivery times.

In March 2003, fifty-two stakeholders—suppliers from Poland, Mexico, and China, the company president and top staff, line people from several countries, and Ektorp customers from Hamburg, Germany (site of the meeting)—came together for three days. Most had never met. Together they described the existing system, documented required changes, agreed on common specs for a new design, created an implementation plan, and obtained buy-in from all relevant levels, functions, and customers at once. In my past experience, such processes took at least six months. IKEA made and launched its pipeline makeover plan with multi-level task forces in a few days.

I was most astonished at the common ground specs for a new system. They included flattening the hierarchy, involving customers and suppliers in design from the start, providing direct contact with suppliers and stores, changing the roles of central staff, and modifying information systems so all could influence the system's coordination and control. I considered it remarkable that people made up their new paradigm solution with no prompting from consultants on systems design principles. By taking seriously customer concerns and matching various designs against their goals, they dismantled a traditional, centralized system.

It was a vivid example of people following Mary Parker Follett's "law of the situation" (Metcalf and Urwick, 1940, p. 59). There was one more thing—leadership. Top executives joined the dialogue without saying what form a new system should take. Rather, the president continually reiterated the importance of the prototype to the company's future. Ektorp—that sofa sitting in the meeting room with a coffee table in front of it—was a means to a larger goal.

Within a month, seven task forces were redoing the system around the world. The main coordination and control mechanism? A regular conference call buttressed by emails. Having all in touch with one another enabled a degree of self-organizing not previously seen. "I learned a lot and also got many insights into how we in IKEA cooperate amidst the complexity, and in how to run a workshop like this one," said Catti Bengtsson, who had no formal line authority. "We have complete documentation at our intranet site, which is updated continuously. The regular telephone conferences are helping us keep the focus and speed!" (Ektorp, incidentally, became the best-selling sofa in the world.)

Training Practitioners

By 1991, having done several Future Searches, Janoff and I seized on an opportunity presented by Gil Levin, director of Albert Einstein College of Medicine's summer Cape Cod Institute. We designed an experiment to see whether we could teach Future Search methods in a seminar. There exists in such training a paradox. Future Search requires interdependent stakeholders. The dynamic tension comes as people find common ground across lines of class, culture, and status, leading to action plans none dreamed possible. Workshop participants' only common concern is learning the method. Diverse and motivated they may be, but they cannot re-create the dynamics when they have no ongoing business with each other.

We approached Cape Cod with skepticism. Nearly one hundred people showed up, a group too large for our purposes. To make things worse, we selected the future of organization development (OD) as a simulation topic, thinking this would provide a common denominator. That turned out to be a little like choosing the future of metaphysical speculation, since OD encompassed infinite methods and its professionals, who advocated collaboration, had little need for it.

Even were Cape Cod not a simulation, an actual Future Search to help non-interdependent, solo professionals do collaborative planning is a dead end. (Knowing this, Janoff and I later ran three Future Searches for professional groups with low interdependence. Lots of talk, little action. Eventually we accepted what we had learned at Cape Cod: ours was not the best meeting design for lone wolf practitioners.)

However, we learned a more important lesson. Many Cape Cod participants later ran successful Future Searches. Somehow they got the principles, tools, and techniques. Most also got a pleasant surprise. Faced with people who needed to cooperate, they had a better experience than during the training.

Launching a Future Search Network

In 1991 we met with a social action group from the Philadelphia Region OD Network, sparked by Marilyn Sifford and the late Ralph Copleman, who wanted to learn Future Search. Together we designed an action research project to see whether consultant teams could run successful Future Searches after three days of training. To maximize chances for success, we invited clients and consultants to learn together. By "success" we meant enabling clients to do things after that they could not do before.

That project resulted in a dozen pro bono Future Searches: an inner-city career agency, a statewide reading program, and a hospital for disturbed children. As clients reported planning breakthroughs, people in other cities requested training. Eventually, we repeated the program sixteen times in North America, resulting in hundreds of Future Searches and many implementation stories.

Thus began Future Search Network in 1993, founded as a nonprofit coalition of volunteer practitioners. Members offered to put on Future Searches in any culture, any language, for whatever people could afford (www.futuresearch.net).

To help fund the Network, we offered public workshops. By 2012, our colleagues and we had trained nearly four thousand people in Asia, Africa, Australia, Europe, and the Americas. Hundreds, perhaps thousands, of Future Searches, in corporations, NGOs, nonprofits, and communities, had been run and results documented.

We decided also that the method, a product of so many hands and brains, would be freely available, unencumbered by certification and market concerns. As the Network grew, its members experimented with time frames, overall length, group size, task sequence, instructions, how to display data, how to manage all size groups, and with the degree to which people could do work formerly done for them by staff. The method became simpler, instructions fewer, groups more diverse, and participants' involvement more passionate as we turned the meetings over to them. All this we put into a detailed action guide now in its third edition (Weisbord and Janoff, 2010).

■ ■ ■

"THE LEARNING CURVE GAVE ME CONFIDENCE..."

MELROSE PARK, PA—When *Productive Workplaces* was first released in 1987, I was working as an internal OD consultant with faculty and staff at the University of Pennsylvania. I found the book powerful and informative. The visual models were thought-provoking, particularly the Learning Curve (page xx) that showed the evolution of consulting styles from "experts solving problems" to "everybody improving whole systems." Although many academic clients expected it of me, I was never comfortable in the expert role. PW gave me the confidence to provide consulting services that fit my personal style while achieving the best results for my clients.

After reading about Future Search back in 1987, Ferne Kuhn and I partnered to manage one. This was years before a specific Future Search design or facilitation training existed. Nonetheless, with PW in our briefcases, we conducted our first Future Search for a government agency in Washington, D.C., to help clarify goals and plan for the coming year. The group was surprised by what they could accomplish in a day by all working together. We found the experience challenging and fun, and we learned a key lesson: one day is too short. Results were present-oriented and tactical. We didn't have time to dream big. We had no outside stakeholders. Still, we learned enough to do more work like this.

I have since managed many FSs in organizations large and small, achieving results that exceeded the clients' expectations and often my own. Now I have built an international consultancy focused on whole systems change. FS principles remain central to my work in peace-building, whether capacity-building with NGOs or in post-conflict communities to rebuild their future. I find it essential to "get the whole system in the room, find common ground, think globally, act locally, and foster personal responsibility and self-management."

—Loretta Raider, principal, The Raider Consulting Group

A Network in Action

A professional Network steeped in shared principles, values, and procedures made possible new forms of social action. In 2002, for example, Future Search Network was invited into a business/community partnership led by Dave Whitwam, then CEO of Whirlpool Corporation, a global giant based in Benton Harbor, Michigan. Whirlpool's motivation was a history of racial tensions between its home town, a once-thriving, largely black community that had lost many businesses, and St. Josephs, its well-to-do, mainly white neighbor across the river. Animosities made it hard for Whirlpool to attract a diverse workforce at its headquarters. Whirlpool Foundation, the company's community action arm, retained Kaleel Jamison Consulting Group (KJCG), a diversity consulting firm led by Fred Miller and Judith Katz, colleagues I had known for years. (See their story on page 105.)

KJCG mobilized hundreds of local citizens in workshops, seminars, and meetings. People met each other across economic and racial boundaries, discovering common stakes in working together. Future Search Network's task was to help channel this emerging energy into joint community projects. Having a Network made possible the mobilizing in a few days of thirty-two members from diverse racial and ethic backgrounds. Working in teams of four with community leaders and a KJCG team led by Marcus Robinson, we ran eight Future Searches in as many weeks, one for the umbrella Council of World Class Communities, and in business, communities of faith, community outreach, economic development, education and learning, government, and health care. More than three hundred local citizens came together on dozens of plans to attract new businesses, open affordable housing, build children's playgrounds, and include many citizens from churches and schools previously left out of local civic life.

Ripples in the Stream of Social Change

I cannot leave this review without noting two phenomena related to the rapid spread of this work. First was the discovery that diverse people could participate in Future Searches without needing new skills and that facilitators could manage them without long apprenticeships. Second, the method bridged cultural boundaries none of us had set out to cross. In the 1970s I learned how problematic it was to adapt business-based methods to medical schools, let alone to cultures not my own. Future Search Network members, following the protocols I have described, had involved participants from an encyclopedic list of the world's cultures.

People were using Future Search to validate their own traditions. Unity Church clergy adapted the method to congregational renewal because the principles embodied core tenets of their faith. Many Episcopal and Methodist ministers came to the same conclusion. The Jewish Reconstructionist Federation undertook a Future Search because it embodied "reconstructionism in action." A director of the U.S. Army leadership center incorporated Future Search into officer training because the balance between structure and open-ended possibility seemed peculiarly suited to military officers. In Hawaii the planning committee for Ko'olau Loa, a community on the North Shore of Oahu, concluded that Future Search enabled a return to traditional Hawaiian values of the oneness of mind, body, and spirit. In Singapore, participants of Chinese descent said they experienced in Future Search a re-creation of traditional community values of mutual support and cooperation.

There were other clues that something out of the ordinary was happening. I was surprised at how many groups adopted their "mind maps" of trends affecting them as totems of a sort, putting them in reports, on the Internet, and on the wall back at the office. I was equally surprised that dramatizing ideal futures gained wide acceptance. In Uganda, Sandra Janoff saw tribal chiefs from remote villages invent a spontaneous ritual, when "the head of one clan started chanting to his ancestors about a better life for his children. The other chiefs joined him and they created a symbol to take back showing they all agreed to this." In the same vein we have seen staid business executives laugh, dance, and play act, displaying a talent for serious fun nobody knew they had. It is as if participants use Future Search to evoke archetypes missing from conventional meetings.

Why Was This Happening?

My friend Bapu Deolalikar, an international development consultant, had called the method "culture free" in 1992 long before Future Search spanned the globe. At the time I mumbled my skepticism that such a thing could be possible. By the mid-1990s, however, it became clear that Future Searches were tapping into something lodged deep in the human psyche. I'm confident this could not happen if people first had to master skills and attitudes they did not already have.

Far from adding new pressures into the field—new theories, concepts, and strategies, conflicts to be managed, problems to be solved—we had stripped away group dynamics technology and language. In Lewin's terms, we had reduced the restraining forces enough so that the skills, experiences, and motivation people already had would sweep them toward the futures they really wanted. We were actualizing Kurt Lewin's values while updating his concepts and techniques for a world of full-time change.

For me, this marked the end of my interest in complex strategic management programs. Cutting through complexity required methods anybody could use based on what they already knew. Many people in the new millennium, caught in a maelstrom of "faster, shorter, cheaper," were trapped in a hunt for techniques to keep up.

Techniques don't do anything. People do. What we called "resistance to change" could be renamed a healthy reaction of organisms pushed beyond their design limits. We didn't need better tools for handling resistance. Future Search offered people a way to transcend the tyranny of technology, the pressure for growth at any cost, and the relentless compression of time. It offered a forum for accepting ourselves and working with each other as is.

To be embraced by so many cultures, this process must be serving universal needs. That realization pointed me toward its mythic aspects. I could imagine FS as a secular rite of passage, enabling people to find capabilities they did not know they had. The rituals were the time lines, mind maps, "prouds and sorries," and "common ground wall." Its myths were fanciful stories dressed up as "preferred future scenarios."

In homogeneous cultures, people used the secular myths and rituals to celebrate familiar community milestones. In cross-cultural Future Searches, diverse people could travel a non-sectarian bridge to find each other. Because the rituals belonged to no one culture, all could own them. It was as if people used the Future Search to project onto an empty screen labeled "past, present, and future" what they valued most. Far from being a "new paradigm," perhaps we had inadvertently tapped into the oldest one of all, dating to when every tribe lived by myth, ritual, and the changing seasons.

Redefining Future Search

Then, in 1995, I was startled to discover parallels between Future Search and the ancient Taoist philosophy underlying traditional Chinese medicine. The catalyst was a seminar on "Redefining Health," a program of TAI-SOPHIA (formerly the Traditional Acupuncture Institute) in Columbia, Maryland, where my son Robert had been clinical director. In the seminar we learned the seasons of five-element acupuncture, each matching an element in nature—fall (metal); winter (water); spring (wood); summer (fire); late summer (earth).

Each season has a condition associated with "effective actions for life." The model had us moving—in relation to the issue we had selected—around the seasons, from "honoring all concerned" in fall, to a place of inquiry and unknowing in winter, to a clear vision in spring, to partnership in summer, and to mutual agreement about what to do in late summer.

(Acupuncturists who practice this way intend that people experience the five conditions during treatment. To be whole and energized is to know all five states.)

We were asked to apply this metaphorical system to situations in our lives. Observing this process, I felt a tingle of excitement. This movement exactly paralleled the phases of Future Search! Future Search started with timelines honoring the experience of every person. We made a mind map of global trends, the basis for inquiry into the complexity of the unknown. We moved to common ground and dramatic visions of a shared future. Finally, we sought voluntary partnerships, agreements, and commitments. This cycle of experience had been known for thousands of years. Over a few decades we had replicated it in planning meetings. Its origins, I concluded, must lie in the collective unconscious (Weisbord, 2001). See "Ancient Wisdom/Future Search."

ANCIENT WISDOM		**FUTURE SEARCH**	
Season	**Ongoing Conditions**	**Phase**	**Purpose**
FALL	Honoring all concerned; insight into who each of us is in this situation.	PAST	Validating every person's experience; developing a shared context.
WINTER	Knowledge; willingness to be in inquiry/ unknowing.	PRESENT	Pooling all perceptions; inquiry; discovery.
SPRING	Seeing what your vision is with clarity about your intent.	FUTURE	Living our dreams; internalizing what we really want.
SUMMER	Opening the heart to create partnership.	COMMON GROUND	Confirming shared values and aspirations.
LATE SUMMER	Mutual agreement about what would be of service.	ACTION	Cooperating on next steps toward a future serving all.

I cannot prove that Future Search does all this. However, I have little doubt that researchers will follow up my hypothesis. Someday we may see formal evidence that Future Search and similar methods succeeded not because they changed the paradigm so much as they helped people refocus on what had always been fundamental to our species—dignity, meaning, community, and productive work. In a tidal wave of change, most of it self-made and much of it self-defeating, many people were eager in the 21st Century to recover those parts of our shared experience that made working together one of life's joys.

■ ■ ■

"STRENGTHENING THE BRIDGE BETWEEN SOUTHERN AFRICA AND EUROPE..."

BRUSSELS, BELGIUM—I rediscovered Future Search during a Learning Exchange meeting in South Africa in 2007, integrating it with Open Space and Appreciative Inquiry in several projects. When I turned fifty that year, my wife and I invited 160 friends, colleagues, family and clients to a feast at the Colonial Palace in Brussels. We had decided to do something useful in Africa. When partygoers asked what I wanted for a present, I said, "Your time." So we created a "time bank" based on people donating time to Africa. In a series of workshops we decided on four principles. We would:

- Create a volunteer Institute of members sharing, exploring, and comparing experiences, knowledge, and desires;
- Focus initially on challenges in Southern Africa;
- Help people connect whilst learning from working together on community, organizational, and personal development.
- Build a bridge between Southern Africa and Europe, with two-way traffic, so that we learn from one another.

We founded Ubuntu4u ("I am because we are" in the Zulu language) in 2008. In an Open Space meeting participants from South Africa, Netherlands, Belgium, Germany, and Turkey decided to explore working with locals from two townships with whom we met to discuss local desires and needs. We organized an Appreciative

Inquiry (AI) workshop in Zamdela township not far from Johannesburg, focused on arts and culture, a sector from which people might generate an income. Participants planned a local theatre initiative, and a director who works with young actors in Germany went to the township in 2009 to help young artists rehearse the fully adapted play from *Goldoni: A Servant of Two Masters.* The group later participated in the National Theater Festival in Grahamstown in 2010. Our South African partners also visited Europe, where we worked together with urban minorities to strengthen the bridge between Southern Africa and Europe.

—Hans Begeer, co-founder, Ubuntu4u

PART FIVE

Learning Then and Now

Dorothy: "How am I to get back to Kansas?"
Wizard of Oz: "We shall have to think about that. There is only one thing that I ask in return for my help. You must keep my secret and tell no one I am a humbug."

—*The Wonderful Wizard of Oz,* Baum, 1990, 1958, p. 118

I come now to the end of my own yellow brick road. I have yet to meet the Wizard, except the one who lives in me. He informs me that each of us follows paths worn by other feet to places only we alone can go. You can devise infinite variations on the modes described in Part Four—team building, work design, and Future Search. Although not interchangeable, any combination might become a potent systems change strategy. Even with identical structures, no two events will ever match. Each time you undertake such a journey you will learn things you did not know you knew.

In Chapter Twenty-Four I sum up what I learned from revisiting my 1987 cases fifteen to thirty years later. I have put to rest for myself now and forever the "sustainable change" myth. Perhaps you too will find here echoes of your own experience.

In Chapter Twenty-Five I offer perspectives on choosing methods for today. The proliferation of large-group activities like Open Space, Appreciative Inquiry Summit, World Cafe, and Whole Scale Change give you many mix-and-match options. By now you have access to a lifetime of ideas for inventing your own strategies.

In the last chapter, I weave twenty-five years' worth of unresolved story fragments—authority, democracy, equity, hierarchy, rewards, risk, training—into my tapestry of economics, technology, and people.

My conclusion is as old as the pyramids. The only way to build a roadway to the future is one yellow brick at a time. Consider anyone a humbug who offers you an exemption.

chapter
TWENTY FOUR

Ten Cases Decades Later: What's Sustainable About "Change"?

"This is not a one walk dog."

—Dianne Connelly, practitioner of traditional Chinese medicine

I built this book from the origins of my practice and a theory of action derived from ten cases I knew first-hand. In the second edition, I followed up these cases fifteen to thirty years later. This volume, with further additions, brings my story up-to-date. The six cases in Part Two were foundations for the "Learning Curve" on page xx. In them I noted my own practice evolving from expert problem solving toward everybody improving whole systems. My insight was that this shift, driven by social, technological, and economic change, called for new ways of managing and consulting.

Revisiting these and four other narratives years later, I wanted to know what happened after I left. More particularly, I wanted to see what I could learn about continuity in a world of unstable workplaces. Ten cases is admittedly a small number. I put these in the book because each involved one to three years of effort with committed clients, a good cross-section of the one hundred or so workplace projects I had done. It's possible, of course, that my experiences are so idiosyncratic they cannot be generalized. Nonetheless, here are answers to some questions I asked myself during this inquiry. See "Ten Projects Summarized."

Ten Projects Summarized

Cases	Dates	What Was Done	Situation 15 to 30 Years Later
Chapter Two			
MW Family Business	1966–1968	Self-managing work teams started; increased productivity and morale, reduced turnover, absenteeism	Company sold twice; part of successful conglomerate; "teams" of one did whole job
Part Two Six Key Cases			
Medical School	1969–1971	Planning process involving all stakeholders, with emphasis on alienated faculty; new mission	Changed owners twice; survived financial scandal; faculty remained involved in planning and budgeting
Food Services	1970–1971	Turnover reduced through Likert survey and manager training	Turnover was still an issue for the company and industry; manager training now key everywhere
Chem Corp	1979–1980	Survey feedback improves R&D/ relations with other functions and increases flow of new products	Old culture resurfaced; few new products

Ten Projects Summarized, Cont'd.

Cases	Dates	What Was Done	Situation 15 to 30 Years Later
Packaging Plant	1978–1979	Packaging system greatly improved	
	1989–1990	Entire plant redesigned by 60 employees	Redesign of 1989–1990 did not outlast leadership changes
Solcorp	1981	Attempt to get R&D, marketing, and manufacturing in synch	Company gone without a trace
Printing Inc.	1981–1983	Reorganization at top followed by redesign of work systems by employees	Facility closed; manufacturing moved
Part Three Whole System Cases			
Bethlehem Steel Sparrows Point Plant	1981–1983	Whole system pilot projects to improve union/management relations and save company greatly improves quality	Plant closings; climate of labor/management cooperation sustained; company filed for Chapter 11 bankruptcy in 2002; assets sold in 2003
McCormack & Dodge	1985	Strategic reorganization by sixty employees in series of conferences	Company merged by new owner, lost money, sold abroad
AECL Medical Products	1985	Failed company saved through employment guarantees and total involvement becomes profitable	Company survived further crisis; sold in 1990s; remained part of large, successful company

Q: What Led People to Undertake These Projects?

A: While statistics can be mustered—there are many in this book—to support involving everyone in improving the whole, I don't believe "the numbers" ever motivated skeptics to do it. Positive measures mainly reassure people who would do this work anyway. In my projects leaders were of two kinds. Some were under the gun to survive and were at the point where they would try anything plausible. Had things been going well, they would not have called consultants. Others believed that involving people was the right thing to do and the prospect of a return on investment made it easier to justify betting with consultants who shared their values.

Of the five motivated by survival, Solcorp's president was driven by an under-developed product and market pressures from his corporate parent. The Sparrows Point Plate Mill superintendent worried about the superiority of Japanese steel. Medical School's president faced financial pressures, an alienated faculty, and conflict between the school and its teaching hospital. The president of AECL Medical had come up against continuing layoffs and a possible shutdown. At Printing Inc. the CEO's own survival was at stake. The company was doing okay, but he had fallen out of favor at corporate headquarters.

In five other cases leaders were blessed by rapid growth and increasing success. This complicates the hypothesis that change projects require a threatening crisis. There is such a thing as a crisis of success. Sometimes an organization outruns the experience of its leaders. This happens more as the work world spins faster, pushing people into novel situations. In such cases putting your values into action offers more certainty than recycling old methods. In the success/high growth cases, all the leaders were value driven, believing that stakeholder engagement, influence, and commitment would improve economic viability.

My family business, for example, was growing 25 percent a year. I wanted a workplace founded on Theory Y assumptions because that touched a deep part of my identity. At Food Services the president gained valuable self-knowledge at a behavioral science seminar. He wanted the same for his managers. The turnover project evolved when a pilot group discovered how much employee attrition cost. The regional president in whose area the research was done, however, had a deep belief in people and did several team-building sessions with me about the same time.

At Chem Corp, the HR manager and his boss, the president, had asked for team building to foster cooperation among functions. The action research project was a spinoff from other team members wanting better relations with a testy R&D chief. The latter, as a scientist, liked the idea of quantifying relationships among departments. At Printing Inc. I came in after the president was pressured by corporate headquarters to shape up his leadership or else. The later work redesign projects were led by a vice president with an affinity for teamwork, openness, and a belief in having people control their work.

Packaging Plant enjoyed rapid growth and market leadership when I first went there in 1979. The manufacturing VP who called me wanted greater responsibility for results shared by managers and workers alike. He believed in opening up the plant and finding new ways to cooperate. The plant manager had no choice but to go along. In the plant redesign for which I returned ten years later, another plant manager valued employee participation and creativity and wanted everyone to have a chance to succeed.

McCormack & Dodge was growing fast, too, and was a leader in mainframe financial systems software. The president had a balky and contentious staff, and he wanted departments to cooperate—an itch that led eventually to a total company reorganization by employees from all levels and functions.

Q: How Did I Decide What Methods to Use?

A: My choices had more to do with my enthusiasms than with existing OD methods. I started my consulting practice after a decade of business experience. I also knew how to interview from my years as a journalist. Combining these experiences, I got through my initial consulting assignments. In year one I said, "Here's what I propose to do," drawing on what I knew. In year two, having added survey feedback to my tool kit, I could say, "Well, there are two ways to go at this." Attending workshops, I brought myself up to speed with process consulting, interpersonal skills, team building, group dynamics, and problem solving. By year five I had a menu that included the above plus intergroup workshops, management-by-objectives, ad hoc meetings, and leadership training, all within an action research framework. Whatever path I suggested, both I and my clients believed we would get the hoped-for results.

I also kept my eyes open for work redesign projects to repeat what I had done as a manager. It took me twelve years of consulting to find the first one, after which I did several more. In each case I proposed plausible methods I was eager to try because they spoke to my sense of adventure. I was looking for the boundaries of social, technological, and economic change. Indeed, until I committed in the early 1990s to Future Search as the embodiment of everything I believed in, I never did the same thing twice. Rather, I tailor-made each project from the whole cloth of my current passions linked to my clients' aspirations.

In my family firm I had just read Douglas McGregor and was eager to start self-managing teams. At Medical School I first interviewed people because that was what I knew how to do. By the time we got to action steps, I had met Rensis Likert at the Institute for Social Research, internalized his "link pin" planning ideas, and saw this as a reassuring structure for a school low on trust.

At Food Services I built further on Likert's work, starting with his concept of human resource accounting wed to survey data feedback because I was eager to prove the bottom line value of social processes in a business not my own. At Chem Corp I saw a chance to develop a new use for the differentiation-integration theories I had absorbed while studying medical schools with Paul Lawrence.

Packaging Plant in 1979 enabled an application of systems thinking, a concept I was attracted to intellectually and wanted to find a way of using with people who were systems operators, not thinkers.

By the time I got to AECL Medical Products and McCormack & Dodge in the mid-1980s I had had twenty years of experience. By the second Packaging Plant effort in 1989, I was doing work redesign in a series of large group meetings, a significant scaling up of earlier efforts. At each stage I was integrating everything I knew into every project, seeking the limits of workplace improvement.

In short, I liked the high wire. My safety net was the certain knowledge that doing projects nobody had done before in each workplace was the only sure path to new levels of both business results and learning. You can't "change" a workplace by repeating familiar patterns. Nor can you do it by comparing an organization's needs with an inventory of all the possible ways for meeting them. I think Harrison Owen's (2008) principle for Open Space meetings applies to all OD strategies. Whatever you did is the only thing you could have done. Choosing a change strategy is like deciding what to wear each morning. You can only pick from what you have. But keep in mind your plan for the day.

Q: What Became of These Workplaces Years Later?

A: Four organizations by 2003 were no more. Solcorp disappeared, having no market viability. Sparrows Point Plate Mill, world class at the end, was closed for strategic reasons when Bethlehem Steel acquired another plate mill, and Bethlehem itself went belly-up in 2004. Printing Inc., successful for a long time, had its manufacturing moved to points south for strategic reasons. McCormack & Dodge, despite its success, was merged with a rival and lost its founding CEO. The parent company, having diluted its economic strength, got rid of a merged entity turned albatross.

Two organizations, Chem Corp R& D and Packaging Plant, enjoyed great short-term success from the OD projects and were ongoing successful businesses. Chem Corp, privately held when I was there, went public within a decade. Packaging plant belonged to a global conglomerate. Twenty years after the successful redesign it had headline-making product recalls and shut down for some months for an overhaul. So much for "sustainable change." These were the only ones of my ten cases to have the same (public) ownership two decades after I had worked with them. Both continued to bring consultants in every few years to revisit turf ploughed years before. Successive generations of managers needed to walk their own dogs.

Three organizations—my family firm, Food Services, and AECL Medical Products—were sold and thrived as part of larger companies. In my former family business, the work system I had installed in 1967 metamorphosed after the sale, obeying the laws of ever-more-powerful technologies. In Food Services, manager training and turnover reduction became institutionalized, although not traceable to 1970. Medical Products was reunited with its sister company in a progressive, well-capitalized firm. All three companies had effective employee- and customer-friendly work systems under new management that knew nothing of earlier programs.

Finally, Medical School changed hands twice, survived scandal and economic mayhem, and went from the smallest private school to become the largest in the United States. Thirty years later, faculty involvement in programs and budgets was a legacy of the 1970 project, although hardly anyone knew it.

Q: Do These Cases Represent "Culture Change"?

A: I don't use the term "culture change," thinking it a bit grandiose for workplaces. Still, many others do, so let me attempt a definition congruent with my beliefs. I'm aware from years of Future Searches that one tangible expression of culture is the circle, that ancient symbol of community. In workplaces, people in the circle are those with information, influence, control, power, and respect. Some sit in the inner circle, some the outer, and some hover on the fringe, hoping to be invited in. Here's my practice theory of culture change: make the circle bigger and things get better; make the circle smaller and things get worse.

As more people become involved, the circles get bigger and the potential for making things better increases. For me the simplest example of "culture change" is when people accustomed to sitting in closed circles find themselves asking, "Who else ought to be here?" or "How can we get people with information, expertise, authority, resources, and need all in one conversation?" If you did that repeatedly, it might become "a way of life." That is a formula for designing and maintaining productive workplaces, where dignity, meaning, and community are enacted as people go about creating wealth (business) or spending it for the public good (nonprofit and public sector).

Q: Did the Circles Get Bigger in the Ten Case Examples?

A: In every case, the circle grew bigger for some people. Indeed, as consulting projects expanded from expert problem solving toward involving everyone in improving the whole, more people got into the loop. Eventually, they provided their own data, analysis, and action plans, using structures and processes managed by consultants. The four cases where consultants did the diagnosis and prescription—Food Services, Chem Corp, Packaging Plant, and Solcorp—saw large numbers in the circle during the surveys and interviews and far fewer when it came to action. At Printing Inc. and Medical School, a great many people participated at every step. These projects had considerable impact, the first resulting in a total reorganizing of the work systems, the second in a strategic change of direction and inclusion of enough faculty to avoid splitting the system beyond repair.

The projects at Bethlehem Steel (Chapter Seventeen) and AECL Medical (Chapter Nineteen) involved the most inclusive circles and, perhaps no coincidence, had the most dramatic impact. Both led to significant changes in work processes, labor-management cooperation, using new technologies, and capability to weather quality and market crises. In both cases employee commitment and involvement staved off disaster—for a while.

In this regard I must also cite the Future Searches I have described. These, I think, encapsulate in one event the dynamics required to get everyone on the same page and acting together. Paradoxically, many Future Searches have had greater long-term impact on a system than months or years of more narrowly focused activity such as team building, leadership training, or surveys. I have many theories about why this could happen and no proof that would stand up in a court of science.

Oddly enough, the metaphors I have used to explain this work are more familiar to cultural anthropologists than to management consultants. "Rite of passage," "secular ritual," and "walk around the seasons" are a few. These suggest for me the smallest containers big enough to hold what is easy to see and hard to believe: whole systems moving themselves in three days to new, more balanced ways of functioning. That has happened often enough in communities and organizations to be noted by thousands of people.

Much remains to be learned about these phenomena. Future Search Network has had an ongoing "ripple" research project to document what people did after Future Searches that they couldn't do before. (See the progress report in Weisbord and Janoff, 2010.) Maybe we'll discover we're doing culture change after all.

Q: How Can I Be so Sure That Making the Circle Bigger Has Both Economic and Social Benefits?

A: I enjoyed both benefits as a manager and for many years saw my consulting clients get both, at least for a while. In my family business I saw a 40 percent increase in productivity within six months after starting self-managed teams and great esprit in the workforce. Food Services saved millions of dollars reducing turnover by attending to employee needs. Chem Corp initially took some new products to market in a shorter time; Packaging Plant and Printing Inc. increased production capability; AECL Medical went from years of losses to years of profits; and Medical School did not go broke until it was taken over by a big for-profit corporation with loose ethics. Bethlehem Steel staved off disaster in the short run with unprecedented labor-management cooperation. It could not outrun the exigencies of a globalized steel industry. McCormack & Dodge did well economically while it had control of its destiny and was eaten alive after its parent company merged it with a despised rival. In every case motivated people produced good economic results. They were not achieved by consulting reports.

Q: What Comes After? Are There Natural Limits to This Work?

A: The "environment," that catchall open systems concept, is what constrains us all. The environment got Taylor's ball-bearing company in the 19th Century and it got Bethlehem Steel and Printing Inc. and Solcorp in the 20th Century. That's the shadow side of participative planning. If you set your mind to it, you can get everybody improving whole systems. You know you can do it because thousands of others already have. But when Humpty-Dumpty, good egg to the core—organic, free range, and all that—falls off the wall, smashing to smithereens in the global marketplace, all the king's horses and all the king's men, even with the king's total commitment, cannot put Humpty-Dumpty back together. That too is a tale reinforced by my cases and confirmed dramatically when the dot.com bubble burst in 2001 and dozens of great places to work went under.

Chasing permanence in an impermanent world, then, is as self-defeating as a cat chasing its tail. We cannot stabilize cultural changes any more than we can get the planets to assume different orbits, the Nile to flow south or the Mississippi north. What's the alternative? Doing each day the best you can with what you know is right. "Shucks," say you, "I learned that in grade school!" Well, here at last is a practical application. Any time you include more people and help them to look at the whole before fixing the parts, any time you get people to focus on shared aspirations rather than problems, any time you set it up so people control and coordinate their work, that's a high order of systems change. Repeat this formula daily for as long as you can, and voila, you have "built in" continuity. You have it, that is, until the environment says "enough."

I believe now that getting everyone improving whole systems is an existentially right goal no matter what comes after.

■ ■ ■

"FUTURE SEARCH WAS A GAME-CHANGING METHODOLOGY..."

SAN FRANCISCO, CA—When Marvin Weisbord was preparing the manuscript for *Productive Workplaces* in 1986 and 1987, I was one of several persons at Jossey-Bass Publishers who provided input on the draft manuscript and helped shape it. I was so impressed by Marvin's ideas that I did something book editors seldom do: as soon as the finished book arrived from the printer, I read it again and made four pages of handwritten notes, which I have kept to this day. I was deeply influenced by the ideas and research that this book presented about learning organizations, community, meaningful work, participative decision making, employee involvement and engagement, and numerous other concepts—long before those concepts had become popularized in the management literature. I sought to practice these ideas in my own work as executive vice president and then president of Jossey-Bass Publishers and then subsequently as founder and president of Berrett-Koehler Publishers. And I noticed that thousands of other books that followed by hundreds of different authors picked up on the themes that were first laid out so compellingly in *Productive Workplaces.*

"Future Search"—a pioneering strategic planning, change, and community-building methodology introduced and popularized by *Productive Workplaces*—has had an especially large impact on my thinking and on the organizations in which I have worked. In 1990, when we were seeking the best process to guide strategic planning at Jossey-Bass, we chose to convene a two-day Future Search Conference, and I can still see the impact of that process and event to this day in the culture and strategies of Jossey-Bass, despite the fact that Jossey-Bass has gone through multiple ownership and leadership changes. I was so personally impressed by the ideas that emerged from the 1990 Jossey-Bass Future Search that many of those ideas later became the foundational concepts of Berrett-Koehler Publishers. Then in 2000, and again in 2008, when we sought the best process to guide strategic planning at Berrett-Koehler, Future Search was again our process of choice. The outcomes of those Future Searches were collective insights, plans, and commitments that have not only guided much of what we have done at Berrett-Koehler over the past ten years but that have also provided the orientation and strategies that enabled Berrett-Koehler to survive two very difficult periods (the "dot.com" bust of 2000 and the global economic recession that began in 2007) and emerge stronger on the other side of these challenging periods.

One of the game-changing perspectives that is developed in *Productive Workplaces* and that underlies the Future Search methodology—and that came as a revelation to me—is the concept of identifying all of an organization's stakeholders and then involving all of those stakeholders in strategic planning, organizational change, and major policy setting. In my letter at the front of the first Berrett-Koehler catalog in 1992, I expressed the founding concept of our company as "a deep sense of responsibility to administer the publishing company for the benefit of all of our 'stakeholder' groups—authors, customers, employees, suppliers and subcontractors, owners, and the societal and environmental communities in which we live and work. Each of these groups contributes to the success of our publishing venture, and each has a 'stake' or investment in its success, whether that investment is time, talent, money, or other resources." This continues to be the guiding concept of Berrett-Koehler Publishers, and it came largely from the concepts I learned from *Productive Workplaces* and from Future Search.

—Steven Piersanti, president and publisher,
Berrett-Koehler Publishers, Inc.

chapter
TWENTY FIVE

Changing the World One Meeting at a Time*

"It ain't bragging if you can do it."

—Dizzy Dean, legendary baseball player (1931)

When I imagined "whole system in the room" in 1987 as the structural building block for productivity, I named work design and Future Search the embodiments I knew best. Now you will find more brand name "large group interventions" than cereals in the supermarket. What can you do in large "whole system" groups? Anything you can imagine. You can unite people across great distances, form coalitions, involve communities, merge corporations, raise money, implement strategic plans, reconcile conflicts, manage crises, restructure organizations, and, when you're done for the day, have a swell party with your new friends.

Could this be the new paradigm eagerly heralded for decades? (Or is that social networking?) In their seminal 1997 book, Barbara Bunker and Billie Alban inventoried twelve large-group methods. By 2007, Peggy Holman, Tom Devane, and Steve Cady had collected sixty-one methods and counting. With so much product on the shelves, how do you decide whether

**Author's Note:* I adapted some of this from my chapter "Large Group Interventions—A Shopper's Guide" in the *ASTD Handbook for Workplace Learning* (Biech, 2009).

to grab Appreciative Inquiry, the Conference Model, Future Search, Open Space, Scenario Planning, Whole Scale Change, World Cafe, or to get a private label hybrid devised just for, or by, you? Will you customize a new strategy for each situation, as I did for twenty-two years in the consulting business, or adapt one framework to every context, as I did with Future Search for twenty years after that? There is no right answer. The best process will always be one that energizes you, somebody will pay for, and can attract a crowd.

The Allure of Ever-Larger Groups

Why have large, larger, and still larger "large-group interventions" appealed to so many people? I plead guilty to my role in the unfolding drama. A radical idea in 1987, "getting everybody improving whole systems" seems like a no-brainer now. A century ago Taylor advocated breaking tasks into small chunks. Fifty years ago human relations advocates touted small groups as the solution to everything, while sociotechnical enthusiasts dismissed such activity as touchy-feely. "OD," one of them told me, "is where the rubber meets the air."

In *Productive Workplaces*, I put this cracked Humpty-Dumpty of orientations together through the lens of my own practice. McGregor's *The Human Side of Enterprise* inspired me in the 1960s because, as Peter Vaill (2009) has written, "there were virtually *no* books back then . . . that were both well-grounded in research and theory and written in a readable style with lots of examples." I embraced McGregor because as a manager I was up to my elbows in cost and technology dilemmas that only people could solve. Vaill wrote that McGregor inadvertently did business a disservice by showcasing "the human side" in his title. "There is no other side," he pointed out. As a consultant, I learned that companies made a big mistake shunting off the collateral damage of oppressive work systems to a human resource department for fixing with training programs. Oddly enough, McGregor knew that in the 1940s.

Whether you manage, consult, teach, or research, you are stuck with wondering how to fulfill yourself while seeking to regulate the unstable equilibrium among economics, technology, and people. In your search for excellence, how do you go from good to great, without—like so many organizations I worked with—going from great to gone? You can be forgiven if, in the big-box large-group intervention store, your eyes glaze trying to figure out which aisle has the best meeting methods. There's no way you can sample so many interactive brands when your smart phone is full of meetings with no names at all. Having been a manager, consultant, researcher, and teacher, I can tell you that nobody ever acquired sixty-one methods. Managers swim in a sea of competing claims. Every staff specialist says, "Do my thing first." Publishers push what's new and hot. Researchers study what interests them. Teachers, the good ones, teach what they most want to learn. Consultants offer what they know how to do and what they have passion for (two criteria that, alas, do not always go together like a horse and carriage).

How do you tell vitamins from sugar coating? This becomes easier as you figure out your own values. In Chapter Ten, defining the concept of "equifinality," I told the story of trying to find the perfect way, amidst conflicting claims, to sharpen woodworking chisels. When I posed this to my wife Dorothy, she instantly cut through the fog of competing methods. "The answer is obvious," she said. "They *all* work."

Seeking the best large-group meeting method, you could do worse than heed Dorothy. They all work. Techniques, however, don't care what you do with them. They remain blithely indifferent, even to those who profess undying love. Consequently, they also all fail. I can define failure precisely by telling you about its opposite, success. A meeting succeeds when people do things afterward that they couldn't or wouldn't do before. If that sounds too simple, try this: a successful method helps a system transform its capability for action. This is NOT the same as transforming organizations so that they stay that way. Nobody does that.

Kurt Lewin, who started this top spinning so many decades back, said that to understand an organization, try to change it. Change means doing something you never did before. Indeed, Russell Ackoff, with his gift for lifting the fog of systemic complexity, said that if you want change you have to take risks. You could fail. You can succeed in groups of improbable size in ways that people once considered impossible. You also can waste everybody's time. Simply bringing platoons of people into a room, physical or virtual, will get you nowhere unless you attend to such basics as worthy tasks, the right people, good leadership, adequate resources, and enough time. There is not one thing on that list that is peculiar to the 21st Century. You could have made up the same story one hundred years ago.

Everybody Improves Whole Systems

To ameliorate alienation and get better, faster outcomes, some of us in the 1980s began redesigning systems in a series of large conferences, sixty people and up. This process involved many more people, cutting implementation time from years to months. It was a principled effort to involve people across levels and functions at the same time. Sometimes customers and suppliers came in. I did this at McCormack & Dodge in 1985 and at "Packaging Plant" in 1989. *The Conference Model* (Axelrod and Axelrod, 2000) describes a notable example the authors have used repeatedly.

I came to a liberating conclusion in the mid-1980s. If we wanted workplaces in which productivity rested on a bedrock of dignity, meaning, and community, we ought to figure out how to get *everybody improving whole systems.* Processes that involved everybody in improving the whole seemed to me the design spec for a diverse world of non-stop change. Such methods would make it possible for everybody to (a) use the brains they were born with, (b) bring their experience to bear, (c) appreciate the whole and their part in it, and (d) be capable of taking responsibility.

How to do that became for me the right question. My answer, going back to 1987, required an attractive goal, a leader with an itch to scratch, and some energized people (Chapter Nineteen). I observed a few practices that seemed to make my elusive goal attainable: get the "whole system" in the room; focus on the future rather than the problem list; and set things up so that people could do the work themselves. In *Discovering Common Ground* (1992) I brought together many cases that I thought pointed toward unifying principles for successful large-group methods.

The Future Search model in Chapters Twenty-Two and Twenty-Three is one outgrowth of that inquiry. When large, diverse groups meet, they effectively redefine a system's boundaries. They turn "systems thinking" into an experiential rather than a conceptual activity. People meet those who *are* their environment. Everybody comes to understand the whole in a way that no one person had done before. Thus they empower themselves. Although these are structural interventions, paradoxically, many people voluntarily change their behavior (Weisbord and Janoff, 2007).

Unless "everyone" is present, people may slough off responsibility to those who aren't there. This last point is not trivial. In a contentious meeting of stakeholders in the air traffic system, for example, a participant looked around the room after a few anxious hours and said, "Well, we're all here. If *we* don't fix this system, no one else will do it." So now you have a key criterion for assessing any large-group method, including those not yet invented. To what extent will Method X help you prepare everybody to act responsibly on behalf of the whole? Anything less, and you run the risk of prescribing more of the medicine that makes people cynical. Even that's not enough. You still need to find all the mundane stuff that preceded cyberspace—leadership, resources, and a worthy task that people cannot do alone.

■ ■ ■

"THEY TEND TO BE HIGHLY COLLABORATIVE, PARTICIPATORY, AND INNOVATIVE..."

LOS ANGELES, CA—Before my career in academia, I had worked in real estate sales and marketing and as an HR manager at The Home Depot. In 2006, as a doctoral student, I volunteered to assist with a research study and was told that I needed to read *Productive Workplaces.* I took the book along on a family weekend in Northern Wisconsin, hoping to find a few minutes to page through it. Instead, I couldn't put it down. A weekend intended for hiking, biking, and shopping turned into reading by the water, on the deck, and on the couch.

The ideas in *Productive Workplaces* changed my perspective. I felt at one time that I had sold out my desire to impact the world by fitting into corporate America. I finally let it sink in that it was possible for me to do both. My skills and interests matched what the world's organizations needed—people using system thinking, ready to change the whole.

Soon after, I became involved in researching the effects of Future Search, attended an FS training workshop, adopted the method for my dissertation research, and began collecting quantitative data on corporate leaders who had undertaken Future Searches. I am discovering that they tend to be highly collaborative, participatory, and innovative.

In 2008, I relocated to Los Angeles, where I became the lead faculty and successfully launched a new master's degree program in industrial/organizational psychology for the Chicago School of Professional Psychology. Now, in my work with student services, I utilize many of the strategies of Future Search in higher education.

—Brigit C. Olsen, director of student services at
The Santa Barbara Graduate Institute in
Santa Barbara, California

What Will Work for YOU?

That somebody did miracles with Appreciative Open Strategic Whole Future Conversations (I made that one up, but just wait) tells you nothing about what *you* could do with my imaginary hybrid. If somebody claimed she got a miracle putting all that together, she probably did. For evidence, check the cases in Bunker's and Alban's large-group methods book. They will knock your socks off. I was involved in one of them and, while I contemplate the others with awe, I can't imagine replicating them. Indeed, I'm not sure I could pull off my own high wire act again.

Knowing that something "worked" before leaves me with no more certainty than believing that because a train arrived on time yesterday the same will be true today. The best way to apply any method is with wonder, high tolerance for anxiety, patience, and an open mind. Still, you need not fly blind. Get the basic principles, whatever you believe them to be, firmly fixed in your psyche. That's your insurance policy. Find a good match among, leader, goal, time frame, and procedure. After that, leave it up to the cosmos—and to the people in the room.

Events Versus Processes

Some people worry themselves over whether a conference represents just an "event," rather than something, larger, grander, nobler, and more far-reaching, that is to say, a "process." Only processes, I have heard tell, result in cultural change that will be self-organizing and self-sustaining, making organizational learning a way of life. (I just slipped in five clichés of the change management business. I bet you didn't even notice!)

Having chased that phantasm to the far side of the galaxy and come back empty-handed, I would rather put the energy that goes into debating processes versus events into real work. That means planning and running the best meeting you have in you, every single time, with as many of the right people as you can squeeze into the best room you can find. Do such events periodically with intention, and, voila, you have a process.

That is a path anyone can choose if he has the authority. What happens after each meeting will depend on who is willing to take responsibility and what resources they have. No matter how much you preplan, such matters are unknowable until people do things purposefully that they didn't used to do.

What You Do Today Resonates Everywhere

Why the proliferation of interactive large groups in the 2000s? Eric Trist observed decades ago that workplace innovations had lives of their own. They rarely spread within the companies that pioneered them. The team-based General Foods pet food factory in Kansas outperformed but did not influence its conventional sibling in Illinois for decades (see Chapter Twenty-Three). Somehow, word of its success got around, and many distant workplaces emulated it. There is a term for this phenomenon—"morphic resonance"—that, despite my distaste for jargon, I like very much. It was coined by Rupert Sheldrake (1989), the molecular biologist and maverick scientist, to describe how (perhaps) things change all by themselves.

Take flying. For thousands of years people aspired to soar like birds. Nobody could do it until the brothers Wright built the right machine and learned to use it. After that nearly anyone could fly. Until Roger Bannister ran a mile in under four minutes in 1954, that feat was thought beyond human limits. Now countless others have done it. In 2009 a bear in New York State's Adirondack Mountains taught itself to open campers' complex "bear proof" food storage containers. In no time many formerly stymied bears were cracking the safe and helping themselves to peanut butter and jelly (Foderero, 2009).

So it is with workplace innovations. Margaret Wheatley (2006) was among the first to show the inherent potential and the beautiful order that exists amid apparent confusion. Before "chaos theory" became management lingo, most people were skeptical of large crowds voluntarily interacting, sharing information, planning, and committing to action. As more people learn to do something, however, it becomes easier for others, even without prior exposure. The capability travels through space and time by processes not well understood, although you can see the results. When we say a trend is "in the air" we are talking about morphic resonance. By the end of the 20th Century, many colleagues and I came to understand the transformative power of "the whole system in the room."

We recognized that inviting the right people to an interactive meeting, something the average person could do without training, opened the door to constructive, time-efficient actions that no one could plan, program, or specify as "deliverables." The more we did it, the easier it was for others. As a result, tens of thousands of people who once had the word "meeting" equate with "frustration" had attended highly productive forums. They had learned first-hand the action potential of what Wheatley called a "self-organizing system." Paradoxically, in an age of shorter, faster, cheaper, the shortest, fastest, cheapest starting place for improving workplaces was a room with a "whole system" in it.

Technology, Again

In the five decades that I have been on this quest, I have learned to work comfortably with groups of a few hundred without resorting to electronics beyond the cordless microphone. I consider myself a technological illiterate in this age of multi-tasking, even though I have lived long enough to see Chloe and Isabel, two of my granddaughters, sitting on the same couch text messaging each other while watching TV and doing their homework.

The integration of the Internet, television, the telephone, art, music, literature, science, blogging, and social networking has made possible astounding interactions. Thanks to morphic resonance, you can work with hundreds or even thousands of people if you have the time, resources, and technology. In every meeting we have more resources a mouse click away than our ancestors could mobilize in a lifetime. People are now experimenting with simultaneous online meetings around the globe, some participants in the same room, others sitting alone. There seems no end to the permutations. Consider, for example, the BBC's involving seventeen thousand people in a drive to make their company the most creative in the world using every known form of interaction (Cheung-Judge and Powley, 2006).

And yet, and yet . . . nobody I know claims that interacting at a distance makes a wholly satisfying substitute for meetings in the flesh. The most successful large-group interventions, now and later, I believe, will involve both forms. Many more methods exist now than did in 1987, making it hard to choose among them. You can sail this sea of possibility to uncharted new worlds. You also can drown in it. I can tell you with the confidence born of decades of chasing rainbows to the far horizon that you will not be able to absorb, let alone use, the proliferating workplace change library. Every method has in it a lifetime of somebody's experience. By the time you master one new trick, people the world over have devised a dozen more. Fortunately, you only need a few good methods to grow on. Seek out the ones that excite you. Then look for places where people resonate to what you know how to do.

Our ancestors gave us priceless gifts, but none has prepared us for a world beyond the Internet, virtual teams, and inedible BlackBerries. I am too much of a historian to imagine that today's trendiest large-group methods are the end of history. Every method has its limits, as we all are destined to learn. More to the point, we live in a global economy that is consuming resources at a rate far beyond our ability to replace them.

Indeed, sustainable organizations have no future in an unsustainable world of our own making.

The future of our organizations, communities, nations, and planet does not rest on particular methods. It lies with what we do every day. With large-group methods, we have the capability to screw up on a grand scale. We can choose to run meetings of any size with key people missing in time frames so short that more meetings are unavoidable, closeted in dungeon rooms that deplete body, mind, and spirit. We can perpetuate the practice of having experts talk at people followed by questions but never action commitments. We can treat anxiety and chaos as problems to be solved rather than the context for productive work.

We also can involve everybody in improving the whole. For most of us the only way we ever will change the world is one meeting at a time. If you can't make a difference every day, what difference will it make if you put it off to tomorrow?

■ ■ ■

"I STARTED BY LOOKING FOR OBSERVABLE SUCCESS FACTORS..."

VLIJMEN, NETHERLANDS—I drew heavily on *Productive Workplaces* for my research into working with "the whole system in the room" after meeting Marvin in South Africa at a Future Search Network workshop and Learning Exchange. The diagram below is the result of my research at Tilburg University on observable success factors in methods such as Future Search, Open Space, World Café, and Real Time Strategic Change. The question I asked was "When and how do what I call Large Scale Interventions (LSI) lead to sustainable change?" *Productive Workplaces Revisited* provided me with valuable input. The diagram shows how LSI principles produce a web of conditions and characteristics of a change process with "the whole system in the room." The diagram also indicates when conditions are not met and you should say "no" to LSI, thus forming the bases for practical guidelines.

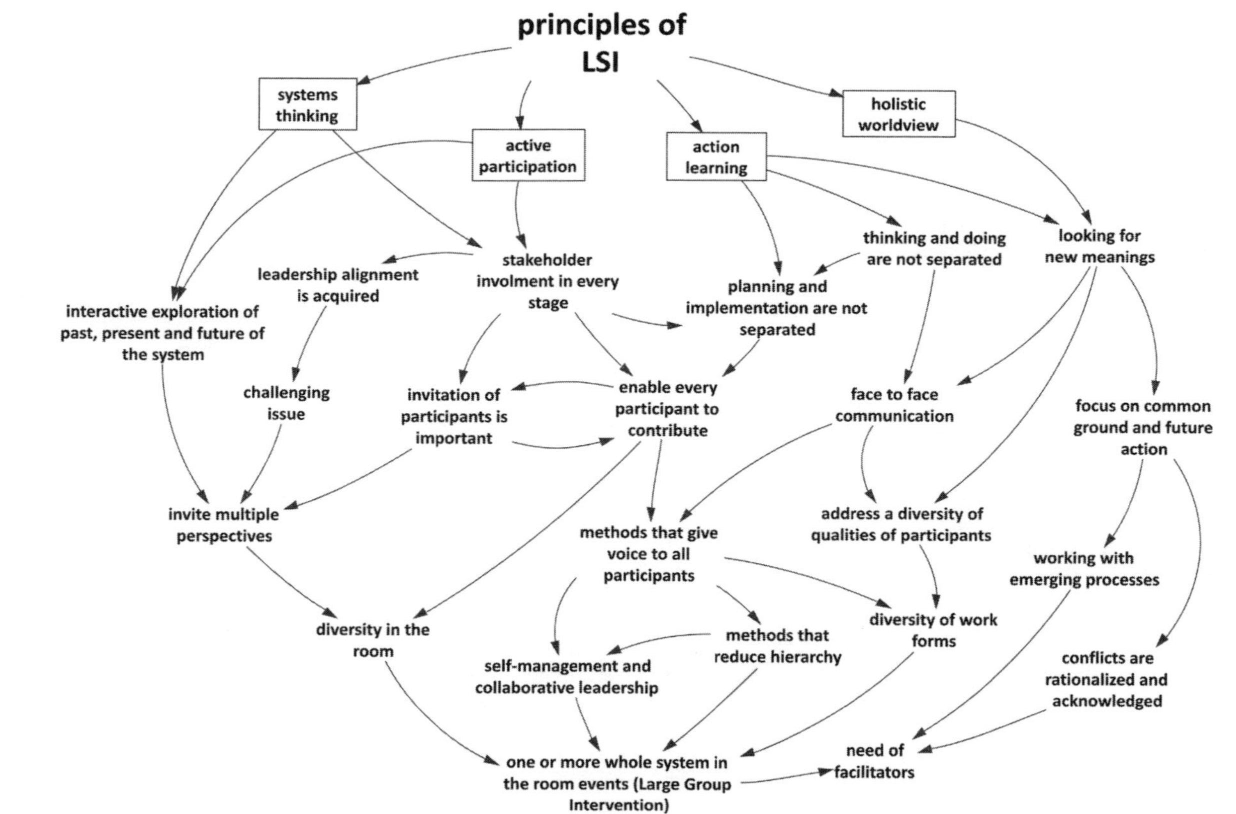

Source: Tonnie Van der Zouwen. Used with author's permission.

Productive Workplaces inspired me to write up my doctoral research as an invitation to discuss LSI dilemmas frankly in order to learn how to deal with them better. I sought to create a practical guide for organizational change with LSI that that does not offer a "how to" empirical model nor recipes for specific methods.

—Tonnie Van der Zouwen, Ph.D., Van der Zouwen Consultancy, author of *Building an Evidence Based Practical Guide to Large Scale Interventions: Towards Sustainable Change with the Whole System*

chapter
TWENTY SIX

The Future Never Comes, It's Already Here

"Can't help but wonder where I'm bound."

—Tom Paxton, folk singer, 1963

When people ask me about the future of the work I have done for the last fifty years, my thoughts go to *The Experts Speak* (Cerf and Navasky, 1984). Here you learn that Wilbur Wright wrote his brother Orville in 1901, two years before doing it, that "man will not fly for fifty years." The British physicist Lord Kelvin proclaimed X-rays "a hoax" in 1907, the managing editor of *Scientific American* told readers in 1913 it was unlikely airplanes would ever carry more than seven passengers, and Albert Einstein in 1932 declared nuclear energy unobtainable. Thomas Watson, IBM's founder, predicted the world market for computers would not exceed five, and *Popular Mechanics* in 1949 assured readers that computers would be reduced in size from 30,000 to just 1,000 vacuum tubes. Darryl F. Zanuck, head of 20th Century Fox Studios, was certain in the late 1940s that "video will not be able to hold onto any market it captures after the first six months." The British Astronomer Royal called space travel "utter bilge" in 1956, and Henry Ford II in 1957 assured his dealers that "the Edsel is here to stay."

In this book in 1987, I quoted Shell Oil's erstwhile futurist Peter Schwartz imagining a long period of stability after the turbulent 1970s. Well, don't bet on it. Stability for decades has been as elusive as rainfall in the Sahara. The longest economic boom in recent memory ended for the United States with the collapse of technology companies just after 2000. There followed earthshaking corporate bankruptcies, notably Enron and WorldCom, driven by deceit, fraud, and mismanagement. By 2008 the whole world, after a housing mortgage scandal and rampant shady banking practices, entered a long recession. Nobody controlled the global marketplace. Indeed, nobody, it seemed, controlled the global corporations. Insatiable for quarterly dividends, some firms substituted dubious accounting for accountability.

Global terrorism became a fact of life, affecting the security and economy of every nation. People were adopting a raft of new technologies—in the arts, biotechnology, communications, education, entertainment, genetics, health care, media, recreation, and warfare—adding great complexity to daily life. Corporations began accepting that green is good for business. Politicians were paralyzed by public debt. Such was the "present" situation informing the work world.

What comes next?

Let me tell you about the future as I have experienced it for the last fifty years. The future never comes. Today is the future you imagined yesterday. It's slipping into the past by the second. When Frederick Taylor was born in 1857, every story in this book lay in the future. Now all are past. You cannot guarantee that what you wish for will happen. Improving companies, NGOs, and communities can be existentially satisfying work if you avoid the megalomania of believing you build for the ages. There are no "secrets," whether from Attila the Hun, Socrates, Joan of Arc, Machiavelli, Freud, Mother Teresa, or Vince Lombardi, that you do not already know. Leave tomorrow to the cosmos. Today's work requires every ounce of energy you have.

Leftover Questions

We have plenty to keep us busy with so many unanswered questions on the right balance among economics, technology, and people in a political democracy; about the difference between authority, essential for security, and authoritarianism, which threatens our survival; about what sort of meal satisfies the hunger for community, dignity, and meaning; about the limits of fast-changing technologies in a world gone global and virtual at the same time; about our positive and negative inner voices tugging us between grit-your-teeth denial and purposeful involvement; about the unique contributions each of us can make. In these closing pages I want to indicate some paths we can take, would take, will take *now* if we care about the future of our workplaces and our planet.

The Virtual Work World. I cannot tell yet all the implications of virtual work and 24/7 tensions between work and family life (Chapter Twenty-One). I'm aware of efforts to put large-group methods on the Internet. Virtual meeting technology enables tens of thousands of people to interact. I believe people in such meetings have the same dynamic issues as those who meet face-to-face, without the safety valve of socializing between sessions. Increasingly people are on their own to meet needs for wholeness, health, and balance in their lives.

By 2000, the work/family tensions virtual teams were experiencing also bedeviled those who serve them. Working in Bangalore with Indian call center staffers supporting computer users in the United States, I heard one say, "I have to take an American name and practice an American accent. I eat fast food all night at my desk, and when I get home in the morning, I don't know who I am!" He and his wife worked long hours and spent their high incomes on TVs and other appliances rarely used. That experience led me to wonder whether the old paradigm sweatshop, largely discredited in the United States, was simply being exported. The customers may have been freed by technology. The service providers may be imprisoned by it. To what extent will people in the world's back office and service centers in Africa, Asia. India, and the Philippines be able to design their own work systems?

People in the Middle. There remains the peculiar plight of redundant people caught in a time warp between paradigms. In 1987, this was each organization's dilemma. Today it is a global phenomenon. Thirty years ago Fred Emery (1980, p. 20) pointed out that any scheme for democratizing factory work is "fraudulent" if it leaves in place that pillar of authoritarianism, the role of foreman. Traditional supervision may be the buggy whip of the 21st Century. It's time to supplement supervisory training with training in self-management. Who needs better buggy whips?

I suggest three tough principles that cast some (admittedly dim) light on this rocky path:

- *Principle 1:* Secure employment is the bedrock of viable organizations. As I write, this is a global problem with no centralized solutions. Work redesign means fewer people have better jobs and produce more. Loyal people who did their best and find the game changed deserve the means and emotional support to obtain new roles and skills.
- *Principle 2:* We ought not be deterred from participative work redesign and a search for new technologies and markets just because those in charge have not done it before. We ought not preserve the special status, autocratic style, or expert turf of holdouts at the cost of motivation, commitment, and growth for 90 percent of a workforce.
- *Principle 3:* There are no sure things, only sure values. If you lead, you have to take a stand without a crystal ball. I remember Don Thompson's admonition to managers when he was an operations vice president managing a shift toward employee-managed work teams. "This thing is a steamroller," he said. "It's a benevolent steamroller. It's only going three miles an hour. If you go five miles an hour you can stay ahead of it. If you go eight miles an hour you can even stop for a beer. But if you only go two, it's going to flatten you."

We are in the midst of an unstoppable historic shift from global competition to cooperation. You can approach it as a workplace warrior, firing and laying off to cut costs (economics), imposing innovations unilaterally (technology), and manipulating decisions already made to "make people feel involved" (human relations). That's the old paradigm, making things worse for all who invoke it.

The new paradigm, I think, will one day be understood as a revolutionary turning point in human history—from expert problem solving circa 1900 to everybody improving whole systems in this millennium. We have been slow to recognize how quickly this strategy is replacing the old one in the workplace, just as automobiles once replaced horses and buggies.

If you believe in involving everybody, you face profound paradoxes. We move, for example, by verbalizing reservations. But skepticism gets you tagged a "change resister." To make it safe for people to voice skepticism, we have to resist calling people resisters. In Taylor's time, making resistance the engineers' problem did not work. In our time, making it the human resource manager's problem still doesn't work.

Change Is Everybody's Fate. It's a reality to face, not a problem to solve. How can we learn to

1. Treat each person as an adult capable of sharing risks and entitled to share rewards?
2. Involve people in creating their own choices instead of offering a week's notice and an outplacement counselor as the outer limits of practicality?
3. Accept individual and corporate responsibility for inventing alternative paths, new economic activity, to reduce the anxiety released by the disappearance of old machinery, markets, and jobs?

Participation is not enough unless all participate. My dilemma includes mountains of evidence that having groups represented helps only the representatives—and not as much as they would like. It has been known for decades—from Israel, Scandinavia, Yugoslavia, and West Germany—that putting workers on boards of directors and worker ownership does not reduce worker apathy or increase output where people do narrow jobs under traditional supervisors (Bucklow, 1966).

Representation in planning enhances democracy. It is not sufficient for productive workplaces. Each person needs real tasks that make a contribution to the whole, a form of democracy still being invented. I believe all of society benefits when people improve whole systems; if you tell me my aspirations are impractical, I can only reply that so was flying before 1903.

Training—When and Where? I installed self-managing teams in the 1960s before I knew anything about training. Fifty-plus years and hundreds of workshops later, I know a lot about training. I wish I could tell you how much is the right amount, or when to do it, or even whether to. For years I found myself too soon or too late. Not only that, but the trainees usually said the wrong people were in the room. I admired Eileen Curtin's ability (see Chapter Twelve) to mix purposeful focus, training, and problem solving so skillfully in a work redesign that people learned just what they needed exactly when they could use it. That is an art I wish I could tie a ribbon around and give to each reader who sends in a postcard. (I wrote that in 1987. Now, I would attach it in response to an email.)

Instead, I leave you with a paradox. We need the best methods we can find for learning new skills. Unless our learning is self-motivated, we are unlikely to use it. Training needs to be voluntary, jointly entered into by people who work together, and safe in the sense that people will not be compromised by others' judgments of them. In short, make it a joint venture between trainees and trainers—a difficult though not impossible move. Putting everybody through this or that program satisfies certain needs. Building productive workplaces is not one of them.

What Managers and Consultants Are Learning to Do

Here is a lifelong agenda for managers and consultants committed to satisfying work and outstanding results:

- Involve others in designing their work.
- Advocate quality and customer service.
- Get rid of dumb jobs.
- Help people make a contribution as well as a living.
- Encourage diversity of people and ideas.
- Be involvers, facilitators, keepers of the learning environment.
- Help others take stands on important economic and technology issues—even when they disagree.
- Hold interactive stakeholder meetings, across levels and departments, and with customers and suppliers.
- Walk the line between too much and too little structure.
- Search for new economic opportunities and secure jobs.
- Live with and accept their own positive and negative voices.
- Help others build power bases, learn skills, talk to one another on equal footing across all cultural and ethnic boundaries.

- Use the whole brain—intuition, values, experience, and rational problem solving.
- Let go the need to know everything; help people write their own textbooks.
- Accept the need for stability and the inevitability of change.

And a hundred other things we forgot, or never knew, and have yet to learn.

Working in Workplaces Means Working on Yourself

I once had a piano teacher who reiterated the same simple lessons year after year: practice; listen. You can never do enough of either. So too you can never have too much self-knowledge.

Risks. You face enormous risks in reaching far. Every stretch toward dignity, meaning, and community is shadowed by what my friend William Schmidt called "the fraughts." Fraught means "burdened," teeming," "weighted," "charged," "loaded." Every business is fraught with the temptation to exploit its workforce on behalf of its shareholders, with manipulating middle managers to preserve power at the top, with technocrats driving people to exclude all else but work from their lives, and with leaders holding on for dear life to a pyramid of status and power independent of results. There is a fine line between exploits and exploitation. I am troubled each time I see companies unilaterally go for layoffs ahead of using their human capital to search out alternatives. I believe 21st-Century managers should embrace methods that hand people back their lives.

Working on Ourselves. I think our limiting assumptions go beyond economics to the negative voices buried in each of us. Profit is far from the only driving force in business. The desire to control, to maintain hierarchy, is so strong that some executives reduce profits to keep their worst assumptions intact. Conversely, freedom may not be the only motive for those who resist structure and commitment. Creating more ambiguity when there is already too much is a subtle bid for control more insidious than authoritarianism. There is a lifetime of personal work for each of us in contacting the shadow side of our natures, integrating the voices that tug us away from creative and humane impulses. We're never finished, and the right time to do it is every day.

Political Democracy and New Technologies

> I know of no safe depository of the ultimate powers of the society but the people themselves, and if we think them not enlightened enough to exercise their control with a wholesome discretion, the remedy is not to take it from them, but to inform their discretion.
>
> —Thomas Jefferson, September 28, 1820

Mediating between us and our personal tensions, we have a democratic political system more than two hundred years old in the United States, a few centuries older in Great Britain, and relatively new to most of the world. Core values of free expression, mutual influence, equity, rationality, and acceptance of differences came to the New World centuries ago.

Thomas Jefferson asserted the worth and dignity of each person as "unalienable" (meaning no one can take them away). He affirmed universal rights to "life, liberty, and the pursuit of happiness" in the Declaration of Independence—the bedrock symbol of U.S. culture. You can read the American Revolution as an ongoing action-research experiment to find a better fit in human society between personal and community needs. What makes the experiment possible is freedom of expression guaranteed by the First Amendment to the U.S. Constitution. Has any society ever sought to reconcile through political equality so many differences across cultures, classes, races, genders, hierarchies, institutions, and vast geography?

What expectations were created! Does it startle you that workers have low commitment to workplaces where they have little to say about their jobs? Were high expectations built by social scientists studying motivation? Or were we socialized to them from kindergarten on, studying the exploits of America's founders? Is it surprising that the central issue of productivity has often been framed as the tension between authoritarian and participative leadership? That's how American revolutionaries defined their conflict with crazy King George III.

The fact that free expression, mutual responsibility, self-control, and employee involvement in work design are associated with higher output, lower stress, and more viable businesses is as much a tribute to democracy as to social science. Frederick Taylor saw the fruitlessness of dictatorial managers and supervisors. Taylor had himself be a peacemaker. He thought rational work systems would cut out abuses of authority common in 19th-Century factories. That his system could not sustain its intentions shows how our baser impulses—control, greed, mechanistic thinking—may trump dignity, meaning, and community when people don't pay attention.

Authority, Not Authoritarianism. We need authority in organizations and communities, people competent to say "yes" or "no." We suffer under authoritarianism—the willful, uninformed exercise of power. In the workplace we need modes consistent with democratic values and more efficient than democratic governments. Perhaps the United States' unique contribution to 21st-Century management is to do business in ways that preserve individual freedom, enhance community, support innovation in methods and markets, and provide each person engaging work. Other nations may inspire us, but the culture we have to work with is peculiarly our own. We have a lot to learn from abroad and a lot to offer. However, no systems exempt us from human failings. Democracy is a way of being easily abused.

For these reasons, I have a hard time calling transforming organizations "cultural change." The values I speak for—a voice in policy, openness, trust, controlling your own work—represent cultural conservation, holding on to what we value most. Company cultures have been compromised by abuses of technology, bureaucracy, and authority. Democratic values came on sailing ships a long time before. We conserve our culture when we seek to extend these values in the workplace, to keep open a creative dialogue between individualism and the common good.

Democracy Takes Learning. Democracy is a tough way to live. With all its flaws, I think it beats the alternatives. I do not wish to have someone else—educated, well-intentioned, wealthy, or wise—decide unilaterally what is best for me. Unless we are deeply involved in our work, we cannot feel good about ourselves. Unless we work with others toward valued goals, we cannot infuse hope and aspiration into our lives. Unless we treat one another as equals, we cannot find satisfaction in work. Unless we make our own mistakes, and learn to forgive ourselves, we cannot learn at all. Unless we cooperate, we cannot survive.

If we care about the future, we must learn to care more about economics and technology, to understand their social uses and abuses here and now. Workplace improvement—viability in world markets—requires that each person learn to accept personal customer responsibility and interdependence with many others. Hundreds, maybe thousands, of organizations have publicly acknowledged that need and are learning the behavior that goes with it.

The Time Is Now

Frederick Taylor observed a century ago that everyone noticed the waste of water, forests, coal, and iron, but not the waste of human capability—acts of "blundering, ill-directed, or inefficient" behavior, appreciation of which "calls for an act of memory, an effort of the imagination" (1915, p. 5).

Now appreciation calls for imagining the unimaginable—the interconnectedness of every last thing under the sun. In choosing to write about dignity, meaning, and community in the workplace, I am uncomfortably aware that we cannot sustain productive work apart from our lives as members of an endangered species on an endangered planet. The whole world is our community. We have become more sophisticated about Taylor's issue: awareness of human resources. We have a long way to go to tie together forests, water, soil, coal, iron, and newer natural resources like oil, gas, sun, wind, and hydrogen with the infinite capacity of the human brain wed to the computer. In chemical wastes, in acid rain, in greenhouse gasses, we have set up our own end game. Only by playing it cooperatively can we hope to win. No boss, no leader, no expert, no person, no group, no company, no nation, no continent can go it alone.

My favorite "Peanuts" cartoon has Good Ole Charlie Brown saying, "I wish I was four years old again knowing what I know now." Would I plunge again into the projects in this book, knowing that for most the half-life would be an eye blink in human history? Yes, I would do them all again knowing—as could anyone who takes on the awesome task of improving systems—that "outcomes" in a sea of non-stop change are as short-lived as butterflies in summer.

I would do this work again because I believe that:

- Dialogue and inquiry are good for us.
- Humane workplaces enjoy greater economic success.
- Helping people gain control of their work engenders hope, and we need hope to get by.
- It is existentially right to encourage cooperation—social, technical, and economic—across lines of age, class, culture, education, ethnicity, gender, national borders, race, status, and occupation.

Finally, I would do this work again for the sake of future generations. Getting everyone improving the whole is a legacy from the ancestors honored in these pages. It continues in the stories by my colleagues, who have made themselves part of that history. Our descendants richly deserve this legacy. In workplaces of the future, actual or virtual, I believe it is the only one they are likely to find worth inheriting.

REFERENCES

Ackoff, R. L. *Redesigning the Future: A Systems Approach to Societal Problems.* Hoboken, NJ: John Wiley & Sons, 1974.

Ackoff, R. L. "The Corporate Rain Dance." *The Wharton Magazine,* 1977, *1* (2), 36–41.

Ackoff, R. L. *Creating the Corporate Future: Plan or Be Planned For.* Hoboken, NJ: John Wiley & Sons, 1981.

Ackoff, R. L. *The Democratic Corporation: A Radical Prescription for Recreating Corporate America and Rediscovering Success.* New York: Oxford University Press, 1994.

Aguren, S., and others. *Volvo Kalmar Revisited: Ten Years of Experience.* Stockholm: Efficiency and Participation Development Council, 1984.

Argyris, C. *Intervention Theory and Method.* Reading, MA: Addison-Wesley, 1970.

Argyris, C. "Actionable Knowledge: Intent Versus Actuality." *Journal of Applied Behavioral Science, 32,* 1996, pp. 441–444.

Argyris, C., and Schön, D. A. *Organizational Learning: A Theory of Action Perspective.* Reading, MA: Addison-Wesley, 1978.

Axelrod, E. M., and Axelrod, R. H. *Collaborating for Change: The Conference Model.* San Francisco: Berrett-Koehler, 2000.

Axelrod, R. H. *Terms of Engagement: Changing the Way We Change Organizations* (2nd ed.). San Francisco: Berrett-Koehler, 2010.

Bartlett, J. (ed.) *Familiar Quotations.* (E. M. Beck, ed.) Boston: Little, Brown, 1980.

Baum, L. F. *The Wizard of Oz.* New York: Grosset & Dunlap, 1900 (Reprinted 1958, New York: Scholastic, Inc.).

Beckhard, R. *Organization Development: Strategies and Models.* Reading, MA: Addison-Wesley, 1969.

Beckhard, R., and Harris, R. T. *Organizational Transitions: Managing Complex Change.* Reading, MA: Addison-Wesley, 1977.

Biech, E. (ed.). *ASTD Handbook for Workplace Learning Professionals.* Arlington, VA: ASTD Press, 2008.

Bellah, R. N., and others. *Habits of the Heart: Individualism and Commitment in American Life.* Berkeley and Los Angeles: University of California Press, 1985.

Bendix, R. *Work and Authority in Industry.* Hoboken, NJ: John Wiley & Sons, 1956.

Benne, K. "The Processes of Re-Education: An Assessment of Kurt Lewin's Views." *Group & Organization Studies,* March 1976, *1* (1), 26–42. (Presented June 28, 1971, at Central Connecticut State University, New Britain, Connecticut.)

Bennis, W. G. *Changing Organizations.* New York: McGraw-Hill, 1966.

Bennis, W. G. "Chairman Mac in Perspective." *Harvard Business Review,* Sept./Oct. 1972, *50* (5), 139–143.

Bennis, W. G. *On Becoming a Leader* (4th ed.). New York: Basic Books, 2009.

Bennis, W. G., Benne, K. D., and Chin, R. *The Planning of Change* (2nd ed.). New York: Holt, Rinehart & Winston, 1969.

Bennis, W. G., and Schein, E. H. (eds.). *Leadership and Motivation: Essays of Douglas McGregor.* Cambridge, MA: MIT Press, 1966.

Bion, W. R. *Experience in Groups and Other Papers.* London: Tavistock, 1961.

Blake, R. R., and Mouton, J. S. *The Managerial Grid.* Houston, TX: Gulf, 1964.

Blanchard, K., and Johnson, S. *The One-Minute Manager.* New York: Morrow, 2003.

Block, P. *The Empowered Manager: Positive Political Skills at Work.* San Francisco: Jossey-Bass, 1991.

Block, P. *Flawless Consulting* (3rd ed.). San Francisco: Pfeiffer, 2011.

Bounds, C. "Senge's Fifth Discipline: An Evaluation of Its Impact on Education," http://cbounds.wordpress.com/2009/07/08/senges-fifth-discipline-an-evaluation-of-its-impact-on-education/.

Bowers, D. G., and Franklin, J. L. *Survey-Guided Development I: Data-Based Organizational Change.* San Diego, CA: University Associates, 1977.

Bradford, D. L., and Cohen, A. R. *Managing for Excellence: The Guide to Developing High Performance in Contemporary Organizations.* Hoboken, NJ: John Wiley & Sons, 1984.

Bradford, L., Gibb, J. R., and Benne, K. D. *T-Group Theory and Laboratory Method: Innovation in Re-Education.* Hoboken, NJ: John Wiley & Sons, 1964.

Brand, S. "The World Information Economy: An Interview with Peter Schwartz and Jay Ogilvy." *Whole Earth Review,* Winter 1986, pp. 88–97.

Brown, J., and Isaacs, D. *The World Cafe: Shaping Our Futures Through Conversations That Matter.* San Francisco: Berrett-Koehler, 2005.

Braverman, H. "Labour and Monopoly Capital." New York: Monthly Review Press, 1974.

Bridges, W. *Transitions: Making Sense of Life's Changes.* Reading, MA: Addison-Wesley, 1980.

Bridges, W. "How to Manage Organizational Transition." *Training*, Sept. 1985, pp. 28–32.

Bucklow, M. "A New Role for the Work Group." *Administrative Science Quarterly*, June 1966, *1* (1), 59–78.

Bunker, B. B., and Alban, B. T. *Large Group Interventions: Engaging the Whole System for Rapid Change.* San Francisco: Jossey-Bass, 1997.

Bunker, B. B., and Alban, B. T. *The Handbook of Large Group Methods: Creating Systemic Change in Organizations and Communities.* San Francisco: Jossey-Bass, 2006.

Bunker, K., and Santana, L. C. "The Learning Premise: A Conversation with Peter B. Vaill." Chapter 2 in K. Bunker, D. T. Hall, and K. Kram (eds.), Extraordinary *Leadership: Addressing the Gaps in Senior Executive Development.* San Francisco: Jossey-Bass, 2010.

Burck, G. "Union Carbide's Patient Schemers." *Fortune*, Dec. 1965, pp. 147–149.

Burke, W. W. *Organization Development: Principles and Practices.* Boston: Little, Brown, 1982.

Buzan, T. *Use Both Sides of Your Brain.* New York: Dutton, 1974.

Bylinsky, G. "What Tomorrow Holds." *Fortune*, Oct. 13, 1986, pp. 42–44.

Cartwright, D. "Kurt Lewin, 1890–1947." *International Journal of Opinion and Attitude Research*, 1947, *1*, 96–99.

Caruso, D. B. "Retirees to Fight Cutoff of Benefits." *The Philadelphia Inquirer*, March 24, 2003, p. B3.

Caruso, D. B. "Bethlehem Steel Asset Sale Okd." *The Philadelphia Inquirer*, April 23, 2003, p. C3.

Cascio, W. *Responsible Restructuring: Creative and Profitable Alternatives to Layoffs.* San Francisco: Berrett-Koehler, 2002.

Castle, P. "PS Restructuring Signals Greater Opportunities for Satisfaction in Workplace." *Canberra Times*, "The Circus" column, May 10, 1986.

Cerf, C., and Navasky, V. S. *The Experts Speak: The Authoritative Compendium of Misinformation.* New York: Pantheon Books, 1984.

Chase, S. "An Authentic Genius." *The New Republic*, Oct. 8, 1924, reprinted in *Bulletin of the Taylor Society*, Feb. 1925, *10* (1), 66–68.

Checkland, P. *Systems Thinking, Systems Practice.* Chichester, UK: John Wiley & Sons, 1981.

Cheung-Judge, M., and Powley, E. H. "Innovation at the BBC: Engaging an Entire Organization." In B. B. Bunker and B. T. Alban (2006), *The Handbook of Large Group Methods: Creating Systemic Change in Organizations and Communities* (pp. 45–61). San Francisco: Jossey-Bass.

Clapp, N., and others. *The Selected Wisdom of New Jersey.* Plainfield, NJ: Block Petrella Weisbord Designed Learning, Inc., 1975.

Clarkson, M. "Search Conferences." Paper presented at the International Quality of Working Life Conference, Toronto, August 1981.

Coch, L., and French, J. R. P., Jr. "Overcoming Resistance to Change." *Human Relations*, 1948, *1*, 512–533.

Cohen, A. "Too Old to Work?" *New York Times Magazine*, March 2, 2003, pp. 54–59.

Cohen, M. D., and March, J. G. "Leadership in an Organized Anarchy." *Leadership and Ambiguity: The American College President.* New York: McGraw-Hill, 1974.

Collins, J. C. *Good to Great.* New York: HarperCollins, 2001.

Collins, J. C., and Porras, J. I. *Built to Last: Successful Habits of Visionary Companies.* New York: Harper, 1997.

Cooperrider, D., Whitney, D., Anderson, H., McNamee, S., Gergen, M., and Gergen, K. J. *Appreciative Organization.* Taos, NM: Taos Institute Publications, 2001.

Copley, F. B. *Frederick W. Taylor: Father of Scientific Management.* 2 vols. New York: Harper & Row, 1923.

Cousins, N. "What You Believe Can Have an Effect on Your Health." *U.S. News & World Report*, Jan. 23, 1984, pp. 61–62.

Dannemiller-Tyson Associates. *Whole-Scale Change: Unleashing the Magic in Organizations.* San Francisco: Berrett-Koehler, 2000.

Davis, L. E. "Job Design Research." *Journal of Industrial Engineering*, Nov./Dec. 1957.

Davis, L. E., Canter, R. R., and Hoffman, J. E. "Current Job Design Criteria." *Journal of Industrial Engineering*, 1955, *6*, 5–11.

Davis, L. E., and Sullivan, C. S. "A Labor-Management Contract and the Quality of Working Life." *Journal of Occupational Behavior*, 1980, *1*, 29–41.

de Geus, A. *The Living Company.* London: Nicholas Brealey, 1997.

de Renzy-Martin, P. Executive Vice President, Shell Solar, www.shell.com. News Release, October 24, 2002.

Dean, Dizzy. www.quotationsbook.com/author/1931/ April 2007.

Deming, W. E. *Quality, Productivity and Competitive Position.* Cambridge, MA: MIT Press, 1982.

Drucker, P. F. *Management: Tasks, Responsibilities, Practices.* New York: Harper & Row, 1974. (Rev. ed. New York: HarperCollins, 2008.)

Drucker, P. F. "The Coming Rediscovery of Scientific Management." *The Conference Board Record*, June 1976, pp. 23–27.

Drury, H. B. *Scientific Management: A History and Criticism.* New York: Columbia University Press, 1915.

Dunn, W. N., and Swierzek, F. W. "Planned Organizational Change: Toward Grounded Theory." *Journal of Applied Behavioral Science*, 1977, *2* (13), 135–157.

Dunnette, M. D. "People Feeling: Joy, More Joy, and the Slough of Despond." *Journal of Applied Behavioral Science*, 1969, *5*, 25–44.

Dupre, J. Former Director of Organization Development, Mattel, Inc. Unpublished manuscript, 2010.

Ebbin, R. "Turnover Takes a Turn for the Better." *Restaurants USA*, March 1999.

Egon Zehnder International. Report of survey noted in *Forbes*, June 30, 1986, p. 9.

Elden, M. "Three Generations of Work Democracy Experiments in Norway: Beyond Classical Socio-Technical Analysis." Institute for Industrial Social Research, Technical University of Trondheim, Norway, 1978.

Elden, M. "Client as Consultant: Work Reform Through Participative Research." *National Productivity Review*, Spring 1983a, pp. 136–147.

Elden, M. "Democratization and Participative Research in Developing Local Theory." *Journal of Occupational Behavior*, 1983b, *4*, 21–33.

Emery, F. E. "Characteristics of Socio-Technical Systems." London: Tavistock Documents #527. Abridged in F. E. Emery, *The Emergence of a New Paradigm of Work*. Canberra: Centre for Continuing Education, Australian National University, 1959.

Emery, F. E. *Report on the Hunsfoss Project*. London: Tavistock Documents Series, 1964.

Emery, F. E. "The Next Thirty Years: Concepts, Methods, and Anticipations." *Human Relations*, 1967, *20*, 199–237.

Emery, F. E. *The Emergence of a New Paradigm of Work*. Canberra: Centre for Continuing Education, Australian National University, 1978.

Emery, F. E. "Designing Socio-Technical Systems for 'Greenfield' Sites." *Journal of Occupational Behavior*, 1980, *1*, 19–27.

Emery, F. E., and Trist, E. L. "Socio-Technical Systems." In C. W. Churchman and others (eds.), *Management Sciences, Models and Techniques*. London: Pergamon, 1960.

Emery, F. E., and Trist, E. L. "The Causal Texture of Organizational Environments." Paper presented to the International Psychology Congress, Washington, D.C., 1963. Reprinted in *Human Relations*, 1964, *18* (1), 21–32.

Emery, F. E., and Trist, E. L. *Toward a Social Ecology*. New York: Plenum, 1973.

Emery, M. *Searching: for New Directions, in New Ways for New Times*. Canberra: Centre for Continuing Education, Australian National University, 1982.

Emery, M. "Learning and the Quality of Working Life." *QWL Focus*, Feb. 1983, *3* (1), 1–7.

Fisher, I. "Scientific Management Made Clear." *Bulletin of the Taylor Society*, Feb. 1925, *10* (1), 41–61.

Fisher, K., and Fisher, M. "Maintaining a Balanced Personal and Work Life," Chapter 17 in *Manager's Guide to Virtual Teams*. New York: McGraw-Hill, 2011.

Flax, S. "Did GM Give Away the Store?" *Fortune*, Oct. 15, 1984, pp. 223–228.

Flint, J. "The Fireproof Man." *Forbes*, Oct. 22, 1984, pp. 94–98.

Foderaro, L. W. "Bear-Proof Can Is Pop-Top Picnic for a Crafty Thief." *The New York Times*, July 25, 2009, page A1.

Forrester, J. W. "Designing the Future." Speech at Universidad de Sevilla, Sevilla, Spain, December 15, 1998.

Fox, R. E, Lippitt, R., and Schindler-Rainman, E. *The Humanized Future: Some New Images.* San Diego, CA: University Associates, 1973.

French, W. L. "Organization Development: Objectives, Assumptions and Strategies." *California Management Review*, Winter 1969, *12* (2), 23–39.

French, W. L., and Bell, C. H., Jr. *Organization Development: Behavioral Science Interventions for Organization Improvement.* Englewood Cliffs, NJ: Prentice-Hall, 1973.

Galbraith, J. R. *Organization Design.* Reading, MA: Addison-Wesley, 1977.

Gantt, H. L. *Work, Wages, and Profits* (2nd ed.). New York: Engineering Magazine Company, 1916.

Gantt, H. L. *Organizing for Work.* New York: Harcourt Brace Jovanovich, 1919.

Garfield, C. *Peak Performers: The New Heroes of American Business.* New York: William Morrow, 1986.

Garson, B. *The Electronic Sweatshop: How Computers Are Transforming the Office of the Future into the Factory of the Past.* New York: Penguin, 1989.

Geertz, C. *The Interpretation of Cultures.* New York: Basic Books, 1973.

Georgopoulos, B. S., and Mann, F. C. *The Community General Hospital.* New York: Macmillan, 1962.

Gibb, J. R. *Trust: A New View of Personal and Organizational Development.* Los Angeles: Guild of Tutors Press, 1978.

Gilmore, T. N. "Overcoming Crisis and Uncertainty: The Search Conference." In L. Hirschhorn and Associates, *Cutting Back: Retrenchment and Redevelopment in Human and Community Services.* San Francisco: Jossey-Bass, 1983.

Gilmore, T., and Krantz, J. *Projective Identification in the Consulting Relationship: Exploring the Unconscious Dimensions of a Client System.* Philadelphia: University of Pennsylvania, Management and Behavioral Science Center, the Wharton School, April 1985.

Goldratt, E., and Cox, J. *The Goal.* Great Barrington, MA: North River Press, 1985.

Gray, S. G. "The Tavistock Institute of Human Relations." In H. V. Dicks, *50 Years of the Tavistock Clinic.* London: Routledge & Kegan Paul, 1970.

Greiner, L. E., and Metzger, R. O. *Consulting to Management.* Englewood Cliffs, NJ: Prentice-Hall, 1983.

Gustavsen, B. "Workplace Reform and Industrial Democratic Dialogue." *Economic and Industrial Democracy*, 1985, *6*, 461–479.

Gutchess, J. *Employment Security in Action: Strategies That Work.* New York: Pergamon Press, 1984.

Hackman, R. J., and Oldham, G. R. *Work Redesign.* Reading, MA: Addison-Wesley, 1980.

Halpern, N. "Sustaining Change in the Shell Sarnia Chemical Plant." *QWL Focus,* May 1982, *2* (1), 5–11.

Hamilton, A., Madison, J., and Jay, J. *The Federalist Papers,* introduction by Clinton Rossiter. New York: New American Library, 1961.

Harrison, R. "Role Negotiation: A Tough-Minded Approach to Team Development." In W. W. Burke and H. A. Hornstein (eds.), *The Social Technology of Organization Development.* San Diego, CA: University Associates, 1972.

Heidorn, R., Jr., and Raghavan, S. "Bethlehem Steel to Close the Last Plant in Its Hometown," *Philadelphia Inquirer,* December 30, 1997, pp. A1, A9.

Herbst, P. G. *Socio-Technical Design.* London: Tavistock, 1974.

Herzberg, F., Mausner, B., and Snyderman, B. *The Motivation to Work* (2nd ed.). Hoboken, NJ: John Wiley & Sons, 1959.

Hickey, J. W. "Productivity Gain Seen in Labor-Management Reversal." *World of Work Report,* April 1986, *11* (4), 3–4.

Hirschhorn, L. *Beyond Mechanization: Work and Technology in a Postindustrial Age.* Cambridge, MA: MIT Press, 1984.

Hirschhorn, L., and Associates. *Cutting Back: Retrenchment and Redevelopment in Human and Community Services.* San Francisco: Jossey-Bass, 1983.

Hjelholt, G. "Training for Reality" and a supplement, "Some Results of Ship's Crew Training," working papers nos. 5 and 5A. Leeds: University of Leeds, Department of Management Studies, September 1968.

Hjelholt, G. "Group Training for Understanding Society: The Mini-Society." *Interpersonal Development, 3,* 140–51, 1972. In B. Madsen and S. Willert (eds.), *Working on Boundaries: Gunnar Hjelholt and Applied Psychology.* Aarhus: Aarhus University Press, 2006, pp. 259–74.

Holman, P., Devane, T., and Cady, S. *The Change Handbook: The Definitive Resource on Today's Best Methods for Engaging Whole Systems* (2nd ed.). San Francisco: Berrett-Koehler, 2007.

Jacobs, R. W. *Real Time Strategic Change.* San Francisco: Berrett-Koehler, 1994.

Janoff, S., and Weisbord, M. "Facilitating the Whole System in the Room." *Seminar on a Philosophy and Method for Transforming Work Groups.* Philadelphia: Future Search Network, 2001.

Janssen, C. *Personlig Dialektik* (2nd ed.). Stockholm: Liber, 1982.

Janssen, C. *The Four Rooms of Change, Part I. A Practical Everyday Psychology.* Stockholm: Ander & Lindstrom, 2011a.

Janssen, C. *The Four Rooms of Change, Part II. Fifteen Years of More Experience.* Stockholm: Ander & Lindstrom, 2011b.

Jaques, E. *The Changing Culture of a Factory.* London: Tavistock, 1951.

Johnson, M. J. "Fred Taylor '83: Giant of Non-Repute." *The Stevens Indicator*, Spring 1980, *97* (2), 4–8.

Kakar, S. *Frederick Taylor: A Study in Personality and Innovation.* Cambridge, MA: MIT Press, 1970.

Karp, H., Fuller, C. S., and Sirias, D. *Bridging the Boomer-Xer Gap: Creating Authentic Teams for High Performance at Work.* Palo Alto, CA: Davis-Black, 2002.

Kast, F. E., and Rosenzweig, J. E. *Organization and Management: A Systems Approach.* New York: McGraw-Hill, 1970.

Kelly, F. C. *The Wright Brothers.* New York: Ballantine Books, 1943.

Kleiner, A. *Fast Company, 3*, June 1996, p. 44.

Knickerbocker, I., and McGregor, D. "Industrial Relations and National Defense: A Change to Management." *Personnel*, July 1941, *18* (1), 49–63.

Knickerbocker, I., and McGregor, D. "Union-Management Cooperation: A Psychological Analysis." *Personnel*, Nov. 1942, *19* (3), 520–539.

Kotter, J. P., with Heskett, J. L. *Corporate Culture and Performance.* New York: The Free Press, 1992.

Kristofferson, K., and Foster, F. "Me and Bobby McGee" (© Combine Music Corp.) From "Kristofferson," © 1970, Columbia/Legacy.

Langewiesche, W. *Stick and Rudder.* New York: McGraw-Hill, 1944.

Lawler, E. E., III. *High-Involvement Management: Participative Strategies for Improving Organizational Performance.* San Francisco: Jossey-Bass, 1986.

Lawrence, P. R., and Lorsch, J. W. *Organization and Environment.* Cambridge, MA: Harvard University Press, 1967.

Lawrence, P. R., and Nohria, N. *Driven: How Human Nature Shapes Our Choices.* San Francisco: Jossey-Bass, 2002.

Lepore, J. "Not So Fast: Scientific Management Started as a Way to Work. How Did It Become a Way of Life?" *The New Yorke*r, October 12, 2009.

Levering, R., Moskowitz, M., and Katz, M. *The 100 Best Companies to Work for in America.* New York: New American Library, 1985.

Lewin, K. "Die Sozialisierung des Taylor systems" [Humanization of the Taylor system]. *Praktischer Sozialismus*, 1920, (4), 5–36.

Lewin, K. *Dynamic Theory of Personality.* New York: McGraw-Hill, 1935.

Lewin, K. "Research on Minority Problems." *The Technology Review*, Jan. 1946, *48* (3).

Lewin, K. "Frontiers in Group Dynamics, part 1: Concept, Method and Reality in Social Science: Social Equilibria and Social Change." *Human Relations*, 1947a, *1*, 5–41.

Lewin, K. "Frontiers in Group Dynamics, part 2: Channels of Group Life: Social Planning and Action Research." *Human Relations*, 1947b, *1*, 143–153.

Lewin, K. *Resolving Social Conflicts: Selected Papers on Group Dynamics.* G. W. Lewin (ed.). New York: Harper & Row, 1948.

Lewin, K. *Field Theory in Social Science: Selected Theoretical Papers.* D. Cartwright (ed.). New York: Harper & Row, 1951.

Lewin, K., and others. "The Practicality of Democracy." In G. Murphy (ed.), *Human Nature and Enduring Peace.* Boston: Houghton-Mifflin, 1945.

Liedtke, M. (2010). " Google's Long-Term Thinking Has Its Investors Wondering." *The Philadelphia Inquirer*, October 13, 2010, p. A11.

Likert, R. *New Patterns of Management.* New York: McGraw-Hill, 1961.

Likert, R. *The Human Organization: Its Management and Value.* New York: McGraw-Hill, 1967.

Likert, R., and Likert, J. G. *New Ways of Managing Conflict.* New York: McGraw-Hill, 1976.

Lindaman, E. *Thinking in the Future Tense.* Nashville, TN.: Broadman Press, 1978.

Lindaman, E., and Lippitt, R. *Choosing the Future You Prefer.* Washington, DC: Development Publications, 1979.

Lippitt, L. *Preferred Futuring.* San Francisco: Berrett-Koehler, 1998.

Lippitt, R. "Kurt Lewin, 1890–1947: Adventures in the Exploration of Interdependence." *Sociometry*, 1947, *10*, 87–97.

Lippitt, R. "Future Before You Plan." *NTL Managers' Handbook.* Arlington, VA: NTL Institute, 1983.

Lippitt, R., Watson, J., and Westley, B. *The Dynamics of Planned Change.* New York: Harcourt Brace Jovanovich, 1958.

Locke, E. A. "The Ideas of Frederick W. Taylor: An Evaluation." *Academy of Management Review*, 1982, *7* (1), 14–24.

Locke, E. A. "Participation in Decision Making: When Should It Be Used?" *Organizational Dynamics*, Winter 1986, pp. 65–79.

Ludema, J. D., and others. *The Appreciative Inquiry Summit: A Practitioner's Guide for Leading Large-Group Change.* San Francisco: Berrett-Koehler, 2009.

Lytle, W. O. *Starting an Organization Design Effort: A Planning and Preparation Guide* (rev. ed.). Englishtown, NJ: BPW Publishing, 1997.

Lytle, W. O. *Designing a High-Performance Organization: A Guide to the Whole-Systems Approach.* Englishtown, NJ: BPW Publishing, 1998.

Lytle, W. O. "Accelerating the Organization Design Process." *Reflections: The SoL Journal*, Winter 2002, MIT Press.

McFarland, M. W. (ed.). *The Papers of Wilbur and Orville Wright.* 2 vols. New York: McGraw-Hill, 1953.

McGregor, D. "A Year at Antioch." Yellow Springs, OH: Antioch College, June 1949.

McGregor, D. "Human Organization and Education." Talk delivered at the University of Michigan, March 23, 1950.

McGregor, D. "On Leadership." *Antioch Notes*, May 1954, pp. 2–3.

McGregor, D. *The Human Side of Enterprise.* New York: McGraw-Hill, 1960.

McGregor, D., Bennis, W. G., and McGregor, C. (eds.). *The Professional Manager.* New York: McGraw-Hill, 1967.

McGregor, D., and Scanlon, J. N. " The Dewey and Almy Chemical Company and the International Chemical Workers Union." Case Study no. 3. Washington, DC: National Planning Association, 1948.

McIntosh-Fletcher, D., and McIntosh-Fletcher, W. T. *Work Alignment for Realizing the Promise of Work.* Scottsdale, AZ: McFletcher Corporation, 2011.

McIntosh-Fletcher, W. T., & McIntosh-Fletcher, D. *Work Style Patterns® Inventory.* Scottsdale, AZ: The McFletcher Corporation, 1979, 1988–2005, 2009; online version 2010.

McKibbon, J. "A Labour Perspective on QWL." Ontario Ministry of Labour. *QWL Focus, The News Journal of the Ontario Quality of Working Life Centre,* Spring 1984, *4* (1).

Madsen, B., and Willert, S. (eds.). *Working on Boundaries: Gunnar Hjelholt and Applied Psychology.* Aarhus, Denmark: Aarhus University Press, 2006, pp. 259–174.

Main, J. "Under the Spell of the Quality Gurus." *Fortune,* Aug. 18, 1986, pp. 30–34.

Mann, F. C. "Studying and Creating Change: A Means to Understanding Social Organization." In C. M. Arensbert and others (eds.), *Research in Industrial Human Relations: A Critical Appraisal.* New York: Harper & Row, 1957.

Marrow, A. F. *The Practical Theorist.* New York: Basic Books, 1969.

Maslow, A. H. *Eupsychian Management.* Homewood, Ill.: Irwin, 1965.

Maslow, A. H., and Murphy, G. (eds.). *Motivation and Personality.* New York: Harper & Row, 1954.

Mathewson, S. B. *Restriction of Output Among Unorganized Workers.* New York: Viking Penguin, 1931.

Mayo, E. *The Social Problems of an Industrial Civilization.* Cambridge, MA: School of Business Administration, Harvard University, 1945.

Mead, M. "Cultural Discontinuities and Personality Transformation." *Journal of Social Issues,* 1983, *39* (4), 161–177; reprinted from *JSI Supplement,* 1954 (8), 3–16.

"Memorial to Douglas McGregor." Cambridge, MA: MIT, October 16, 1964.

Metcalf, H. C., and Urwick, L. (eds.). *Dynamic Administration: The Collected Works of Mary Parker Follett.* New York: Harper & Row, 1940.

Miller, E. J. "The Open System Approach to Organizational Analysis, with Specific Reference to the Work of A. K. Rice." In G. Hofstede and M. S. Kassem (eds.), *European Contributions to Organization Theory.* Assen, Netherlands: Van Gorcum, Mulder, Mauk, 1975.

Miller, F. A., and Katz, J. H. *The Inclusion Breakthrough: Unleashing the Real Power of Diversity.* San Francisco: Berrett-Koehler, 2002.

Miller, R. S. Quoted in Bethlehem Steel news release, Public Affairs Department, July 9, 2002.

Mintzberg, H. "Planning on the Left Side and Managing on the Right." *Harvard Business Review*, July/Aug. 1976, *54* (4), 49–58.

Mohrman, S. A., Cohen, S. G., and Mohrman, A., Jr. *Designing Team-Based Organizations.* San Francisco: Jossey-Bass, 1995.

Moore, B. E., and Ross, T. L. *The Scanlon Way to Improved Productivity: A Practical Guide.* Hoboken, NJ: John Wiley & Sons, 1978.

Nadworny, M. J. *Scientific Management and the Unions: 1900–1923.* Cambridge, MA: Harvard University Press, 1955.

Naisbitt, J. *Megatrends.* New York: Warner Books, 1982.

Neilsen, E. H. *Becoming an OD Practitioner.* Englewood Cliffs, NJ: Prentice-Hall, 1984.

Nelson, B. "Bosses Face Less Risk Than Bossed." *The New York Times*, April 1983.

Nelson, D. *Frederick W. Taylor and the Rise of Scientific Management.* Madison: University of Wisconsin Press, 1980.

Noer, D. M. *Healing the Wounds: Overcoming the Trauma of Layoffs and Revitalizing Downsized Corporations.* San Francisco: Jossey-Bass, 2009.

Nord, W. "Theory Y Assumptions in a Non-Theory Y World." *Interfaces*, Feb. 1978, *8* (2), 61–66.

Oshry, B. *Seeing Systems: Unlocking the Mysteries of Organizational Life.* San Francisco: Berrett-Koehler, 1996.

Ouchi, W. *Theory Z.* Reading, MA: Addison-Wesley, 1981.

Owen, H. "Let the Spirit Soar." Unpublished manuscript, 1984.

Owen, H. *Open Space Technology: A User's Guide* (3rd ed.). San Francisco: Berrett-Koehler, 2008.

Papanek, M. L. "Kurt Lewin and His Contributions to Modern Management Theory." *Academy of Management Proceedings*, Aug. 1973, pp. 317–321.

Pasmore, W., and others. "Sociotechnical Systems: A North American Reflection on Empirical Studies of the Seventies." *Human Relations*, 1982, *35* (12).

Patterson, D. "A Labour Perspective on QWL." Ontario Ministry of Labour. *QWL Focus, The News Journal of the Ontario Quality of Working Life Centre*, Spring 1984, *4* (1).

Pava, C.H.P. *Managing New Age Technology: An Organizational Strategy.* New York: The Free Press, 1983.

Paxton, T. "I Can't Help But Wonder (Where I'm Bound)" © 1963; Renewed 1991 Cherry Lane Music Publishing Company, Inc. (ASCAP) and DreamWorks Songs (ASCAP).

Pearce, J. C. *The Crack in the Cosmic Egg.* New York: Julian Press, 1971.

Perls, F., Hefferline, R., and Goodman, F. *Gestalt Therapy.* New York: Julian Press, 1951.

Perrow, C. *Complex Organizations: A Critical Essay* (2nd ed.). New York: Random House, 1979.

Peters, T. J., and Waterman, R. H. *In Search of Excellence.* New York: Harper & Row, 1982.

Petrella, T. "Managing with Teams." Plainfield, NJ: Block Petrella Associates, 1974.

Pfeffer, J. "Lay Off the Layoffs." *Newsweek*, February 15, 2010, pp. 35–37.

Picker, W. J. "Douglas McGregor (A Study Guide)." Unpublished manuscript, December 1967, rev. June 1968.

Renier, J. J. "'Ethical Infrastructure' Vital to Productivity Gains." *World of Work Report*, Jan. 1986, *11* (1), 4–5.

Revans, R. W. *The Origins and Development of Action Learning.* Bromley, UK: Chartwell Bratt Ltd., 1982.

Rice, A. K. *Productivity and Social Organization: The Ahmedabad Experiment.* London: Tavistock, 1958.

Richman, T. "Peering into Tomorrow." *INC.*, Oct. 1982, pp. 45–48.

Roethlisberger, E. J., and Dickson, W. J. *Management and the Worker.* Cambridge, MA: Harvard University Press, 1939.

Sashkin, M. "Interview [with] Eric Trist, British Interdisciplinarian." *Group & Organization Studies*, June 1980, *5* (2), 144–166.

Sashkin, M. "Participative Management Is an Ethical Imperative." *Organizational Dynamics*, Spring 1984, pp. 4–22.

Schein, E. *Process Consultation: Lessons for Managers and Consultants*, Volume II (Prentice Hall Organization Development Series). New York: Prentice Hall, 1987.

Schindler-Rainmann, E., and Lippitt, R. *Building the Collaborative Community: Mobilizing Citizens for Action.* Riverside, CA: University of California Press, 1980.

Schön, D. *Beyond the Stable State.* New York: Random House, 1971.

Senge, P. *The Fifth Discipline: The Art and Practice of the Learning Organization* (rev. ed.). New York: Doubleday, 2006.

Sheldrake, R. *The Presence of the Past: Morphic Resonance and the Habits of Nature.* New York: Vintage Books, 1989.

Simmons, J., and Mares, W. *Working Together.* New York: Knopf, 1983.

Sisan, C., and Sisan, K. (eds.). *The Oxford Book of 20th Century Verse.* London: Oxford University Press, 1973.

Sorensen, K. H. "Technology and Industrial Democracy: An Inquiry into Some Theoretical Issues and Their Social Basis." *Organization Studies*, 1986, *2* (6), 139–160.

Stark, C. "U.S. Judge Gives Green Light to Allegheny Racketeering Lawsuit." *Philadelphia Inquirer*, December 24, 1999, p. C1.

Tannenbaum, R., and Hanna, R. W. "Holding On, Letting Go, and Moving On: Understanding a Neglected Perspective on Change." In R. Tannenbaum,

N. Margulies, E. Massarik, and Associates (eds.), *Human Systems Development: New Perspectives on People and Organizations.* San Francisco: Jossey-Bass, 1985.

Tarbell, I. "Making the Most of Men." *Saturday Review of Literature*, Oct. 25, 1924, reprinted in *Bulletin of the Taylor Society*, Feb. 1925, *10* (1), 80–81.

Taylor, F. W. "A Piece Rate System: A Step Toward Partial Solution of the Labor Problem." Paper for the American Society of Mechanical Engineers, 1895.

Taylor, F. W. *Shop Management.* New York: Harper & Row, 1911.

Taylor, F. W. *The Principles of Scientific Management.* New York: Harper & Row, 1915.

Tead, O. "Taylor's Intellectual Contribution." *American Review*, July/Aug. 1924, reprinted in *Bulletin of the Taylor Society*, Feb. 1925, *10* (1), 62–65.

Thorsrud, E. "The Scandinavian Model: Strategies of Organizational Democratization in Norway." In B. Wilpert and A. Sorge (eds.), *International Perspectives on Organizational Democracy.* Hoboken, NJ: John Wiley & Sons, 1984.

Tocqueville, A. de. *Democracy in America.* 2 vols. (J. P. Mayer and A. P. Kerr, eds.) New York: Doubleday, 1969. (Originally published 1835.)

Toffier, A. T*he Third Wave.* New York: McGraw-Hill, 1980.

Toffier, A. *The Adaptive Corporation.* New York: McGraw-Hill, 1984.

Tolstoy, L. *Anna Karenina.* Translated by David Magarshack. New York: New American Library, 1961. (Originally published 1877.)

Tonn, J. C. *Mary Parker Follett: Creating Democracy, Transforming Management.* New Haven, CT: Yale University Press, 2003.

Trist, E. L. "Critique of Scientific Management in Terms of Socio-Technical Theory." In M. Weir (ed.), *Job Satisfaction.* Glasgow: Fontana/Collins, 1976. Reprinted from *Prakseologia*, 1971, 39–40, 159–174.

Trist, E. L. Speech presented at the European Economic Community Conference, Brussels, 1974.

Trist, E. L. "Adapting to a Changing World." In G. E. Sanderson (ed.), *Readings in Quality of Working Life.* Ottawa: Labour Canada, 1978, pp. 10–20.

Trist, E. L. *The Evolution of Socio-Technical Systems: A Conceptual Framework and an Action Research Program.* Occasional paper no. 2. Ontario Quality of Working Life Centre, June 1981.

Trist, E. L. "Intervention Strategies for Inter-organizational Domains." In R. Tannenbaum and others (eds.), *Human Systems Development: New Perspectives on People and Organizations.* San Francisco: Jossey-Bass, 1985a.

Trist, E. L. "Working with Bion in the 1940s: The Group Decade." In M. Pines (ed.), *Bion and Group Psychotherapy.* London: Routledge & Kegan Paul, 1985b.

Trist, E. L., and Dwyer, C. " The Limits of Laissez-Faire as a Sociotechnical Strategy." In R. Zager and M. F. Rosow (eds.), *The Innovative Organization.* New York: Pergamon Press, 1982.

Trist, E. L., and Emery, F. E. " Report on the Barford Conference for Bristol/Siddeley, Aero-Engine Corp." Document no. 598, July 10–16, 1960. London: Tavistock.
Trist, E. L., with F. Emery and H. Murray. *The Social Engagement of Social Science: A Tavistock Anthology (Vol. III: The Socio-Ecological Perspective).* Philadelphia: The University of Pennsylvania Press, 1997.
Trist, E. L., Higgin, G. W., Murray, H., and Pollock, A. B. *Organizational Choice: The Loss, Re-discovery, and Transformation of a Work Tradition.* London: Tavistock, 1963.
Trist, E. L., with J. Eldred and R. Keidel. "A New Approach to Economic Development." *Human Futures,* 1977, (1), 8–12.
Trist, E. L., with H. Murray. *The Social Engagement of Social Science: A Tavistock Anthology (Vol. I: The Socio-Psychological Perspective).* Philadelphia: The University of Pennsylvania Press, 1990.
Trist, E. L., with Murray, H. *The Social Engagement of Social Science: A Tavistock Anthology (Vol. II: The Socio-Technical Perspective).* Philadelphia: The University of Pennsylvania Press, 1993.
United Steel Workers of America. " Summary: Proposed Agreement with National Steel Corporation." Pittsburgh, April 9, 1986.
Vaill, P. B. "Cook Book Auction and Clap Trap Cocoons." *Exchange: The Organizational Behavior Teaching Journal,* 1979, *4* (1), 4.
Vaill, P. B. *Managing as a Performing Art.* San Francisco: Jossey-Bass, 1989.
Vaill, P. B. *Learning as a Way of Being: Strategies for Survival in a World of Permanent White Water.* San Francisco: Jossey-Bass, 1996.
Vaill, P. B. *Spirited Leading and Learning: Process Wisdom for a New Age.* San Francisco: Jossey-Bass, 1998.
Vaill, P. B. "An Annotated Bibliography of Foundational Literature in Organizational Behavior and Development," 1996, manuscript revised by author, 2009.
van Beinum, H. Speech introducing Emery at "Explorations in Human Features" Conference, 1985.
Van De Ven, A. H., and Ferry, D. L. *Measuring and Assessing Organizations.* Hoboken, NJ: John Wiley & Sons, 1980.
Van der Zouwen, A. *Building an Evidence-Based Practical Guide to Large Scale Interventions. Towards Sustainable Change with the Whole System.* Delft, Netherlands: Eburon Academic Publishers, 2011.
Vansina, L. "Improving International Relations Within Multinational Organizations." In J. D. Adams (ed.), *Theory and Method in Organization Development: An Evolutionary Process.* Arlington, VA: NTL Institute of Applied Behavioral Science, 1974, pp. 331–363.
Vansina, L., and Vansina-Cobbaert, M.-J. *Psychodynamics for Consultants and Managers: Leading Meaningful Change.* Chichester, England: Wiley-Blackwell, 2008.

Vickers, G. *The Art of Judgment.* Thousand Oaks, CA: Sage, 1995. Originally published, 1965d.

von Bertalanffy, L. "The Theory of Open Systems in Physics and Biology." *Science,* 1950, (3), 23–29.

von Bertalanffy, L. *Problems of Life.* Hoboken, NJ: John Wiley & Sons, 1952.

Walton, R. E. "The Diffusion of New Work Structures: Explaining Why Success Didn't Take." *Organizational Dynamics,* 1975, *3* (3), 2–22.

Walton, R. E. "The Topeka Work System: Optimistic Vision, Pessimistic Hypotheses, and Reality." In R. Zager and M. P. Rosow (eds.), *The Innovative Organization.* New York: Pergamon Press, 1982.

Weisbord, M. R. "Management in Crisis: Must You Liquidate People?" An interview with Dr. Rensis Likert. *The Conference Board Record,* February 1970.

Weisbord, M. R. "A Mixed Model for Medical Centers: Changing Structure and Behavior." In *Theory and Method in Organization Development: An Evolutionary Process.* Washington, DC: NTL Institute, 1974.

Weisbord, M. R. "Why Organization Development Hasn't Worked (So Far) in Medical Centers." *Health Care Management Review,* Spring 1976, *1* (2), 17–28.

Weisbord, M. R. "How Do You Know It Works If You Don't Know What It Is?" *OD Practitioner,* Oct. 1977, *9* (3), 1–80.

Weisbord, M. R. "Input- Versus Output-Focused Organizations: Notes on a Contingency Theory of Practice." In W. W. Burke (ed.), *The Cutting Edge: Current Theory and Practice in Organization Development.* San Diego, CA: University Associates, 1978a.

Weisbord, M. R. *Organizational Diagnosis: A Workbook of Theory and Practice.* Reading, MA: Addison-Wesley, 1978b.

Weisbord, M. R. "Some Reflections on OD's Identity Crisis." *Group & Organization Studies,* June 1981, *6* (2), 161–175.

Weisbord, M. R. "Future Search: Innovative Business Conference." *Planning Review,* July 1984, *12* (4), 16–20.

Weisbord, M. R. "Participative Work Design: A Personal Odyssey." *Organizational Dynamics,* Spring 1985, pp. 4–20.

Weisbord, M. R. "Future Search: A 'New Paradigm'? Maybe Not." *SearchNEWS, 6,* Winter 1996.

Weisbord, M. R. "Resolving a New Paradox with Old Wisdom." In P. Block and 30 Flawless Consultants, *The Flawless Consulting Fieldbook and Companion.* San Francisco: Pfeiffer, 2001.

Weisbord, M. R. *Productive Workplaces: Organizing and Managing for Dignity Meaning and Community.* San Francisco: Jossey-Bass, 1987.

Weisbord, M. R. *Productive Workplaces Revisited: Dignity, Meaning, and Community in the 21st Century* (2nd ed.). San Francisco: Jossey-Bass, 2004.

Weisbord, M. R. "Large Group Interventions—A Shopper's Guide." In E. Biech (ed.), *ASTD Handbook for Workplace Learning Professionals.* Arlington, VA: ASTD Press, 2008.

Weisbord, M. R., and Janoff, S. "Faster, Shorter, Cheaper May Be Simple, It's Never Easy." *Journal of Applied Behavioral Science, 41* (1), 70–82, 2005.

Weisbord, M. R., and Janoff, S. *Don't Just Do Something, Stand There! Ten Principles for Leading Meetings That Matter.* San Francisco: Berrett-Koehler, 2007.

Weisbord, M. R., and Janoff, S. *Future Search: Getting the Whole System in the Room for Vision, Action and Commitment* (3rd ed.). San Francisco: Berrett-Koehler, 2010.

Weisbord, M. R., Lamb, H., and Drexler, A. *Improving Police Department Management Through Problem-Solving Task Forces.* Reading, MA: Addison-Wesley, 1974.

Weisbord, M. R., Lawrence, E. R., and Charns, M. E. "Three Dilemmas of Academic Medical Centers." *The Journal of Applied Behavioral Science,* 1978, *14* (3), 284–304.

Weisbord, M. R., and Maselko, J. C. "Learning How to Influence Others." *Supervisory Management,* May 1981, *26* (5), 2–10.

Weisbord, M. R., and Stoelwinder, J. "Linking Physicians, Hospital Management, Cost Containment, and Better Medical Care." *Health Care Management Review,* Spring 1979, 7–13.

Weisbord, M. R., and 35 International Authors. *Discovering Common Ground.* San Francisco: Berrett-Koehler, 1992.

Westcott, L., and Degen, P. *Wind and Sand: The Story of the Wright Brothers at Kitty Hawk.* New York: Abrams, 1983.

Wheatley, M. *Leadership and the New Science* (3rd ed.). San Francisco: Berrett-Koehler, 2006.

Whitfield, E., and McGregor, D. *As We See It: Antioch, 1950.* Yellow Springs, OH: Antioch College, 1950.

Whyte, W. F. *Money and Motivation.* New York: Harper & Row, 1955.

Whyte, W. F., with Whyte, K. K. *Learning from the Field: A Guide from Experience.* Chapter 10, "Types of Applied Social Research." Thousand Oaks, CA: Sage, 1984.

Wilenski, P. "The SES Manager of the Future." Address to the Australian Government Senior Executives Association, Victorian Branch, July 25, 1986.

Wilson, A.T.M. "Some Aspects of Social Process." *Journal of Social Issues,* 1983, *39* (4), 91–107 (1951 Kurt Lewin Memorial Lecture).

Wolf, W. B. "The Impact of Kurt Lewin on Management Thought." *Academy of Management Proceedings,* August 1973, pp. 322–325.

Wolfe, T. *The Right Stuff.* New York: Bantam, 1980.

Wrege, C. D., and Perroni, A. G. "Taylor's Pig-Tale: A Historical Analysis of Frederick W. Taylor's Pig-Iron Experiments." *Academy of Management Journal,* March 1974, *17* (1), 6–27.

Wrege, C. D., and Stotka, A. M. "Cooke Creates a Classic: The Story Behind F. W. Taylor's Principles of Scientific Management." *Academy of Management Review,* Oct. 1978, *3* (4), 736–749.

Wren, D. A. *The Evolution of Management Thought* (2nd ed.). Hoboken, NJ: John Wiley & Sons, 1979.

Zager, R., and Rosow, M. P. *The Innovative Organization: Productivity Programs in Action.* New York: Pergamon Press, 1982.

Zaleznik, A. "Management of Disappointment." *Harvard Business Review,* Nov./Dec. 1967, pp. 59–70.

Zand, D. E., Miles, M. B., and Lytle, W. O., Jr. "Enlarging Organizational Choice Through Use of a Temporary Problem-Solving System." Unpublished paper, 1970.

ACKNOWLEDGMENTS

During the past fifty years I worked as a manager, consultant, researcher, and teacher with thousands of people. Certain colleagues gave to the original work in large ways that call for special thanks. These include Eric Trist and Ronald Lippitt, William J. Schmidt, Claudia Chowaniec, Robert S. Tannenbaum, Max Elden, Leonard Goodstein, Edwin C. Nevis, Richard Beckhard, Fred Emery, Edith Whitfield Seashore, and Sandra Janoff, my workshop partner for more than twenty years. I'm grateful to Morley Segal for access to his files on Douglas McGregor, and to Merrelyn Emery for useful materials on her and Fred Emery's work.

Others colleagues read chapters of earlier editions and made helpful comments—Peter Block, Barbara Benedict Bunker, Douglas Bunker, Per Engelstad, Henry Gautier, Thomas North Gilmore, William S. Hatton, Larry Hirschhorn, Harry Hughes, J. Myron Johnson, Peter Koestenbaum, Jack Sherwood, and Peter Vaill. Also Richard Axelrod, Jean-Pierre Beaulieu, Mary Broad, Claudia Cohen, Drusilla Copeland, Robert Dilworth, Peggy Holman, Ken Hultman, Rick Lent, Kim Martens, Ed Olson, Michael Randel, Donna Singer, and Sandy Weiner. Members of the consulting firm Block Petrella Weisbord had a hand in this too—C. James Maselko, Dominick Volini, John Dupre, Philip Grosnick, Jill Janov, Eileen Curtin, Maurice Dubras, Davidson Jones, Carol Meyers, and Kathleen Emery. My erstwhile assistant, Gloria Co, put the original manuscript through endless drafts.

I thank those who provided help with my second edition revisits to workplaces, notably Timothy Althof, Donald Bell, Donald Cooper, Jacqueline Ewer, Connie Fuller, David Kahn, June Klinghoffer, Frank Dodge,

David Evans, Phyllis Marciano, Tina Nickerson, William Rathgeber, John Rockstroh, Robert Scarpa, Bernard Sigel, Paul Staley, David Vassar, Michael Vogel, Frank Warland, and especially my friend of so many decades, David Wagner.

Nobody makes a career of consulting without a big boost from others. Mike Blansfield got me into the NTL Institute, and W. Warner Burke, who barely knew me, put me on NTL training staffs long years ago. I am fortunate in having many fruitful partnerships—twenty-plus years with Peter Block and Tony Petrella, who taught me the consulting business starting in 1971, action research in medical schools and hospitals with Paul Lawrence and Martin Charns from 1971 to 1976, many projects with Allan Drexler in the 1970s, an annual NTL Institute Consultation Skills Laboratory with Gail Silverman from 1975 to 1981, the "Men at Work" personal growth laboratories with John Weir and Michael Merrill from 1991 to 1995, Blue Sky Productions with Allan Kobernick from 1987 to 1995, and Future Search Network with Sandra Janoff since 1993.

I would not be doing this work were it not for Donald Kirchhoffer and Bob Maddox, who started me on self-managing work teams in the 1960s, nor the magazine writer and author Bernard Asbell, who invited me to join him in my first consulting assignment at Ford Foundation.

For decades I've been inspired by friends and colleagues world-wide, including Billie Alban, Jan Asplind, Håkan Behrendtz, Bapu Deolalikar, George Doris, Maurice Dubras, Gunnar Hjelholt, Jan Johansson, Bill Lytle, Rolf Lynton, Mary Beth Peters, Larry Porter, Eva Schindler-Rainman, Tony Richardson, Leopold Vansina, Neil Watson, John and Joyce Weir, and Margaret Wheatley—master practitioners all. Then I must thank the many colleagues who added their stories to mine and whose names are listed in the table of contents under "Updates from the Field." I also thank Larry Starr, who set up the video archive at the University of Pennsylvania that brings to life people and cases from the book.

I am indebted to scores of members in the NTL Institute, The European Institute for Transnational Studies (eit), the Organization Development Network, and Future Search Network. Thanks to Steven Piersanti, former president of Jossey-Bass, who encouraged me to write this book. I am grateful to Leslie Stephen for her insightful editorial help with two editions and to Wiley editor Matthew Davis for his encouragement. Peter Rubin, a practitioner of traditional Chinese medicine, helped me in subtle ways.

I also acknowledge colleagues who created ingenious methods to get everyone improving whole systems—Richard Axelrod with The Conference Model®, Januita Brown and David Isaacs with The World Cafe, David Cooperrider with Appreciative Inquiry, Kathie Dannemiller with Whole Scale Change®, Barry Oshry with the Power and Systems Laboratory®, and Harrison Owen with Open Space Technology. Their methods and many others are described in Billie Alban and Barbara Bunker's *Large Group Interventions* and in Peggy Holman and Tom Devane's *The Change Handbook*. That any of us are reducing global uncertainty is arguable. That this journey is worth taking I have no doubt.

Finally, I could not do this work without the love and support of Dorothy Barclay Weisbord, my wife and best friend since 1956. I dedicated the original edition to our fathers, one an entrepreneur, the other a union machinist, both of whom died during the writing of it. The second edition I dedicated to the next generation, our grandchildren. I wrote this edition for Dorothy.

M.R.W.

ABOUT THE AUTHOR

Marvin Weisbord is an internationally known consultant, author, and co-founder of Future Search Network, which involves people worldwide in serving society. He was for more than twenty years a partner in the consulting firm Block Petrella Weisbord, working with business firms, government agencies, medical schools, and hospitals. Weisbord serves as a resource faculty member in the Organization Systems Renewal Program at Seattle University. He was an emeritus member of the late European Institute for Transnational Studies and is an elected member of the World Confederation of Productivity Science. The Organization Development Network gave him a Lifetime Achievement Award in 2004 and voted *Productive Workplaces* among the field's five most influential works. He was for twenty years a member of NTL Institute, running workshops in consulting skills, organizational diagnosis, sociotechnical systems, and team building.

Weisbord wrote *Organizational Diagnosis* (1978), conceived and co-authored *Discovering Common Ground* (1992), and is co-author with Sandra Janoff of *Future Search: An Action Guide* (2010) and *Don't Just Do Something, Stand There!* (2007).

He and Dorothy Barclay Weisbord live in Pennsylvania with a dog named Toto. They have four children and eight grandchildren. Weisbord also is an avid jazz pianist.

INDEX

A

B

D

E

F

G

H

I

J

K

L

M

Q

R

S

T

U

V

W

Y

Z